HEWLETT & MARTIN

TANK GIRL ONE

TITAN BOOKS

TANK GIRL ONE (REMASTERED)
ISBN: 9781845767570

Published by
Titan Books
A division of Titan Publishing Group Ltd.
144 Southwark St
London
SE1 0UP

First edition: April 2009
10 9 8 7 6 5 4

A CIP catalogue record for this title is available from the British Library.

Cover illustration by Jamie Hewlett.

Printed in Italy.

Visit our website: www.titanbooks.com

Did you enjoy this book? We love to hear from our readers. Please email us at: readerfeedback@titanemail.com or write to us at the above address.
To receive advance information, news, competitions, and exclusive Titan offers online, please register by clicking the "Sign up" button on our website: www.titanbooks.com

Checkout the official Tank Girl website at:
WWW.TANK-GIRL.COM

THE COMPLETE CLASSIC TANK GIRL COLLECTION

CHAPTER INDEX

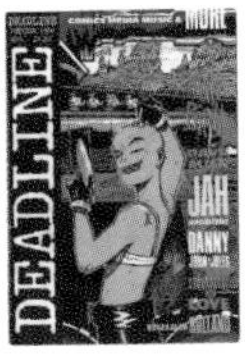
DEADLINE

EPISODE ONE – OCTOBER 1988

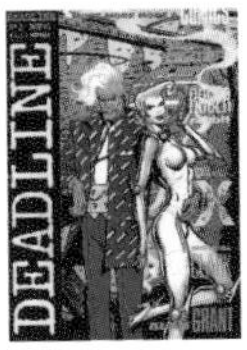
DEADLINE

EPISODE TWO – NOVEMBER 1988

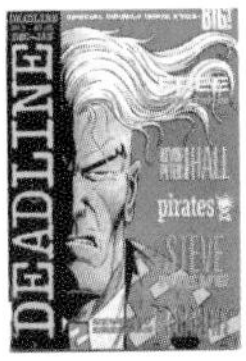
DEADLINE

EPISODE THREE: BIG MOUTH STRIKES AGAIN – DECEMBER 1988

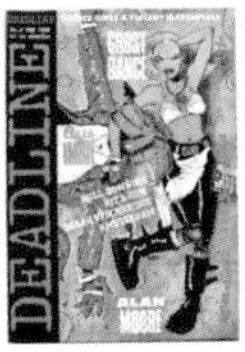
DEADLINE

EPISODE FOUR – FEBRUARY 1989

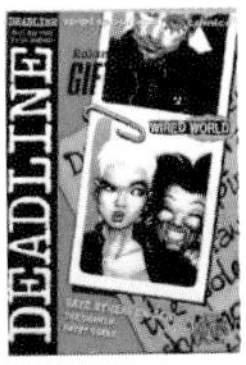
DEADLINE

EPISODE FIVE – MARCH 1989

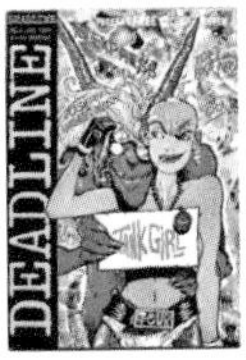
DEADLINE

EPISODE SIX – APRIL 1989

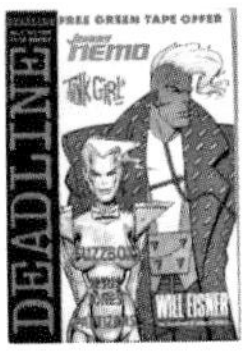
DEADLINE

EPISODE SEVEN – MAY 1989

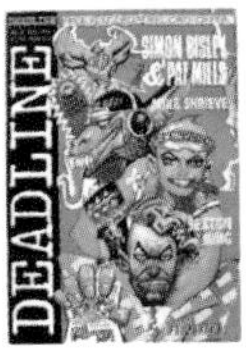
DEADLINE

EPISODE EIGHT: THE AUSTRALIAN JOB PART ONE – JUNE 1989

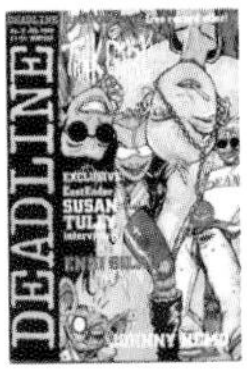
DEADLINE

EPISODE NINE: THE AUSTRALIAN JOB PART TWO – JULY 1989

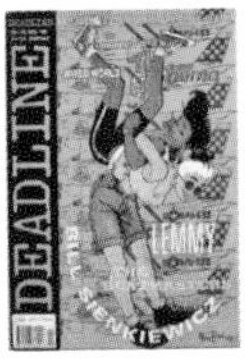
DEADLINE

EPISODE TEN – AUGUST 1989

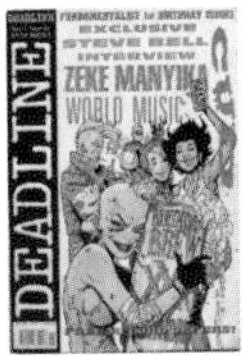
DEADLINE

EPISODE ELEVEN – SEPTEMBER 1989

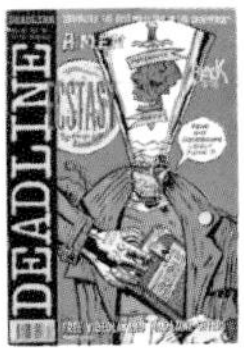
DEADLINE

EPISODE TWELVE – OCTOBER 1989

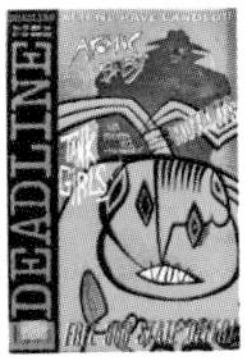
DEADLINE

EPISODE THIRTEEN: THE PREPOSTEROUS BOLLOX OF THE SITUATION – NOVEMBER 1989

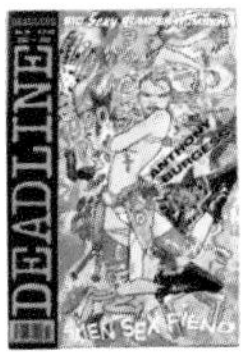
DEADLINE

EPISODE FOURTEEN – DECEMBER 1989

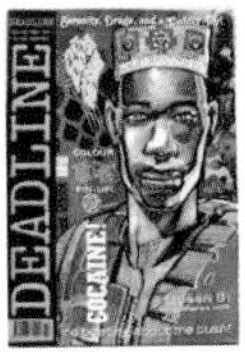
DEADLINE

EPISODE FIFTEEN – FEBRUARY 1990

INTRO

Hello friends and welcome to this glorious collection of the first year (ish) of Tank Girl comic strips. These date back to the late 1980's - an era of much barrel-scraping for art and culture (people say that the seventies were devoid of taste, but, to me anyway, it was the eighties that really sucked) - when Reagan and Thatcher were making life miserable for poor people (a huge generalisation, I know, but as you will soon discover, this introduction isn't exactly intellectual) and the music charts were giving credence to the most hideous soft rock, New Romantic, and dross-MTV monsters (and Michael Jackson). As in the past (with the likes of do-it-yourself-punk, the Pre-Raphaelites, and the US/UK psychedelic scenes), such epochs drive the spirited among us to self-invented and self-sufficient forms of entertainment and expression, which (having the need here to set the stage for our opening chapters) is where our story begins…

Spring 1987. Worthing. Sussex. We'd been at art college for far too long and art fatigue was beginning to set in. We had descended from high-minded intellectual pursuit into that lowest form of dunder-headed media – the comic fanzine.

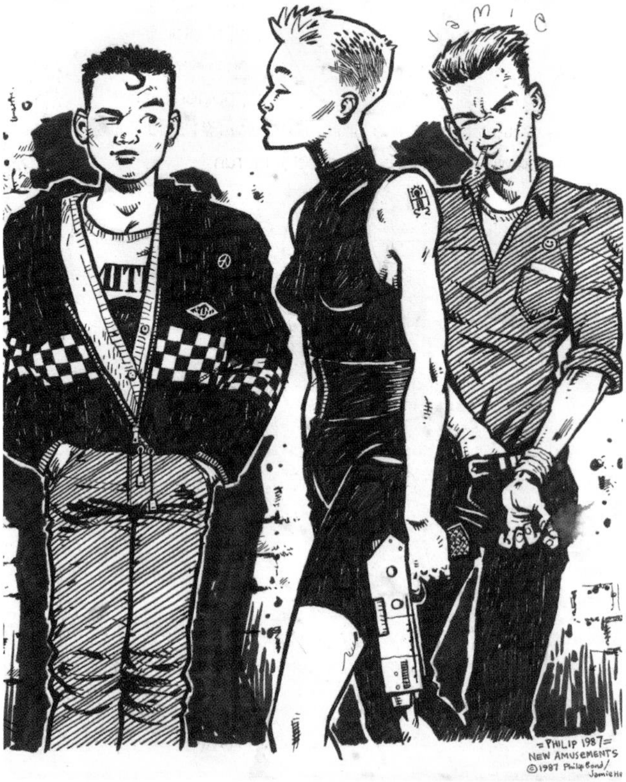

=PHILIP 1987=
NEW AMUSEMENTS
©1987 Philip Bond/
Jamie H

Curly and Spike (a.k.a. Alan and Jamie), watching the ladies go by. From a poster for the unpublished Hewlett and Bond semi-autobiographical strip *New Amusements*.

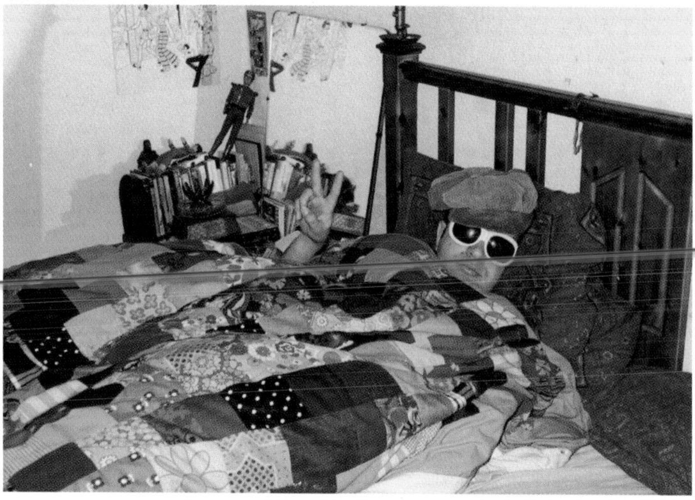

All in a day's work for Alan C. Martin.

I'd met Philip Bond at high school and eight years later I found myself still sitting next to him in class. Jamie Hewlett was a relative newcomer, being a couple of years below us in college, but he slotted seamlessly into our exclusive little gang. We all had some skills: Jamie and Philip were by far the best comic artists our college had ever seen and had gravitated to each other accordingly; I could write a little and had a background in graphic design and fine art; and an enthusiastic collection of our friends brought their own idiosyncratic creations to the table. We "borrowed" the key to the staff photocopier and ran off fifty copies of the first issue of our very own comic *Atomtan*. Filled with comics, poems, posters and countless references to The Smiths, *Atomtan* #1 sold out in days and we went into our second print run.

Our creation was met with hearty applause from family and friends alike. However, nobody took too much notice of the poster tucked away on page twenty of the comic - a hefty looking broad with a big gun, big knockers, and a tag line that simply read, "Tank Girl, she'll break your back and your balls!"

A year and a half later she was plucked from her fanzine obscurity and fleshed out for the inaugural issue of the music/culture/comics/weirdness mash-up that was *Deadline Magazine*.

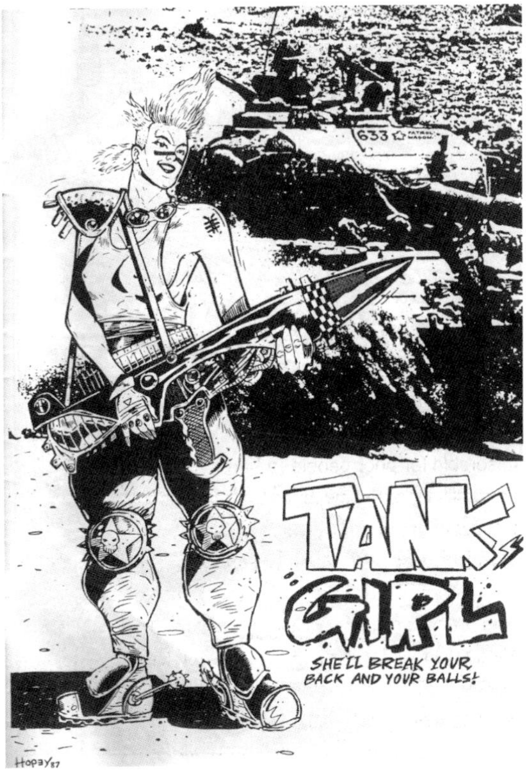
TANK GIRL
SHE'LL BREAK YOUR BACK AND YOUR BALLS!
HOPEY 87

The original *Atomtan* ad that inspired Brett Ewins to commission Tank Girl for *Deadline*.

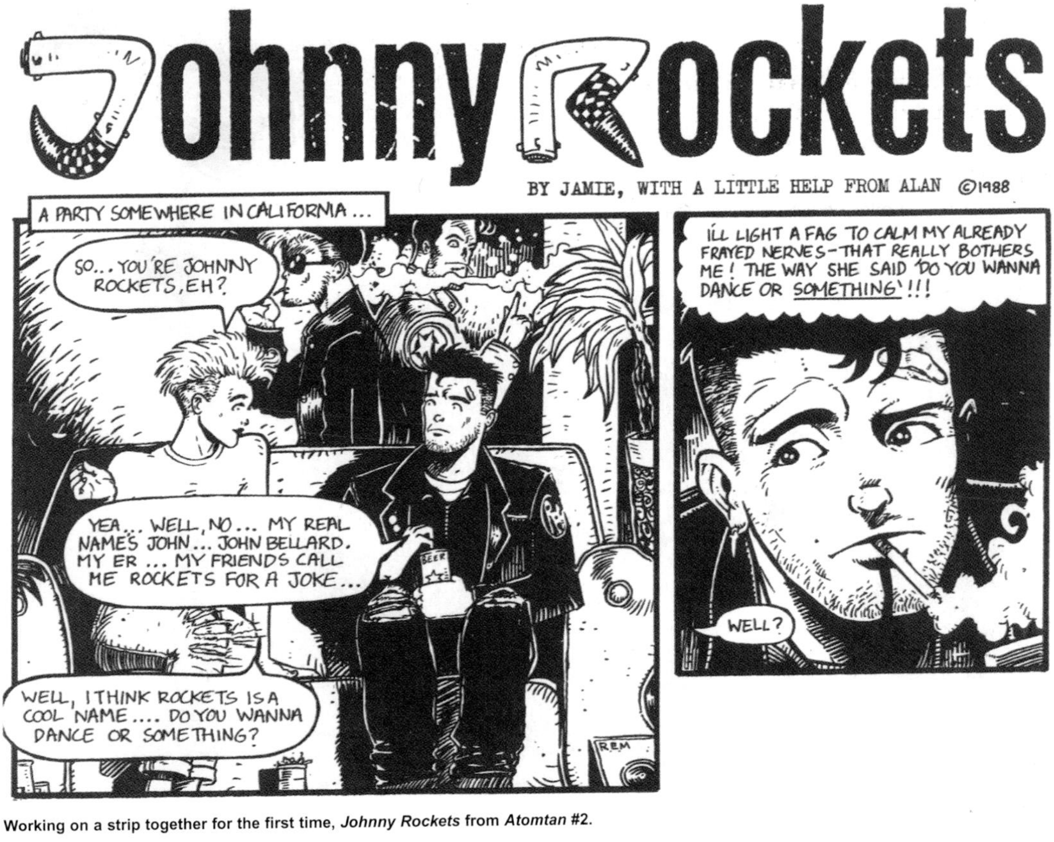
Johnny Rockets
BY JAMIE, WITH A LITTLE HELP FROM ALAN ©1988
A PARTY SOMEWHERE IN CALIFORNIA...
SO... YOU'RE JOHNNY ROCKETS, EH?
YEA... WELL, NO... MY REAL NAME'S JOHN... JOHN BELLARD. MY ER... MY FRIENDS CALL ME ROCKETS FOR A JOKE...
WELL, I THINK ROCKETS IS A COOL NAME.... DO YOU WANNA DANCE OR SOMETHING?
REM
I'LL LIGHT A FAG TO CALM MY ALREADY FRAYED NERVES - THAT REALLY BOTHERS ME! THE WAY SHE SAID 'DO YOU WANNA DANCE OR SOMETHING'!!!
WELL?

Working on a strip together for the first time, *Johnny Rockets* from *Atomtan* #2.

With all iconic characters and ideas, there comes a certain amount of controversy as to how they came into being: Who thought he should wear his pants on the outside? Who invented the big boots? Who decided to put the stripe down the side of the car? Who coined the phrase, "I love it when a plan comes together"? Careers are forged and broken on such otherwise inconsequential points, and a good ligger can dine out for decades on a concept to which he has only a tenuous connection. I may well be one of these people, I'm not sure; my long-term memory started to deteriorate just as Tank Girl's star started to ascend. All I know for certain is that I was there at the very beginning, I was there when the character came to life for the first time proper, and that I continued to be there feeding random and anarchic ideas and storylines into the project as it rolled along. So please read the following in the knowledge that it has been written with the hindsight of someone looking into a fogged-up rear-view mirror, wearing bi-focals, driving in the dark, with no lights, and a terrible hang-over. These, in no particular order, are the subjects concerning the comic that we are asked about the most:

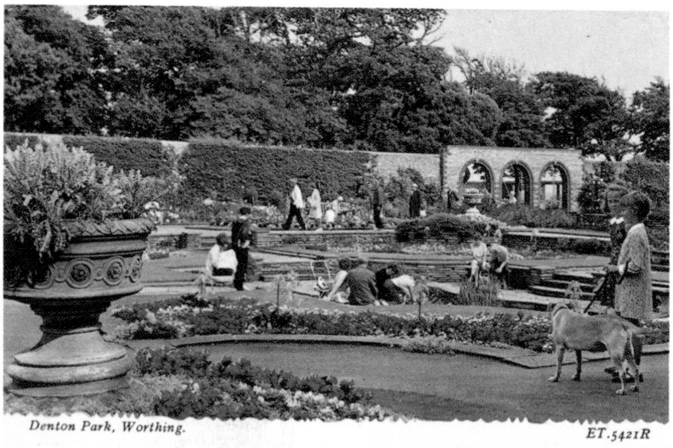
Denton Park, Worthing.
ET.5421R

The magical Denton Gardens, just over the road from our student residence. A source of much inspiration, many midnight feasts, and only a stone's throw from the public bar at The Egremont Hotel.

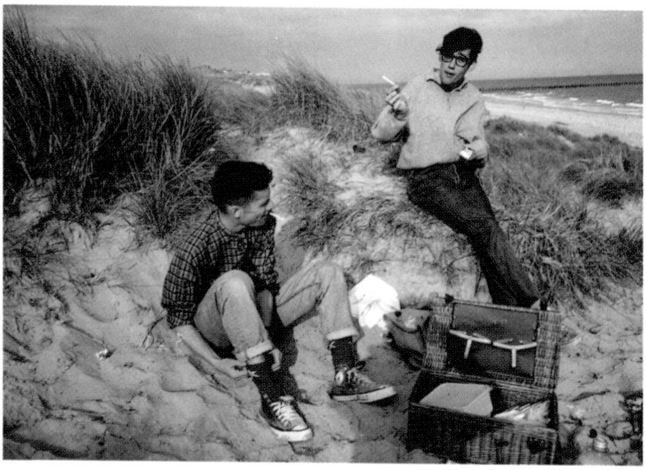

Low tar or no ta? Jamie and the lovely Matt Williams, Climping Sands, Littlehampton. Summer 1988.

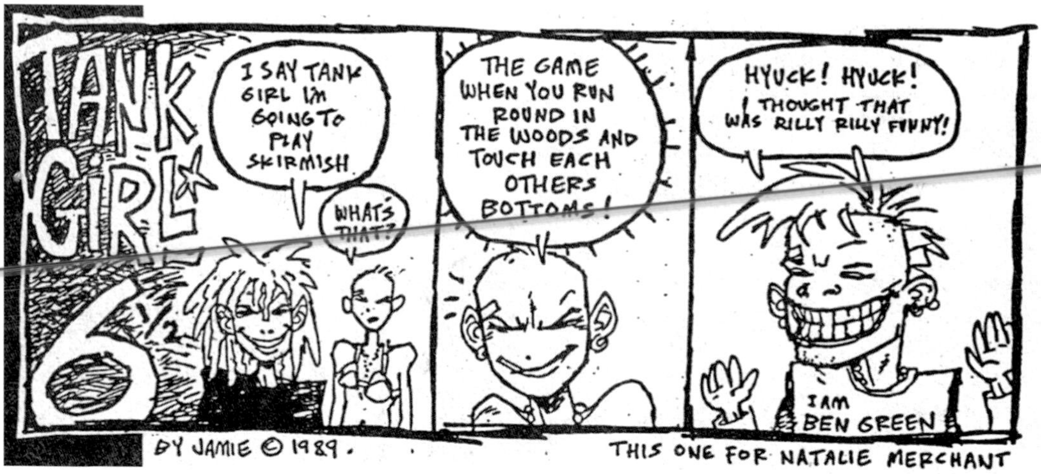
TANK GIRL
6 1/2
I SAY TANK GIRL I'M GOING TO PLAY SKIRMISH
WHAT'S THAT?
THE GAME WHEN YOU RUN ROUND IN THE WOODS AND TOUCH EACH OTHERS BOTTOMS!
HYUCK! HYUCK! I THOUGHT THAT WAS RILLY RILLY FUNNY!
I AM BEN GREEN
BY JAMIE © 1989.
THIS ONE FOR NATALIE MERCHANT

1. The tank. Being kids from the seventies, we all naturally loved tanks; weekend and holiday-time television was awash with war films, some favourites being *The Great Escape*, *The Battle of Britain*, and the tank filled semi-spoof *Kelly's Heroes*. Although this childish affection was ingrained in our hearts, it was an act of serendipitous fortune that put the tank and the girl together: we had been using the suffix "girl" for a long time (since the great advent of the *Supergirl* film, a few years earlier), and Philip already had a character called Rocket Girl (inspired by a girl at college who bore a resemblance to a character from the *Love and Rockets* comics), so when a stray photocopy of a tank picture found its way onto the *Atomtan* page, behind Jamie's chunky-thighed gun-toting femme, she had to be Tank Girl. I mean, what the hell else could we have called her?

Buying a house...? Buy DEADLINE
DEADLINE
no beating about the bush!
DEADLINE
PARTY TIME!
TANK GIRL
JAMIE HEWLETT ©1990
£1•50 MONTHLY
Available from all HIP newsagents & comic shops.
18 years later and the search is still on for a hip newsagent.

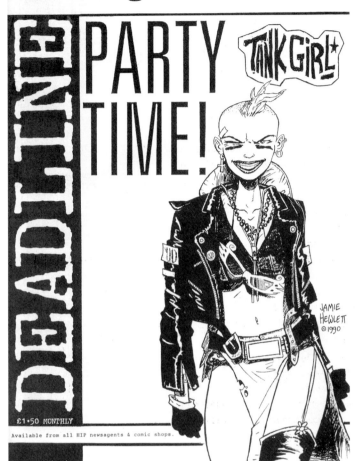

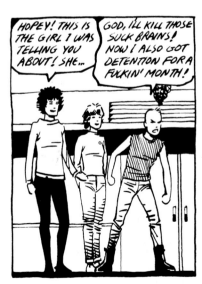

2. The hair. There are several sources for Tank Girl's shaven crown and sprouting front-clump: **a**. Mick Lynch, lead singer from the C86 band Stump (go find a computer and look up "Stump - Buffalo" on YouTube, and you'll see exactly what I'm talking about). **b**. our suede-headed friend Becky from Worthing Art College. **c**. a flashback sequence in issue 2 of the *Love and Rockets* series Mechanix, in which we find Hopey (a *nom-de plume* that Jamie adopted for a few weeks in 1988) sporting said hair-do and wearing a big pair of biker boots. Thinking about it now, there were a lot of people with that very hairstyle in the mid/late eighties; had a survey been carried out, the numbers would probably have run into millions, so to claim any kind of exclusive invention would be preposterous.

HOPEY! THIS IS THE GIRL I WAS TELLING YOU ABOUT! SHE...
GOD, I'LL KILL THOSE SUCK BRAINS! NOW I ALSO GOT DETENTION FOR A FUCKIN' MONTH!
The hair, the boots, the potty-mouth. Hopey kicks things off in Los Bros Hernandez *Love and Rockets* from 1982.

3. Australia. Jamie always maintained that he chose the outback as the setting for Tank Girl's adventures because it was flat and empty of buildings, and therefore very easy to draw. I think it might also have had something to do with Paul Hogan's first *Crocodile Dundee* movie that we were big fans of at the time.

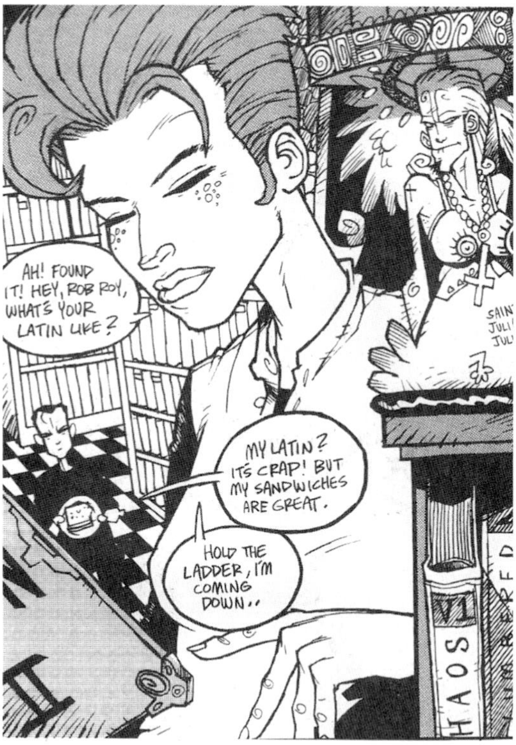
AH! FOUND IT! HEY, ROB ROY, WHAT'S YOUR LATIN LIKE?
MY LATIN? IT'S CRAP! BUT MY SANDWICHES ARE GREAT.
HOLD THE LADDER, I'M COMING DOWN..

A panel from the Hewlett & Martin strip *Hell City*, that originally appeared in book #4 of Garry Leach and Dave Elliott's comics anthology *A1*. Yet another female lead, but this time with added freckles.

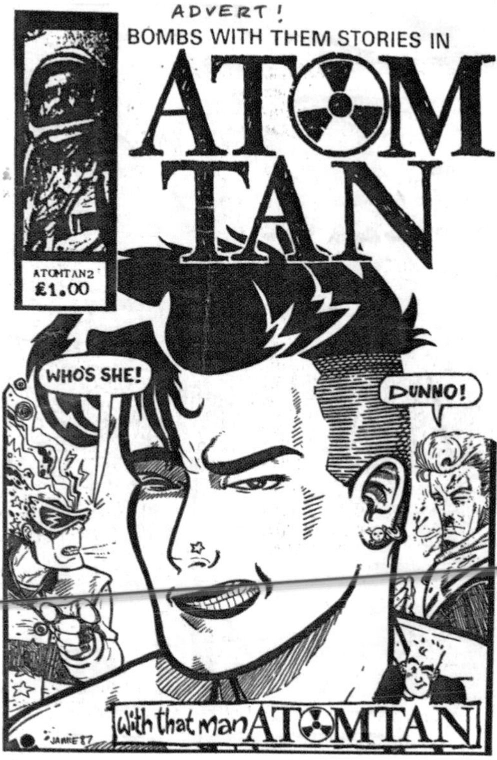
ADVERT!
BOMBS WITH THEM STORIES IN
ATOM TAN
ATOMTAN2
£1.00
WHO'S SHE!
DUNNO!
With that man ATOMTAN

An advert for a never-completed *Atomtan* #3. More hard-arsed, smart-mouthed, indestructible female comic characters, anyone?

And, of course, *Mad Max*. At any rate, it was far enough away from Worthing to seem like another planet to us – a perfect stage for us to imagine our leading lady living her demented life.

4. Popular culture references. Filling every available crevice of the page with song lyrics and name-checks to an eclectic mixture of film and television stars was an extension of our everyday lives. Being such obsessive, pop-culture-gobbling beasts, it was only natural that some of it spilled out onto the page. The majority of the lyrics we quoted would come from what we were listening to as we drew and wrote the strip; Jamie would make mix tapes of all our current favourites and give them strange, homoerotic album names like "Young Men Together Volume 3".

5. Kangaroos. There are lots of kangaroos in Australia. Plus kangaroos are cool.

Over the years there have been umpteen incarnations of this book; this is the latest in a long line. I'm not claiming that this is the "definitive" version or anything so sophisticated. What we have tried to do here is bring together the original work, in correct chronological order, presented as it was first seen (in this case, mainly black and white, with none of the computer colouring that was added later in the mid-nineties), with facts, figures, and release dates for anyone who cares about that kind of shit. We've also included the pages of artwork that Jamie produced for the first Penguin edition back in 1990 (that have been missing from subsequent versions) and a covers gallery of the USA reprints that were published by Dark Horse around that time.

I hope you'll stay with us as we "re-master" the rest of the series and unearth several comic artefacts that have remained unseen and undiscovered for over a decade.

Peace, Love and Rock 'n' Roll,

Alan C. Martin
Nether Largie South burial chamber
Kilmartin
Argyll
Scotland
Feb 2009

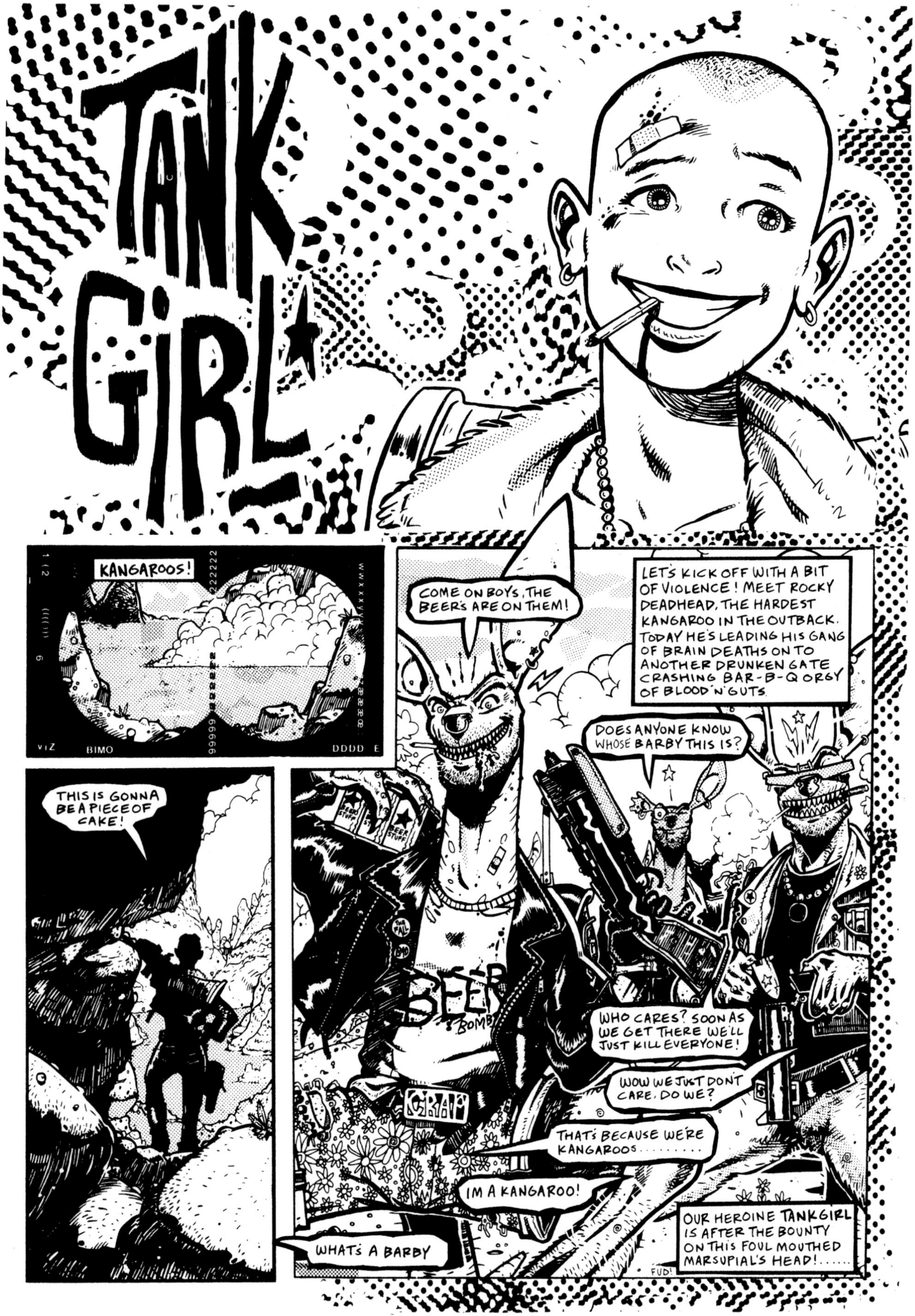
TANK GIRL
KANGAROOS!
THIS IS GONNA BE A PIECE OF CAKE!
COME ON BOYS, THE BEER'S ARE ON THEM!
LET'S KICK OFF WITH A BIT OF VIOLENCE! MEET ROCKY DEADHEAD, THE HARDEST KANGAROO IN THE OUTBACK. TODAY HE'S LEADING HIS GANG OF BRAIN DEATHS ON TO ANOTHER DRUNKEN GATE CRASHING BAR-B-Q ORGY OF BLOOD 'N' GUTS.
DOES ANYONE KNOW WHOSE BARBY THIS IS?
WHO CARES? SOON AS WE GET THERE WE'LL JUST KILL EVERYONE!
WOW WE JUST DONT CARE, DO WE?
THAT'S BECAUSE WE'RE KANGAROOS.........
IM A KANGAROO!
WHAT'S A BARBY
OUR HEROINE TANKGIRL IS AFTER THE BOUNTY ON THIS FOUL MOUTHED MARSUPIAL'S HEAD!......
BEER
BOMB
CRAP
FUD!

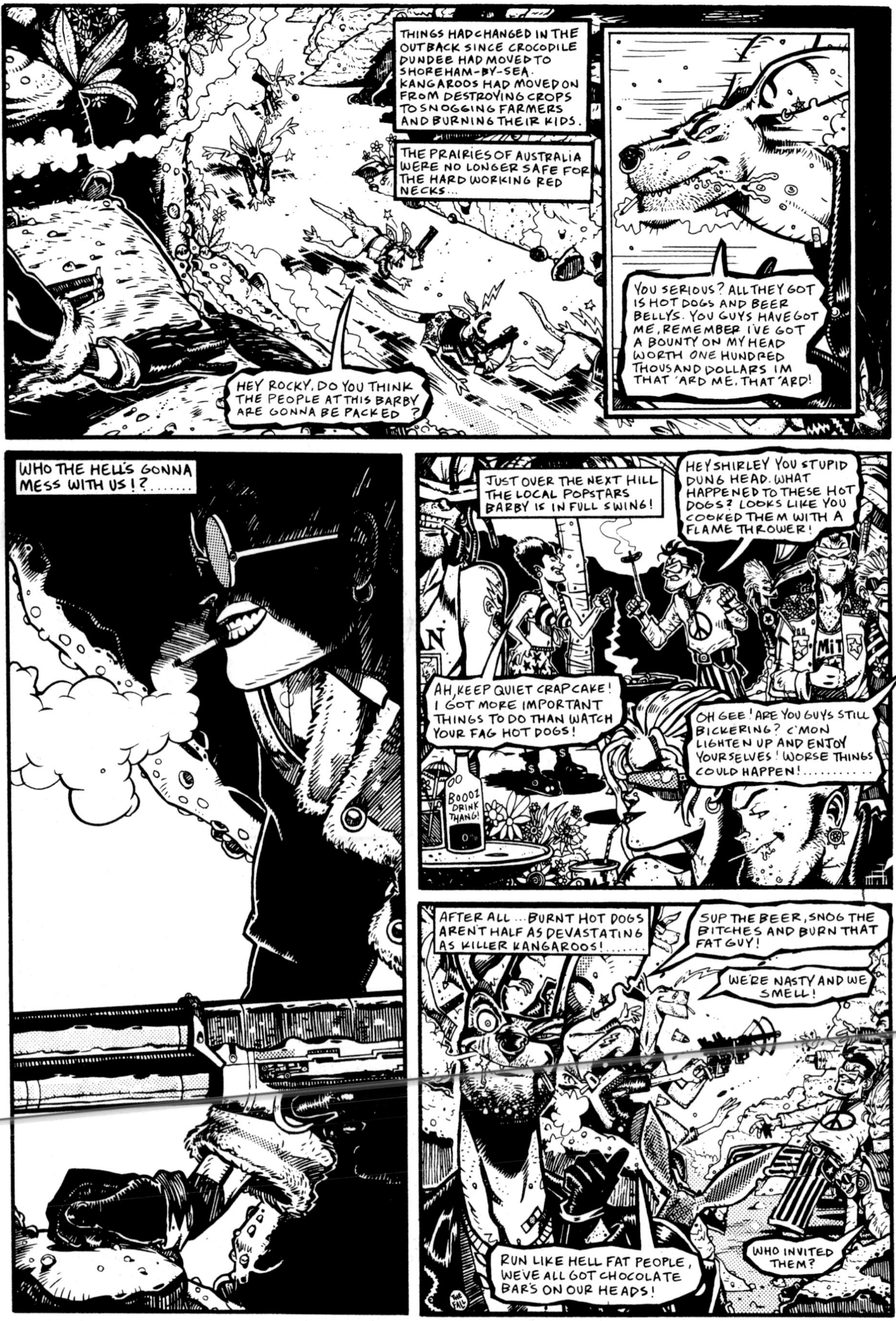
THINGS HAD CHANGED IN THE OUTBACK SINCE CROCODILE DUNDEE HAD MOVED TO SHOREHAM-BY-SEA. KANGAROOS HAD MOVED ON FROM DESTROYING CROPS TO SNOGGING FARMERS AND BURNING THEIR KIDS.
THE PRAIRIES OF AUSTRALIA WERE NO LONGER SAFE FOR THE HARD WORKING RED NECKS...
HEY ROCKY, DO YOU THINK THE PEOPLE AT THIS BARBY ARE GONNA BE PACKED?
YOU SERIOUS? ALL THEY GOT IS HOT DOGS AND BEER BELLYS. YOU GUYS HAVE GOT ME, REMEMBER I'VE GOT A BOUNTY ON MY HEAD WORTH ONE HUNDRED THOUSAND DOLLARS I'M THAT 'ARD ME, THAT 'ARD!
WHO THE HELL'S GONNA MESS WITH US!?.......
JUST OVER THE NEXT HILL THE LOCAL POPSTARS BARBY IS IN FULL SWING!
HEY SHIRLEY YOU STUPID DUNG HEAD. WHAT HAPPENED TO THESE HOT DOGS? LOOKS LIKE YOU COOKED THEM WITH A FLAME THROWER!
AH, KEEP QUIET CRAPCAKE! I GOT MORE IMPORTANT THINGS TO DO THAN WATCH YOUR FAG HOT DOGS!
OH GEE! ARE YOU GUYS STILL BICKERING? C'MON LIGHTEN UP AND ENJOY YOURSELVES! WORSE THINGS COULD HAPPEN!..........
BOOOZ DRINK THANG!
AFTER ALL... BURNT HOT DOGS AREN'T HALF AS DEVASTATING AS KILLER KANGAROOS!......
SUP THE BEER, SNOG THE BITCHES AND BURN THAT FAT GUY!
WE'RE NASTY AND WE SMELL!
RUN LIKE HELL FAT PEOPLE, WE'VE ALL GOT CHOCOLATE BAR'S ON OUR HEADS!
WHO INVITED THEM?

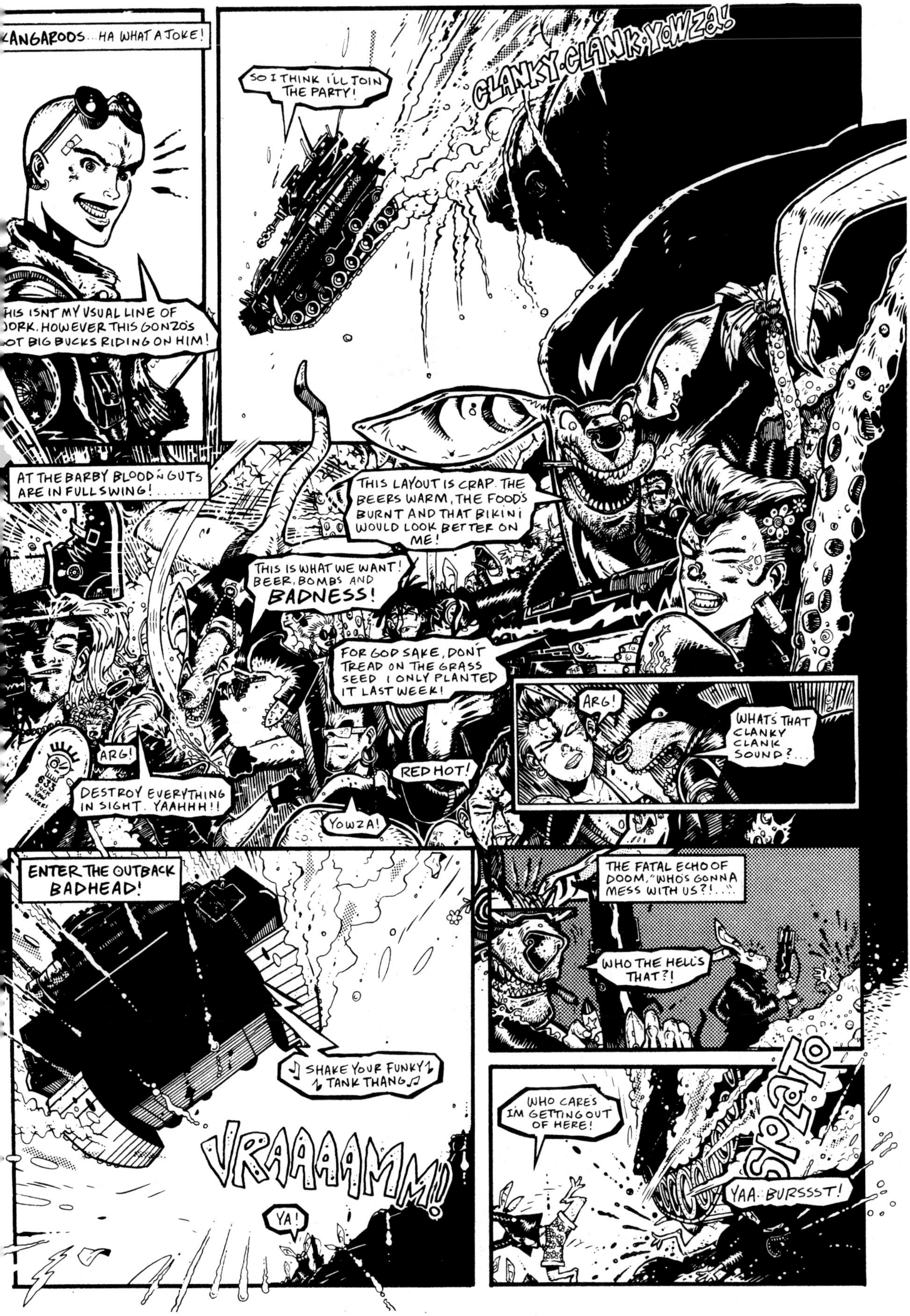
KANGAROOS...HA WHAT A JOKE!
THIS ISNT MY USUAL LINE OF WORK. HOWEVER THIS GONZO'S GOT BIG BUCKS RIDING ON HIM!
SO I THINK I'LL JOIN THE PARTY!
CLANKY·CLANK·YOWZA!
AT THE BARBY BLOOD 'N' GUTS ARE IN FULL SWING!......
THIS LAYOUT IS CRAP. THE BEERS WARM, THE FOOD'S BURNT AND THAT BIKINI WOULD LOOK BETTER ON ME!
THIS IS WHAT WE WANT! BEER, BOMBS AND BADNESS!
FOR GOD SAKE, DON'T TREAD ON THE GRASS SEED I ONLY PLANTED IT LAST WEEK!
ARG!
WHAT'S THAT CLANKY CLANK SOUND?..
ARG!
DESTROY EVERYTHING IN SIGHT. YAAHHH!!
RED HOT!
YOWZA!
ENTER THE OUTBACK BADHEAD!
SHAKE YOUR FUNKY TANK THANG
VRAAAAMM!
YA!
THE FATAL ECHO OF DOOM, "WHO'S GONNA MESS WITH US?!"...
WHO THE HELL'S THAT?!
WHO CARES I'M GETTING OUT OF HERE!
SPLATO
YAA·BURSSST!

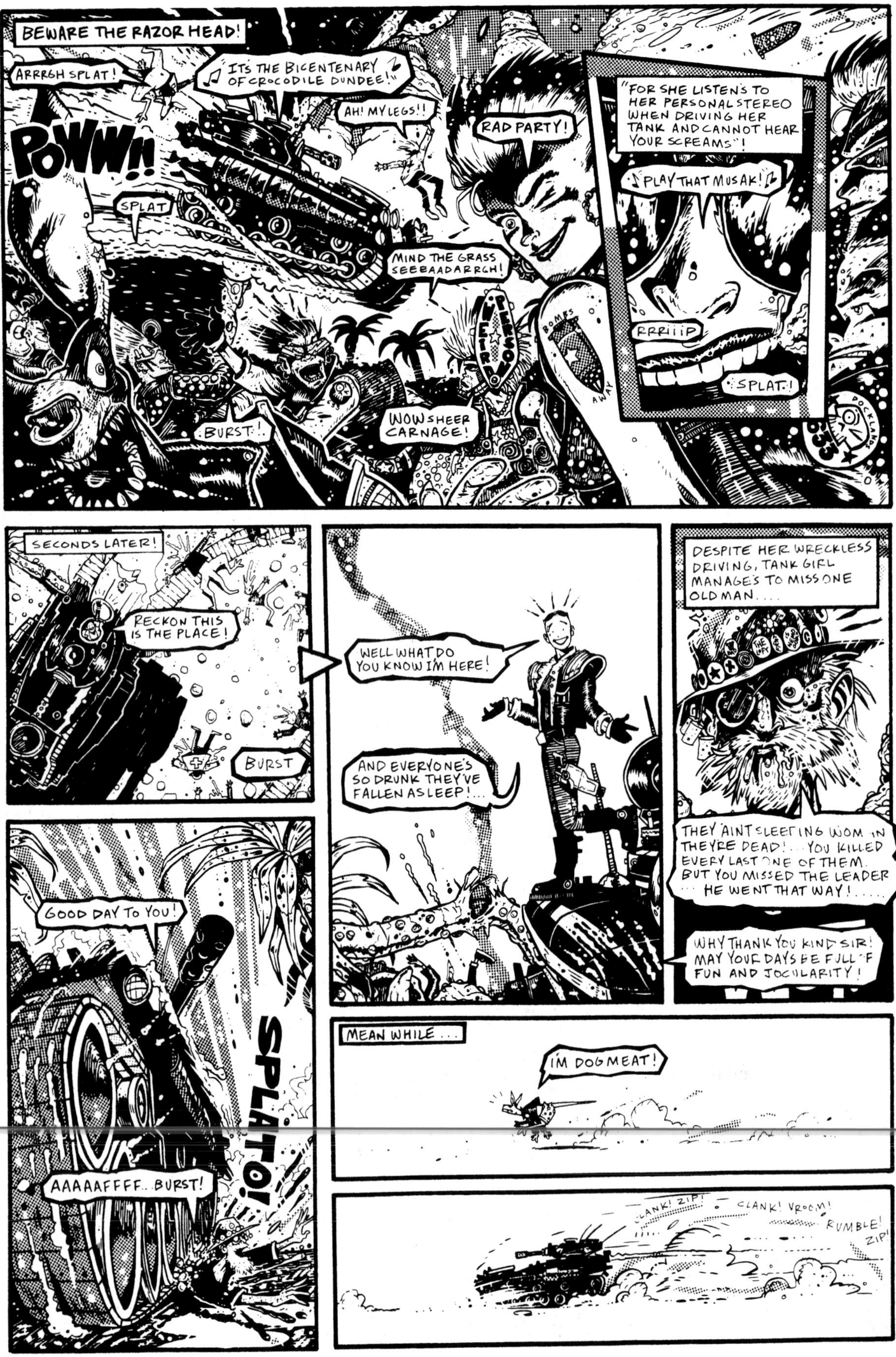

BEWARE THE RAZOR HEAD!
ARRRGH SPLAT!
IT'S THE BICENTENARY OF CROCODILE DUNDEE!
AH! MY LEGS!!
RAD PARTY!
"FOR SHE LISTENS TO HER PERSONAL STEREO WHEN DRIVING HER TANK AND CANNOT HEAR YOUR SCREAMS"!
PLAY THAT MUSAK!
POWW!!
SPLAT
MIND THE GRASS SEEEAADARRGH!
WETRI PERSON
BOMBS AWAY
RRRIIIP
SPLAT!
BURST!
WOW SHEER CARNAGE!
DOCKLANDS 333
SECONDS LATER!
RECKON THIS IS THE PLACE!
BURST
WELL WHAT DO YOU KNOW I'M HERE!
AND EVERYONE'S SO DRUNK THEY'VE FALLEN ASLEEP!...
DESPITE HER WRECKLESS DRIVING, TANK GIRL MANAGES TO MISS ONE OLD MAN....
THEY AINT SLEEPING WOMAN THEY'RE DEAD!... YOU KILLED EVERY LAST ONE OF THEM. BUT YOU MISSED THE LEADER HE WENT THAT WAY!.....
WHY THANK YOU KIND SIR! MAY YOUR DAYS BE FULL OF FUN AND JOCULARITY!
GOOD DAY TO YOU!
SPLATOO!
AAAAAFFFF.. BURST!
MEAN WHILE...
I'M DOGMEAT!
CLANK! ZIP!
CLANK! VROOM!
RUMBLE!
ZIP!

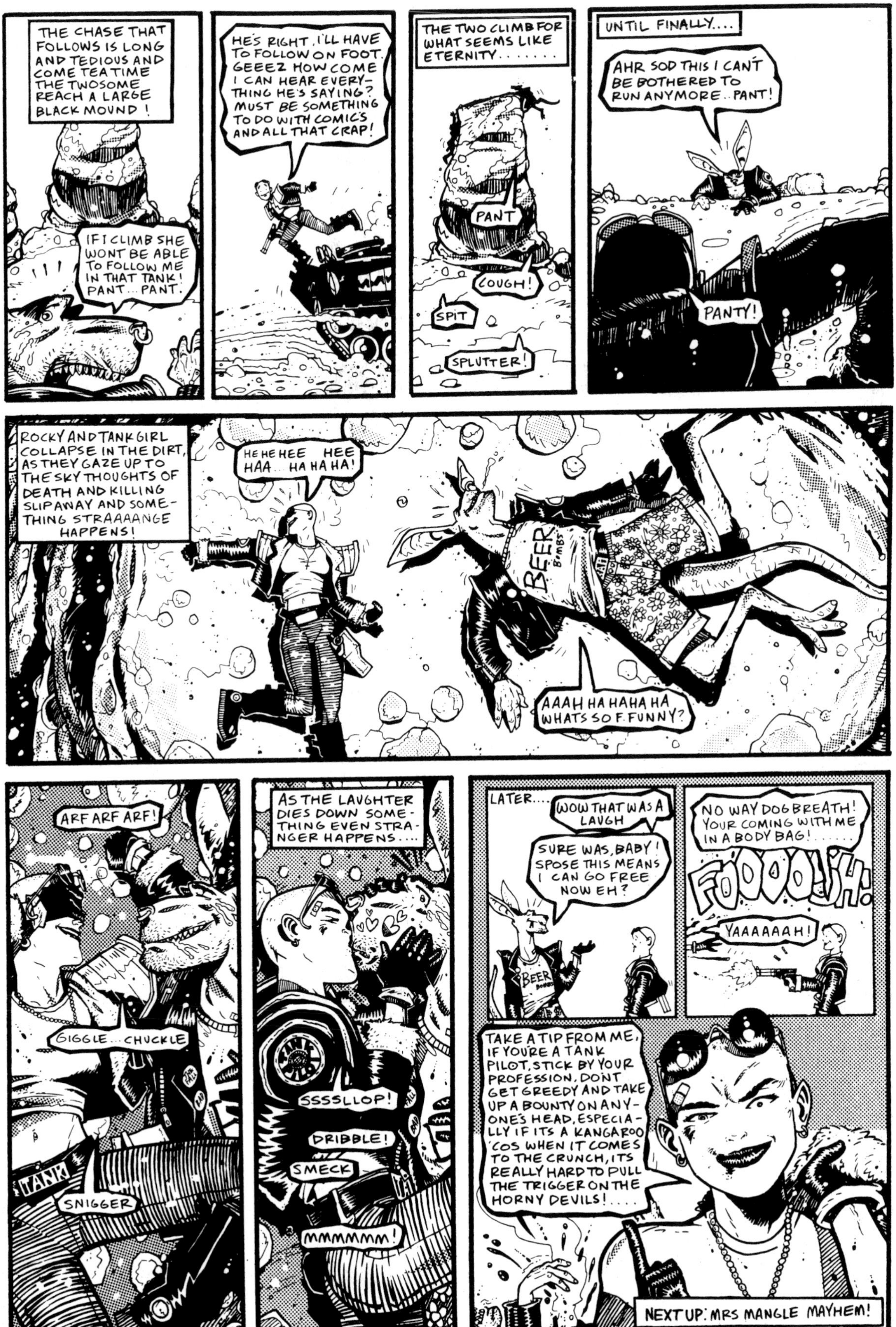
THE CHASE THAT FOLLOWS IS LONG AND TEDIOUS AND COME TEA TIME THE TWOSOME REACH A LARGE BLACK MOUND!
IF I CLIMB SHE WONT BE ABLE TO FOLLOW ME IN THAT TANK! PANT... PANT.
HE'S RIGHT, I'LL HAVE TO FOLLOW ON FOOT. GEEEZ HOW COME I CAN HEAR EVERYTHING HE'S SAYING? MUST BE SOMETHING TO DO WITH COMICS AND ALL THAT CRAP!
THE TWO CLIMB FOR WHAT SEEMS LIKE ETERNITY.......
PANT
COUGH!
SPIT
SPLUTTER!
UNTIL FINALLY....
AHR SOD THIS I CAN'T BE BOTHERED TO RUN ANYMORE.. PANT!
PANTY!
ROCKY AND TANK GIRL COLLAPSE IN THE DIRT, AS THEY GAZE UP TO THE SKY THOUGHTS OF DEATH AND KILLING SLIPAWAY AND SOMETHING STRAAAANGE HAPPENS!
HE HE HEE HEE HAA... HA HA HA!
BEER
AAAH HA HAHAHA HA WHATS SO F. FUNNY?
ARF ARF ARF!
GIGGLE... CHUCKLE
TANK
SNIGGER
AS THE LAUGHTER DIES DOWN SOMETHING EVEN STRANGER HAPPENS....
SSSSLLOP!
DRIBBLE!
SMECK
MMMMMMM!
LATER....
WOW THAT WAS A LAUGH
SURE WAS, BABY! SPOSE THIS MEANS I CAN GO FREE NOW EH?
BEER
NO WAY DOG BREATH! YOUR COMING WITH ME IN A BODY BAG!......
FOOOOSH!
YAAAAAAH!
TAKE A TIP FROM ME, IF YOU'RE A TANK PILOT, STICK BY YOUR PROFESSION, DONT GET GREEDY AND TAKE UP A BOUNTY ON ANYONE'S HEAD, ESPECIALLY IF ITS A KANGAROO 'COS WHEN IT COMES TO THE CRUNCH, ITS REALLY HARD TO PULL THE TRIGGER ON THE HORNY DEVILS!...
NEXT UP: MRS MANGLE MAYHEM!

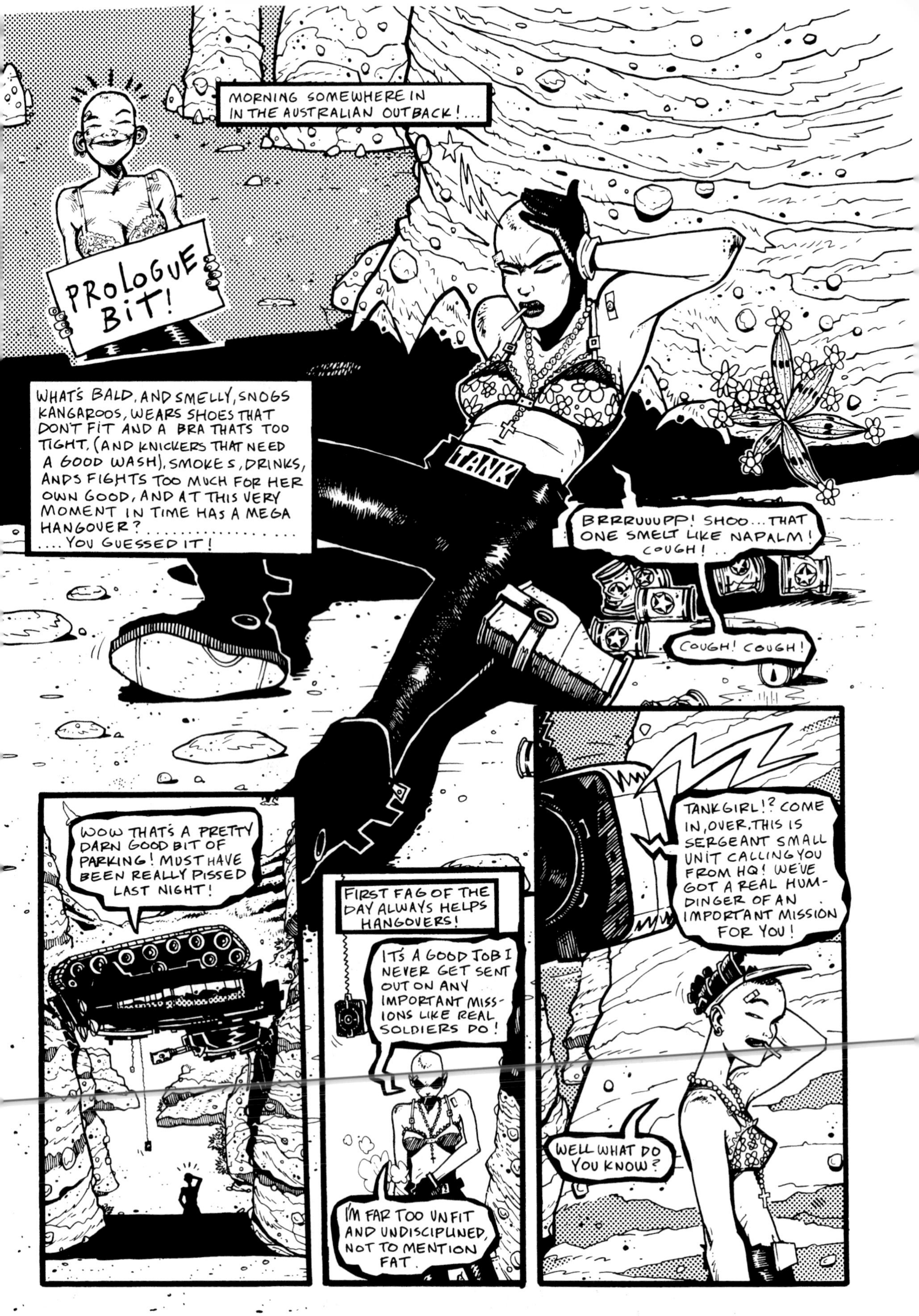
PROLOGUE BIT!
MORNING SOMEWHERE IN IN THE AUSTRALIAN OUTBACK!...
WHAT'S BALD, AND SMELLY, SNOGS KANGAROOS, WEARS SHOES THAT DON'T FIT AND A BRA THATS TOO TIGHT, (AND KNICKERS THAT NEED A GOOD WASH), SMOKES, DRINKS, ANDS FIGHTS TOO MUCH FOR HER OWN GOOD, AND AT THIS VERY MOMENT IN TIME HAS A MEGA HANGOVER? ....YOU GUESSED IT!
TANK
BRRRUUUPP! SHOO... THAT ONE SMELT LIKE NAPALM! COUGH!
COUGH! COUGH!
WOW THAT'S A PRETTY DARN GOOD BIT OF PARKING! MUST HAVE BEEN REALLY PISSED LAST NIGHT!
FIRST FAG OF THE DAY ALWAYS HELPS HANGOVERS!
IT'S A GOOD JOB I NEVER GET SENT OUT ON ANY IMPORTANT MISSIONS LIKE REAL SOLDIERS DO!
I'M FAR TOO UNFIT AND UNDISCIPLINED, NOT TO MENTION FAT
TANKGIRL!? COME IN, OVER. THIS IS SERGEANT SMALL UNIT CALLING YOU FROM HQ! WE'VE GOT A REAL HUMDINGER OF AN IMPORTANT MISSION FOR YOU!
WELL WHAT DO YOU KNOW?

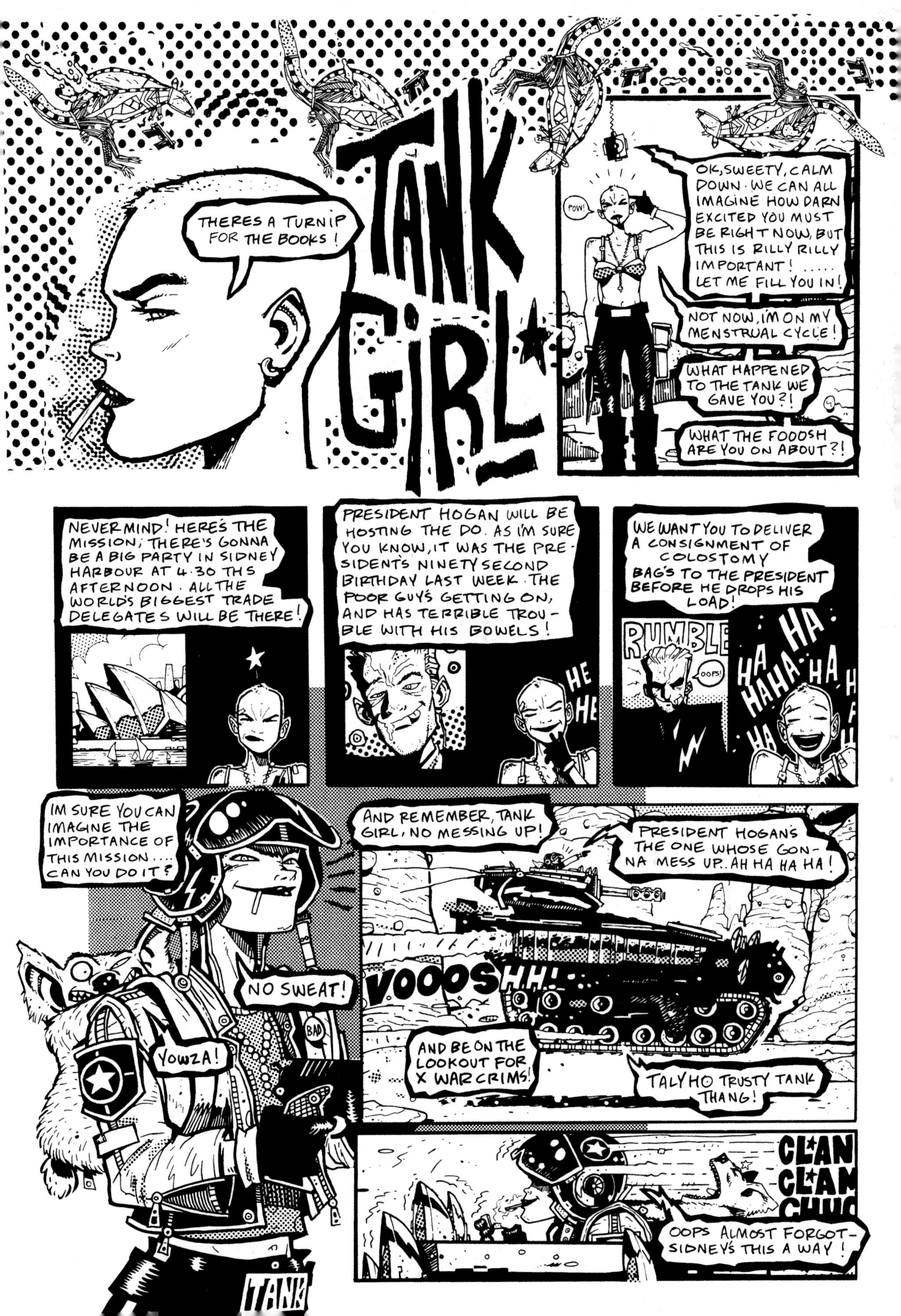
TANK GIRL
THERES A TURNIP FOR THE BOOKS!
OK, SWEETY, CALM DOWN. WE CAN ALL IMAGINE HOW DARN EXCITED YOU MUST BE RIGHT NOW, BUT THIS IS RILLY RILLY IMPORTANT! ..... LET ME FILL YOU IN!
POW!
NOT NOW, I'M ON MY MENSTRUAL CYCLE!
WHAT HAPPENED TO THE TANK WE GAVE YOU?!
WHAT THE FOOOSH ARE YOU ON ABOUT?!
NEVERMIND! HERE'S THE MISSION; THERE'S GONNA BE A BIG PARTY IN SIDNEY HARBOUR AT 4.30 THS AFTERNOON. ALL THE WORLD'S BIGGEST TRADE DELEGATES WILL BE THERE!
PRESIDENT HOGAN WILL BE HOSTING THE DO. AS I'M SURE YOU KNOW, IT WAS THE PRESIDENT'S NINETY SECOND BIRTHDAY LAST WEEK. THE POOR GUY'S GETTING ON, AND HAS TERRIBLE TROUBLE WITH HIS BOWELS!
HE HE
WE WANT YOU TO DELIVER A CONSIGNMENT OF COLOSTOMY BAG'S TO THE PRESIDENT BEFORE HE DROPS HIS LOAD!
RUMBLE
OOPS!
HA HA HA HA HA HAHA HA HA
IM SURE YOU CAN IMAGINE THE IMPORTANCE OF THIS MISSION... CAN YOU DO IT?
NO SWEAT!
BAD
YOWZA!
TANK
AND REMEMBER, TANK GIRL, NO MESSING UP!
PRESIDENT HOGAN'S THE ONE WHOSE GONNA MESS UP.. AH HA HA HA!
VOOOSHH!
AND BE ON THE LOOKOUT FOR X WAR CRIMS!
TALY HO TRUSTY TANK THANG!
CLAN CLAN CHUG
OOPS ALMOST FORGOT - SIDNEY'S THIS A WAY!

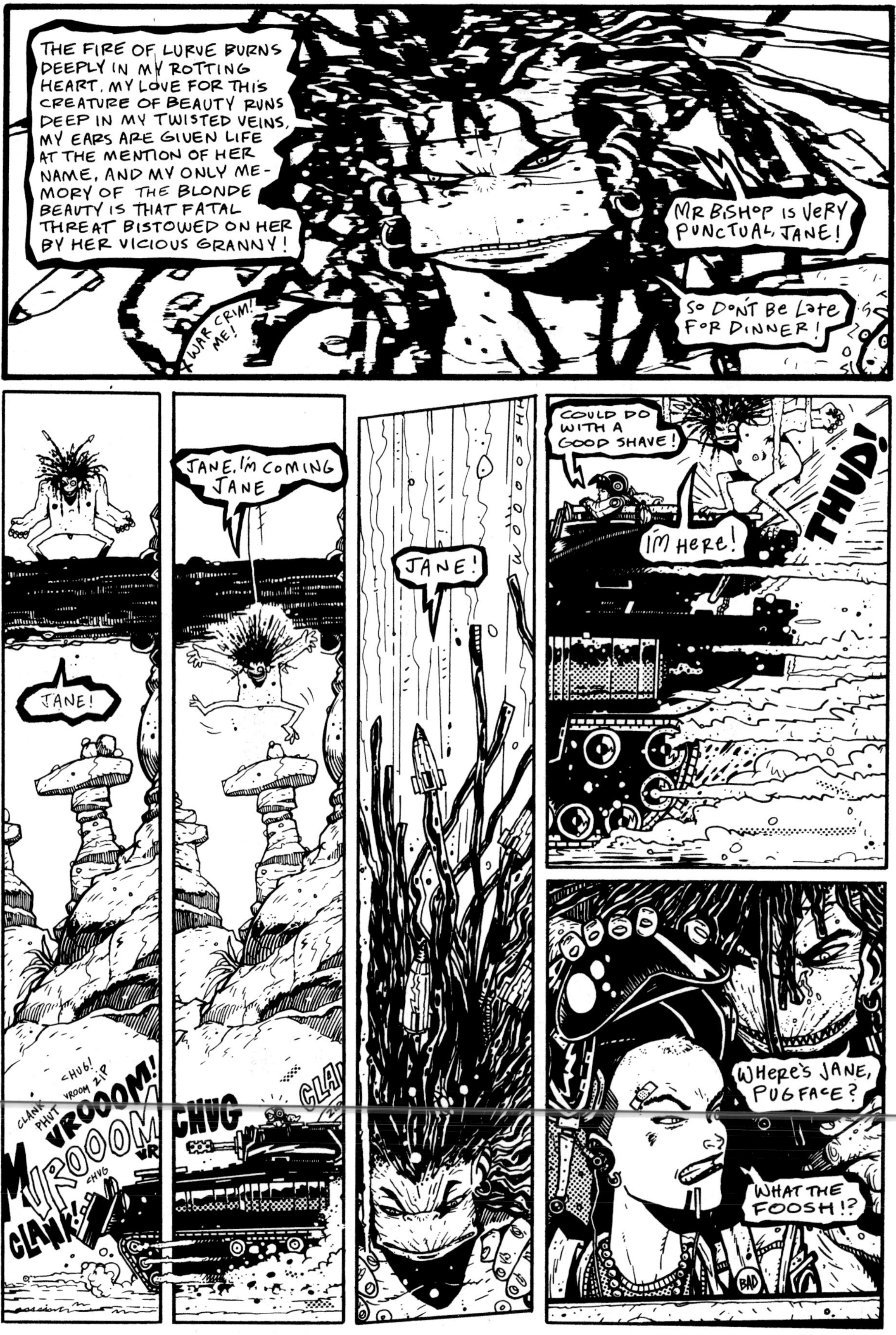
THE FIRE OF LURVE BURNS DEEPLY IN MY ROTTING HEART, MY LOVE FOR THIS CREATURE OF BEAUTY RUNS DEEP IN MY TWISTED VEINS, MY EARS ARE GIVEN LIFE AT THE MENTION OF HER NAME, AND MY ONLY MEMORY OF THE BLONDE BEAUTY IS THAT FATAL THREAT BISTOWED ON HER BY HER VICIOUS GRANNY!
MR BISHOP IS VERY PUNCTUAL, JANE!
SO DON'T BE LATE FOR DINNER!
WAR CRIM! ME!
JANE!
CHUG!
VROOM ZIP
CLANK
PHUT
VROOOM!
VROOOM
CHUG
CLANK!
CLANK
JANE, I'M COMING JANE
JANE!
WOOOOOSH
COULD DO WITH A GOOD SHAVE!
I'M HERE!
THUD!
WHERE'S JANE, PUGFACE?
WHAT THE FOOSH!?
BAD

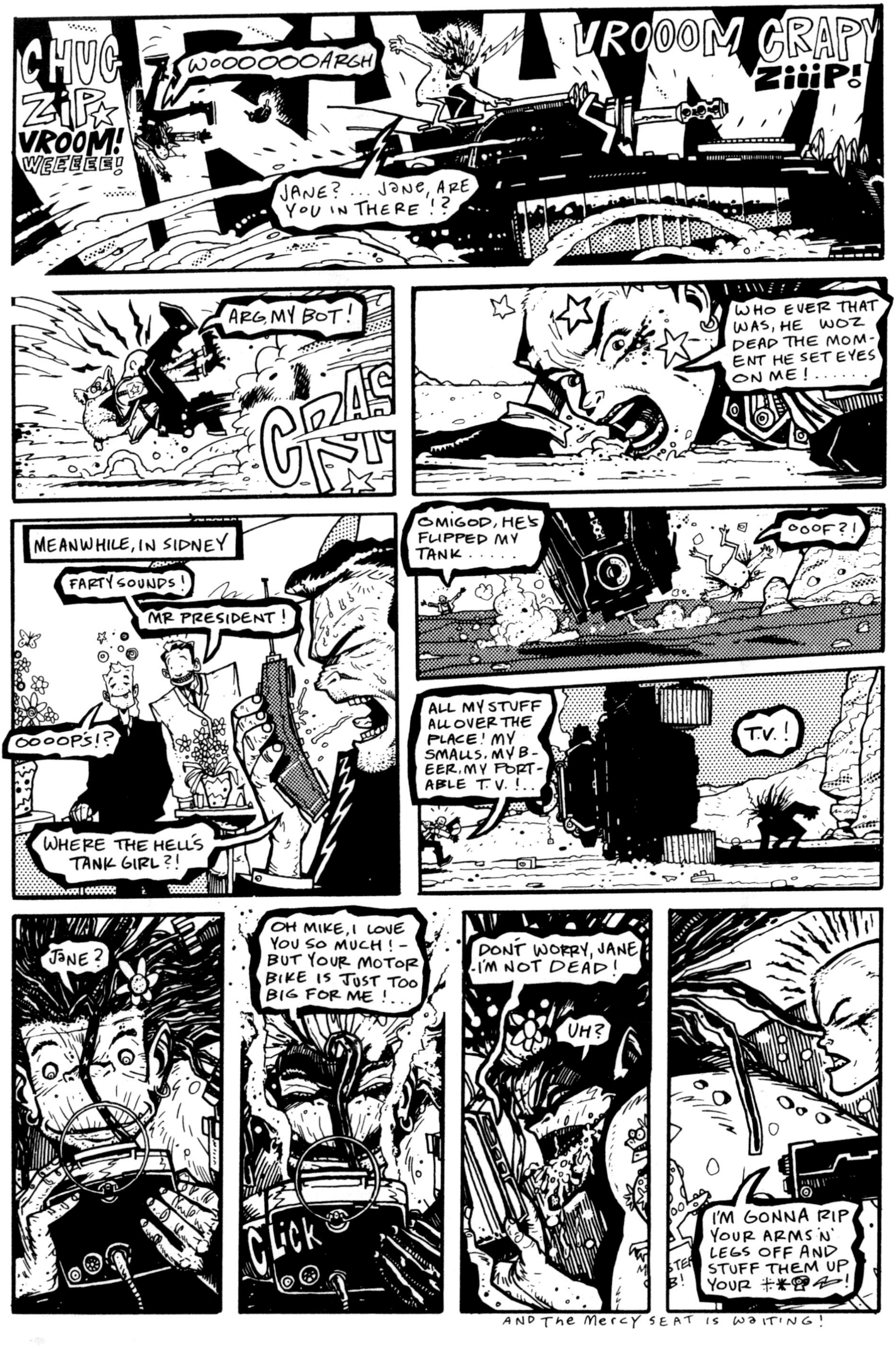
CHUG
ZIP
VROOM!
WEEEEE!
WOOOOOOOARGH
VROOOM CRAPY
ZIIIP!
JANE? ... JANE, ARE YOU IN THERE!?
ARG, MY BOT!
CRAS
WHO EVER THAT WAS, HE WOZ DEAD THE MOMENT HE SET EYES ON ME!.....
MEANWHILE, IN SIDNEY
FARTY SOUNDS!
MR PRESIDENT!
OOOOPS!?
WHERE THE HELL'S TANK GIRL?!
OMIGOD, HE'S FLIPPED MY TANK.....
OOOF?!
ALL MY STUFF ALL OVER THE PLACE! MY SMALLS, MY BEER, MY PORTABLE T.V.!..
T.V.!
JANE?
OH MIKE, I LOVE YOU SO MUCH! - BUT YOUR MOTOR BIKE IS JUST TOO BIG FOR ME!..
CLICK
DON'T WORRY, JANE I'M NOT DEAD!
UH?
I'M GONNA RIP YOUR ARMS 'N' LEGS OFF AND STUFF THEM UP YOUR #*@!
AND THE MERCY SEAT IS WAITING!

POW!

SPLAMBO!

BUG OFF, PUG FACE!

OOOF

IN THE COMMOTION TANK GIRL GRABS THE NEAREST THING!

ARHH!

SUCK-THIS

ALAS DEAR YORICK- I KNEW HIS SHELF!

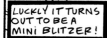

LUCKLY IT TURNS OUT TO BE A MINI BLITZER!

DOOOSH!

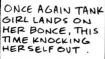

ONCE AGAIN TANK GIRL LANDS ON HER BONCE, THIS TIME KNOCKING HERSELF OUT.

YOW OOOF! CRUNCH!!!

UNTIL NEXTDAY!

SHEESH! YOU'RE LOOKING A MESS, TANK GIRL. WHAT HAPPENED?

SURE IS!

LOOKS LIKE WE BOTH MESSED UP!

CHRIST KNOWS. CAN'T REMEMBER A THING THAT'S HAPPENED IN THE LAST TWO DAYS!

$

YLY NEWSPAPER

DUMP MASTER

PRESIDENT DROPS HIS LOAD!

TANK GIRL TO BLAME!

GUESS THAT MEANS YOU DON'T KNOW YOUR FACE IS ALL OVER THE PAPERS?

SOUNDS LIKE FAME! (AGAIN)

NEXT TIME: THE SACK!?

☆ JAMIE (TANKBOY) 88 ©

TANK

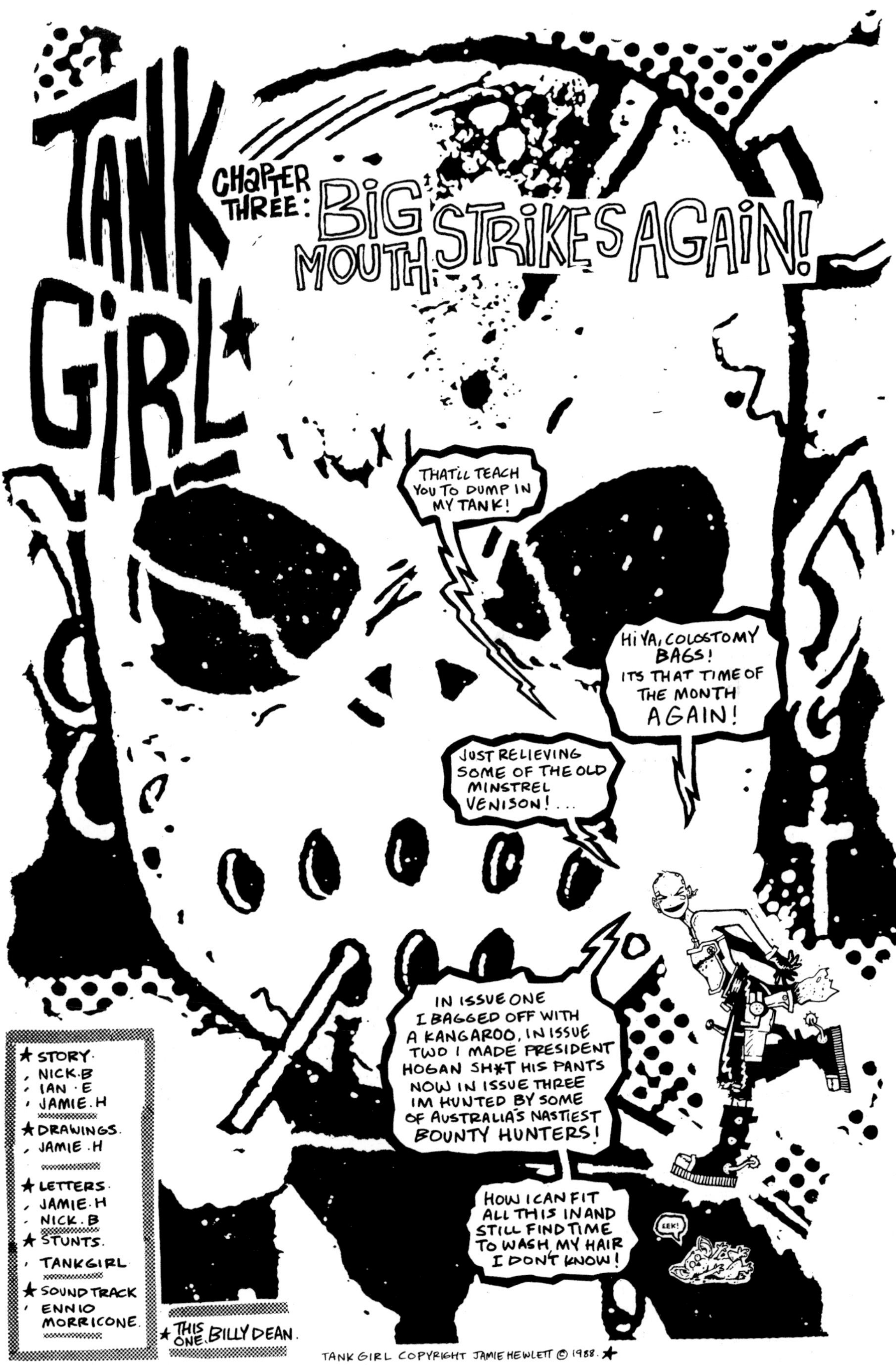
TANK GIRL
CHAPTER THREE: BIG MOUTH STRIKES AGAIN!
THAT'LL TEACH YOU TO DUMP IN MY TANK!
HI YA, COLOSTOMY BAGS! ITS THAT TIME OF THE MONTH AGAIN!
JUST RELIEVING SOME OF THE OLD MINSTREL VENISON!...
IN ISSUE ONE I BAGGED OFF WITH A KANGAROO, IN ISSUE TWO I MADE PRESIDENT HOGAN SH*T HIS PANTS NOW IN ISSUE THREE IM HUNTED BY SOME OF AUSTRALIA'S NASTIEST BOUNTY HUNTERS!
HOW I CAN FIT ALL THIS IN AND STILL FIND TIME TO WASH MY HAIR I DON'T KNOW!
EEK!
★ STORY. NICK.B IAN.E JAMIE.H
★ DRAWINGS. JAMIE.H
★ LETTERS. JAMIE.H NICK.B
★ STUNTS. TANKGIRL
★ SOUND TRACK ENNIO MORRICONE.
★ THIS ONE. BILLY DEAN.

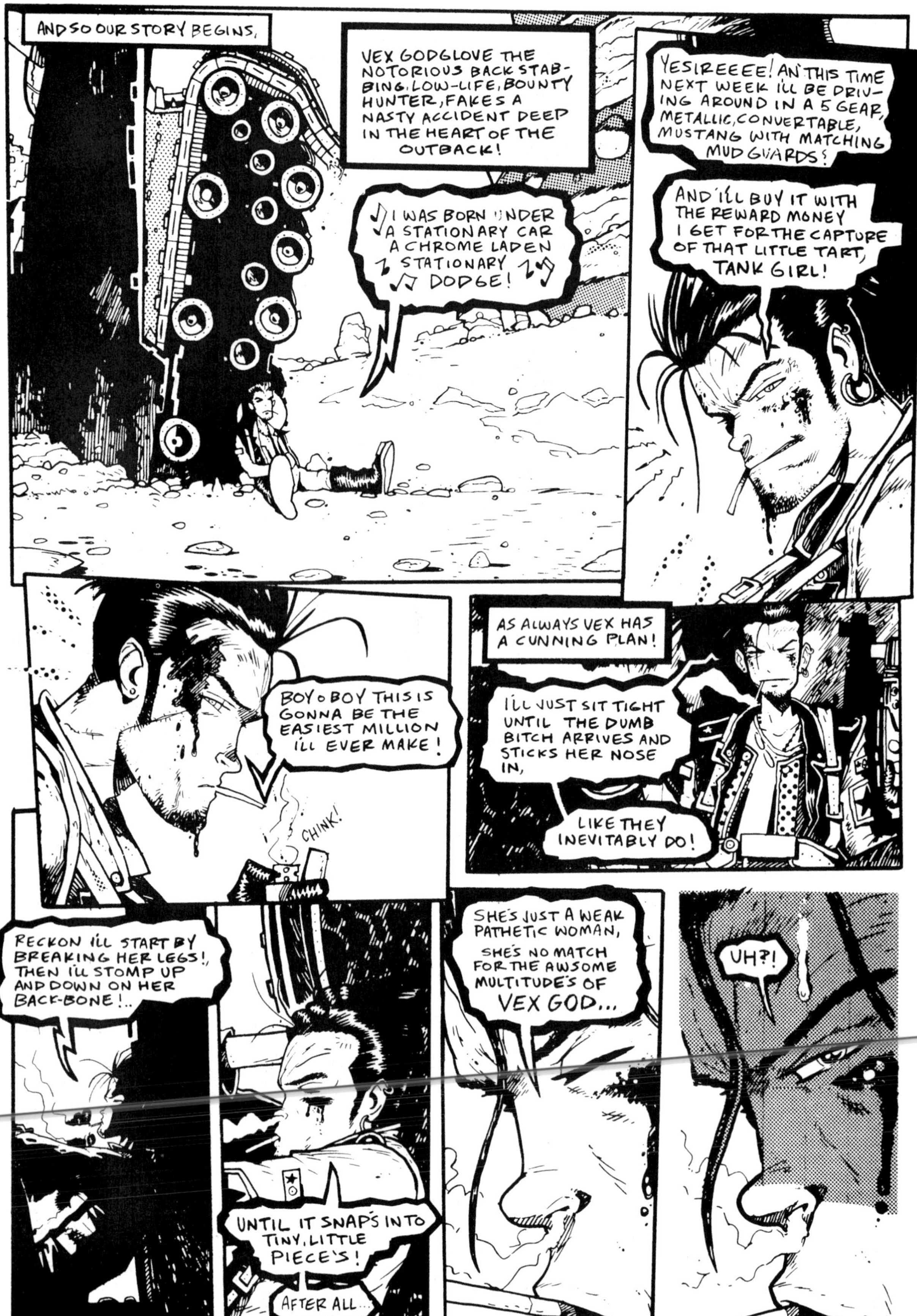
AND SO OUR STORY BEGINS,
VEX GODGLOVE THE NOTORIOUS BACK STABBING, LOW-LIFE, BOUNTY HUNTER, FAKES A NASTY ACCIDENT DEEP IN THE HEART OF THE OUTBACK!
I WAS BORN UNDER A STATIONARY CAR A CHROME LADEN STATIONARY DODGE!
YESIREEEE! AN' THIS TIME NEXT WEEK I'LL BE DRIVING AROUND IN A 5 GEAR, METALLIC, CONVERTABLE, MUSTANG WITH MATCHING MUD GUARDS!
AND I'LL BUY IT WITH THE REWARD MONEY I GET FOR THE CAPTURE OF THAT LITTLE TART, TANK GIRL!
BOY o BOY THIS IS GONNA BE THE EASIEST MILLION I'LL EVER MAKE!
CHINK!
AS ALWAYS VEX HAS A CUNNING PLAN!
I'LL JUST SIT TIGHT UNTIL THE DUMB BITCH ARRIVES AND STICKS HER NOSE IN,
LIKE THEY INEVITABLY DO!
RECKON I'LL START BY BREAKING HER LEGS! THEN I'LL STOMP UP AND DOWN ON HER BACK-BONE!..
UNTIL IT SNAP'S INTO TINY, LITTLE PIECE'S!
AFTER ALL...
SHE'S JUST A WEAK PATHETIC WOMAN,
SHE'S NO MATCH FOR THE AWSOME MULTITUDE'S OF VEX GOD...
UH?!

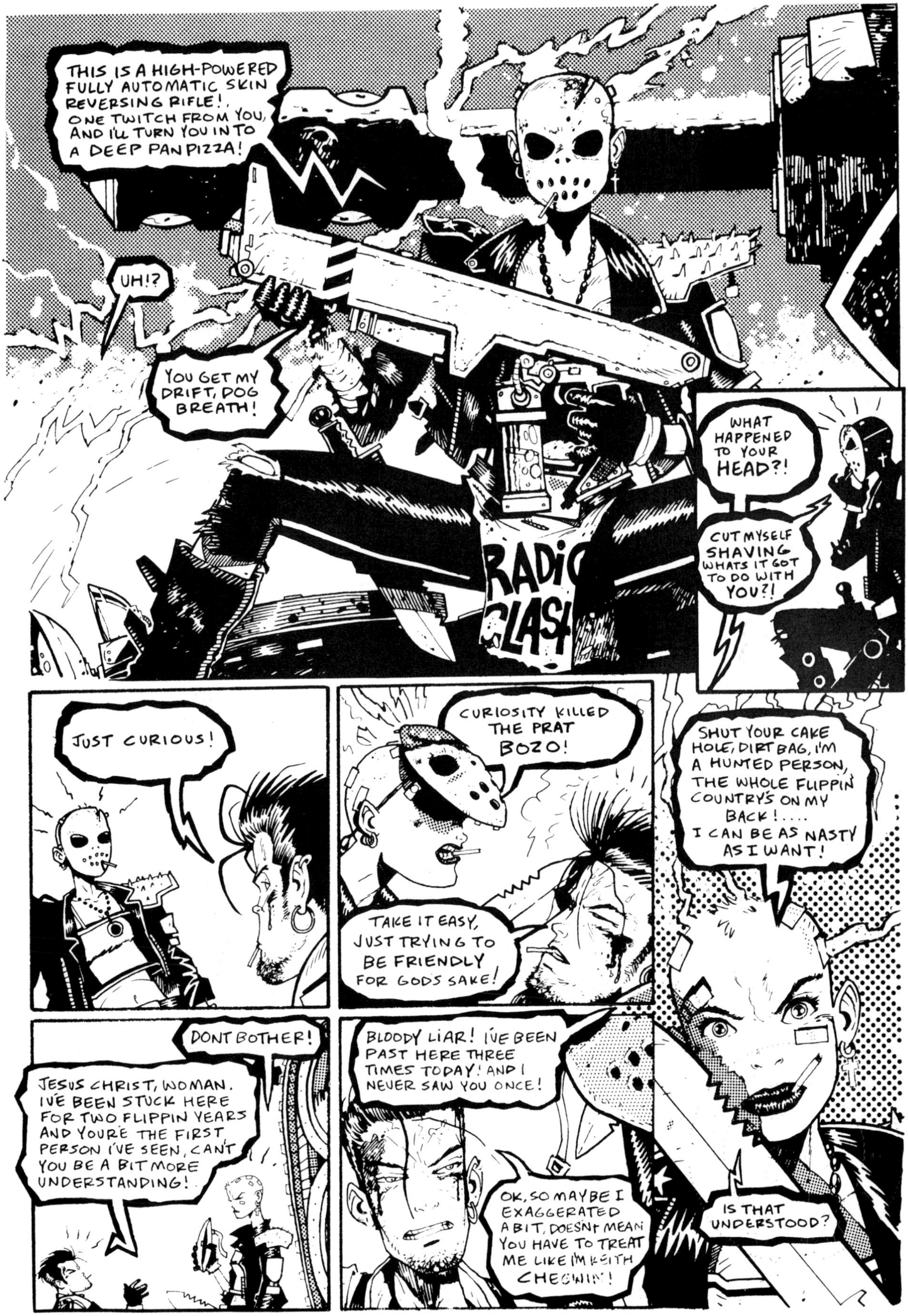
THIS IS A HIGH-POWERED FULLY AUTOMATIC SKIN REVERSING RIFLE! ONE TWITCH FROM YOU, AND I'LL TURN YOU IN TO A DEEP PAN PIZZA!
UH!?
YOU GET MY DRIFT, DOG BREATH!
RADIO CLASH
WHAT HAPPENED TO YOUR HEAD?!
CUT MYSELF SHAVING WHATS IT GOT TO DO WITH YOU?!
JUST CURIOUS!
CURIOSITY KILLED THE PRAT BOZO!
TAKE IT EASY, JUST TRYING TO BE FRIENDLY FOR GODS SAKE!
SHUT YOUR CAKE HOLE, DIRT BAG, I'M A HUNTED PERSON, THE WHOLE FLIPPIN COUNTRY'S ON MY BACK!.... I CAN BE AS NASTY AS I WANT!
DONT BOTHER!
JESUS CHRIST, WOMAN. I'VE BEEN STUCK HERE FOR TWO FLIPPIN YEARS AND YOU'RE THE FIRST PERSON I'VE SEEN, CAN'T YOU BE A BIT MORE UNDERSTANDING!
BLOODY LIAR! I'VE BEEN PAST HERE THREE TIMES TODAY! AND I NEVER SAW YOU ONCE!
OK, SO MAYBE I EXAGGERATED A BIT, DOESN'T MEAN YOU HAVE TO TREAT ME LIKE I'M KEITH CHEGWIN!
IS THAT UNDERSTOOD?

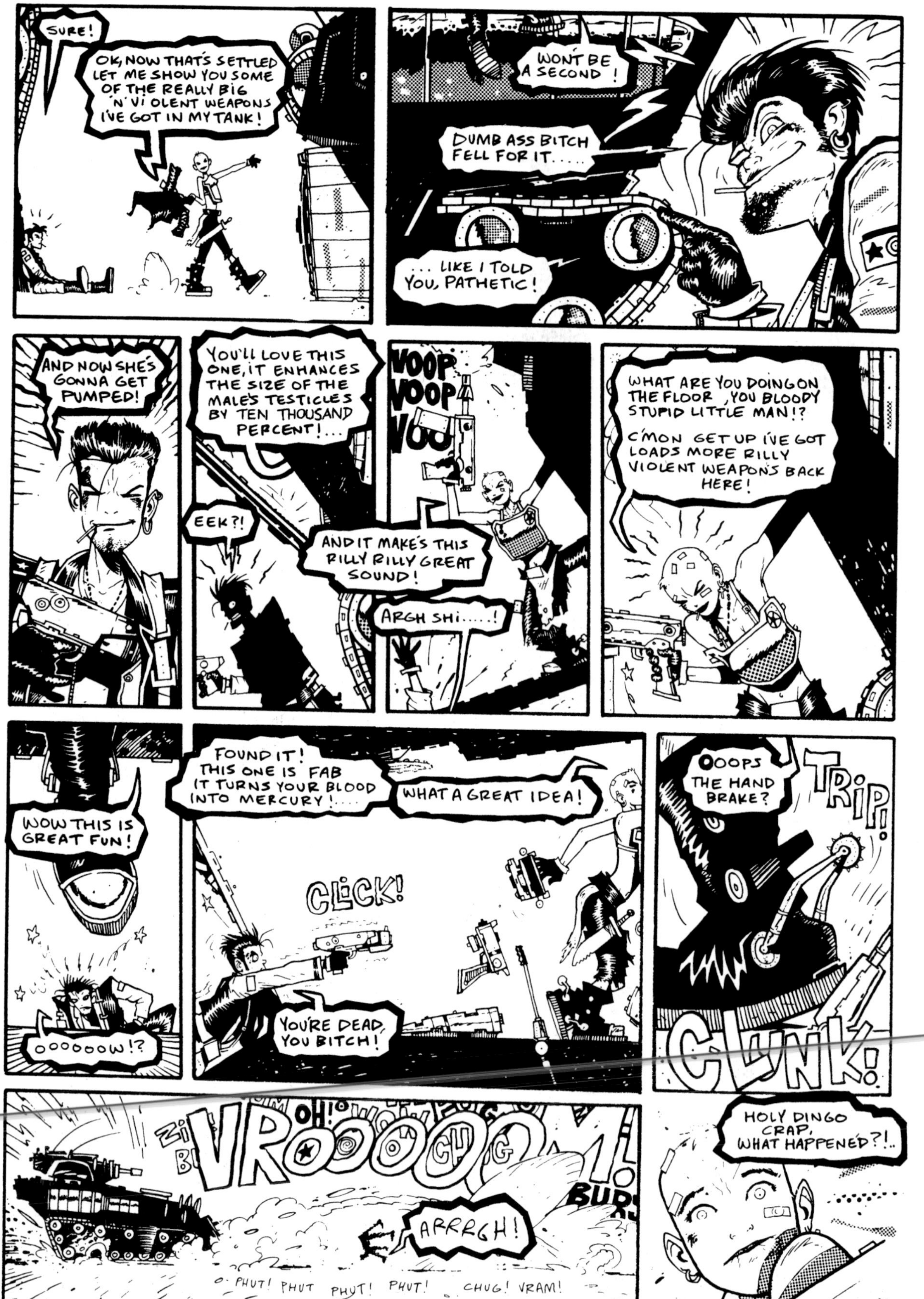
SURE!
OK, NOW THAT'S SETTLED LET ME SHOW YOU SOME OF THE REALLY BIG 'N' VIOLENT WEAPONS I'VE GOT IN MY TANK!
WON'T BE A SECOND!
DUMB ASS BITCH FELL FOR IT.....
...LIKE I TOLD YOU, PATHETIC!
AND NOW SHE'S GONNA GET PUMPED!
YOU'LL LOVE THIS ONE, IT ENHANCES THE SIZE OF THE MALE'S TESTICLES BY TEN THOUSAND PERCENT!...
EEK?!
VOOP VOOP VOO
AND IT MAKE'S THIS RILLY RILLY GREAT SOUND!
ARGH SHI.....!
WHAT ARE YOU DOING ON THE FLOOR, YOU BLOODY STUPID LITTLE MAN!?
C'MON GET UP I'VE GOT LOADS MORE RILLY VIOLENT WEAPONS BACK HERE!
WOW THIS IS GREAT FUN!
OOOOOOW!?
FOUND IT! THIS ONE IS FAB IT TURNS YOUR BLOOD INTO MERCURY!....
WHAT A GREAT IDEA!
CLICK!
YOU'RE DEAD, YOU BITCH!
OOOPS THE HAND BRAKE?
TRIP!
CLUNK!
VROOOOOOM!
OH!
ARRRGH!
PHUT! PHUT PHUT! PHUT! CHUG! VRAM!
HOLY DINGO CRAP, WHAT HAPPENED?!..

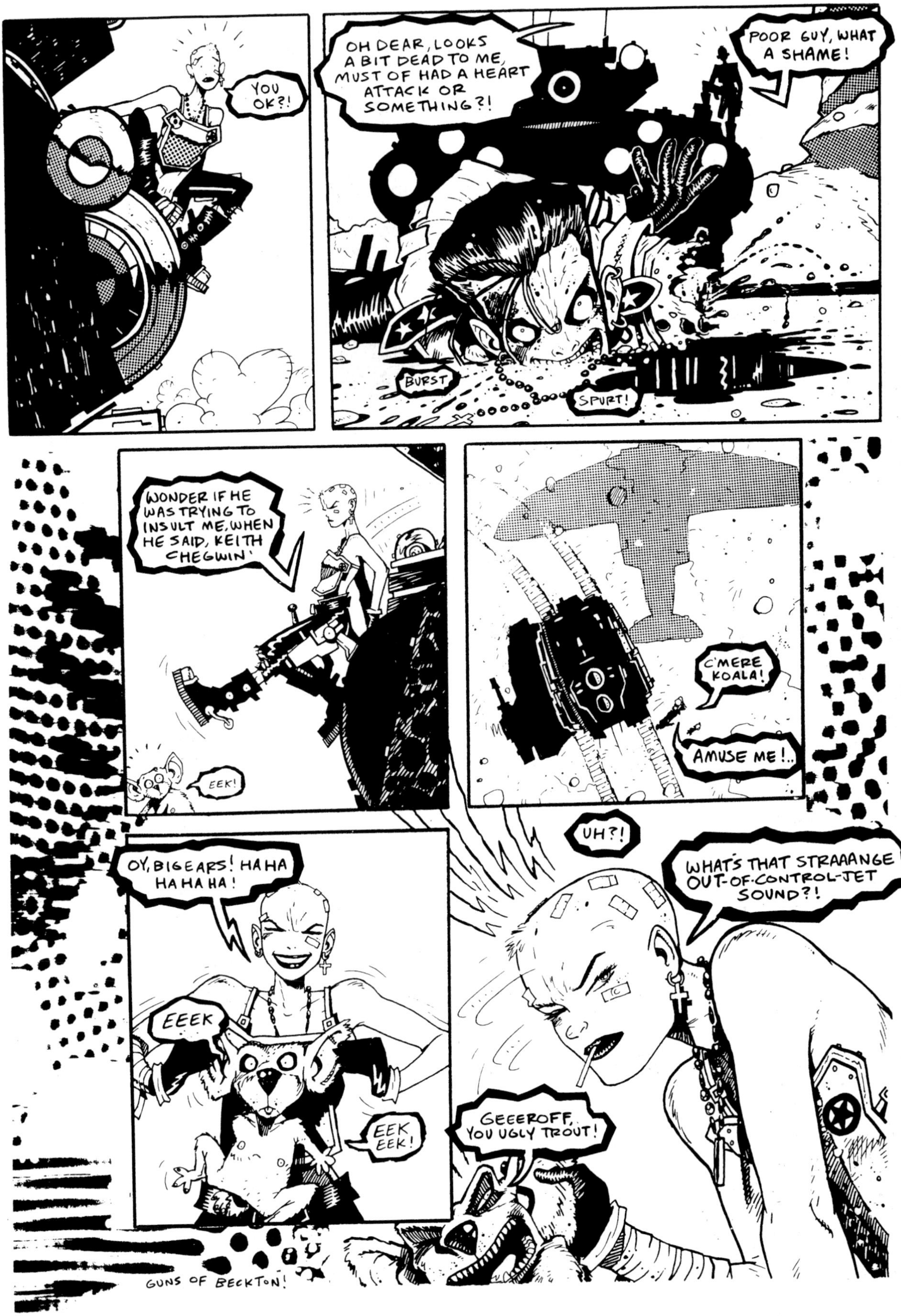

YOU OK?!
OH DEAR, LOOKS A BIT DEAD TO ME, MUST OF HAD A HEART ATTACK OR SOMETHING?!
POOR GUY, WHAT A SHAME!
BURST
SPURT!
WONDER IF HE WAS TRYING TO INSULT ME, WHEN HE SAID, 'KEITH CHEGWIN'
EEK!
C'MERE KOALA!
AMUSE ME!..
OY, BIGEARS! HAHA HAHAHA!
EEEK
EEK EEK!
UH?!
WHAT'S THAT STRAAAANGE OUT-OF-CONTROL-JET SOUND?!
GEEEROFF, YOU UGLY TROUT!
GUNS OF BECKTON!

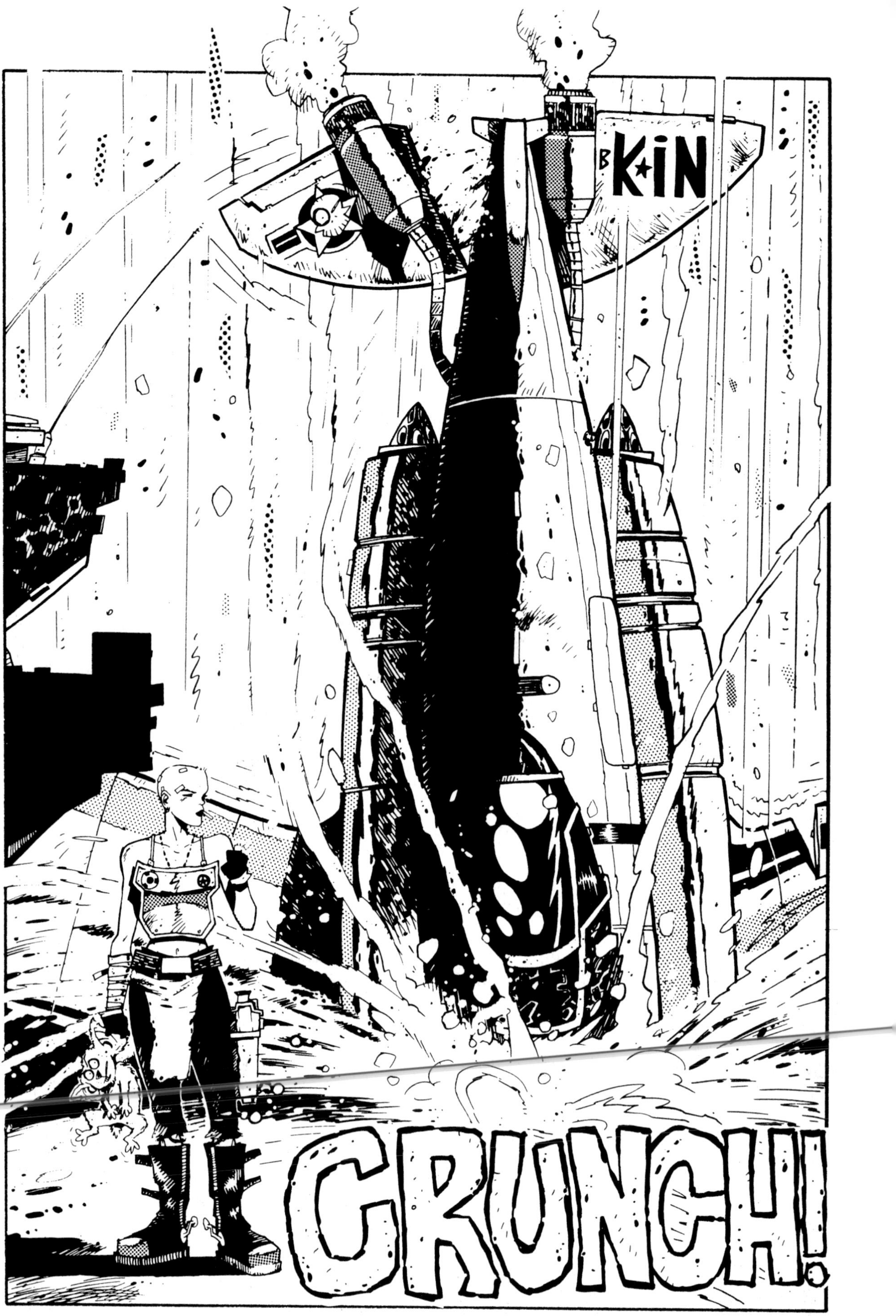
B K★IN
CRUNCH!

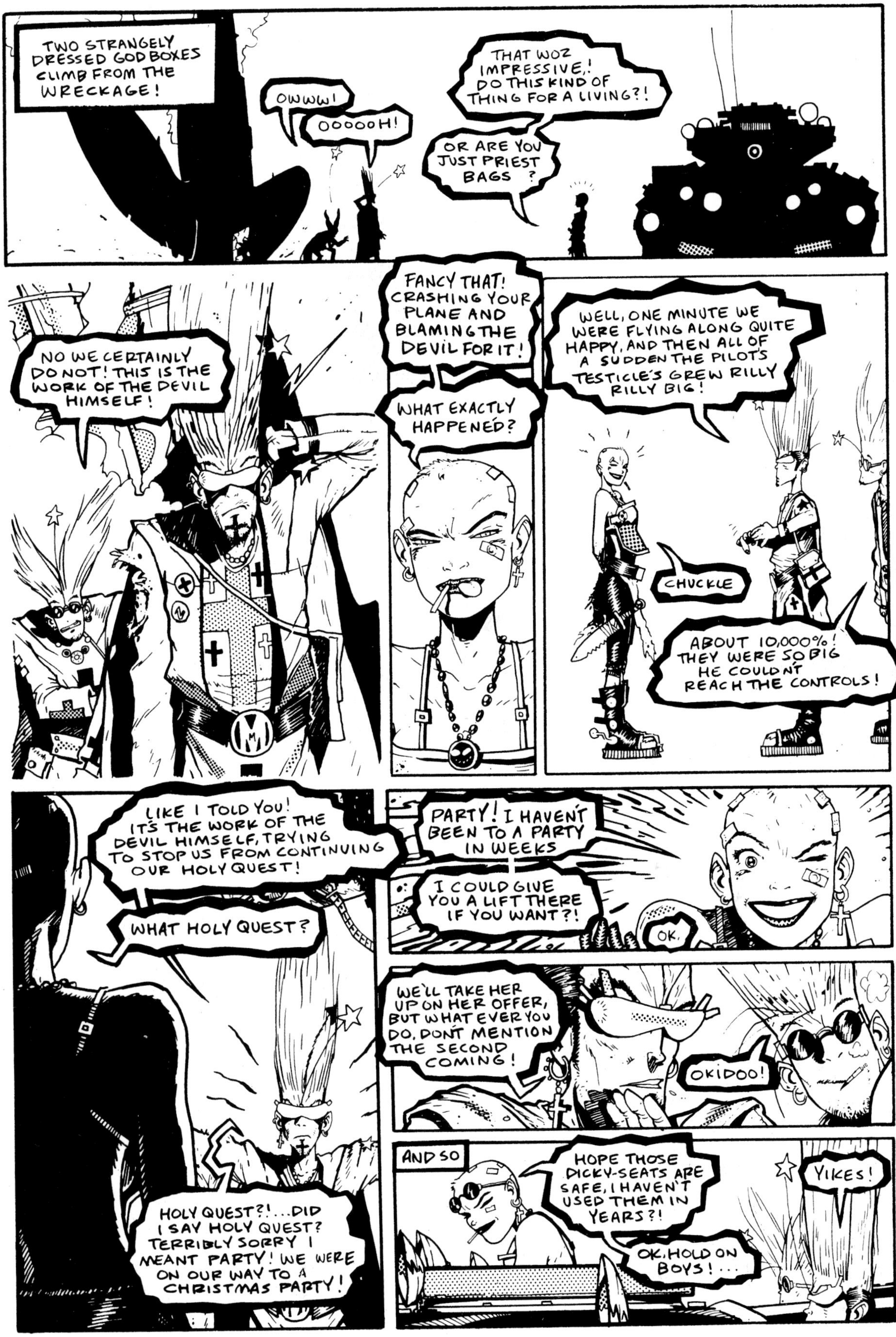
TWO STRANGELY DRESSED GOD BOXES CLIMB FROM THE WRECKAGE!
OWWW!
OOOOOH!
THAT WOZ IMPRESSIVE! DO THIS KIND OF THING FOR A LIVING?!
OR ARE YOU JUST PRIEST BAGS ?
NO WE CERTAINLY DO NOT! THIS IS THE WORK OF THE DEVIL HIMSELF!
FANCY THAT! CRASHING YOUR PLANE AND BLAMING THE DEVIL FOR IT!
WHAT EXACTLY HAPPENED?
WELL, ONE MINUTE WE WERE FLYING ALONG QUITE HAPPY, AND THEN ALL OF A SUDDEN THE PILOT'S TESTICLE'S GREW RILLY RILLY BIG!
CHUCKLE
ABOUT 10,000%! THEY WERE SO BIG HE COULDN'T REACH THE CONTROLS!
LIKE I TOLD YOU! IT'S THE WORK OF THE DEVIL HIMSELF, TRYING TO STOP US FROM CONTINUING OUR HOLY QUEST!
WHAT HOLY QUEST?
HOLY QUEST?!...DID I SAY HOLY QUEST? TERRIBLY SORRY I MEANT PARTY! WE WERE ON OUR WAY TO A CHRISTMAS PARTY!
PARTY! I HAVEN'T BEEN TO A PARTY IN WEEKS
I COULD GIVE YOU A LIFT THERE IF YOU WANT?!
OK.
WE'LL TAKE HER UP ON HER OFFER, BUT WHAT EVER YOU DO, DON'T MENTION THE SECOND COMING!
OKIDOO!
AND SO
HOPE THOSE DICKY-SEATS ARE SAFE, I HAVEN'T USED THEM IN YEARS?!
YIKES!
OK, HOLD ON BOYS!...

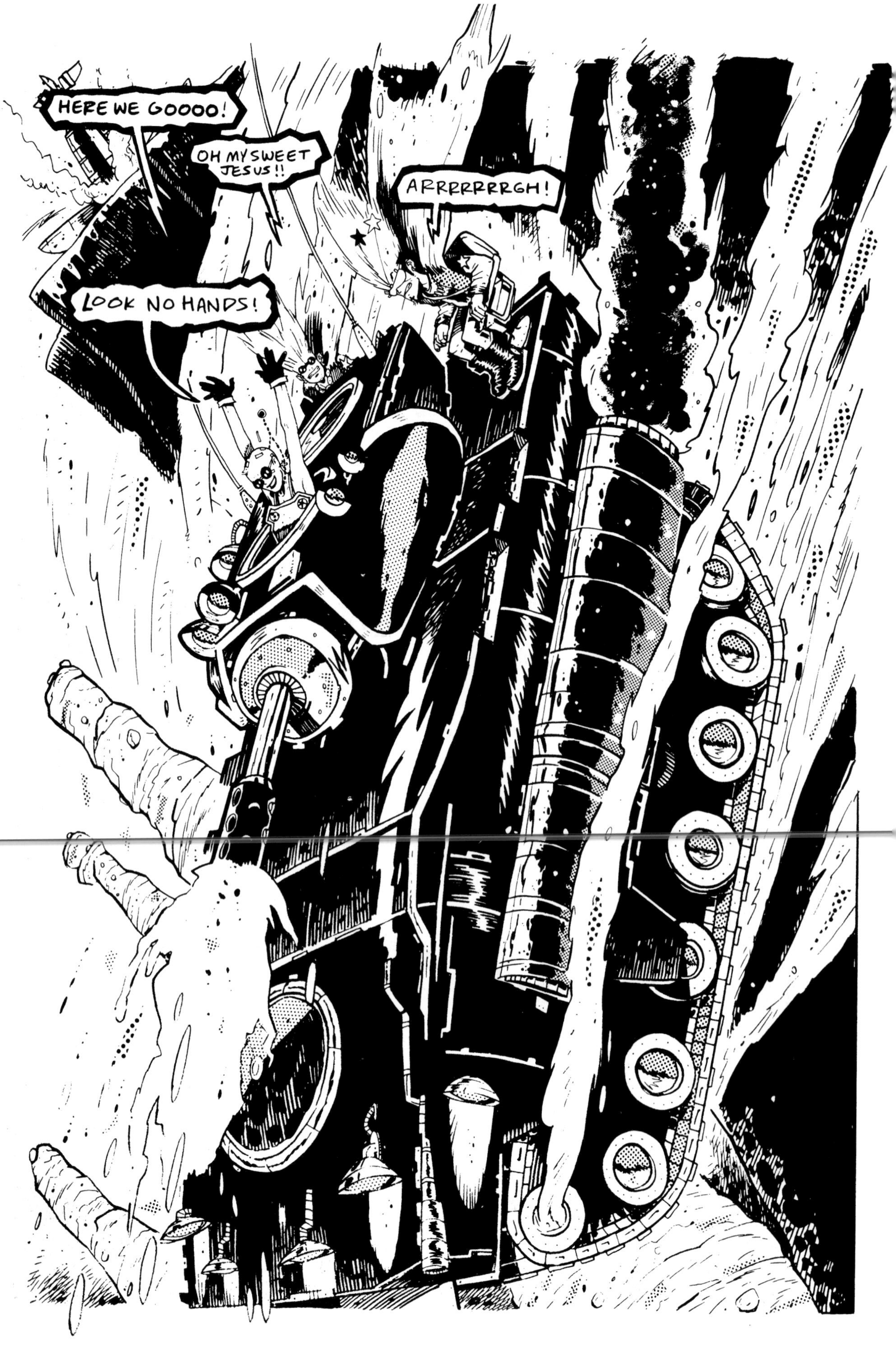
HERE WE GOOOO!
OH MY SWEET JESUS!!
ARRRRRRRGH!
LOOK NO HANDS!

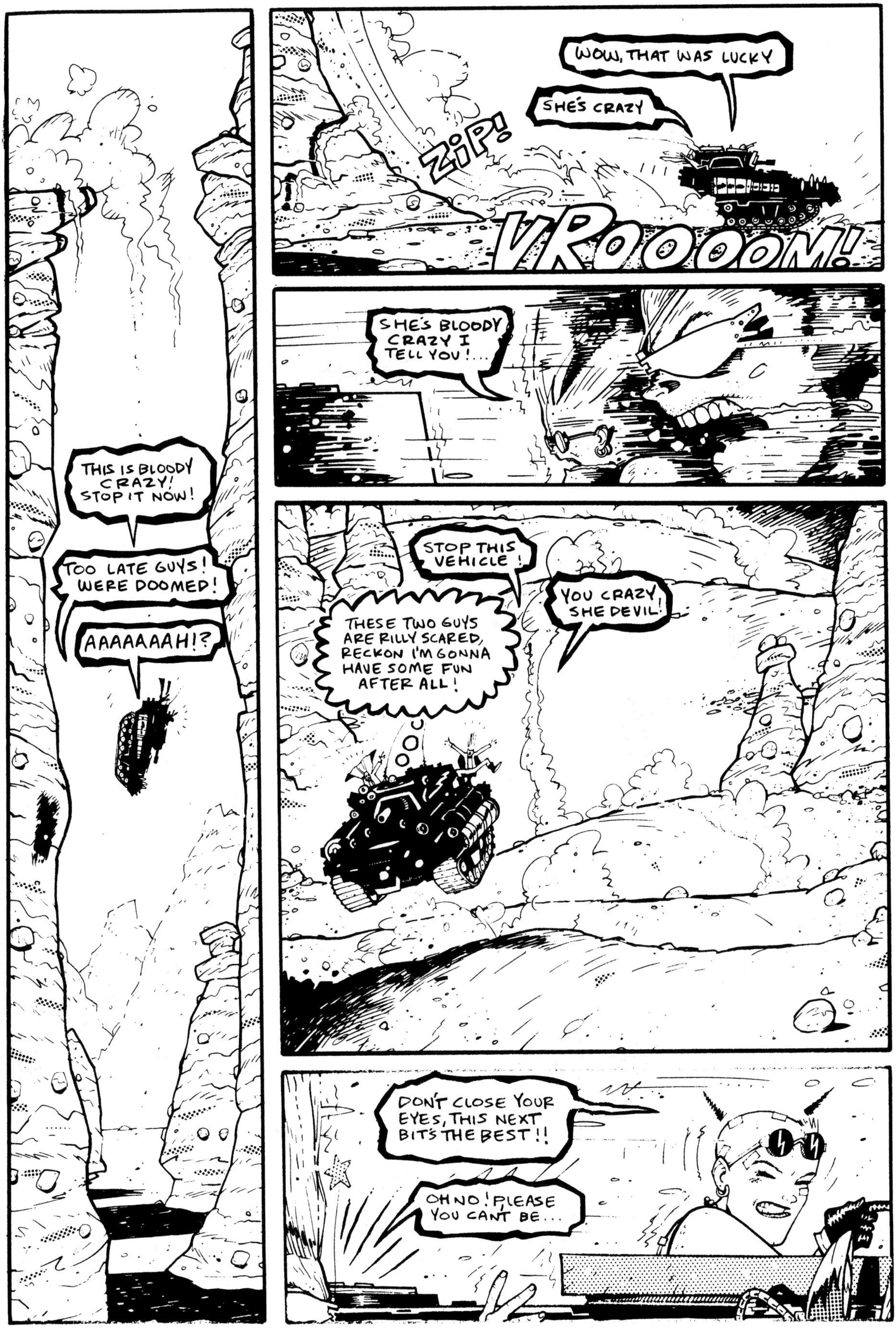
THIS IS BLOODY CRAZY! STOP IT NOW!
TOO LATE GUYS! WERE DOOMED!
AAAAAAAH!?
WOW, THAT WAS LUCKY
SHE'S CRAZY
ZIP!
VROOOOM!
SHE'S BLOODY CRAZY I TELL YOU!...
STOP THIS VEHICLE!
YOU CRAZY SHE DEVIL!
THESE TWO GUYS ARE RILLY SCARED, RECKON I'M GONNA HAVE SOME FUN AFTER ALL!
DON'T CLOSE YOUR EYES, THIS NEXT BIT'S THE BEST!!
OH NO! PLEASE YOU CAN'T BE...

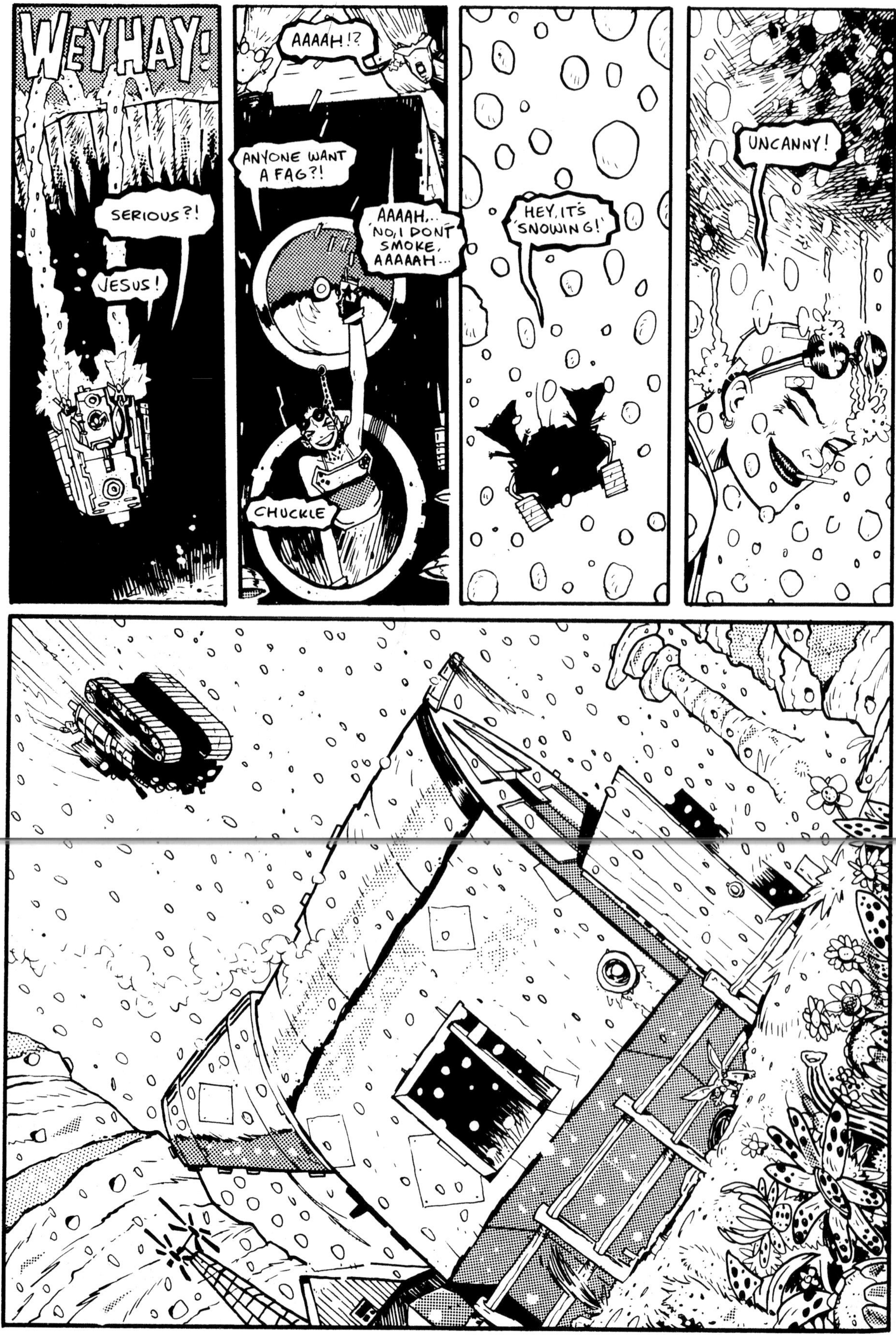
WEYHAY!
SERIOUS?!
JESUS!
AAAAH!?
ANYONE WANT A FAG?!
AAAAH... NO, I DON'T SMOKE, AAAAAH...
CHUCKLE
HEY, IT'S 'SNOWING!'
UNCANNY!

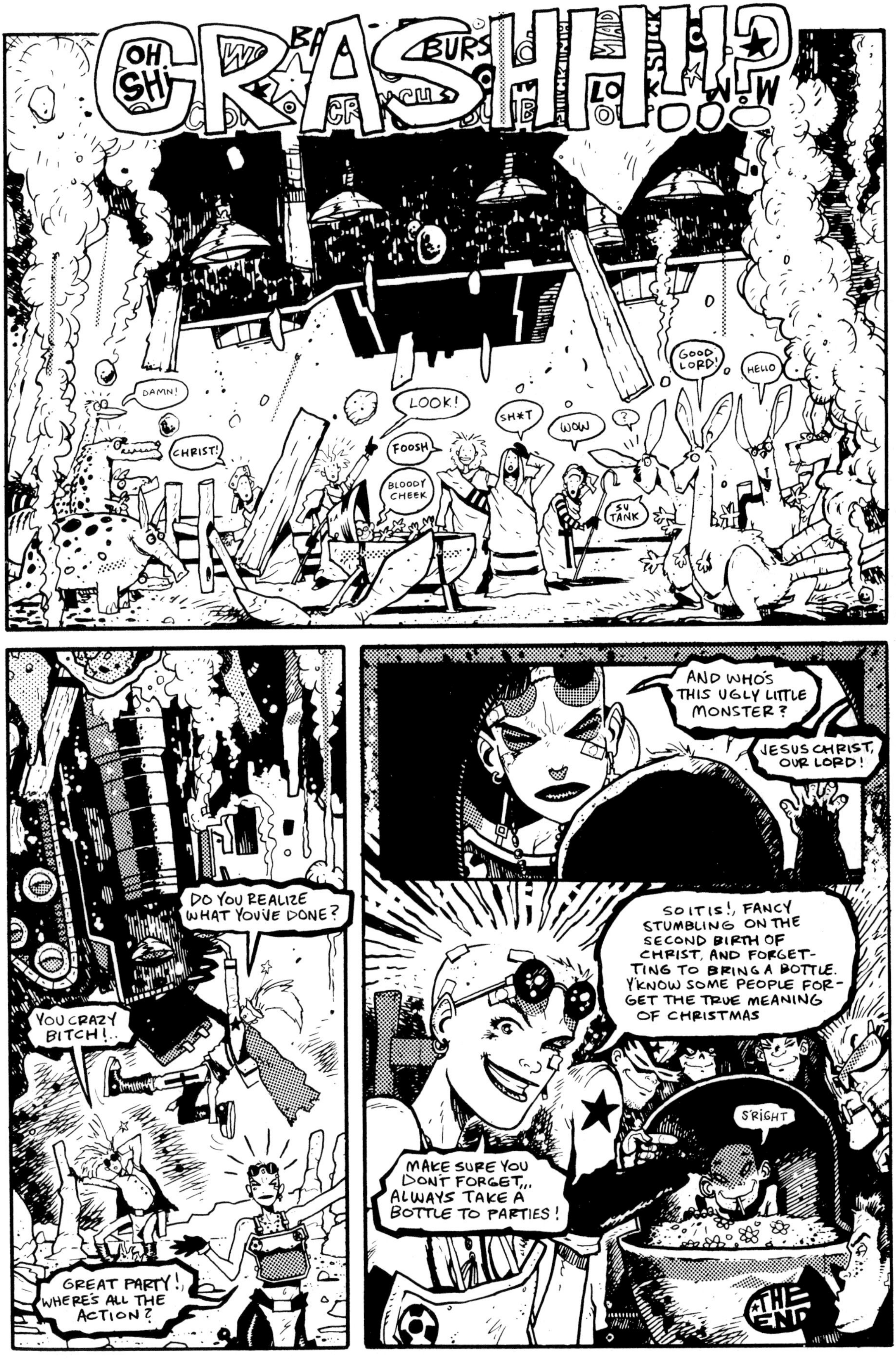
CRASHH!!?
OH SHI
DAMN!
CHRIST!
LOOK!
FOOSH
BLOODY CHEEK
SH*T
WOW
?
SU TANK
GOOD LORD!
HELLO
DO YOU REALIZE WHAT YOU'VE DONE?
YOU CRAZY BITCH!
GREAT PARTY! WHERE'S ALL THE ACTION?
AND WHO'S THIS UGLY LITTLE MONSTER?
JESUS CHRIST, OUR LORD!
SO IT IS!, FANCY STUMBLING ON THE SECOND BIRTH OF CHRIST, AND FORGETTING TO BRING A BOTTLE. Y'KNOW SOME PEOPLE FORGET THE TRUE MEANING OF CHRISTMAS
MAKE SURE YOU DON'T FORGET,,, ALWAYS TAKE A BOTTLE TO PARTIES!
S'RIGHT
THE END

How to draw Tank Girl the Jamie way

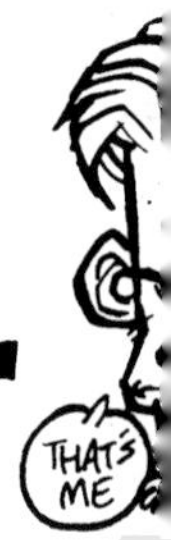
THAT'S ME

1 PENCIL IN A NUDE FIGURE WITH AN HB PENCIL ENSURING THE PROPORTIONS ARE CORRECT....

2 ... ADD THE APPROPRIATE CLOTHES, BOOTS, T-SHIRT, HAT AND PANTIES....

3 ... THEN INK THE BASTARD!....

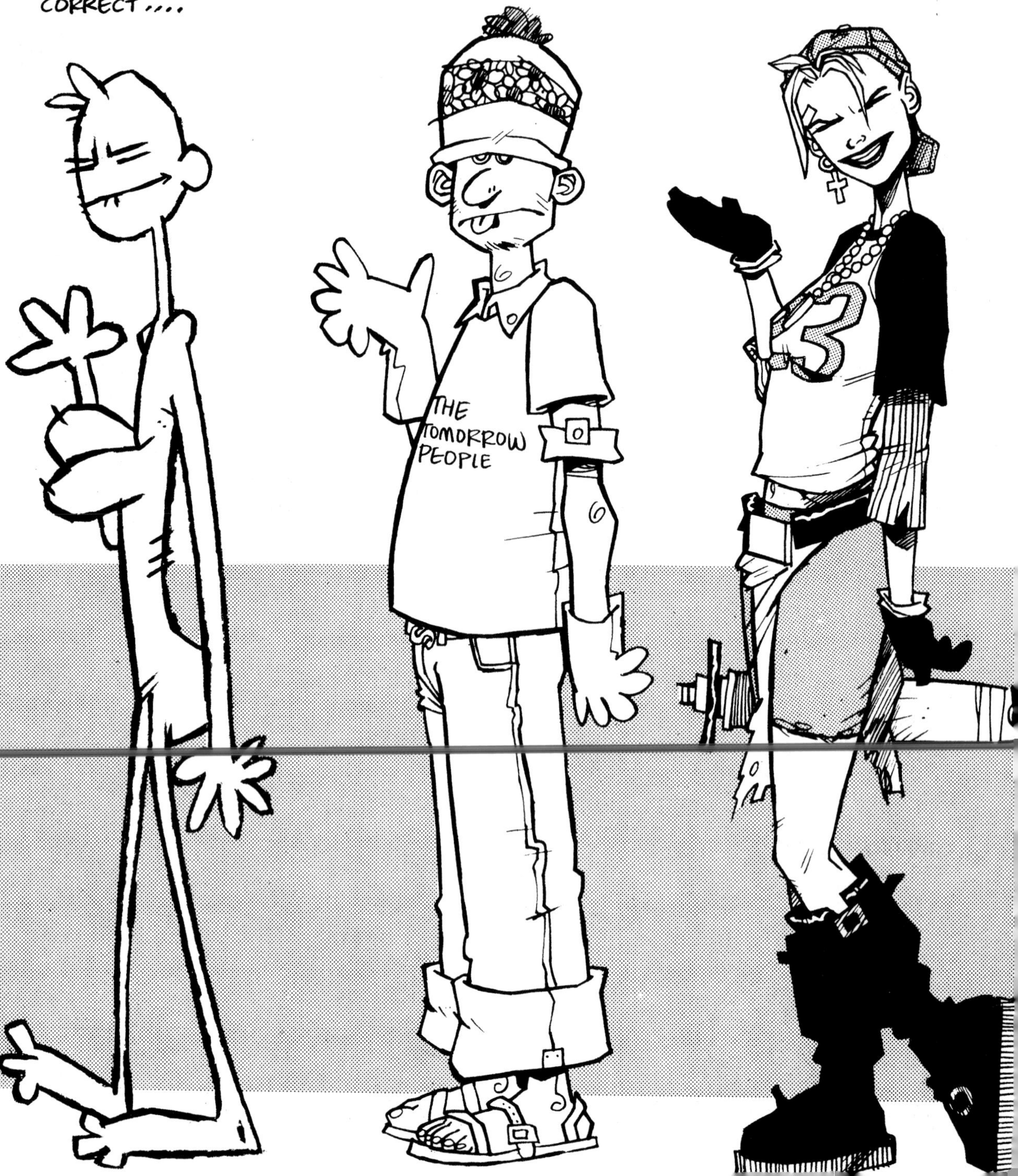
THE TOMORROW PEOPLE

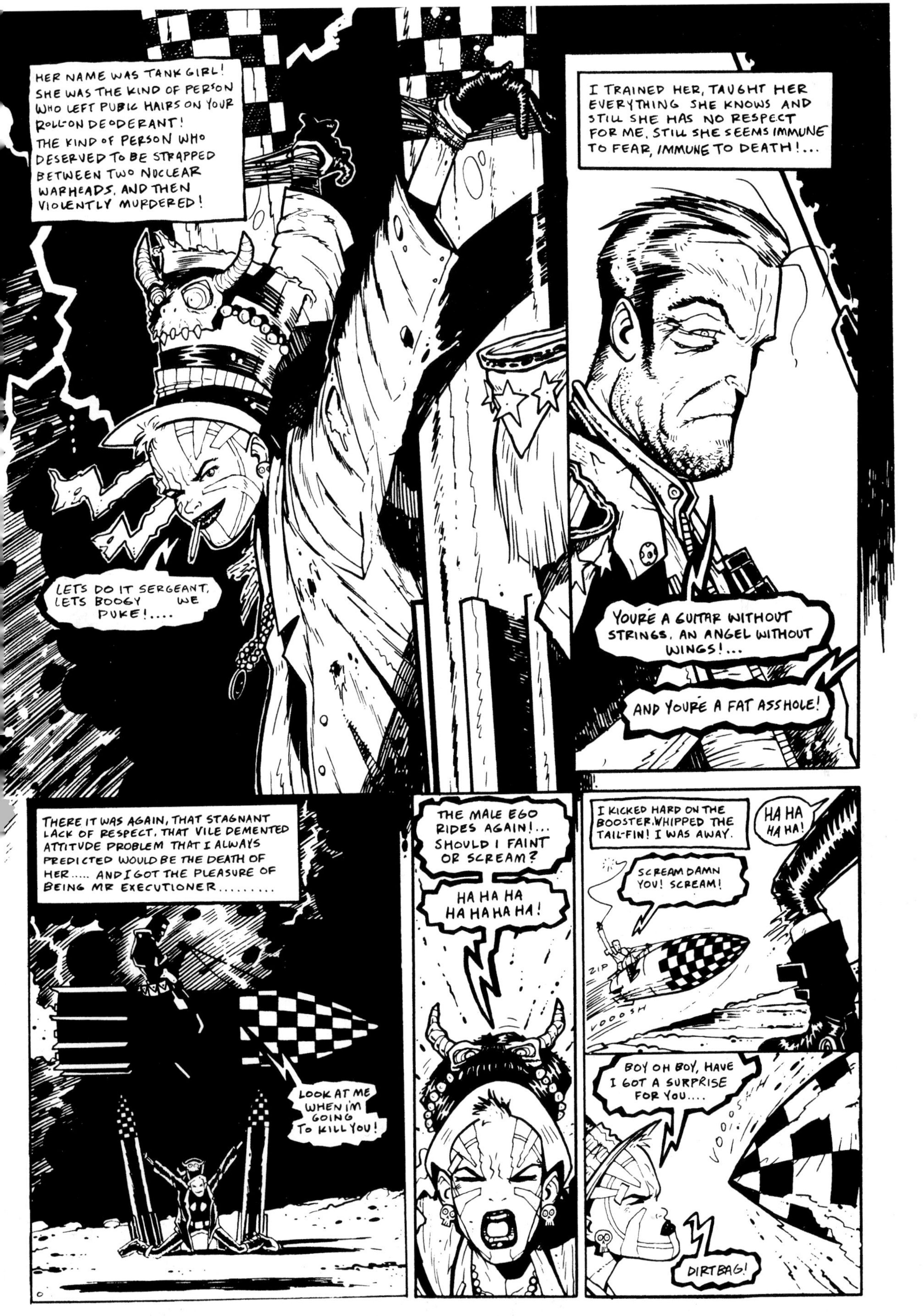

HER NAME WAS TANK GIRL! SHE WAS THE KIND OF PERSON WHO LEFT PUBIC HAIRS ON YOUR ROLL-ON DEODERANT! THE KIND OF PERSON WHO DESERVED TO BE STRAPPED BETWEEN TWO NUCLEAR WARHEADS, AND THEN VIOLENTLY MURDERED!
LETS DO IT SERGEANT, LETS BOOGY WE PUKE!....
I TRAINED HER, TAUGHT HER EVERYTHING SHE KNOWS AND STILL SHE HAS NO RESPECT FOR ME, STILL SHE SEEMS IMMUNE TO FEAR, IMMUNE TO DEATH!...
YOU'RE A GUITAR WITHOUT STRINGS, AN ANGEL WITHOUT WINGS!...
AND YOU'RE A FAT ASSHOLE!
THERE IT WAS AGAIN, THAT STAGNANT LACK OF RESPECT, THAT VILE DEMENTED ATTITUDE PROBLEM THAT I ALWAYS PREDICTED WOULD BE THE DEATH OF HER..... AND I GOT THE PLEASURE OF BEING MR EXECUTIONER.........
LOOK AT ME WHEN I'M GOING TO KILL YOU!
THE MALE EGO RIDES AGAIN!... SHOULD I FAINT OR SCREAM?
HA HA HA HA HA HA HA!
I KICKED HARD ON THE BOOSTER, WHIPPED THE TAIL-FIN! I WAS AWAY.
HA HA HA HA!
SCREAM DAMN YOU! SCREAM!
ZIP
VOOOSH
BOY OH BOY, HAVE I GOT A SURPRISE FOR YOU....
VOOOSHH
DIRTBAG!

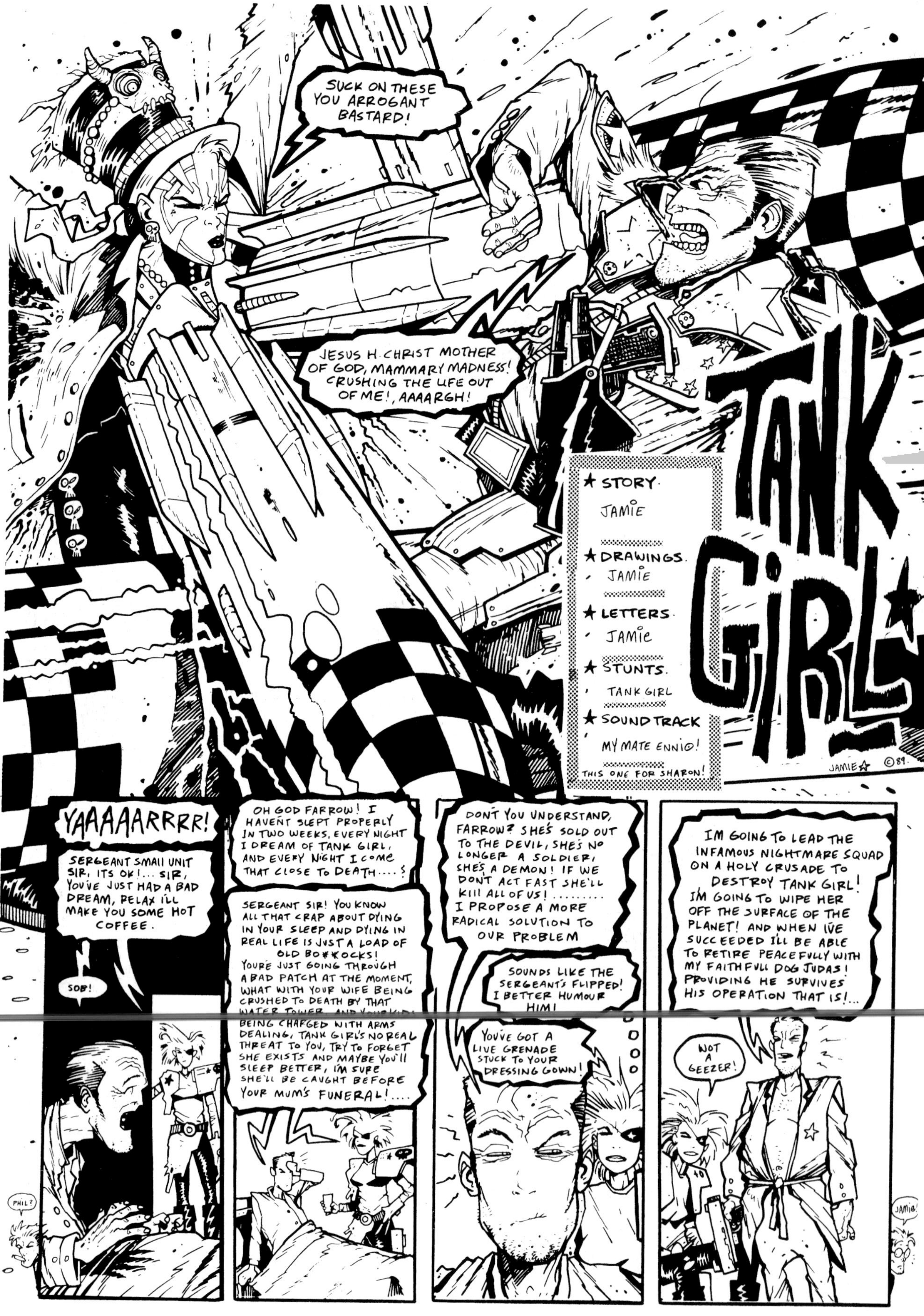
SUCK ON THESE YOU ARROGANT BASTARD!
JESUS H. CHRIST MOTHER OF GOD, MAMMARY MADNESS! CRUSHING THE LIFE OUT OF ME!, AAAARGH!
TANK GIRL
★ STORY. JAMIE
★ DRAWINGS. JAMIE
★ LETTERS. JAMIE
★ STUNTS. TANK GIRL
★ SOUNDTRACK MY MATE ENNIO!
THIS ONE FOR SHARON!
JAMIE ©89.
YAAAAARRRR!
SERGEANT SMALL UNIT SIR, ITS OK!... SIR, YOU'VE JUST HAD A BAD DREAM, RELAX I'LL MAKE YOU SOME HOT COFFEE.
SOB!
OH GOD FARROW! I HAVEN'T SLEPT PROPERLY IN TWO WEEKS, EVERY NIGHT I DREAM OF TANK GIRL, AND EVERY NIGHT I COME THAT CLOSE TO DEATH....
SERGEANT SIR! YOU KNOW ALL THAT CRAP ABOUT DYING IN YOUR SLEEP AND DYING IN REAL LIFE IS JUST A LOAD OF OLD BO✱✱OCKS! YOU'RE JUST GOING THROUGH A BAD PATCH AT THE MOMENT, WHAT WITH YOUR WIFE BEING CRUSHED TO DEATH BY THAT WATER TOWER, AND YOUR KIDS BEING CHARGED WITH ARMS DEALING, TANK GIRL'S NO REAL THREAT TO YOU, TRY TO FORGET SHE EXISTS AND MAYBE YOU'LL SLEEP BETTER, I'M SURE SHE'LL BE CAUGHT BEFORE YOUR MUM'S FUNERAL!...
DON'T YOU UNDERSTAND, FARROW? SHE'S SOLD OUT TO THE DEVIL, SHE'S NO LONGER A SOLDIER, SHE'S A DEMON! IF WE DON'T ACT FAST SHE'LL KILL ALL OF US!......... I PROPOSE A MORE RADICAL SOLUTION TO OUR PROBLEM
SOUNDS LIKE THE SERGEANT'S FLIPPED! I BETTER HUMOUR HIM!
YOU'VE GOT A LIVE GRENADE STUCK TO YOUR DRESSING GOWN!
I'M GOING TO LEAD THE INFAMOUS NIGHTMARE SQUAD ON A HOLY CRUSADE TO DESTROY TANK GIRL! I'M GOING TO WIPE HER OFF THE SURFACE OF THE PLANET! AND WHEN I'VE SUCCEEDED I'LL BE ABLE TO RETIRE PEACEFULLY WITH MY FAITHFULL DOG JUDAS! PROVIDING HE SURVIVES HIS OPERATION THAT IS!...
NOT A GEEZER!
PHIL?
JAMIE!

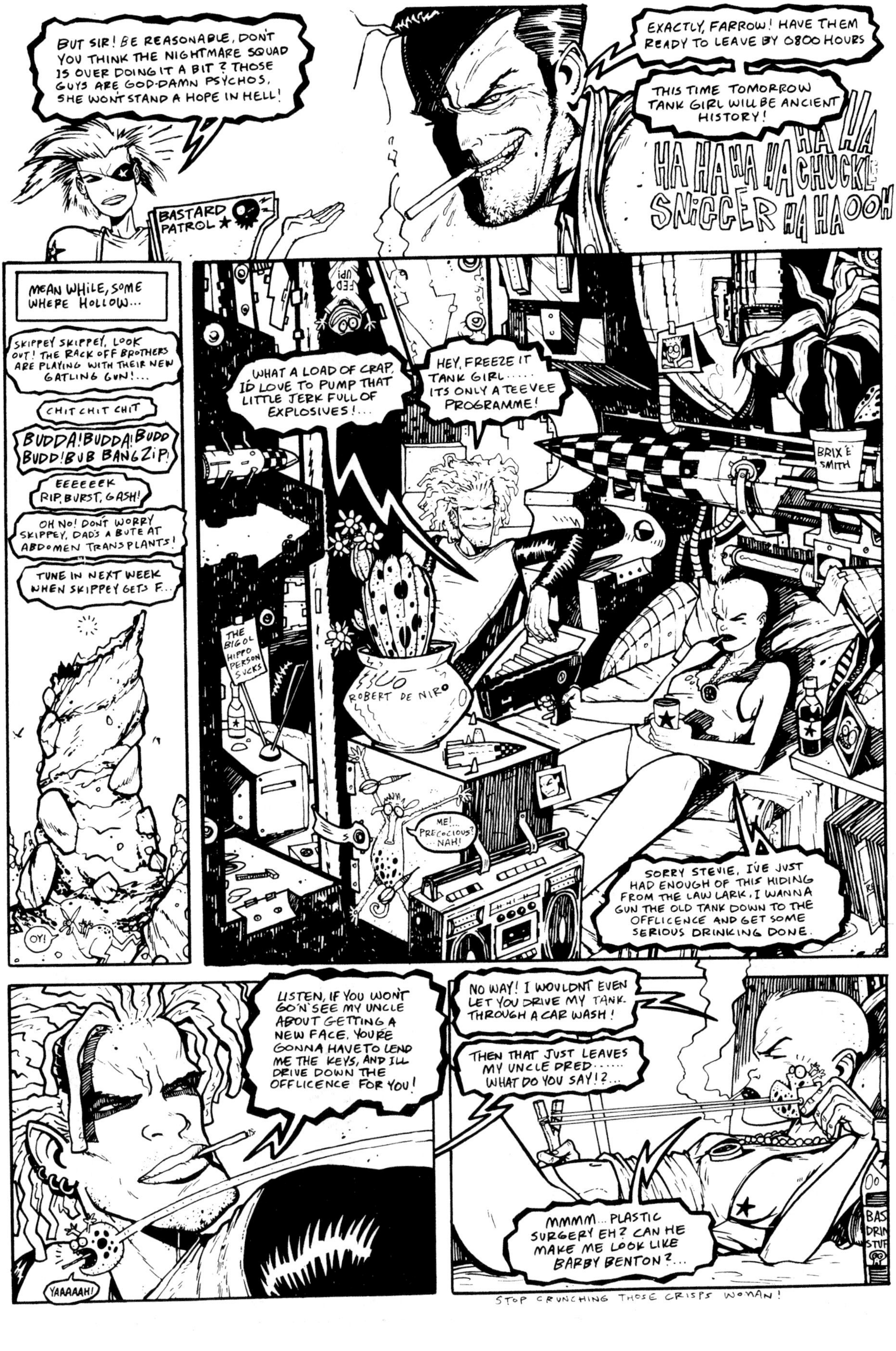
BUT SIR! BE REASONABLE, DON'T YOU THINK THE NIGHTMARE SQUAD IS OVER DOING IT A BIT? THOSE GUYS ARE GOD-DAMN PSYCHOS, SHE WON'T STAND A HOPE IN HELL!
BASTARD PATROL
EXACTLY, FARROW! HAVE THEM READY TO LEAVE BY 0800 HOURS
THIS TIME TOMORROW TANK GIRL WILL BE ANCIENT HISTORY!
HA HA HAHA HA HA HA CHUCKLE SNIGGER HA HA OOH
MEAN WHILE, SOME WHERE HOLLOW...
SKIPPEY SKIPPEY, LOOK OUT! THE RACK OFF BROTHERS ARE PLAYING WITH THEIR NEW GATLING GUN!...
CHIT CHIT CHIT
BUDDA! BUDDA! BUDD BUDD! BUB BANG ZIP!
EEEEEEK RIP, BURST, GASH!
OH NO! DON'T WORRY SKIPPEY, DAD'S A BUTE AT ABDOMEN TRANSPLANTS!
TUNE IN NEXT WEEK WHEN SKIPPEY GETS F...
OY!
FED UP!
WHAT A LOAD OF CRAP, I'D LOVE TO PUMP THAT LITTLE JERK FULL OF EXPLOSIVES!...
HEY, FREEZE IT TANK GIRL..... ITS ONLY A TEEVEE PROGRAMME!
BRIX 'E' SMITH
THE BIG OL HIPPO PERSON SUCKS
ROBERT DE NIRO
ME!... PRECOCIOUS? ...NAH!
SORRY STEVIE, I'VE JUST HAD ENOUGH OF THIS HIDING FROM THE LAW LARK. I WANNA GUN THE OLD TANK DOWN TO THE OFFLICENCE AND GET SOME SERIOUS DRINKING DONE.
LISTEN, IF YOU WON'T GO 'N' SEE MY UNCLE ABOUT GETTING A NEW FACE, YOU'RE GONNA HAVE TO LEND ME THE KEYS, AND I'LL DRIVE DOWN THE OFFLICENCE FOR YOU!
YAAAAAH!
NO WAY! I WOULDN'T EVEN LET YOU DRIVE MY TANK THROUGH A CAR WASH!
THEN THAT JUST LEAVES MY UNCLE DRED...... WHAT DO YOU SAY!?...
MMMM... PLASTIC SURGERY EH? CAN HE MAKE ME LOOK LIKE BARBY BENTON?...
STOP CRUNCHING THOSE CRISPS WOMAN!

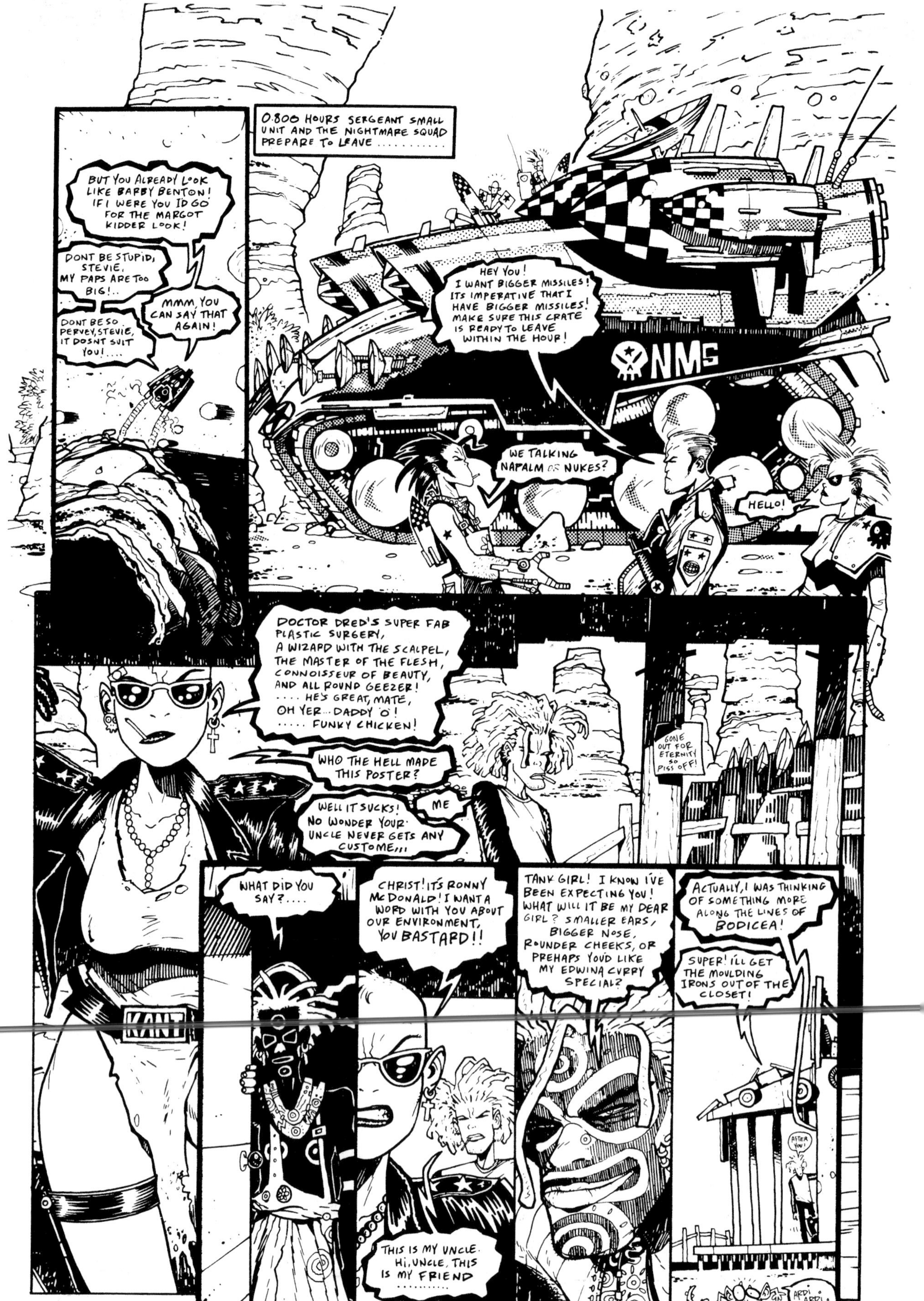
0.800 HOURS SERGEANT SMALL UNIT AND THE NIGHTMARE SQUAD PREPARE TO LEAVE ....
BUT YOU ALREADY LOOK LIKE BARBY BENTON! IF I WERE YOU I'D GO FOR THE MARGOT KIDDER LOOK!
DONT BE STUPID, STEVIE. MY PAPS ARE TOO BIG!..
MMM, YOU CAN SAY THAT AGAIN!
DONT BE SO PERVEY, STEVIE, IT DOSNT SUIT YOU!....
HEY YOU! I WANT BIGGER MISSILES! ITS IMPERATIVE THAT I HAVE BIGGER MISSILES! MAKE SURE THIS CRATE IS READY TO LEAVE WITHIN THE HOUR!
NMS
WE TALKING NAPALM OR NUKES?
HELLO!
DOCTOR DRED'S SUPER FAB PLASTIC SURGERY, A WIZARD WITH THE SCALPEL, THE MASTER OF THE FLESH, CONNOISSEUR OF BEAUTY, AND ALL ROUND GEEZER! .... HE'S GREAT, MATE, OH YER...DADDY O! ..... FUNKY CHICKEN!
WHO THE HELL MADE THIS POSTER?
ME
WELL IT SUCKS! NO WONDER YOUR UNCLE NEVER GETS ANY CUSTOME,,,
GONE OUT FOR ETERNITY SO PISS OFF!
KANT
WHAT DID YOU SAY?....
CHRIST! IT'S RONNY McDONALD! I WANT A WORD WITH YOU ABOUT OUR ENVIRONMENT, YOU BASTARD!!
THIS IS MY UNCLE. HI, UNCLE, THIS IS MY FRIEND ....
TANK GIRL! I KNOW I'VE BEEN EXPECTING YOU! WHAT WILL IT BE MY DEAR GIRL? SMALLER EARS, BIGGER NOSE, ROUNDER CHEEKS, OR PREHAPS YOU'D LIKE MY EDWINA CURRY SPECIAL?
ACTUALLY, I WAS THINKING OF SOMETHING MORE ALONG THE LINES OF BODICEA!
SUPER! I'LL GET THE MOULDING IRONS OUT OF THE CLOSET!
AFTER YOU!
ARDI. ARDI. ARDI

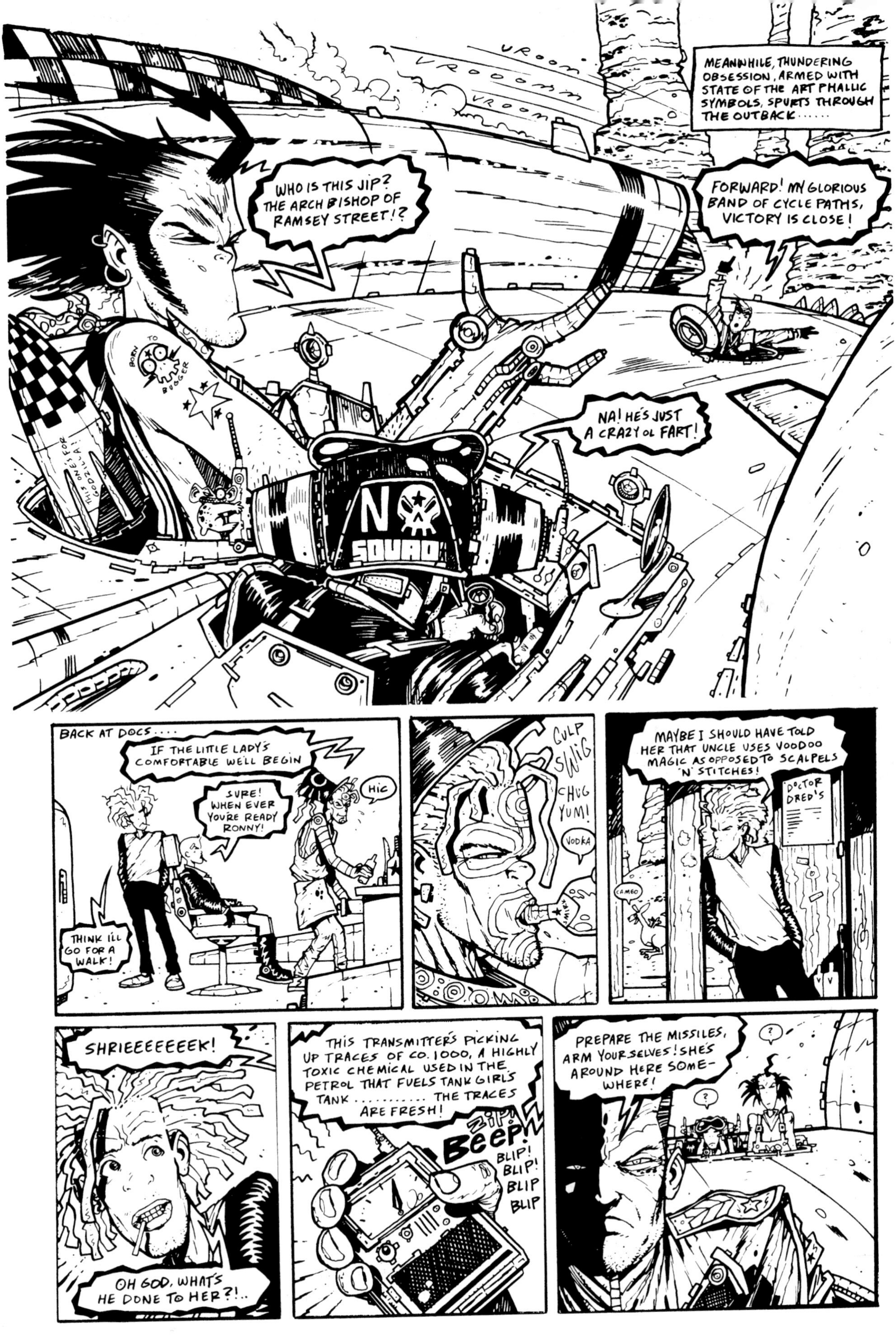
VROOOOM
VROOOOMM
VROOOM
MEANWHILE, THUNDERING OBSESSION, ARMED WITH STATE OF THE ART PHALLIC SYMBOLS, SPURTS THROUGH THE OUTBACK......
WHO IS THIS JIP? THE ARCH BISHOP OF RAMSEY STREET!?
FORWARD! MY GLORIOUS BAND OF CYCLE PATHS, VICTORY IS CLOSE!
BORN TO BUGGER
THIS ONE'S FOR GODZILLA!
NA! HE'S JUST A CRAZY OL FART!
N SQUAD
BACK AT DOCS....
IF THE LITTLE LADY'S COMFORTABLE WE'LL BEGIN
SURE! WHEN EVER YOU'RE READY RONNY!
HIC
THINK I'LL GO FOR A WALK!
GULP
SWIG
CHUG
YUM!
VODKA
MAYBE I SHOULD HAVE TOLD HER THAT UNCLE USES VOODOO MAGIC AS OPPOSED TO SCALPELS 'N' STITCHES!
DOCTOR DRED'S
CAMEO
SHRIEEEEEEEK!
OH GOD, WHAT'S HE DONE TO HER?!..
THIS TRANSMITTER'S PICKING UP TRACES OF CO. 1000, A HIGHLY TOXIC CHEMICAL USED IN THE PETROL THAT FUELS TANK GIRL'S TANK.......... THE TRACES ARE FRESH!
ZIP!
BEEP!
BLIP!
BLIP!
BLIP
BLIP
PREPARE THE MISSILES, ARM YOURSELVES! SHE'S AROUND HERE SOME-WHERE!
?
?

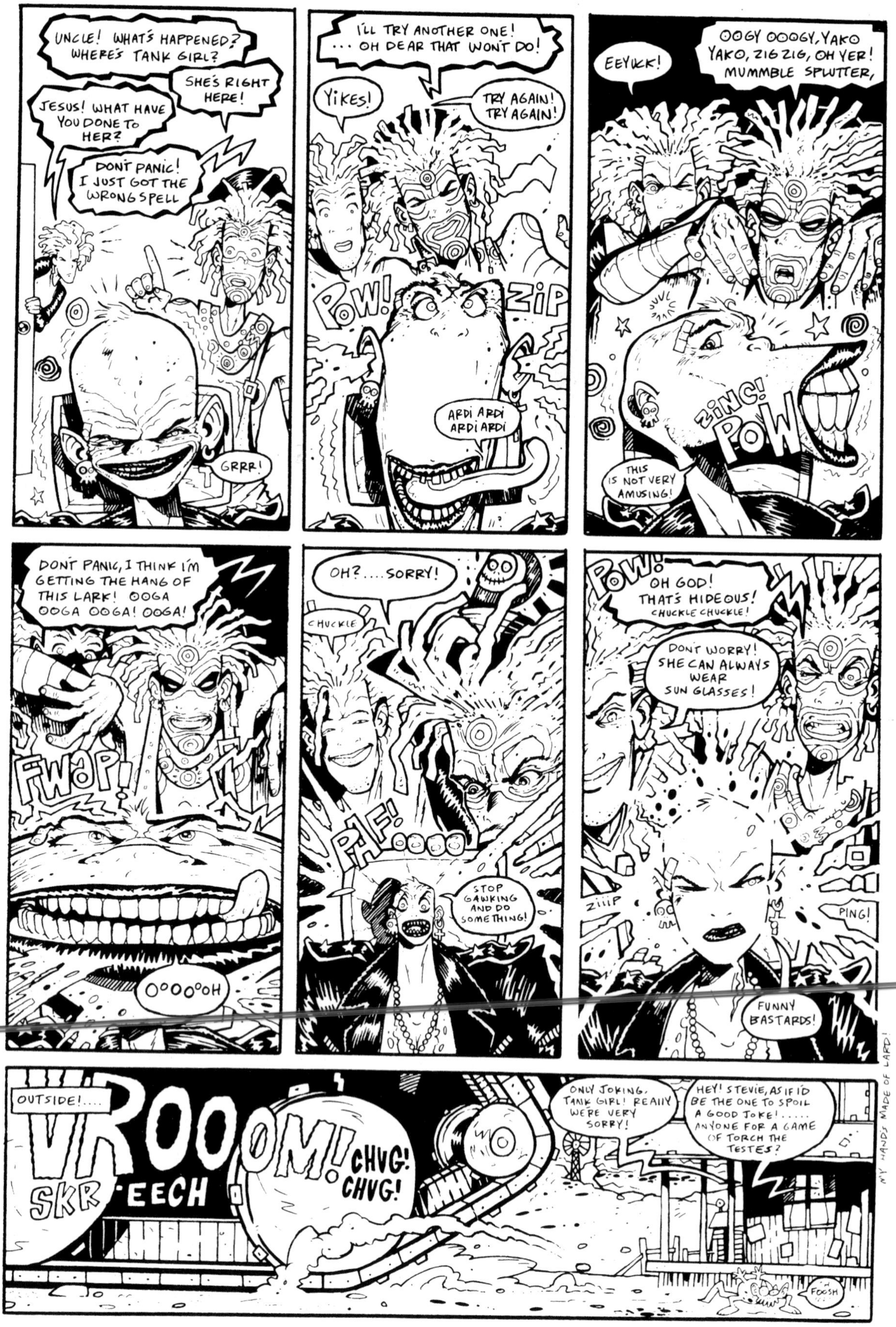
UNCLE! WHAT'S HAPPENED? WHERE'S TANK GIRL?
SHE'S RIGHT HERE!
JESUS! WHAT HAVE YOU DONE TO HER?
DON'T PANIC! I JUST GOT THE WRONG SPELL
GRRR!
I'LL TRY ANOTHER ONE! ... OH DEAR THAT WON'T DO!
YIKES!
TRY AGAIN! TRY AGAIN!
POW!
ZIP
ARDI ARDI ARDI ARDI
EEYUCK!
OOGY OOOGY, YAKO YAKO, ZIG ZIG, OH YER! MUMMBLE SPLUTTER,
ZINC! POW
THIS IS NOT VERY AMUSING!
DON'T PANIC, I THINK I'M GETTING THE HANG OF THIS LARK! OOGA OOGA OOGA! OOGA!
FWAP!
OOOOOH
OH?.... SORRY!
CHUCKLE
PAF!
STOP GAWKING AND DO SOMETHING!
POW!
OH GOD! THAT'S HIDEOUS! CHUCKLE CHUCKLE!
DON'T WORRY! SHE CAN ALWAYS WEAR SUN GLASSES!
ZIIIP
PING!
FUNNY BASTARDS!
OUTSIDE!....
VROOOOM!
SKR-EECH
CHUG! CHUG!
ONLY JOKING, TANK GIRL! REALLY WE'RE VERY SORRY!
HEY! STEVIE, AS IF I'D BE THE ONE TO SPOIL A GOOD JOKE!..... ANYONE FOR A GAME OF TORCH THE TESTES?
FOOSH
MY HANDS MADE OF LARD!

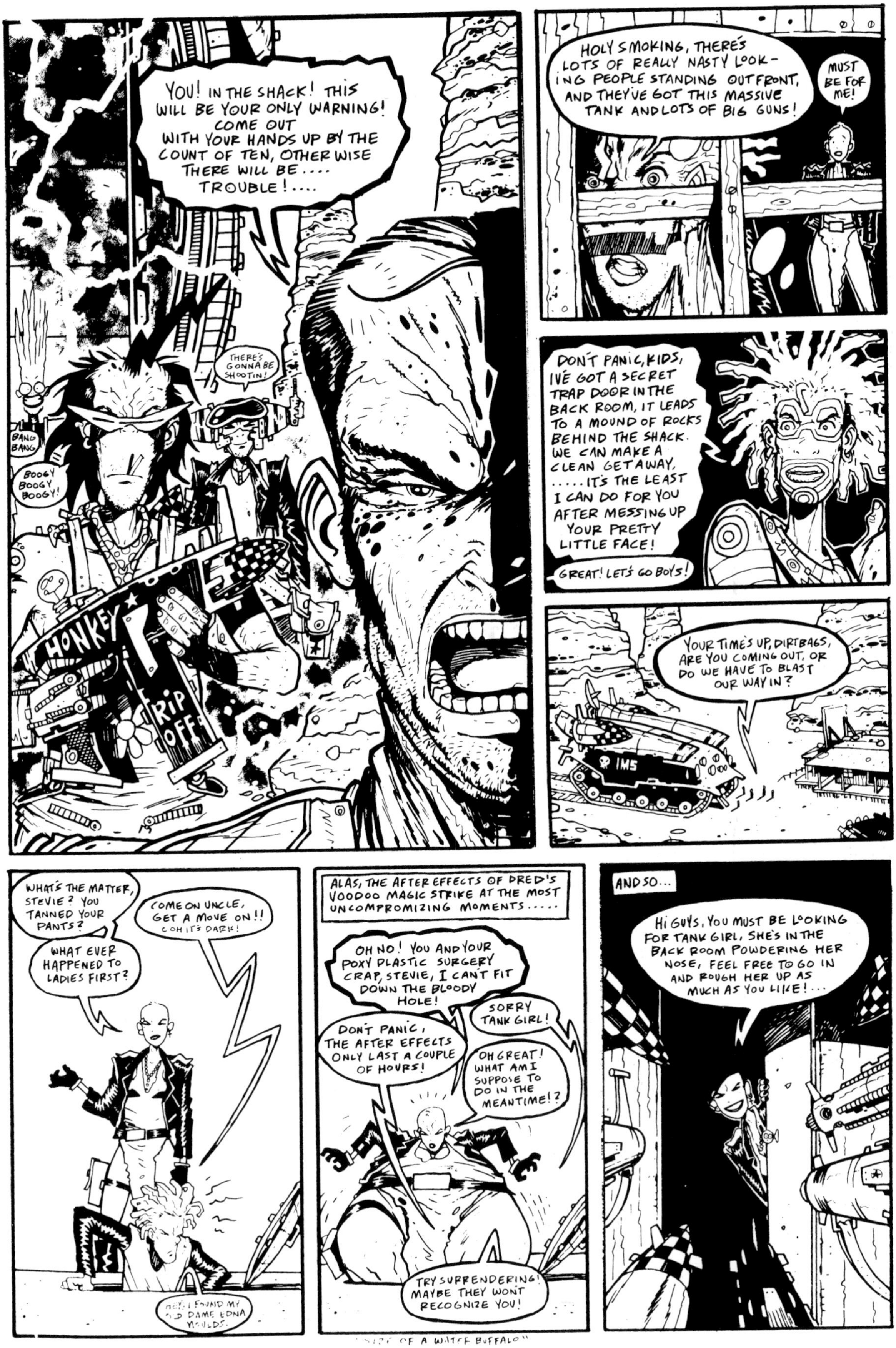
YOU! IN THE SHACK! THIS WILL BE YOUR ONLY WARNING! COME OUT WITH YOUR HANDS UP BY THE COUNT OF TEN, OTHER WISE THERE WILL BE.... TROUBLE!....
THERE'S GONNA BE SHOOTIN!
BANG BANG
BOOGY BOOGY BOOGY!
HONKEY
RIP OFF
HOLY SMOKING, THERE'S LOTS OF REALLY NASTY LOOK-ING PEOPLE STANDING OUTFRONT, AND THEY'VE GOT THIS MASSIVE TANK AND LOTS OF BIG GUNS!
MUST BE FOR ME!
DON'T PANIC, KIDS, I'VE GOT A SECRET TRAP DOOR IN THE BACK ROOM, IT LEADS TO A MOUND OF ROCKS BEHIND THE SHACK. WE CAN MAKE A CLEAN GETAWAY. .....IT'S THE LEAST I CAN DO FOR YOU AFTER MESSING UP YOUR PRETTY LITTLE FACE!
GREAT! LET'S GO BOYS!
YOUR TIME'S UP, DIRTBAGS, ARE YOU COMING OUT, OR DO WE HAVE TO BLAST OUR WAY IN?
IMS
WHAT'S THE MATTER, STEVIE? YOU TANNED YOUR PANTS?
WHAT EVER HAPPENED TO LADIES FIRST?
COME ON UNCLE, GET A MOVE ON!! (OH IT'S DARK!
HEY! I FOUND MY OLD DAME EDNA MOULDS.
ALAS, THE AFTER EFFECTS OF DRED'S VOODOO MAGIC STRIKE AT THE MOST UNCOMPROMIZING MOMENTS.....
OH NO! YOU AND YOUR POXY PLASTIC SURGERY CRAP, STEVIE, I CAN'T FIT DOWN THE BLOODY HOLE!
SORRY TANK GIRL!
DON'T PANIC, THE AFTER EFFECTS ONLY LAST A COUPLE OF HOURS!
OH GREAT! WHAT AM I SUPPOSE TO DO IN THE MEANTIME!?
TRY SURRENDERING! MAYBE THEY WON'T RECOGNIZE YOU!
AND SO...
HI GUYS, YOU MUST BE LOOKING FOR TANK GIRL, SHE'S IN THE BACK ROOM POWDERING HER NOSE, FEEL FREE TO GO IN AND ROUGH HER UP AS MUCH AS YOU LIKE!...

"SIZE OF A WATER BUFFALO"

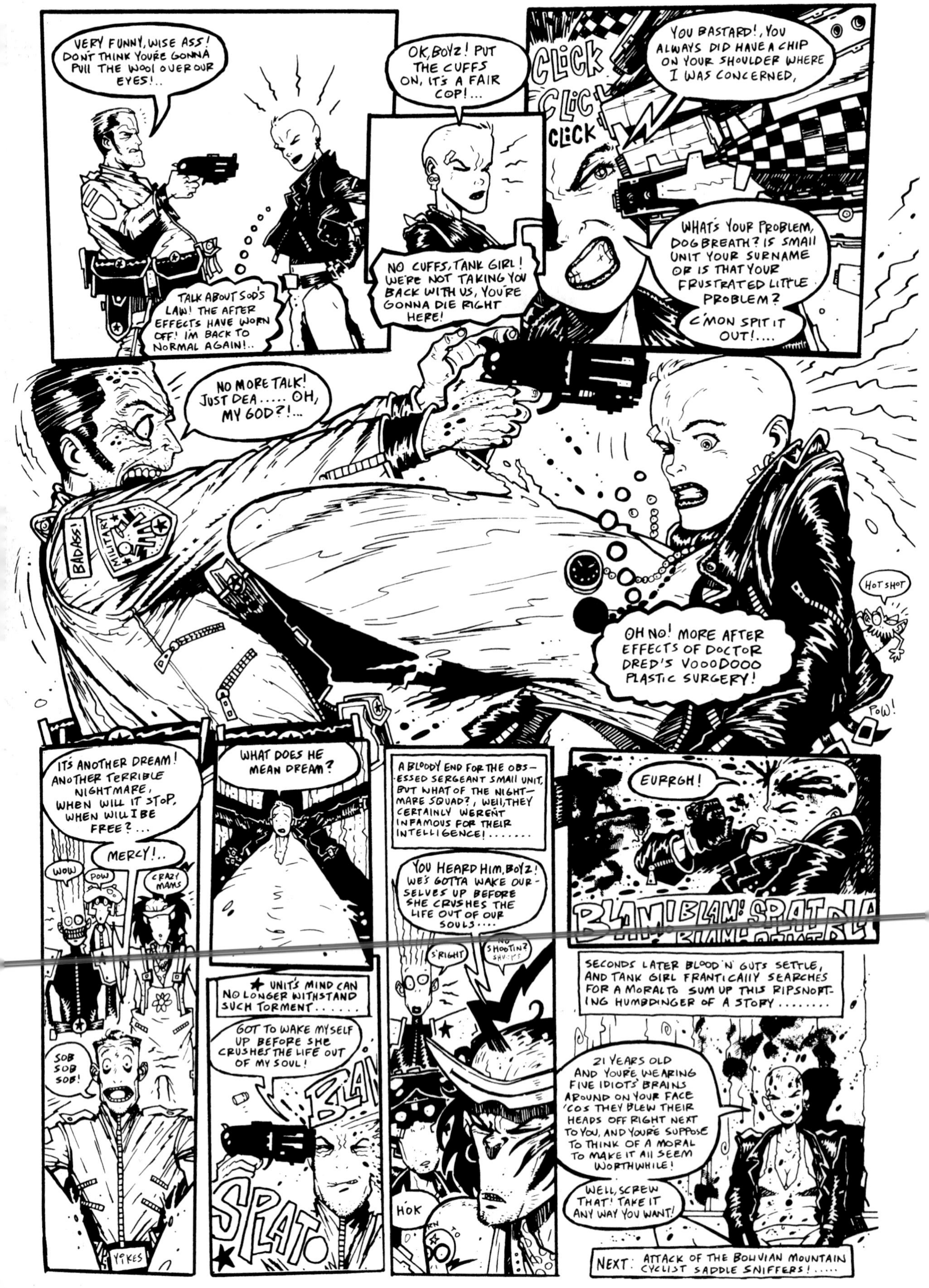
VERY FUNNY, WISE ASS! DON'T THINK YOU'RE GONNA PULL THE WOOL OVER OUR EYES!..
TALK ABOUT SOD'S LAW! THE AFTER EFFECTS HAVE WORN OFF! I'M BACK TO NORMAL AGAIN!..
OK, BOYZ! PUT THE CUFFS ON, IT'S A FAIR COP!...
NO CUFFS, TANK GIRL! WE'RE NOT TAKING YOU BACK WITH US, YOU'RE GONNA DIE RIGHT HERE!
CLICK CLICK CLICK
YOU BASTARD!, YOU ALWAYS DID HAVE A CHIP ON YOUR SHOULDER WHERE I WAS CONCERNED,
WHAT'S YOUR PROBLEM, DOG BREATH? IS SMALL UNIT YOUR SURNAME OR IS THAT YOUR FRUSTRATED LITTLE PROBLEM?
C'MON SPIT IT OUT!....
NO MORE TALK! JUST DEA..... OH, MY GOD?!...
BADASS!
MILITARY
HOTSHOT
OH NO! MORE AFTER EFFECTS OF DOCTOR DRED'S VOOODOOO PLASTIC SURGERY!
POW!
ITS ANOTHER DREAM! ANOTHER TERRIBLE NIGHTMARE, WHEN WILL IT STOP, WHEN WILL I BE FREE?...
MERCY!..
WOW
POW
CRAZY MAMS
SOB SOB SOB!
YIKES
WHAT DOES HE MEAN DREAM?
★ UNIT'S MIND CAN NO LONGER WITHSTAND SUCH TORMENT........
GOT TO WAKE MYSELF UP BEFORE SHE CRUSHES THE LIFE OUT OF MY SOUL!
BLAM
SPLAT
A BLOODY END FOR THE OBSESSED SERGEANT SMALL UNIT, BUT WHAT OF THE NIGHTMARE SQUAD?, WELL, THEY CERTAINLY WEREN'T INFAMOUS FOR THEIR INTELLIGENCE!.......
YOU HEARD HIM, BOYZ! WE'S GOTTA WAKE OURSELVES UP BEFORE SHE CRUSHES THE LIFE OUT OF OUR SOULS....
S'RIGHT
NO SHOOTIN?
HOK
EURRGH!
BLAM! BLAM! SPLAT BLA
SECONDS LATER BLOOD 'N' GUTS SETTLE, AND TANK GIRL FRANTICALLY SEARCHES FOR A MORAL TO SUM UP THIS RIPSNORTING HUMDINGER OF A STORY........
21 YEARS OLD AND YOU'RE WEARING FIVE IDIOTS' BRAINS AROUND ON YOUR FACE 'COS THEY BLEW THEIR HEADS OFF RIGHT NEXT TO YOU, AND YOU'RE SUPPOSE TO THINK OF A MORAL TO MAKE IT ALL SEEM WORTHWHILE!
WELL, SCREW THAT! TAKE IT ANY WAY YOU WANT!
NEXT: ATTACK OF THE BOLIVIAN MOUNTAIN CYCLIST SADDLE SNIFFERS!.....

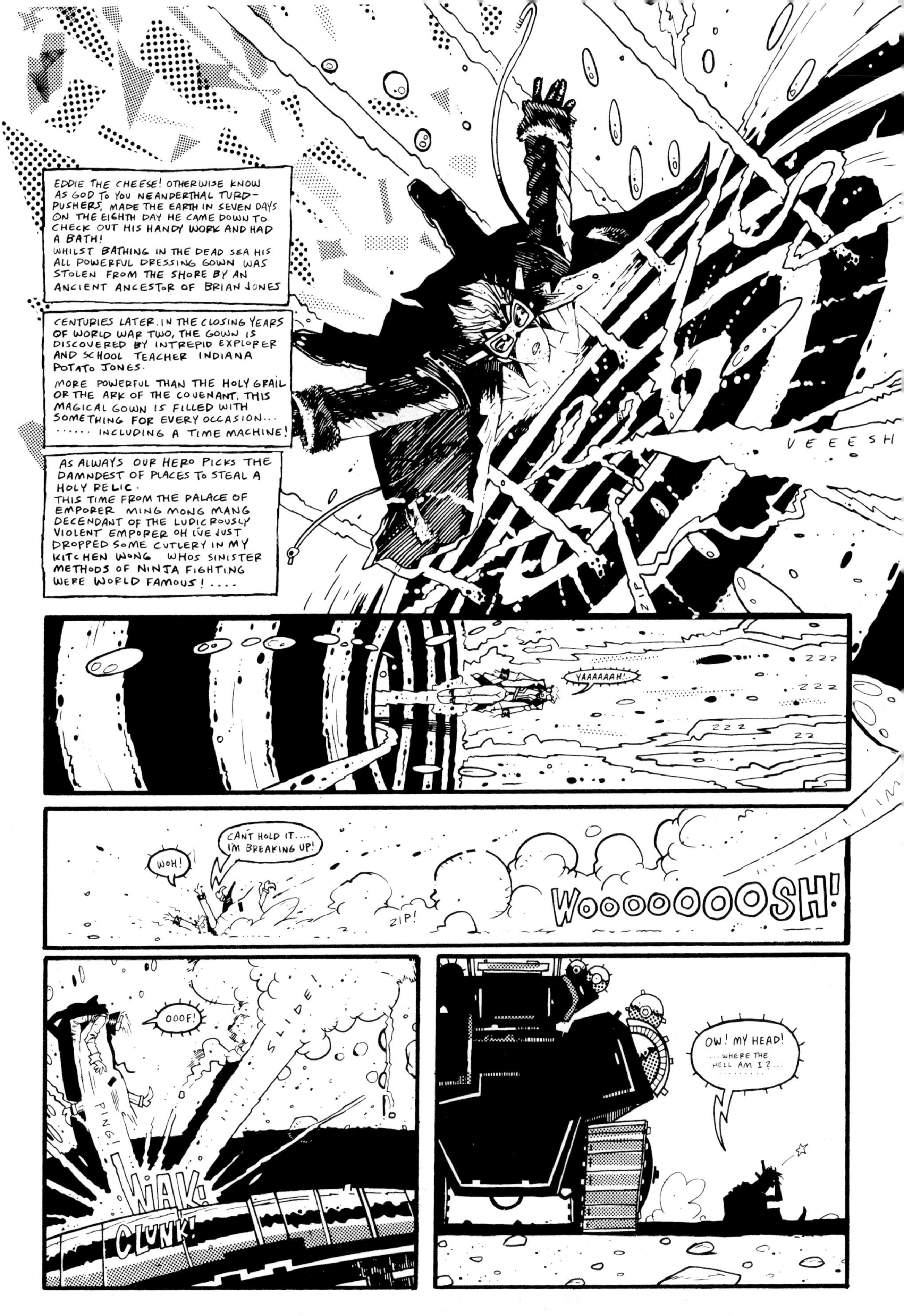

EDDIE THE CHEESE! OTHERWISE KNOW AS GOD TO YOU NEANDERTHAL TURD-PUSHERS, MADE THE EARTH IN SEVEN DAYS ON THE EIGHTH DAY HE CAME DOWN TO CHECK OUT HIS HANDY WORK AND HAD A BATH! WHILST BATHING IN THE DEAD SEA HIS ALL POWERFUL DRESSING GOWN WAS STOLEN FROM THE SHORE BY AN ANCIENT ANCESTOR OF BRIAN JONES
CENTURIES LATER, IN THE CLOSING YEARS OF WORLD WAR TWO, THE GOWN IS DISCOVERED BY INTREPID EXPLORER AND SCHOOL TEACHER INDIANA POTATO JONES. MORE POWERFUL THAN THE HOLY GRAIL OR THE ARK OF THE COVENANT, THIS MAGICAL GOWN IS FILLED WITH SOMETHING FOR EVERY OCCASION... ...... INCLUDING A TIME MACHINE!
AS ALWAYS OUR HERO PICKS THE DAMNDEST OF PLACES TO STEAL A HOLY RELIC. THIS TIME FROM THE PALACE OF EMPORER MING MONG MANG DECENDANT OF THE LUDICROUSLY VIOLENT EMPORER OH I'VE JUST DROPPED SOME CUTLERY IN MY KITCHEN WONG WHOS SINISTER METHODS OF NINJA FIGHTING WERE WORLD FAMOUS!....
VEEESH
ZIP
YAAAAAAH!
ZZZ
ZZZ
ZZZ
ZZ
WOH!
CAN'T HOLD IT.... I'M BREAKING UP!
ZIP!
WOOOOOOOOSH!
OOOF!
SLIDE!
PING!
WAK!
CLUNK!
OW! MY HEAD! ...WHERE THE HELL AM I?...

★ CONCEPT: JAMIE, ALAN ★ SCRIPT: JAMIE, ★ DRAWINGS: JAMIE ★ LETTERS: JAMIE

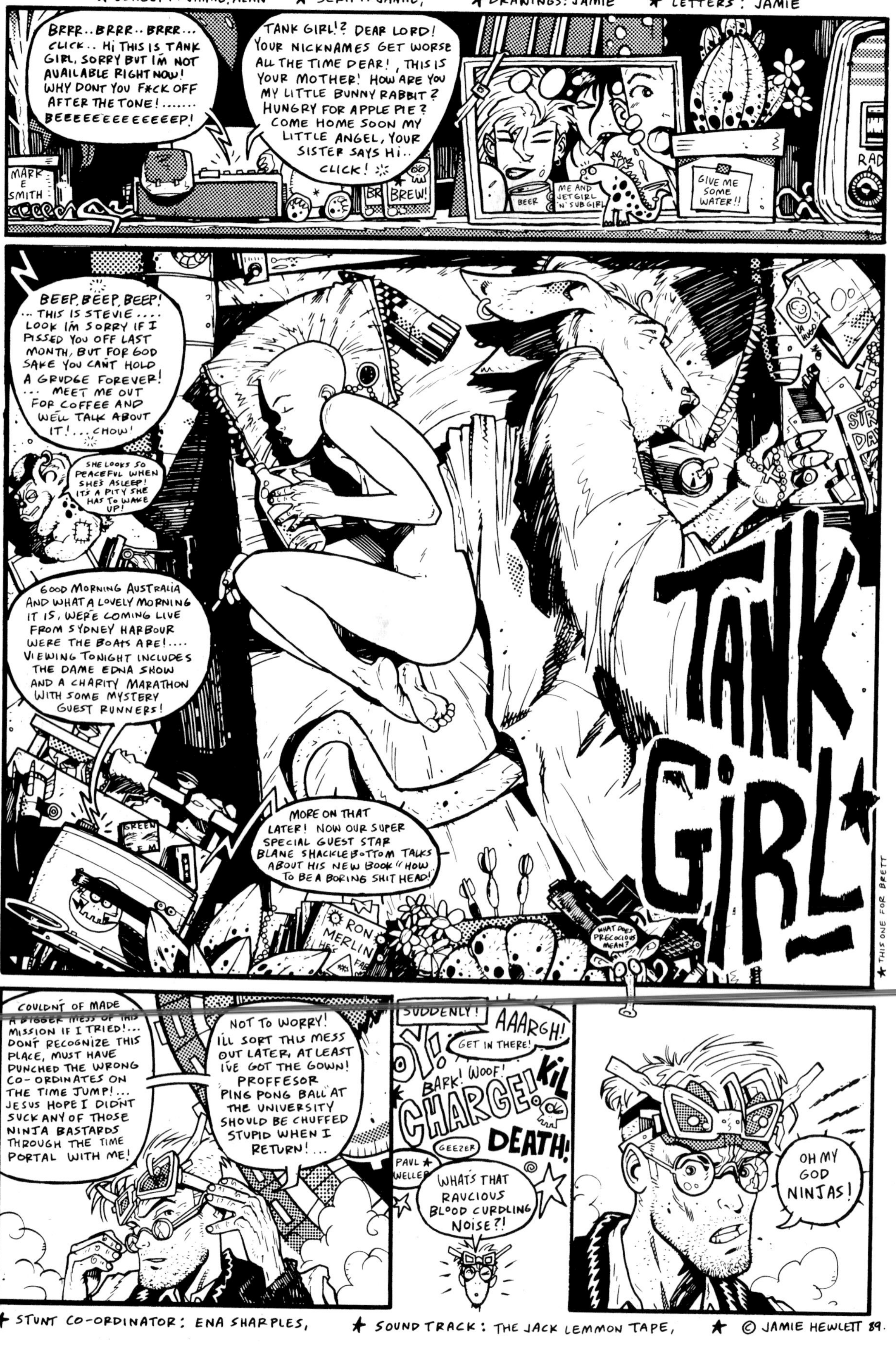

BRRR.. BRRR.. BRRR... CLICK.. HI THIS IS TANK GIRL, SORRY BUT I'M NOT AVAILABLE RIGHT NOW! WHY DONT YOU F*CK OFF AFTER THE TONE! .... BEEEEEEEEEEEEEP!
TANK GIRL!? DEAR LORD! YOUR NICKNAMES GET WORSE ALL THE TIME DEAR!, THIS IS YOUR MOTHER! HOW ARE YOU MY LITTLE BUNNY RABBIT? HUNGRY FOR APPLE PIE? COME HOME SOON MY LITTLE ANGEL, YOUR SISTER SAYS HI.. CLICK!
MARK E SMITH
BREW!
BEER
ME AND JETGIRL 'N' SUBGIRL
GIVE ME SOME WATER!!
BEEP, BEEP, BEEP! ... THIS IS STEVIE ... LOOK I'M SORRY IF I PISSED YOU OFF LAST MONTH, BUT FOR GOD SAKE YOU CAN'T HOLD A GRUDGE FOREVER! ... MEET ME OUT FOR COFFEE AND WE'LL TALK ABOUT IT! ... CHOW!
SHE LOOKS SO PEACEFUL WHEN SHE'S ASLEEP! ITS A PITY SHE HAS TO WAKE UP!
GOOD MORNING AUSTRALIA AND WHAT A LOVELY MORNING IT IS, WE'RE COMING LIVE FROM SYDNEY HARBOUR WERE THE BOATS ARE! .... VIEWING TONIGHT INCLUDES THE DAME EDNA SHOW AND A CHARITY MARATHON WITH SOME MYSTERY GUEST RUNNERS!
MORE ON THAT LATER! NOW OUR SUPER SPECIAL GUEST STAR BLANE SHACKLEBOTTOM TALKS ABOUT HIS NEW BOOK "HOW TO BE A BORING SHIT HEAD!"
TANK GIRL
RON MERLIN
WHAT DOES PRECOCIOUS MEAN?
★ THIS ONE FOR BRETT
COULDN'T OF MADE A BIGGER MESS OF THIS MISSION IF I TRIED! ... DON'T RECOGNIZE THIS PLACE, MUST HAVE PUNCHED THE WRONG CO-ORDINATES ON THE TIME JUMP! ... JESUS HOPE I DIDN'T SUCK ANY OF THOSE NINJA BASTARDS THROUGH THE TIME PORTAL WITH ME!
NOT TO WORRY! I'LL SORT THIS MESS OUT LATER, AT LEAST I'VE GOT THE GOWN! PROFFESOR PING PONG BALL AT THE UNIVERSITY SHOULD BE CHUFFED STUPID WHEN I RETURN! ...
SUDDENLY!
AAARGH!
GET IN THERE!
OY!
BARK! WOOF!
KIL
CHARGE!
GEEZER
DEATH!
PAUL ★ WELLER
WHAT'S THAT RAUCIOUS BLOOD CURDLING NOISE?!
OH MY GOD NINJAS!

★ STUNT CO-ORDINATOR: ENA SHARPLES, ★ SOUND TRACK: THE JACK LEMMON TAPE, ★ © JAMIE HEWLETT 89.

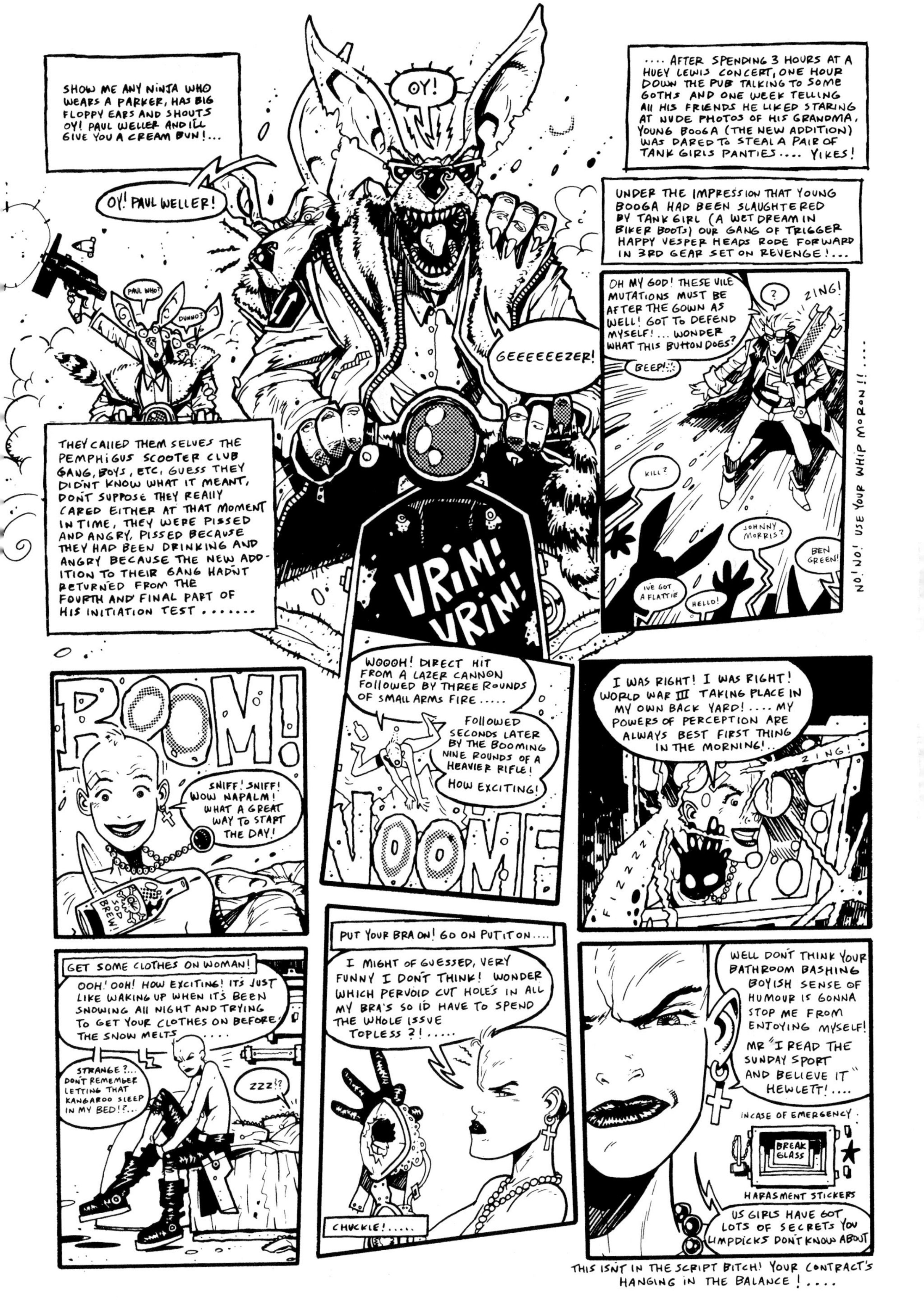
SHOW ME ANY NINJA WHO WEARS A PARKER, HAS BIG FLOPPY EARS AND SHOUTS OY! PAUL WELLER AND I'LL GIVE YOU A CREAM BUN!...
OY!
OY! PAUL WELLER!
PAUL WHO?
DUNNO?
GEEEEEEZER!
....AFTER SPENDING 3 HOURS AT A HUEY LEWIS CONCERT, ONE HOUR DOWN THE PUB TALKING TO SOME GOTHS AND ONE WEEK TELLING ALL HIS FRIENDS HE LIKED STARING AT NUDE PHOTOS OF HIS GRANDMA, YOUNG BOOGA (THE NEW ADDITION) WAS DARED TO STEAL A PAIR OF TANK GIRLS PANTIES.... YIKES!
UNDER THE IMPRESSION THAT YOUNG BOOGA HAD BEEN SLAUGHTERED BY TANK GIRL (A WET DREAM IN BIKER BOOTS) OUR GANG OF TRIGGER HAPPY VESPER HEADS RODE FORWARD IN 3RD GEAR SET ON REVENGE!...
THEY CALLED THEM SELVES THE PEMPHIGUS SCOOTER CLUB GANG, BOYS, ETC, GUESS THEY DIDN'T KNOW WHAT IT MEANT, DON'T SUPPOSE THEY REALLY CARED EITHER AT THAT MOMENT IN TIME, THEY WERE PISSED AND ANGRY, PISSED BECAUSE THEY HAD BEEN DRINKING AND ANGRY BECAUSE THE NEW ADDITION TO THEIR GANG HADN'T RETURNED FROM THE FOURTH AND FINAL PART OF HIS INITIATION TEST.......
VRIM! VRIM!
OH MY GOD! THESE VILE MUTATIONS MUST BE AFTER THE GOWN AS WELL! GOT TO DEFEND MYSELF!... WONDER WHAT THIS BUTTON DOES?
?
ZING!
BEEP!
KILL?
JOHNNY MORRIS?
BEN GREEN!
I'VE GOT A FLATTIE
HELLO!
NO! NO! USE YOUR WHIP MORON!!....
BOOM!
SNIFF! SNIFF! WOW NAPALM! WHAT A GREAT WAY TO START THE DAY!
SOD BREW
WOOOH! DIRECT HIT FROM A LAZER CANNON FOLLOWED BY THREE ROUNDS OF SMALL ARMS FIRE.....
FOLLOWED SECONDS LATER BY THE BOOMING NINE ROUNDS OF A HEAVIER RIFLE!
HOW EXCITING!
VOOMF
I WAS RIGHT! I WAS RIGHT! WORLD WAR III TAKING PLACE IN MY OWN BACK YARD!.... MY POWERS OF PERCEPTION ARE ALWAYS BEST FIRST THING IN THE MORNING!..
ZING!
FIZZZZZ!
GET SOME CLOTHES ON WOMAN!
OOH! OOH! HOW EXCITING! ITS JUST LIKE WAKING UP WHEN ITS BEEN SNOWING ALL NIGHT AND TRYING TO GET YOUR CLOTHES ON BEFORE THE SNOW MELTS.....
STRANGE?... DON'T REMEMBER LETTING THAT KANGAROO SLEEP IN MY BED!?...
ZZZ!?
PUT YOUR BRA ON! GO ON PUT IT ON....
I MIGHT OF GUESSED, VERY FUNNY I DON'T THINK! WONDER WHICH PERVOID CUT HOLES IN ALL MY BRA'S SO I'D HAVE TO SPEND THE WHOLE ISSUE TOPLESS?!.....
CHUCKLE!.....
WELL DON'T THINK YOUR BATHROOM BASHING BOYISH SENSE OF HUMOUR IS GONNA STOP ME FROM ENJOYING MYSELF!
MR "I READ THE SUNDAY SPORT AND BELIEVE IT" HEWLETT!....
INCASE OF EMERGENCY
BREAK GLASS
HARASMENT STICKERS
US GIRLS HAVE GOT LOTS OF SECRETS YOU LIMPDICKS DON'T KNOW ABOUT
THIS ISN'T IN THE SCRIPT BITCH! YOUR CONTRACT'S HANGING IN THE BALANCE!....

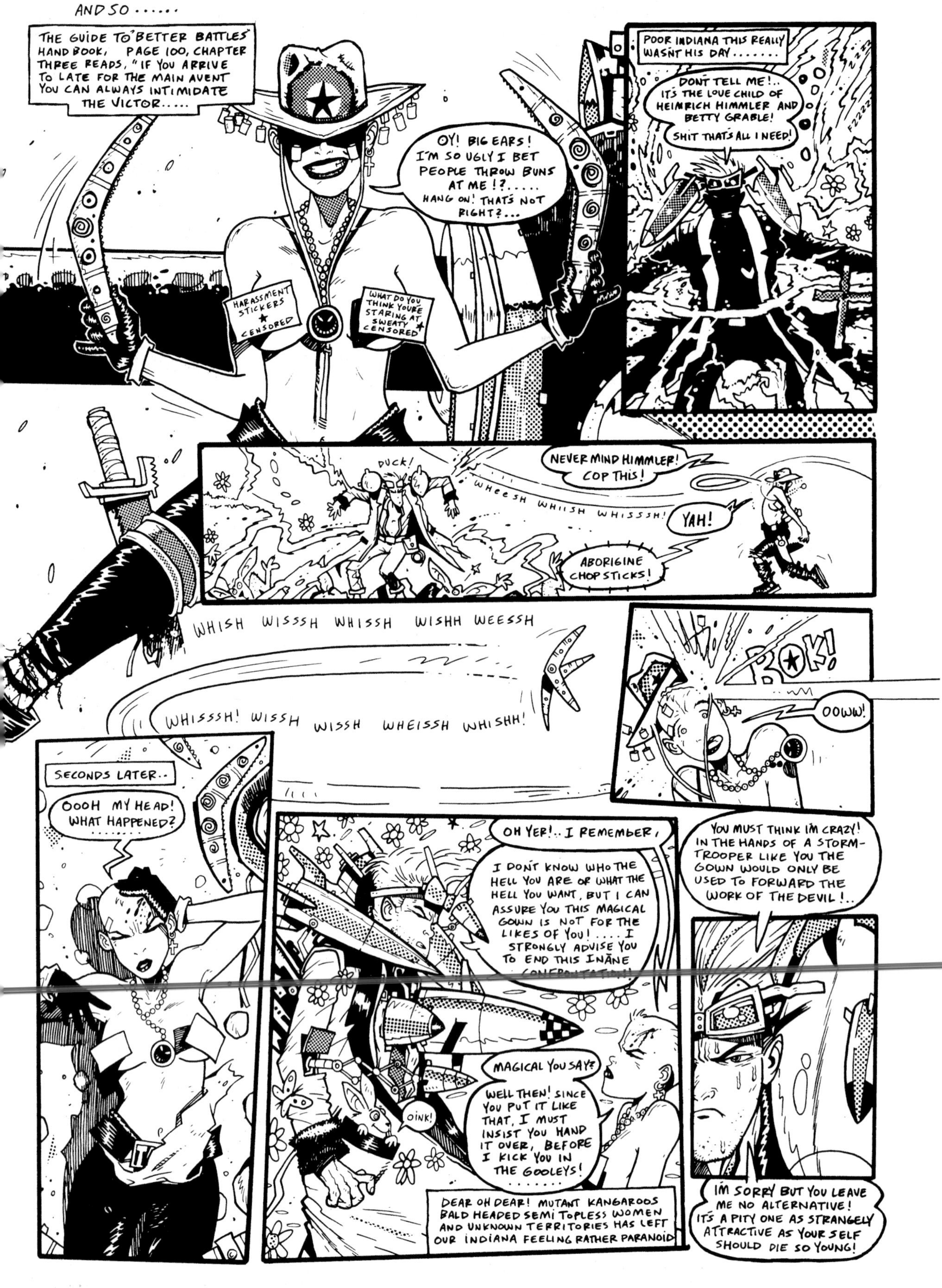
AND SO......
THE GUIDE TO 'BETTER BATTLES' HAND BOOK, PAGE 100, CHAPTER THREE READS, "IF YOU ARRIVE TO LATE FOR THE MAIN AVENT YOU CAN ALWAYS INTIMIDATE THE VICTOR.....
OY! BIG EARS! I'M SO UGLY I BET PEOPLE THROW BUNS AT ME!?..... HANG ON! THAT'S NOT RIGHT?...
HARASSMENT STICKERS ★ CENSORED
WHAT DO YOU THINK YOU'RE STARING AT SWEATY ★ CENSORED
POOR INDIANA THIS REALLY WASN'T HIS DAY.......
DON'T TELL ME!.. IT'S THE LOVE CHILD OF HEIMRICH HIMMLER AND BETTY GRABLE!
SHIT THAT'S ALL I NEED!
DUCK!
NEVER MIND HIMMLER! COP THIS!
WHEESH WHIISH WHISSSH!
YAH!
ABORIGINE CHOP STICKS!
WHISH WISSSH WHISSH WISHH WEESSH
WHISSSH! WISSH WISSH WHEISSH WHISHH!
BOK!
OOWW!
SECONDS LATER..
OOOH MY HEAD! WHAT HAPPENED?
OH YER!.. I REMEMBER,
I DON'T KNOW WHO THE HELL YOU ARE OR WHAT THE HELL YOU WANT, BUT I CAN ASSURE YOU THIS MAGICAL GOWN IS NOT FOR THE LIKES OF YOU!.... I STRONGLY ADVISE YOU TO END THIS INANE CONFRONTATION!
MAGICAL YOU SAY?
WELL THEN! SINCE YOU PUT IT LIKE THAT, I MUST INSIST YOU HAND IT OVER, BEFORE I KICK YOU IN THE GOOLEYS!
OINK!
DEAR OH DEAR! MUTANT KANGAROOS BALD HEADED SEMI TOPLESS WOMEN AND UNKNOWN TERRITORIES HAS LEFT OUR INDIANA FEELING RATHER PARANOID
YOU MUST THINK I'M CRAZY! IN THE HANDS OF A STORM-TROOPER LIKE YOU THE GOWN WOULD ONLY BE USED TO FORWARD THE WORK OF THE DEVIL!..
I'M SORRY BUT YOU LEAVE ME NO ALTERNATIVE! IT'S A PITY ONE AS STRANGELY ATTRACTIVE AS YOUR SELF SHOULD DIE SO YOUNG!

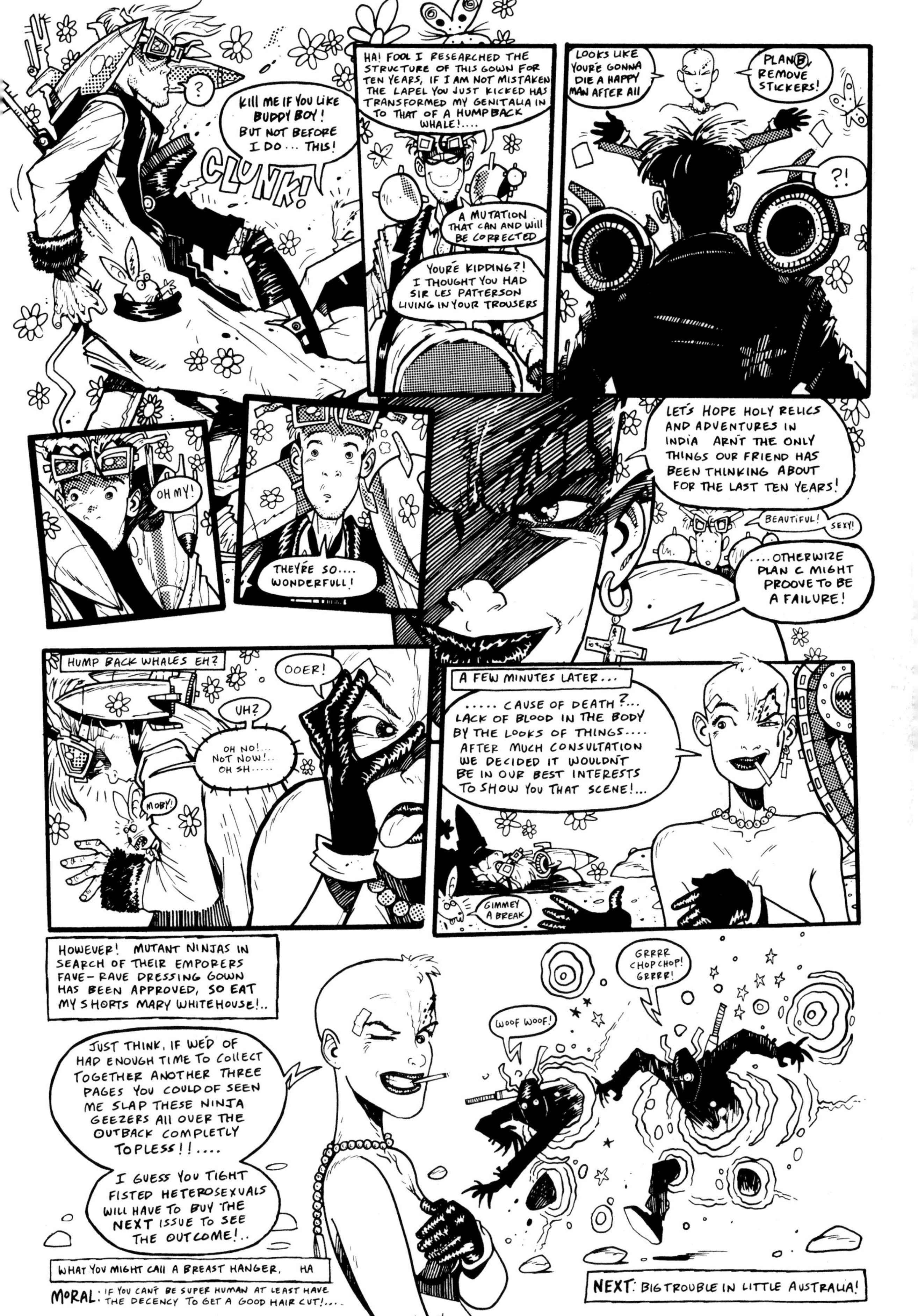
?
KILL ME IF YOU LIKE BUDDY BOY! BUT NOT BEFORE I DO... THIS!
CLUNK!
HA! FOOL I RESEARCHED THE STRUCTURE OF THIS GOWN FOR TEN YEARS, IF I AM NOT MISTAKEN THE LAPEL YOU JUST KICKED HAS TRANSFORMED MY GENITALIA IN TO THAT OF A HUMPBACK WHALE!....
A MUTATION THAT CAN AND WILL BE CORRECTED
YOU'RE KIDDING?! I THOUGHT YOU HAD SIR LES PATTERSON LIVING IN YOUR TROUSERS
LOOKS LIKE YOU'RE GONNA DIE A HAPPY MAN AFTER ALL
PLAN B, REMOVE STICKERS!
?!
OH MY!
THEY'RE SO.... WONDERFULL!
LET'S HOPE HOLY RELICS AND ADVENTURES IN INDIA ARN'T THE ONLY THINGS OUR FRIEND HAS BEEN THINKING ABOUT FOR THE LAST TEN YEARS!
BEAUTIFUL!
SEXY!
....OTHERWIZE PLAN C MIGHT PROOVE TO BE A FAILURE!
HUMP BACK WHALES EH?
OOER!
UH?
OH NO!... NOT NOW!... OH SH.....
MOBY!
A FEW MINUTES LATER...
..... CAUSE OF DEATH?... LACK OF BLOOD IN THE BODY BY THE LOOKS OF THINGS.... AFTER MUCH CONSULTATION WE DECIDED IT WOULDN'T BE IN OUR BEST INTERESTS TO SHOW YOU THAT SCENE!...
GIMMEY A BREAK
HOWEVER! MUTANT NINJAS IN SEARCH OF THEIR EMPORERS FAVE-RAVE DRESSING GOWN HAS BEEN APPROVED, SO EAT MY SHORTS MARY WHITEHOUSE!..
GRRRR CHOP CHOP! GRRRR!
WOOF WOOF!
JUST THINK, IF WE'D OF HAD ENOUGH TIME TO COLLECT TOGETHER ANOTHER THREE PAGES YOU COULD OF SEEN ME SLAP THESE NINJA GEEZERS ALL OVER THE OUTBACK COMPLETLY TOPLESS!!....
I GUESS YOU TIGHT FISTED HETEROSEXUALS WILL HAVE TO BUY THE NEXT ISSUE TO SEE THE OUTCOME!..
WHAT YOU MIGHT CALL A BREAST HANGER, HA
MORAL: IF YOU CAN'T BE SUPER HUMAN AT LEAST HAVE THE DECENCY TO GET A GOOD HAIR CUT!....
NEXT: BIG TROUBLE IN LITTLE AUSTRALIA!

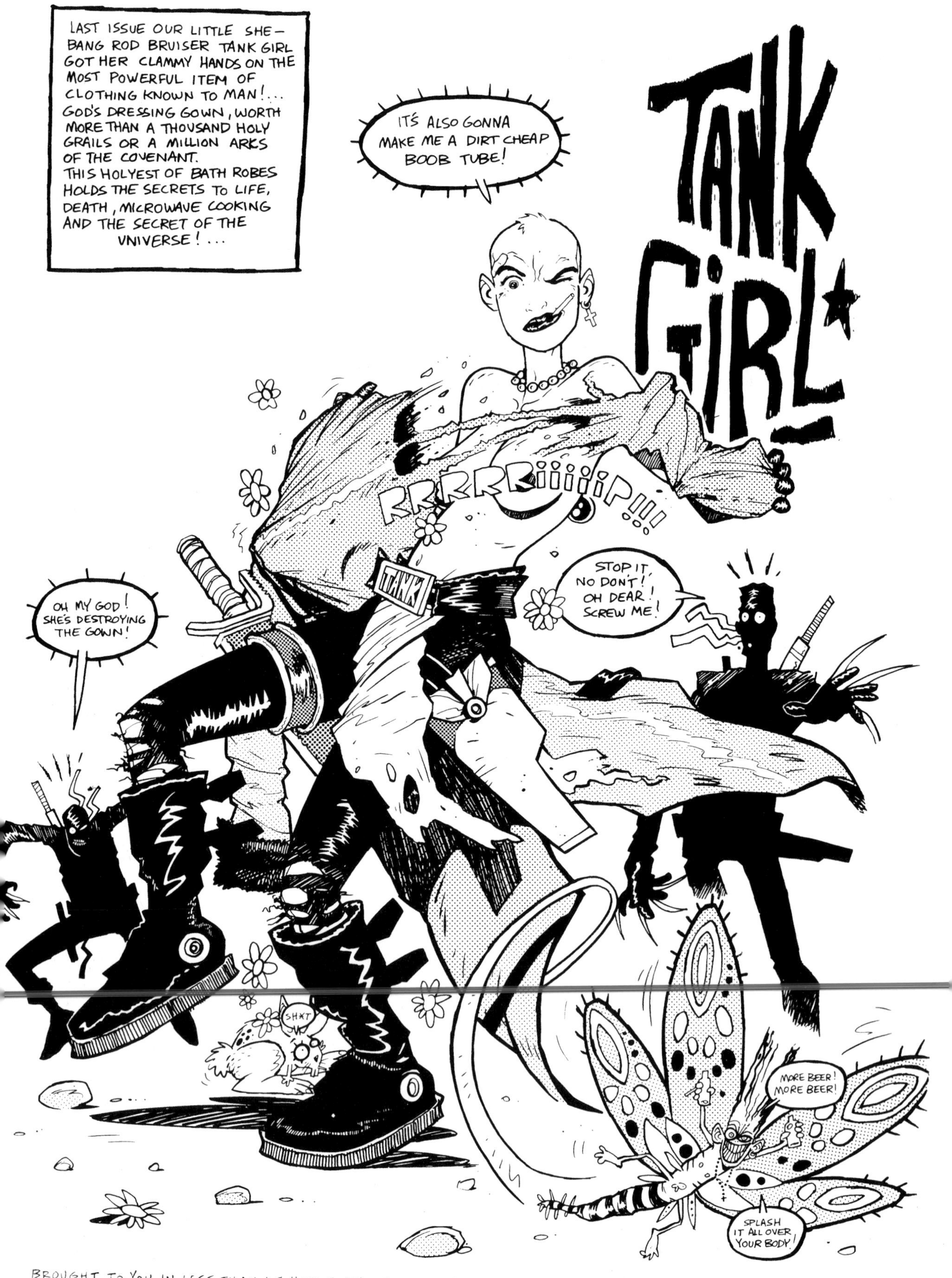
LAST ISSUE OUR LITTLE SHE-BANG ROD BRUISER TANK GIRL GOT HER CLAMMY HANDS ON THE MOST POWERFUL ITEM OF CLOTHING KNOWN TO MAN!... GOD'S DRESSING GOWN, WORTH MORE THAN A THOUSAND HOLY GRAILS OR A MILLION ARKS OF THE COVENANT.
THIS HOLYEST OF BATH ROBES HOLDS THE SECRETS TO LIFE, DEATH, MICROWAVE COOKING AND THE SECRET OF THE UNIVERSE!...
TANK GIRL
IT'S ALSO GONNA MAKE ME A DIRT CHEAP BOOB TUBE!
RRRRRiiiiiP!!!
TANK
OH MY GOD! SHE'S DESTROYING THE GOWN!
STOP IT, NO DON'T! OH DEAR! SCREW ME!
SH*T
MORE BEER! MORE BEER!
SPLASH IT ALL OVER YOUR BODY!

BROUGHT TO YOU IN LESS THAN 48 HOURS BY HEWLETT 'N' MARTIN
THIS ONE FOR STEVE DILLON AND FAMILY

© JAMIE 89.

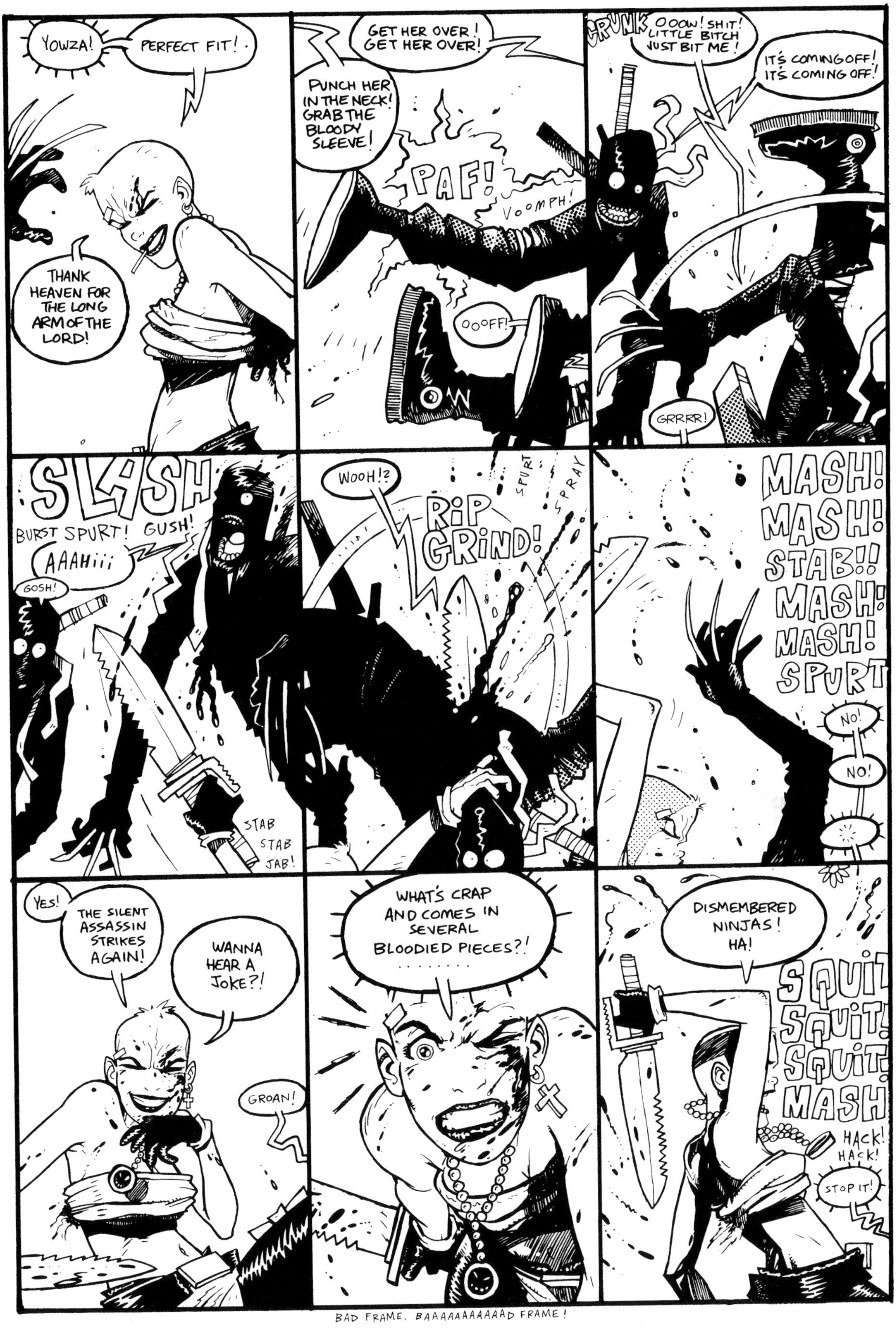
YOWZA!
PERFECT FIT!
THANK HEAVEN FOR THE LONG ARM OF THE LORD!
GET HER OVER! GET HER OVER!
PUNCH HER IN THE NECK! GRAB THE BLOODY SLEEVE!
PAF!
VOOMPH!
OOOFF!
CRUNK
OOOW! SHIT! LITTLE BITCH JUST BIT ME!
IT'S COMING OFF! IT'S COMING OFF!
GRRRR!
SLASH
BURST SPURT! GUSH!
AAAHiii
GOSH!
STAB STAB JAB!
WOOH!?
RIP GRIND!
SPURT
SPRAY
MASH! MASH! STAB!! MASH! MASH! SPURT
NO!
NO!
YES!
THE SILENT ASSASSIN STRIKES AGAIN!
WANNA HEAR A JOKE?!
GROAN!
WHAT'S CRAP AND COMES IN SEVERAL BLOODIED PIECES?!
....
DISMEMBERED NINJAS! HA!
SQUIT SQUIT! SQUIT! MASH
HACK! HACK!
STOP IT!

BAD FRAME, BAAAAAAAAAAAD FRAME!

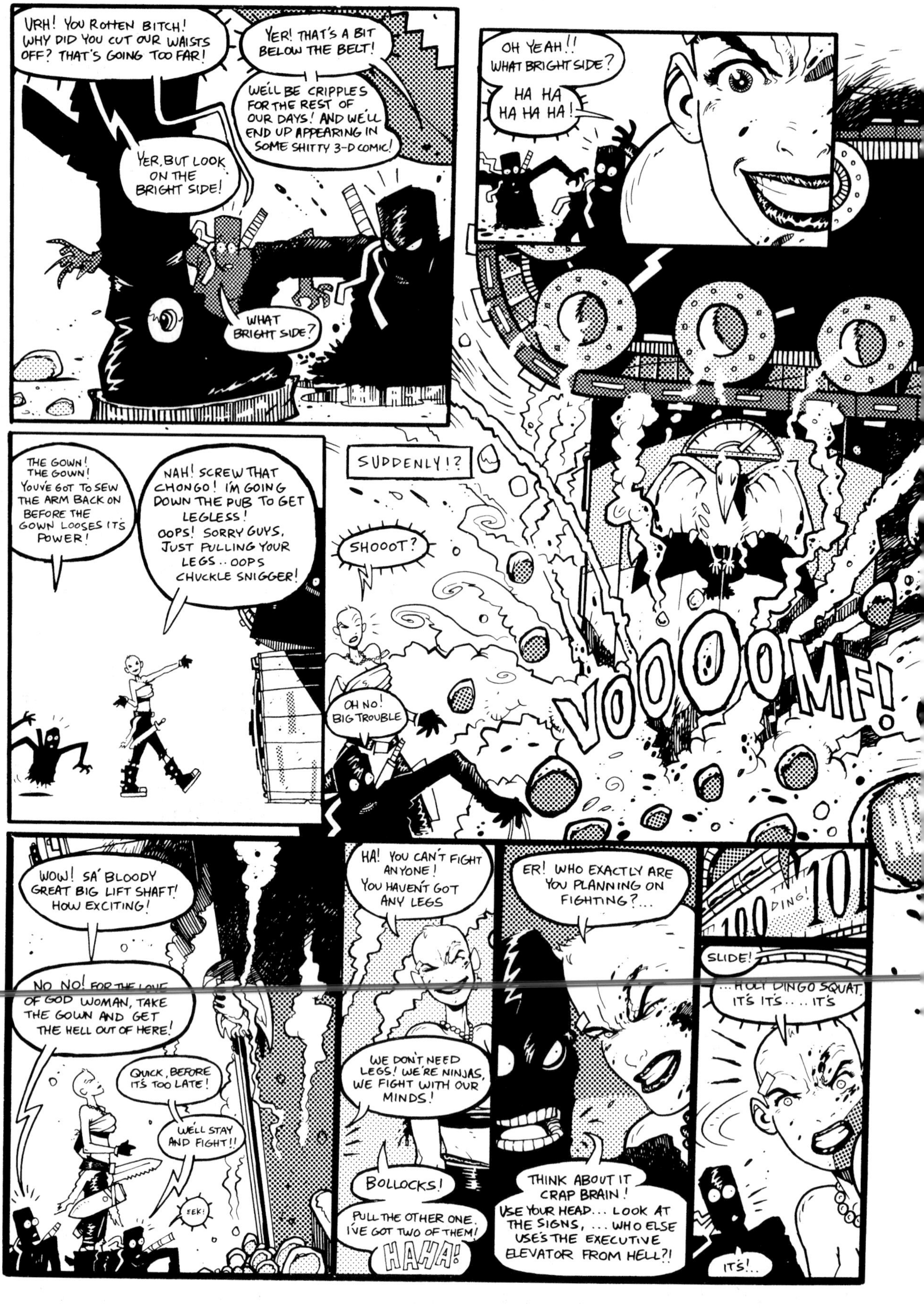
URH! YOU ROTTEN BITCH! WHY DID YOU CUT OUR WAISTS OFF? THAT'S GOING TOO FAR!
YER! THAT'S A BIT BELOW THE BELT!
WE'LL BE CRIPPLES FOR THE REST OF OUR DAYS! AND WE'LL END UP APPEARING IN SOME SHITTY 3-D COMIC!
YER, BUT LOOK ON THE BRIGHT SIDE!
WHAT BRIGHT SIDE?
OH YEAH!! WHAT BRIGHT SIDE?
HA HA HA HA HA!
THE GOWN! THE GOWN! YOU'VE GOT TO SEW THE ARM BACK ON BEFORE THE GOWN LOOSES ITS POWER!
NAH! SCREW THAT CHONGO! I'M GOING DOWN THE PUB TO GET LEGLESS! OOPS! SORRY GUYS, JUST PULLING YOUR LEGS.. OOPS CHUCKLE SNIGGER!
SUDDENLY!?
SHOOOT?
OH NO! BIG TROUBLE
VOOOOOMF!
WOW! SA' BLOODY GREAT BIG LIFT SHAFT! HOW EXCITING!
NO NO! FOR THE LOVE OF GOD WOMAN, TAKE THE GOWN AND GET THE HELL OUT OF HERE!
QUICK, BEFORE IT'S TOO LATE!
WE'LL STAY AND FIGHT!!
EEK!
HA! YOU CAN'T FIGHT ANYONE! YOU HAVEN'T GOT ANY LEGS
WE DON'T NEED LEGS! WE'RE NINJAS, WE FIGHT WITH OUR MINDS!
BOLLOCKS!
PULL THE OTHER ONE. I'VE GOT TWO OF THEM!
HAHA!
ER! WHO EXACTLY ARE YOU PLANNING ON FIGHTING?...
THINK ABOUT IT CRAP BRAIN! USE YOUR HEAD... LOOK AT THE SIGNS, ... WHO ELSE USE'S THE EXECUTIVE ELEVATOR FROM HELL?!
100
10
DING!
SLIDE!
...HOLY DINGO SQUAT. IT'S IT'S.... IT'S
IT'S!..

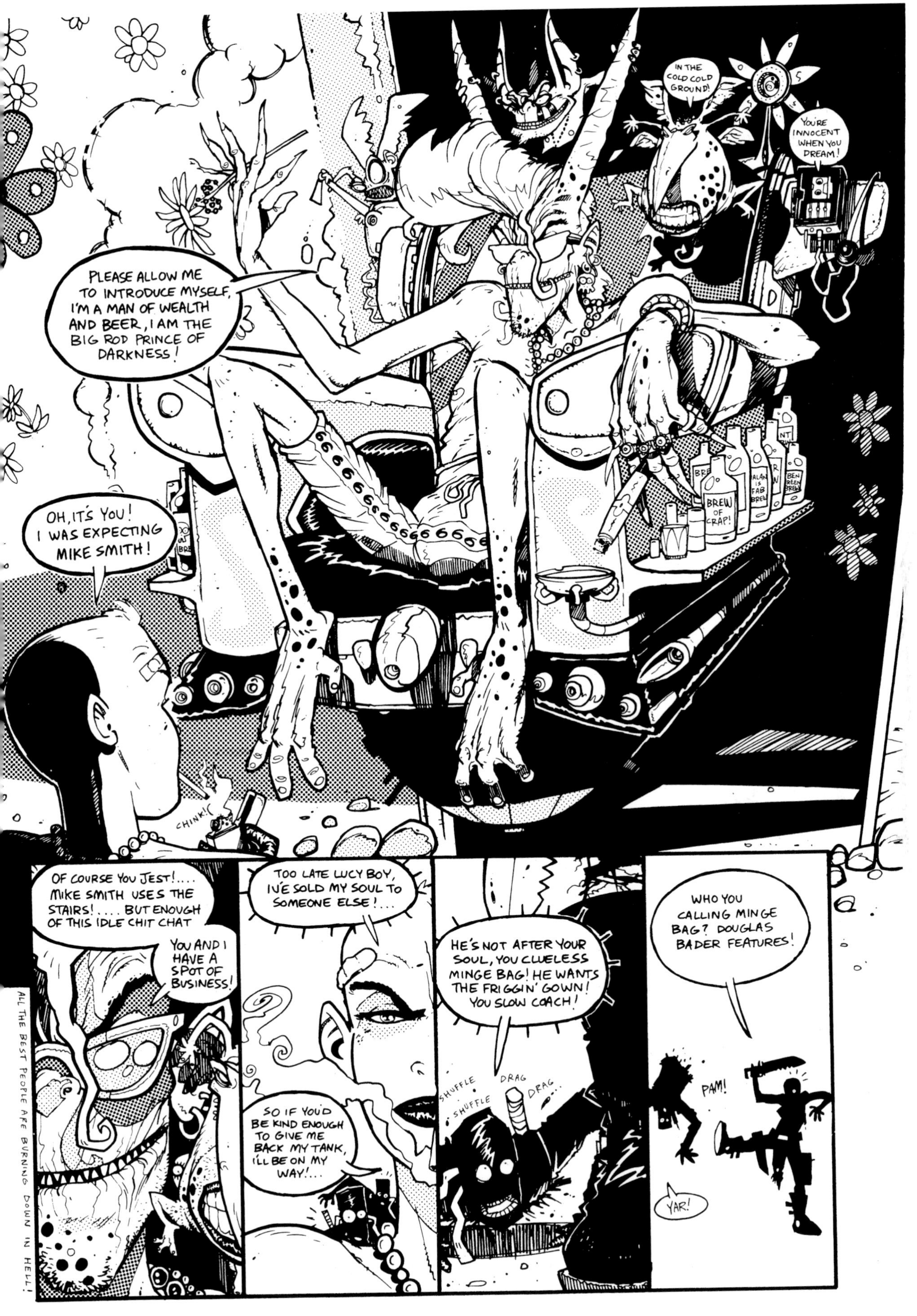
IN THE COLD COLD GROUND!
YOU'RE INNOCENT WHEN YOU DREAM!
PLEASE ALLOW ME TO INTRODUCE MYSELF, I'M A MAN OF WEALTH AND BEER, I AM THE BIG ROD PRINCE OF DARKNESS!
OH, IT'S YOU! I WAS EXPECTING MIKE SMITH!
ALAN IS FAB BREW
BEN GREEN BREW
BREW OF CRAP!
CHINK!
OF COURSE YOU JEST!.... MIKE SMITH USES THE STAIRS!.... BUT ENOUGH OF THIS IDLE CHIT CHAT
YOU AND I HAVE A SPOT OF BUSINESS!
TOO LATE LUCY BOY, I'VE SOLD MY SOUL TO SOMEONE ELSE!...
SO IF YOU'D BE KIND ENOUGH TO GIVE ME BACK MY TANK, I'LL BE ON MY WAY!...
HE'S NOT AFTER YOUR SOUL, YOU CLUELESS MINGE BAG! HE WANTS THE FRIGGIN' GOWN! YOU SLOW COACH!
SHUFFLE
SHUFFLE
DRAG
DRAG
WHO YOU CALLING MINGE BAG? DOUGLAS BADER FEATURES!
PAM!
YAR!

ALL THE BEST PEOPLE ARE BURNING DOWN IN HELL!

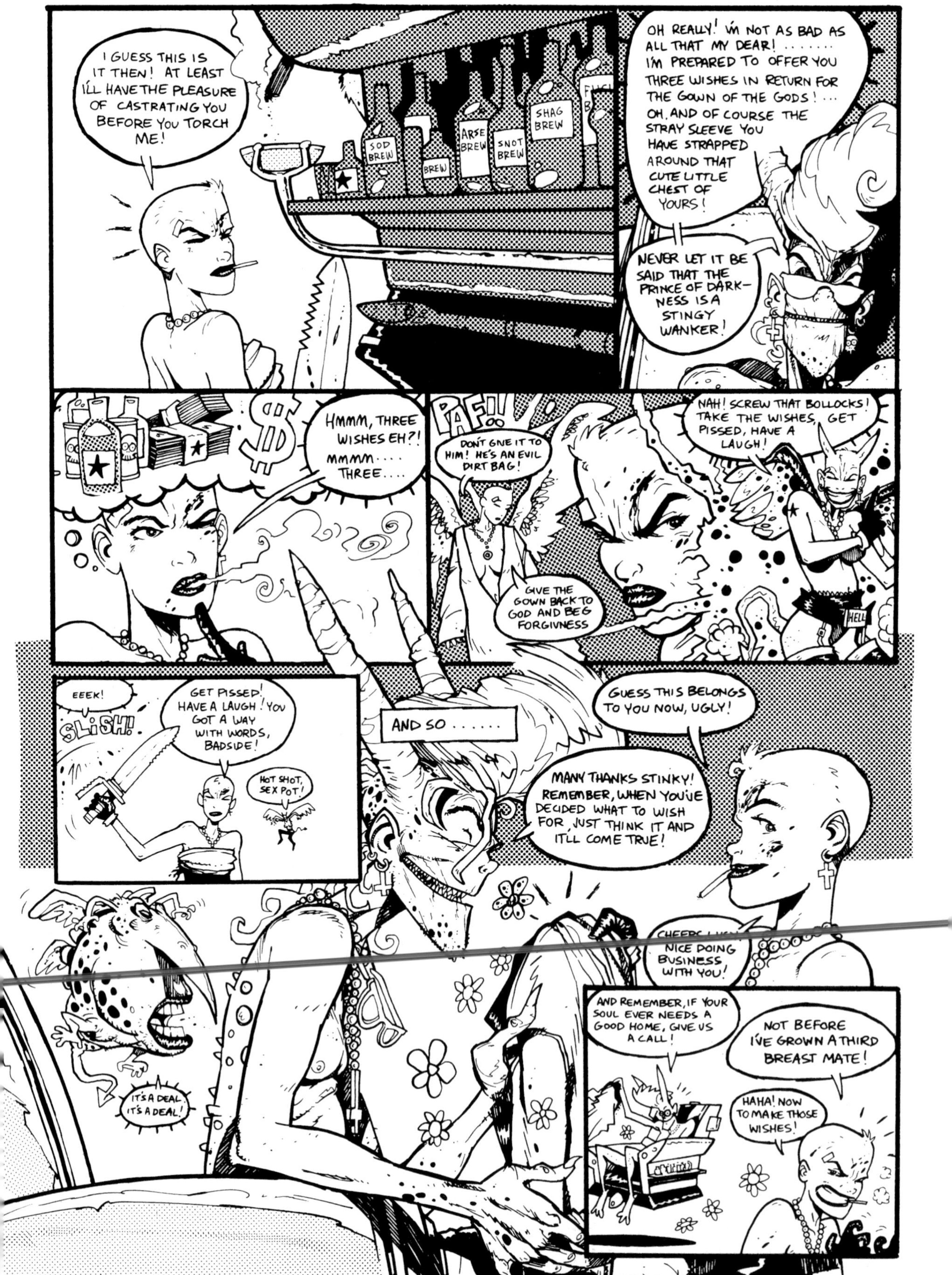
I GUESS THIS IS IT THEN! AT LEAST I'LL HAVE THE PLEASURE OF CASTRATING YOU BEFORE YOU TORCH ME!
SOD BREW
BREW
ARSE BREW
SNOT BREW
SHAG BREW
OH REALLY! I'M NOT AS BAD AS ALL THAT MY DEAR! .... I'M PREPARED TO OFFER YOU THREE WISHES IN RETURN FOR THE GOWN OF THE GODS! ... OH, AND OF COURSE THE STRAY SLEEVE YOU HAVE STRAPPED AROUND THAT CUTE LITTLE CHEST OF YOURS!
NEVER LET IT BE SAID THAT THE PRINCE OF DARKNESS IS A STINGY WANKER!
HMMM, THREE WISHES EH?! MMMM.... THREE....
PAF!!
DON'T GIVE IT TO HIM! HE'S AN EVIL DIRT BAG!
GIVE THE GOWN BACK TO GOD AND BEG FORGIVNESS
NAH! SCREW THAT BOLLOCKS! TAKE THE WISHES, GET PISSED, HAVE A LAUGH!
HELL
EEEK!
SLISH!
GET PISSED! HAVE A LAUGH! YOU GOT A WAY WITH WORDS, BADSIDE!
HOT SHOT, SEX POT!
AND SO ......
GUESS THIS BELONGS TO YOU NOW, UGLY!
MANY THANKS STINKY! REMEMBER, WHEN YOU'VE DECIDED WHAT TO WISH FOR, JUST THINK IT AND IT'LL COME TRUE!
NICE DOING BUSINESS WITH YOU!
IT'S A DEAL! IT'S A DEAL!
AND REMEMBER, IF YOUR SOUL EVER NEEDS A GOOD HOME, GIVE US A CALL!
NOT BEFORE I'VE GROWN A THIRD BREAST MATE!
HAHA! NOW TO MAKE THOSE WISHES!

HI MAN! I'VE COME ABOUT A CHOICES PENSION

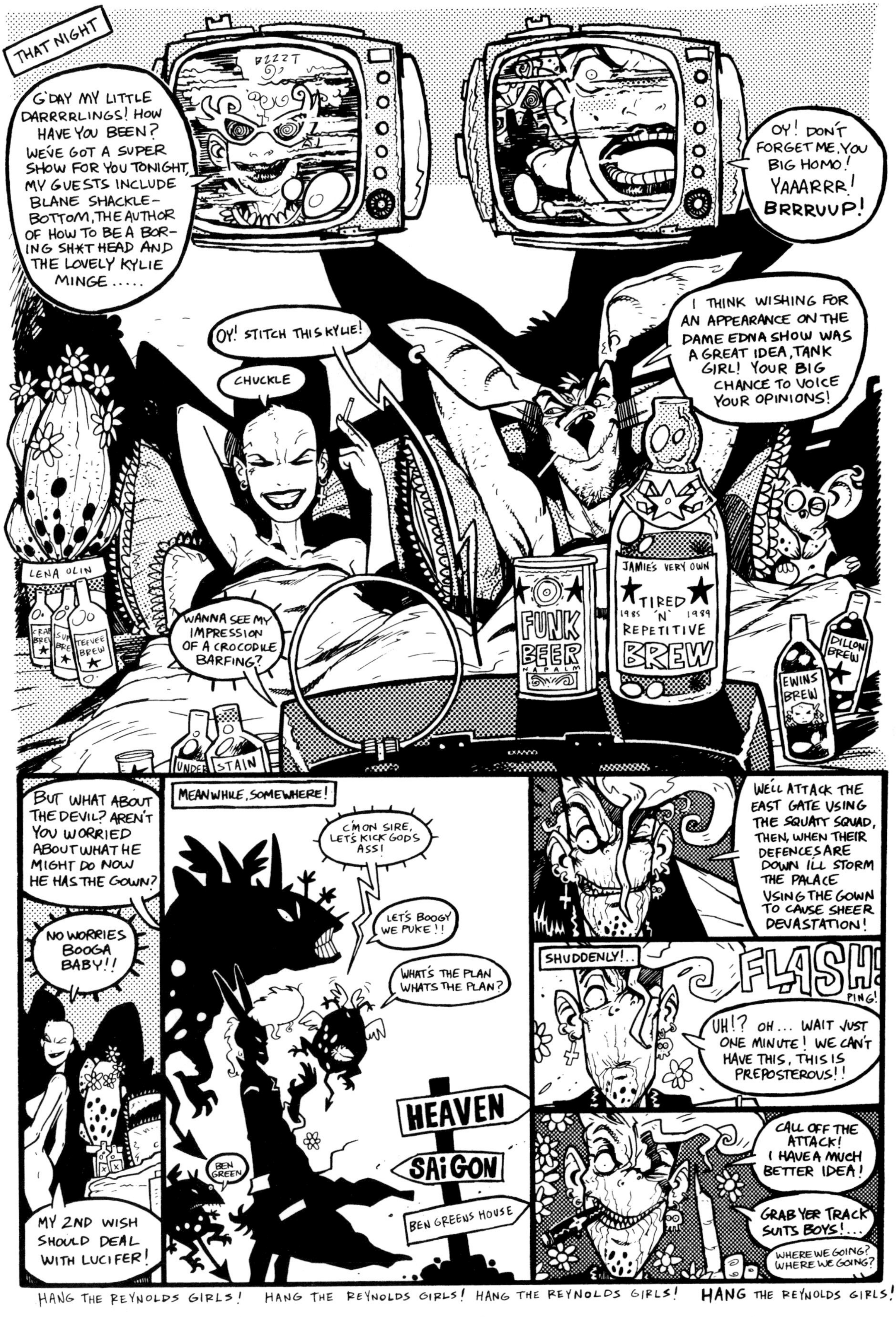
THAT NIGHT
BZZZT
G'DAY MY LITTLE DARRRRLINGS! HOW HAVE YOU BEEN? WE'VE GOT A SUPER SHOW FOR YOU TONIGHT, MY GUESTS INCLUDE BLANE SHACKLE-BOTTOM, THE AUTHOR OF HOW TO BE A BORING SH*T HEAD AND THE LOVELY KYLIE MINGE.....
OY! DON'T FORGET ME, YOU BIG HOMO! YAAARRR! BRRRUUP!
I THINK WISHING FOR AN APPEARANCE ON THE DAME EDNA SHOW WAS A GREAT IDEA, TANK GIRL! YOUR BIG CHANCE TO VOICE YOUR OPINIONS!
OY! STITCH THIS KYLIE!
CHUCKLE
WANNA SEE MY IMPRESSION OF A CROCODILE BARFING?
LENA OLIN
TEEVEE BREW
FUNK BEER
NAPALM
JAMIE'S VERY OWN TIRED 'N' REPETITIVE BREW
1985 1989
DILLON BREW
EWINS BREW
STAIN
BUT WHAT ABOUT THE DEVIL? AREN'T YOU WORRIED ABOUT WHAT HE MIGHT DO NOW HE HAS THE GOWN?
NO WORRIES BOOGA BABY!!
MY 2ND WISH SHOULD DEAL WITH LUCIFER!
MEANWHILE, SOMEWHERE!
C'MON SIRE, LET'S KICK GOD'S ASS!
LET'S BOOGY WE PUKE!!
WHAT'S THE PLAN WHATS THE PLAN?
BEN GREEN
HEAVEN
SAIGON
BEN GREENS HOUSE
WE'LL ATTACK THE EAST GATE USING THE SQUATT SQUAD, THEN, WHEN THEIR DEFENCES ARE DOWN I'LL STORM THE PALACE USING THE GOWN TO CAUSE SHEER DEVASTATION!
SHUDDENLY!..
FLASH!
PING!
UH!? OH... WAIT JUST ONE MINUTE! WE CAN'T HAVE THIS, THIS IS PREPOSTEROUS!!
CALL OFF THE ATTACK! I HAVE A MUCH BETTER IDEA!
GRAB YER TRACK SUITS BOYS!...
WHERE WE GOING? WHERE WE GOING?

HANG THE REYNOLDS GIRLS! HANG THE REYNOLDS GIRLS! HANG THE REYNOLDS GIRLS! HANG THE REYNOLDS GIRLS!

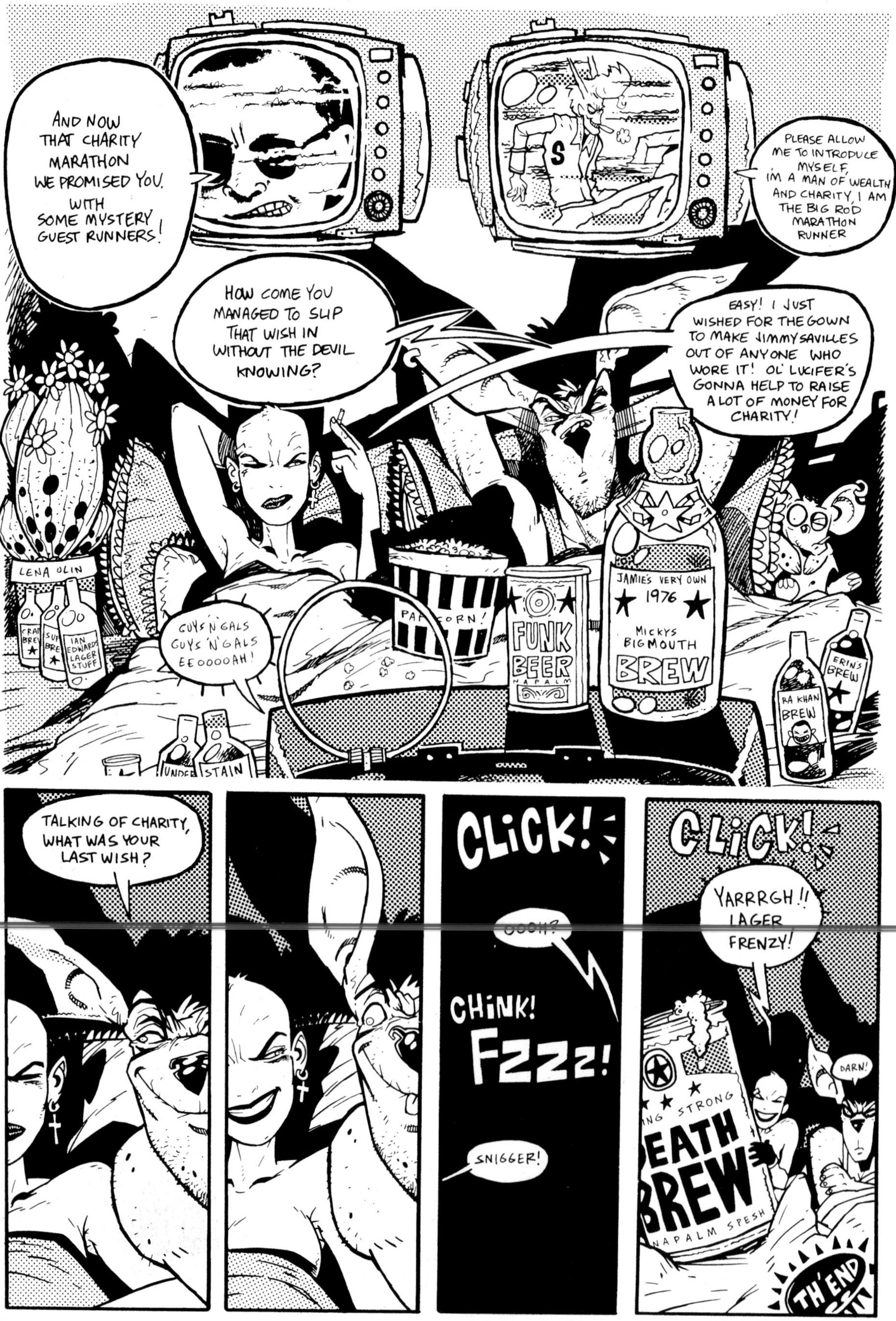
AND NOW THAT CHARITY MARATHON WE PROMISED YOU. WITH SOME MYSTERY GUEST RUNNERS!
S
PLEASE ALLOW ME TO INTRODUCE MYSELF, I'M A MAN OF WEALTH AND CHARITY, I AM THE BIG ROD MARATHON RUNNER
HOW COME YOU MANAGED TO SLIP THAT WISH IN WITHOUT THE DEVIL KNOWING?
EASY! I JUST WISHED FOR THE GOWN TO MAKE JIMMY SAVILLES OUT OF ANYONE WHO WORE IT! OL' LUCIFER'S GONNA HELP TO RAISE A LOT OF MONEY FOR CHARITY!
LENA OLIN
IAN EDWARDS LAGER STUFF
GUYS 'N' GALS GUYS 'N' GALS EEOOOOAH!
POPCORN!
FUNK BEER NAPALM
JAMIE'S VERY OWN 1976 MICKYS BIGMOUTH BREW
RA KHAN BREW
ERIN'S BREW
STAIN
TALKING OF CHARITY, WHAT WAS YOUR LAST WISH?
CLICK!
OOOH?
CHINK!
FZZZ!
SNIGGER!
CLICK!
YARRRGH!! LAGER FRENZY!
DARN!
NAPALM SPESH
TH' END

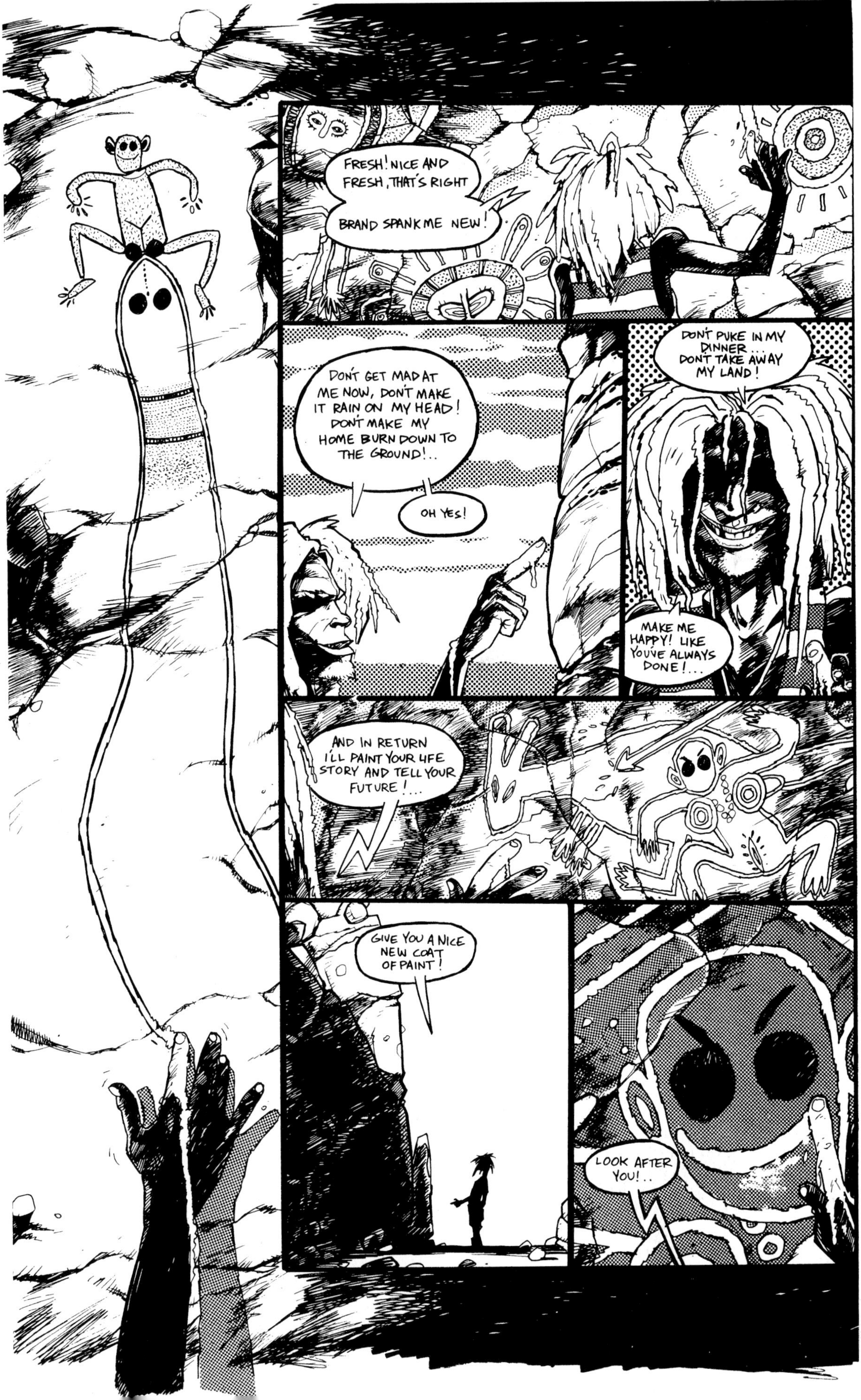
FRESH! NICE AND FRESH, THAT'S RIGHT
BRAND SPANK ME NEW!
DON'T GET MAD AT ME NOW, DON'T MAKE IT RAIN ON MY HEAD! DON'T MAKE MY HOME BURN DOWN TO THE GROUND!..
OH YES!
DON'T PUKE IN MY DINNER... DON'T TAKE AWAY MY LAND!
MAKE ME HAPPY! LIKE YOU'VE ALWAYS DONE!...
AND IN RETURN I'LL PAINT YOUR LIFE STORY AND TELL YOUR FUTURE!...
GIVE YOU A NICE NEW COAT OF PAINT!
LOOK AFTER YOU!..

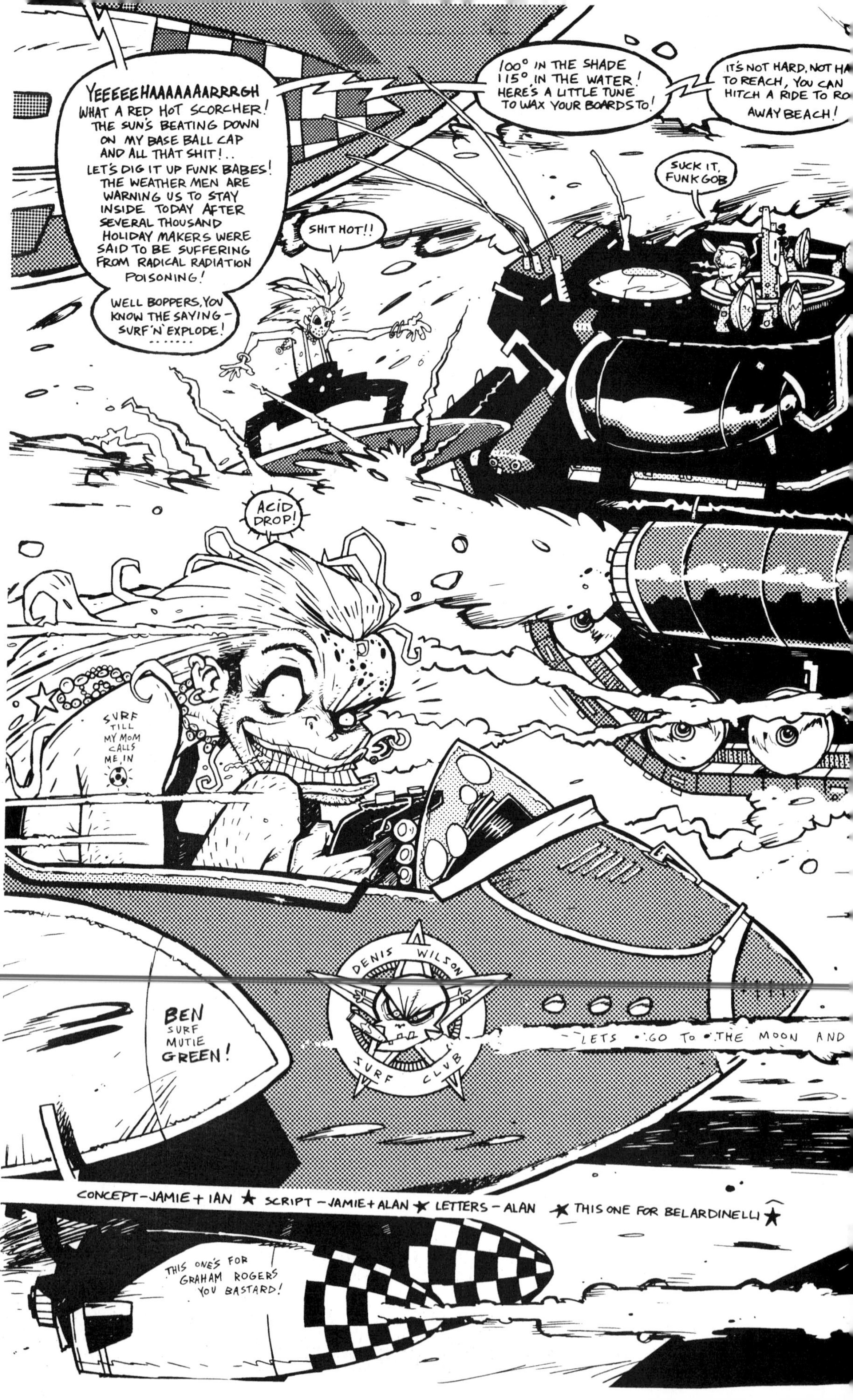

YEEEEEHAAAAAAARRRGH WHAT A RED HOT SCORCHER! THE SUN'S BEATING DOWN ON MY BASE BALL CAP AND ALL THAT SHIT!.. LET'S DIG IT UP FUNK BABES! THE WEATHER MEN ARE WARNING US TO STAY INSIDE TODAY AFTER SEVERAL THOUSAND HOLIDAY MAKERS WERE SAID TO BE SUFFERING FROM RADICAL RADIATION POISONING!
WELL BOPPERS, YOU KNOW THE SAYING - SURF 'N' EXPLODE! ......
100° IN THE SHADE 115° IN THE WATER! HERE'S A LITTLE TUNE TO WAX YOUR BOARDS TO!
IT'S NOT HARD, NOT HA TO REACH, YOU CAN HITCH A RIDE TO RO AWAY BEACH!
SUCK IT, FUNK GOB
SHIT HOT!!
ACID DROP!
SURF TILL MY MOM CALLS ME IN
DENIS WILSON SURF CLUB
BEN SURF MUTIE GREEN!
LETS GO TO THE MOON AND
CONCEPT - JAMIE + IAN ★ SCRIPT - JAMIE + ALAN ★ LETTERS - ALAN ★ THIS ONE FOR BELARDINELLI ★
THIS ONE'S FOR GRAHAM ROGERS YOU BASTARD!

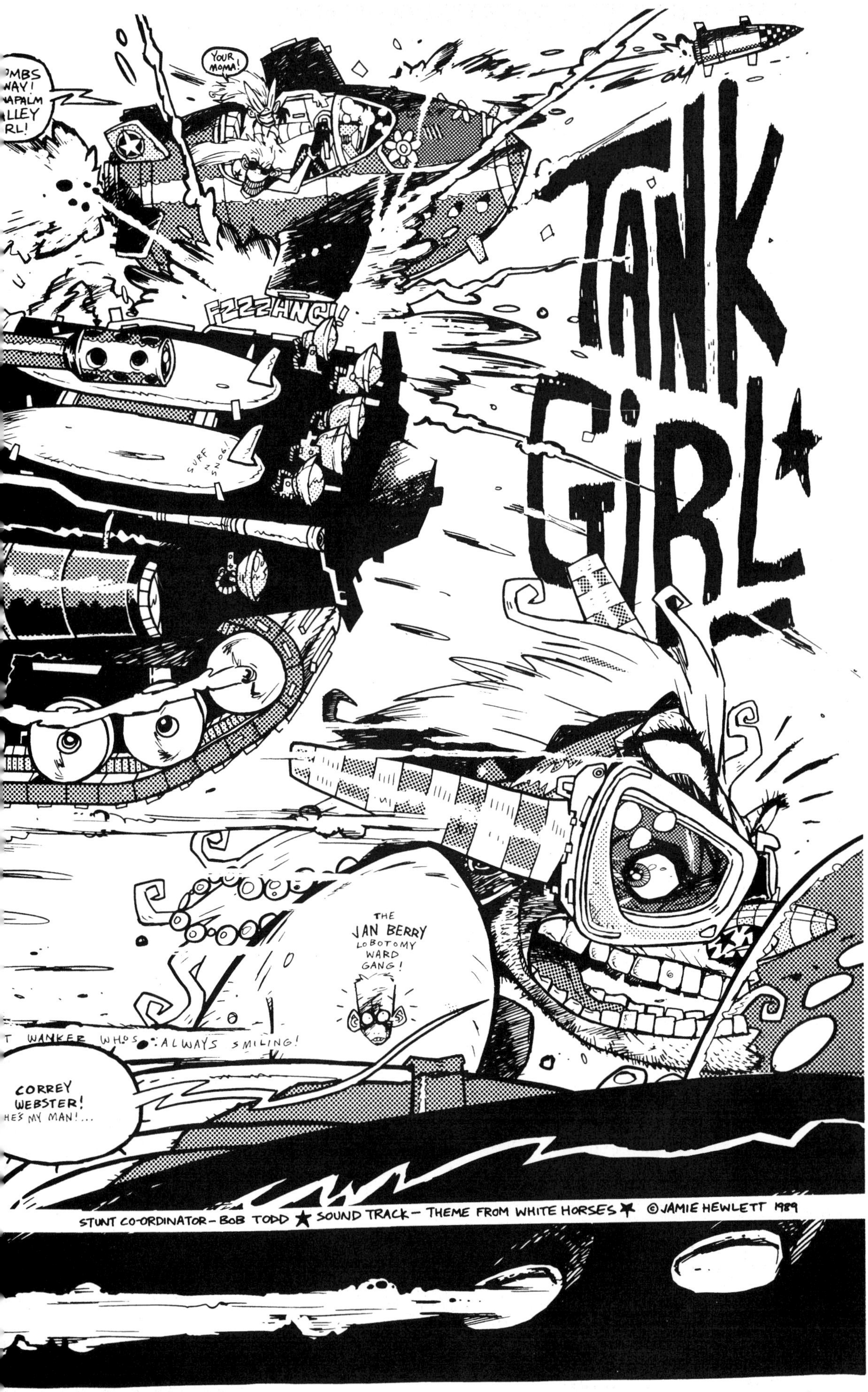

OMBS WAY! NAPALM LLEY RL!
YOUR MOMA!
TANK GIRL
FZZZANG!!
THE JAN BERRY LOBOTOMY WARD GANG!
T WANKER WHO'S ALWAYS SMILING!
CORREY WEBSTER! HE'S MY MAN!...
STUNT CO-ORDINATOR – BOB TODD ★ SOUND TRACK – THEME FROM WHITE HORSES ★ © JAMIE HEWLETT 1989

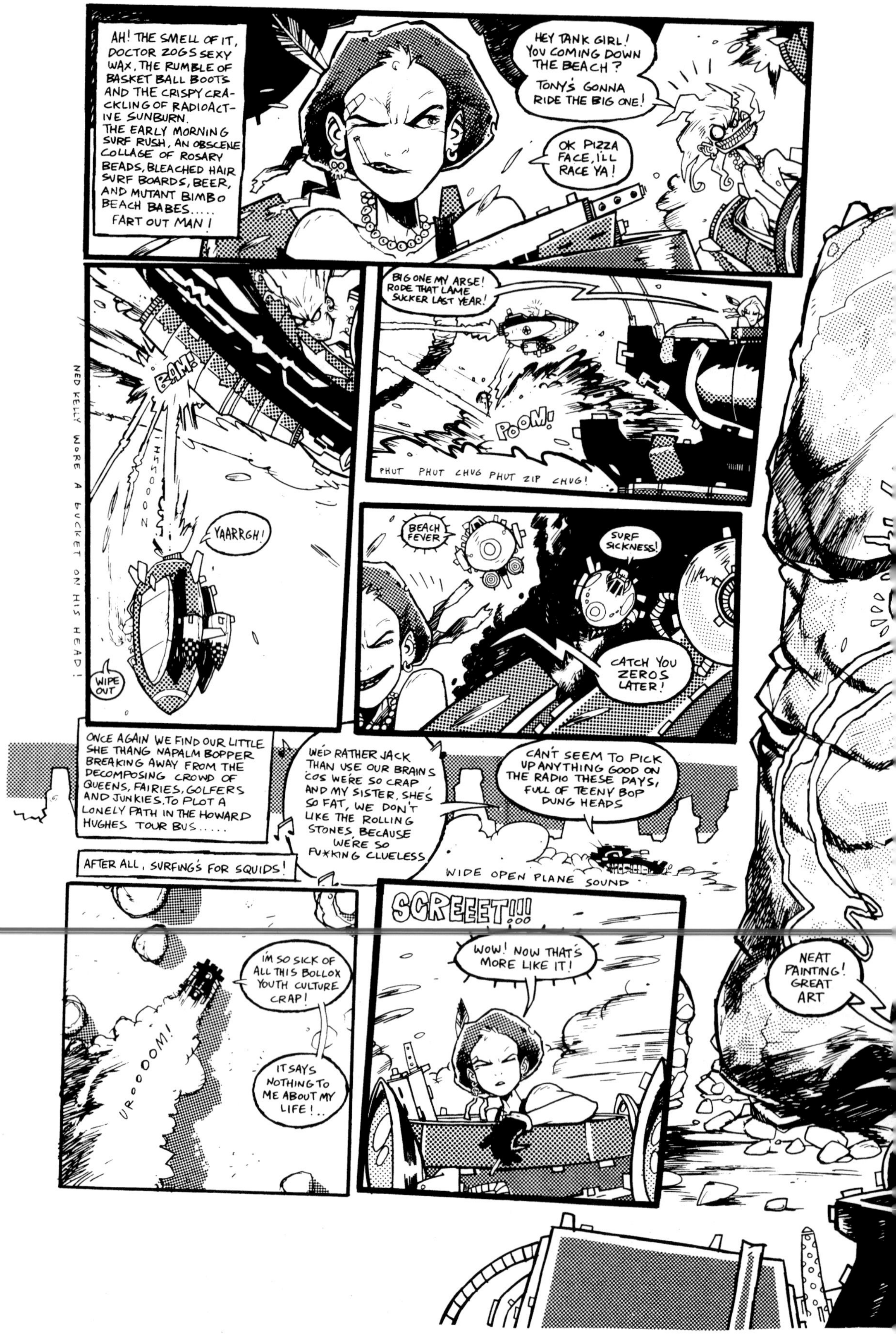

AH! THE SMELL OF IT, DOCTOR ZOGS SEXY WAX, THE RUMBLE OF BASKET BALL BOOTS AND THE CRISPY CRACKLING OF RADIOACTIVE SUNBURN. THE EARLY MORNING SURF RUSH, AN OBSCENE COLLAGE OF ROSARY BEADS, BLEACHED HAIR SURF BOARDS, BEER, AND MUTANT BIMBO BEACH BABES..... FART OUT MAN!
HEY TANK GIRL! YOU COMING DOWN THE BEACH?
TONY'S GONNA RIDE THE BIG ONE!
OK PIZZA FACE, I'LL RACE YA!
BAM!
YAARRGH!
WIPE OUT
NED KELLY WORE A BUCKET ON HIS HEAD!
BIG ONE MY ARSE! RODE THAT LAME SUCKER LAST YEAR!
POOM!
PHUT PHUT CHUG PHUT ZIP CHUG!
BEACH FEVER
SURF SICKNESS!
CATCH YOU ZEROS LATER!
ONCE AGAIN WE FIND OUR LITTLE SHE THANG NAPALM BOPPER BREAKING AWAY FROM THE DECOMPOSING CROWD OF QUEENS, FAIRIES, GOLFERS AND JUNKIES, TO PLOT A LONELY PATH IN THE HOWARD HUGHES TOUR BUS.....
AFTER ALL, SURFING'S FOR SQUIDS!
WE'D RATHER JACK THAN USE OUR BRAINS 'COS WE'RE SO CRAP AND MY SISTER, SHE'S SO FAT, WE DON'T LIKE THE ROLLING STONES BECAUSE WE'RE SO FU*KING CLUELESS
CAN'T SEEM TO PICK UP ANYTHING GOOD ON THE RADIO THESE DAYS, FULL OF TEENY BOP DUNG HEADS
WIDE OPEN PLANE SOUND
UROOOOOM!
I'M SO SICK OF ALL THIS BOLLOX YOUTH CULTURE CRAP!
IT SAYS NOTHING TO ME ABOUT MY LIFE!..
SCREEET!!!
WOW! NOW THAT'S MORE LIKE IT!
NEAT PAINTING! GREAT ART

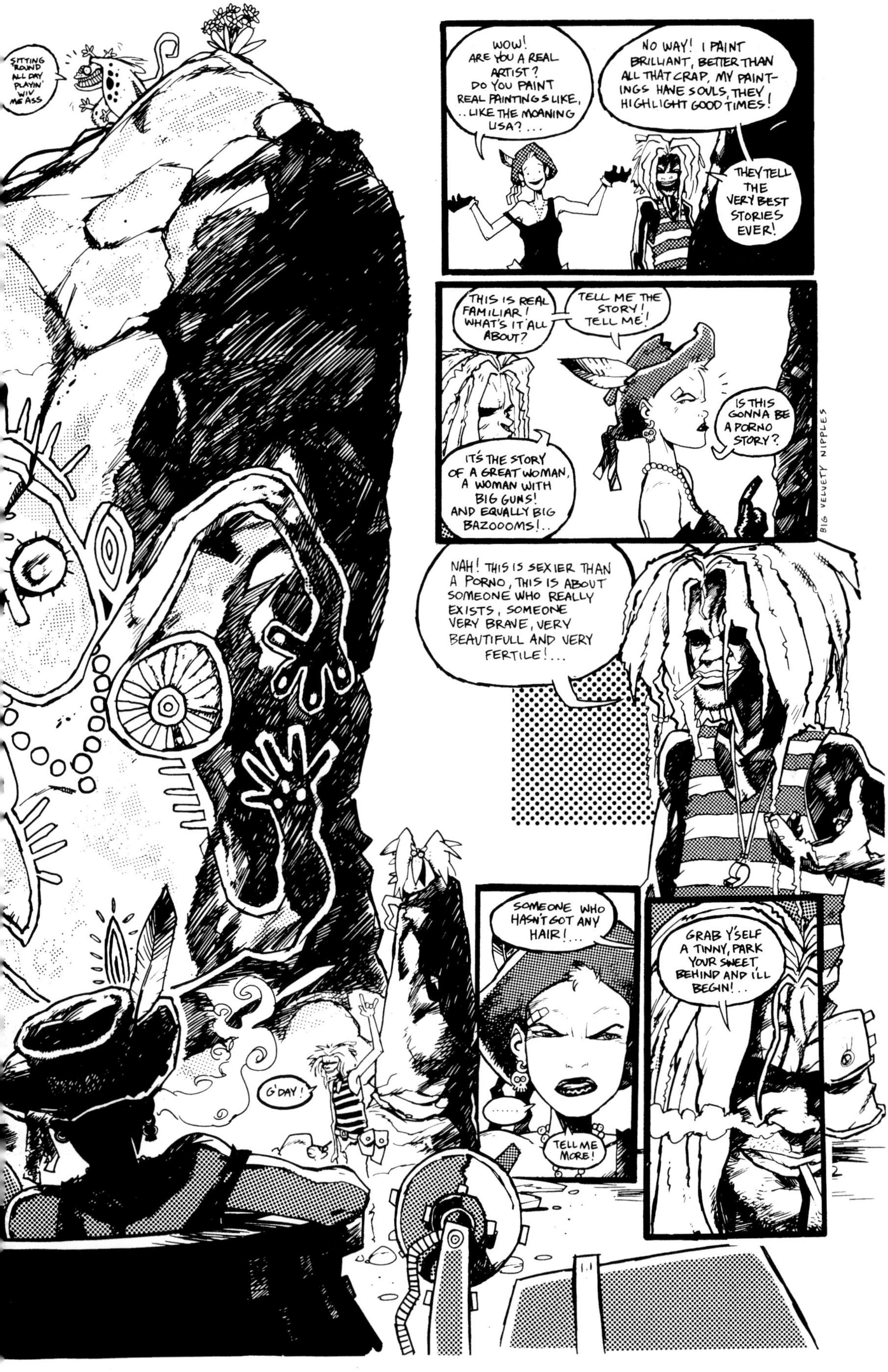
SITTING ROUND ALL DAY PLAYIN' WIV ME ASS
WOW! ARE YOU A REAL ARTIST? DO YOU PAINT REAL PAINTINGS LIKE, .. LIKE THE MOANING LISA? ...
NO WAY! I PAINT BRILLIANT, BETTER THAN ALL THAT CRAP, MY PAINTINGS HAVE SOULS, THEY HIGHLIGHT GOOD TIMES!
THEY TELL THE VERY BEST STORIES EVER!
THIS IS REAL FAMILIAR! WHAT'S IT ALL ABOUT?
TELL ME THE STORY! TELL ME!
IS THIS GONNA BE A PORNO STORY?
IT'S THE STORY OF A GREAT WOMAN, A WOMAN WITH BIG GUNS! AND EQUALLY BIG BAZOOOMS!..
BIG VELVETY NIPPLES
NAH! THIS IS SEXIER THAN A PORNO, THIS IS ABOUT SOMEONE WHO REALLY EXISTS, SOMEONE VERY BRAVE, VERY BEAUTIFULL AND VERY FERTILE!...
SOMEONE WHO HASN'T GOT ANY HAIR!...
......
TELL ME MORE!
GRAB Y'SELF A TINNY, PARK YOUR SWEET BEHIND AND I'LL BEGIN!..
G'DAY!

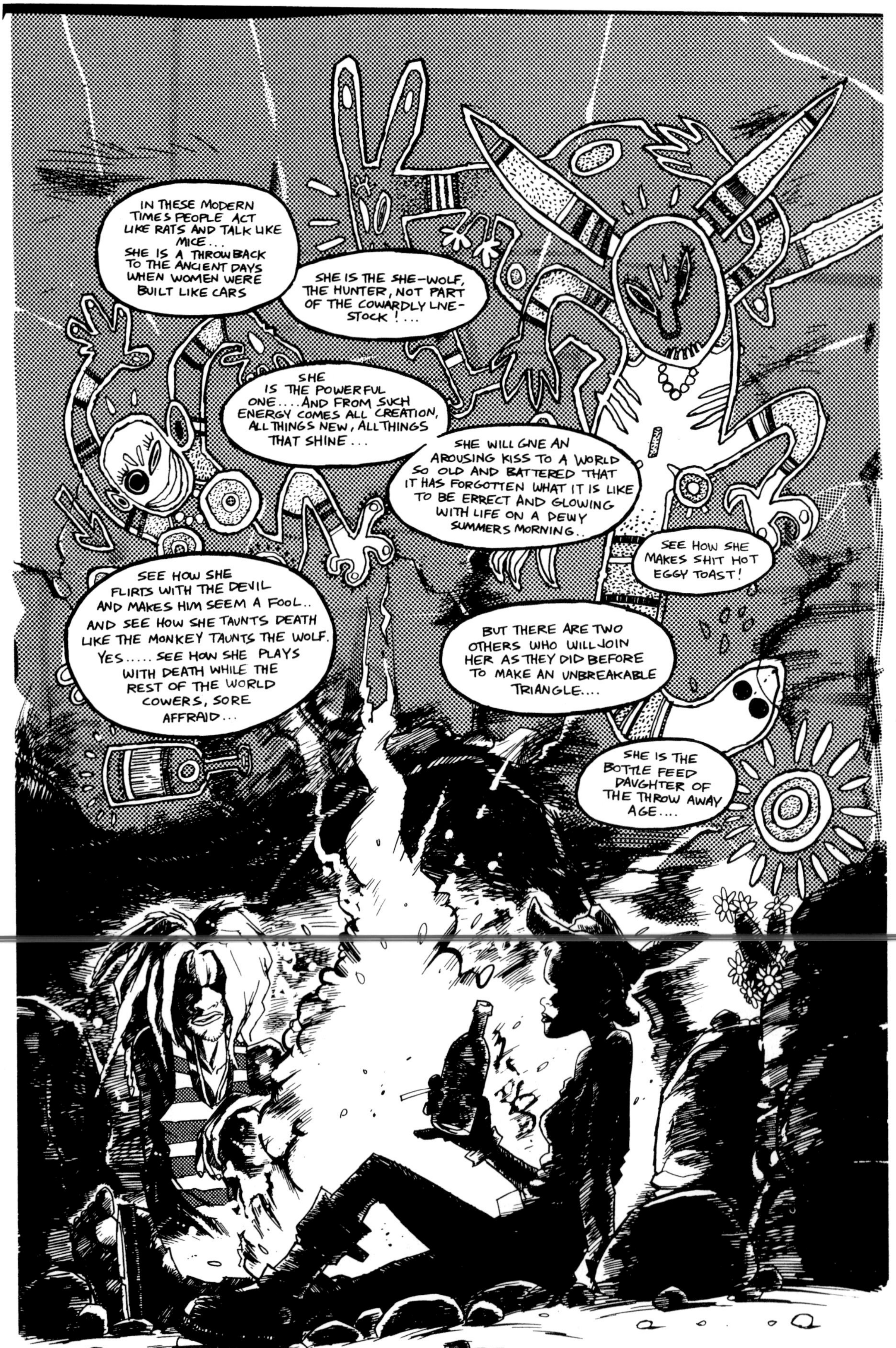
IN THESE MODERN TIMES PEOPLE ACT LIKE RATS AND TALK LIKE MICE... SHE IS A THROWBACK TO THE ANCIENT DAYS WHEN WOMEN WERE BUILT LIKE CARS
SHE IS THE SHE-WOLF, THE HUNTER, NOT PART OF THE COWARDLY LIVE-STOCK!...
SHE IS THE POWERFUL ONE....AND FROM SUCH ENERGY COMES ALL CREATION, ALL THINGS NEW, ALL THINGS THAT SHINE...
SHE WILL GIVE AN AROUSING KISS TO A WORLD SO OLD AND BATTERED THAT IT HAS FORGOTTEN WHAT IT IS LIKE TO BE ERRECT AND GLOWING WITH LIFE ON A DEWY SUMMERS MORNING..
SEE HOW SHE MAKES SHIT HOT EGGY TOAST!
SEE HOW SHE FLIRTS WITH THE DEVIL AND MAKES HIM SEEM A FOOL.. AND SEE HOW SHE TAUNTS DEATH LIKE THE MONKEY TAUNTS THE WOLF. YES..... SEE HOW SHE PLAYS WITH DEATH WHILE THE REST OF THE WORLD COWERS, SORE AFFRAID...
BUT THERE ARE TWO OTHERS WHO WILL JOIN HER AS THEY DID BEFORE TO MAKE AN UNBREAKABLE TRIANGLE....
SHE IS THE BOTTLE FEED DAUGHTER OF THE THROW AWAY AGE....

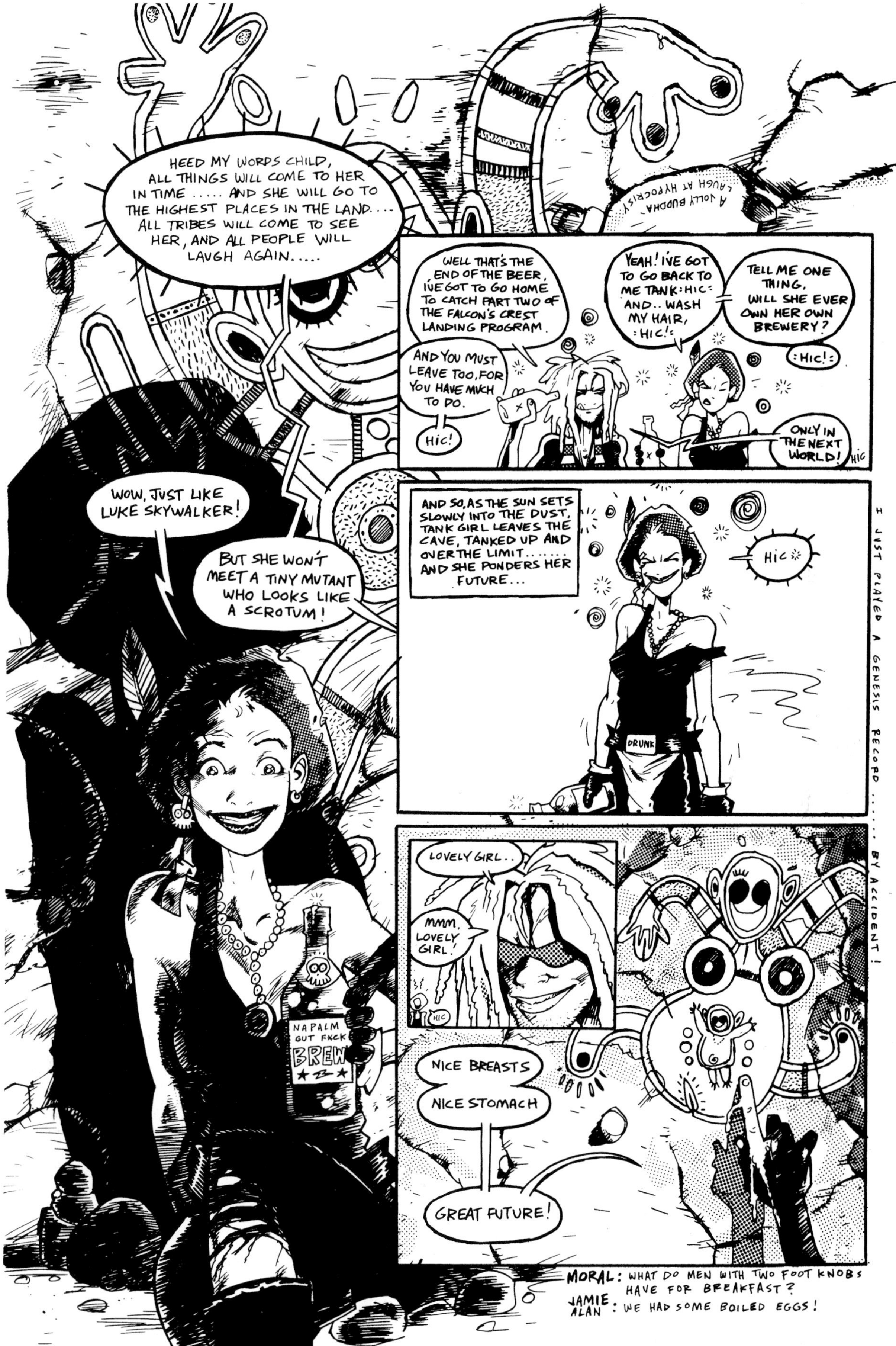
HEED MY WORDS CHILD, ALL THINGS WILL COME TO HER IN TIME ..... AND SHE WILL GO TO THE HIGHEST PLACES IN THE LAND.... ALL TRIBES WILL COME TO SEE HER, AND ALL PEOPLE WILL LAUGH AGAIN.....
A JOLLY BUDDHA LAUGH AT HYPOCRISY
WELL THAT'S THE END OF THE BEER, I'VE GOT TO GO HOME TO CATCH PART TWO OF THE FALCON'S CREST LANDING PROGRAM.
YEAH! I'VE GOT TO GO BACK TO ME TANK :HIC: AND.. WASH MY HAIR, :HIC!:
TELL ME ONE THING, WILL SHE EVER OWN HER OWN BREWERY?
:HIC!:
AND YOU MUST LEAVE TOO, FOR YOU HAVE MUCH TO DO.
HIC!
ONLY IN THE NEXT WORLD!
HIC
WOW, JUST LIKE LUKE SKYWALKER!
BUT SHE WON'T MEET A TINY MUTANT WHO LOOKS LIKE A SCROTUM!
AND SO, AS THE SUN SETS SLOWLY INTO THE DUST, TANK GIRL LEAVES THE CAVE, TANKED UP AND OVER THE LIMIT...... AND SHE PONDERS HER FUTURE...
HIC
DRUNK
NAPALM GUT FXCK BREW
LOVELY GIRL..
MMM. LOVELY GIRL.
HIC
NICE BREASTS
NICE STOMACH
GREAT FUTURE!
I JUST PLAYED A GENESIS RECORD ...... BY ACCIDENT!
MORAL: WHAT DO MEN WITH TWO FOOT KNOBS HAVE FOR BREAKFAST?
JAMIE ALAN: WE HAD SOME BOILED EGGS!

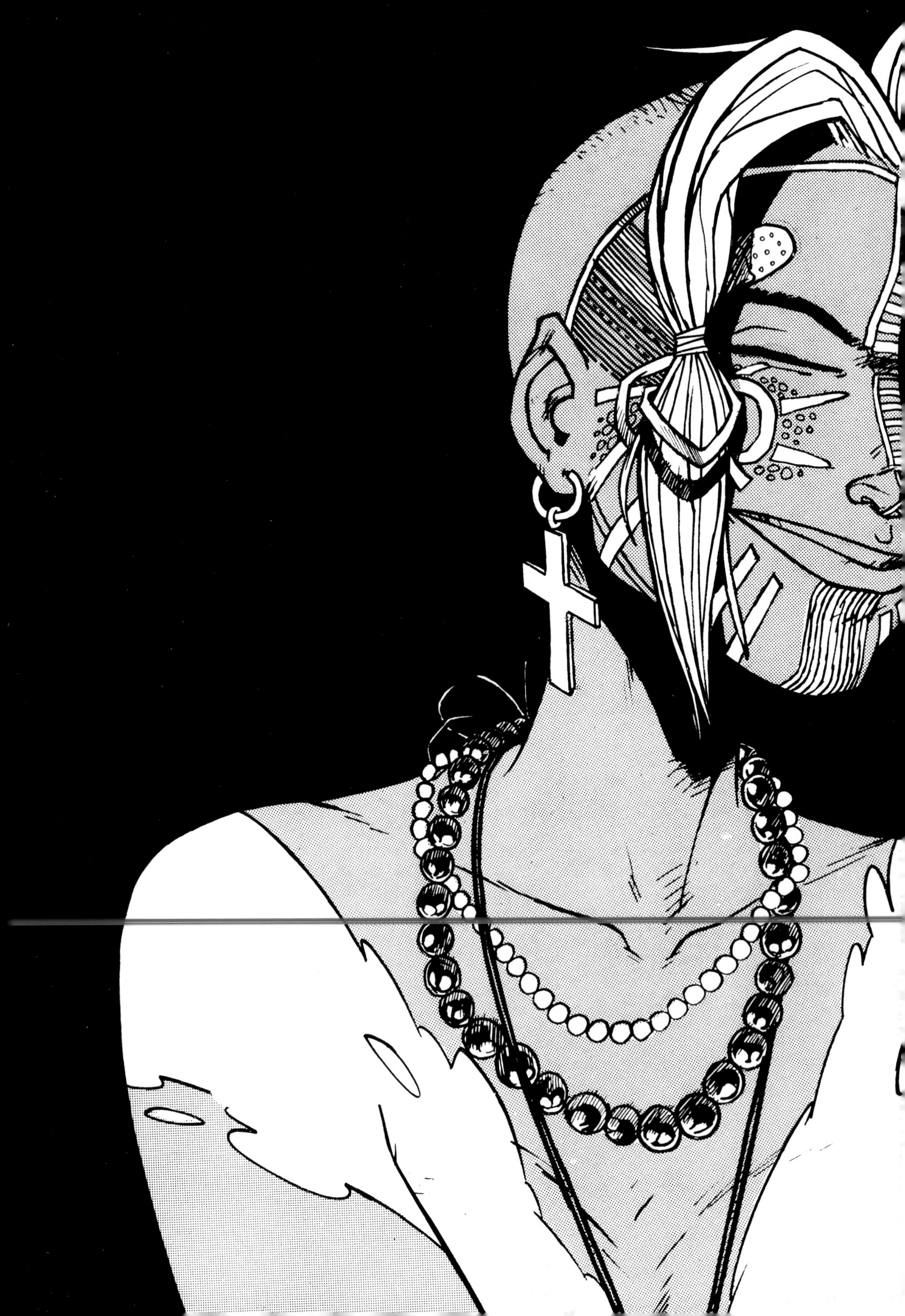

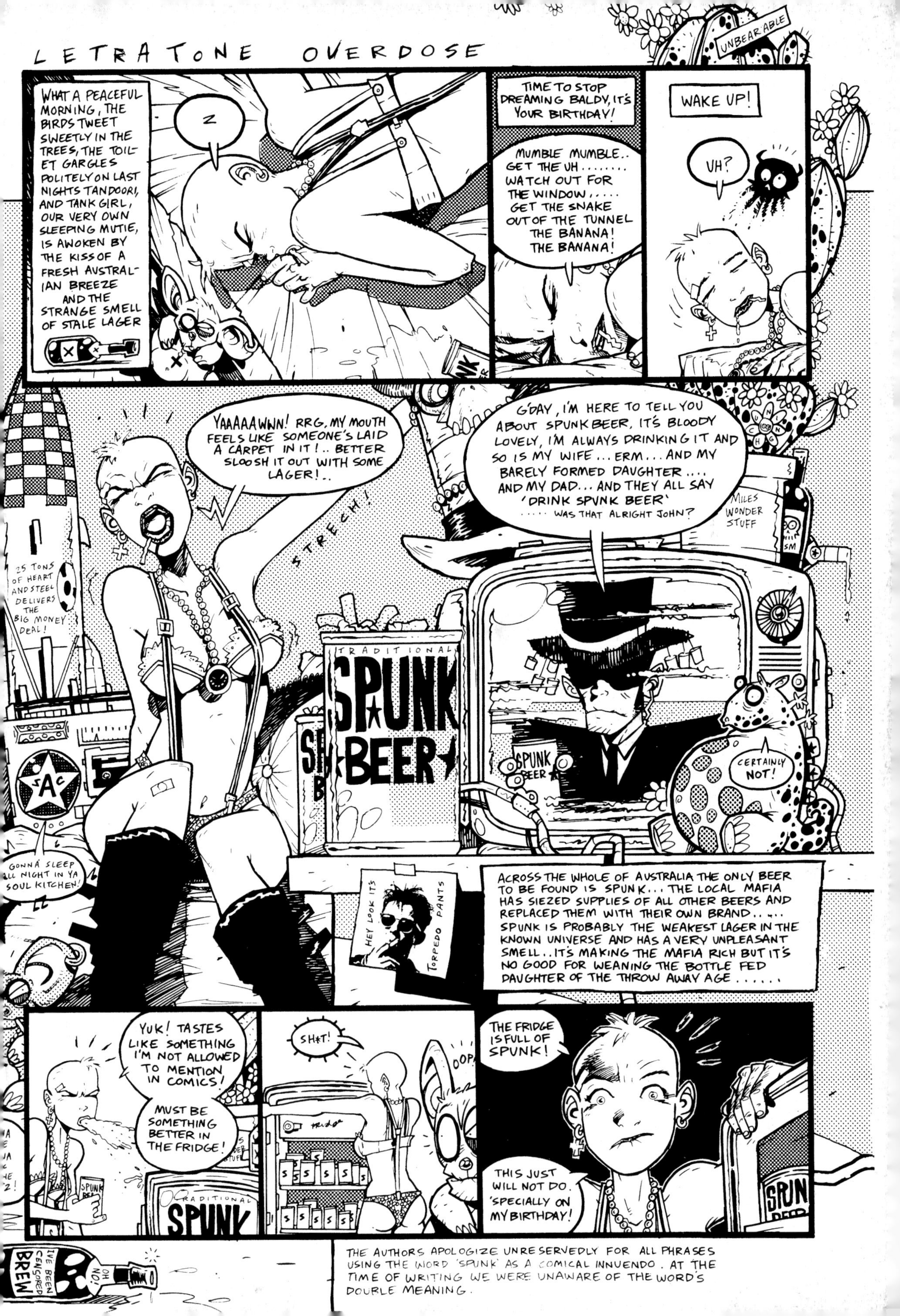

LETRATONE OVERDOSE
UNBEARABLE
WHAT A PEACEFUL MORNING, THE BIRDS TWEET SWEETLY IN THE TREES, THE TOILET GARGLES POLITELY ON LAST NIGHTS TANDOORI, AND TANK GIRL, OUR VERY OWN SLEEPING MUTIE, IS AWOKEN BY THE KISS OF A FRESH AUSTRALIAN BREEZE AND THE STRANGE SMELL OF STALE LAGER
Z
TIME TO STOP DREAMING BALDY, IT'S YOUR BIRTHDAY!
MUMBLE MUMBLE.. GET THE UH .... WATCH OUT FOR THE WINDOW .... GET THE SNAKE OUT OF THE TUNNEL THE BANANA! THE BANANA!
WAKE UP!
UH?
YAAAAAWWN! RRG, MY MOUTH FEELS LIKE SOMEONE'S LAID A CARPET IN IT!.. BETTER SLOOSH IT OUT WITH SOME LAGER!..
STRECH!
G'DAY, I'M HERE TO TELL YOU ABOUT SPUNK BEER, IT'S BLOODY LOVELY, I'M ALWAYS DRINKING IT AND SO IS MY WIFE ... ERM ... AND MY BARELY FORMED DAUGHTER .... AND MY DAD ... AND THEY ALL SAY 'DRINK SPUNK BEER' ..... WAS THAT ALRIGHT JOHN?
CERTAINLY NOT!
MILES WONDER STUFF
25 TONS OF HEART AND STEEL DELIVERS THE BIG MONEY DEAL!
TRADITIONAL SPUNK BEER
SPUNK BEER
GONNA SLEEP ALL NIGHT IN YA SOUL KITCHEN!
HEY LOOK ITS TORPEDO PANTS
ACROSS THE WHOLE OF AUSTRALIA THE ONLY BEER TO BE FOUND IS SPUNK... THE LOCAL MAFIA HAS SIEZED SUPPLIES OF ALL OTHER BEERS AND REPLACED THEM WITH THEIR OWN BRAND...... SPUNK IS PROBABLY THE WEAKEST LAGER IN THE KNOWN UNIVERSE AND HAS A VERY UNPLEASANT SMELL..IT'S MAKING THE MAFIA RICH BUT IT'S NO GOOD FOR WEANING THE BOTTLE FED DAUGHTER OF THE THROW AWAY AGE ......
YUK! TASTES LIKE SOMETHING I'M NOT ALLOWED TO MENTION IN COMICS!
MUST BE SOMETHING BETTER IN THE FRIDGE!
TRADITIONAL SPUNK
SH*T!
OOPS
THE FRIDGE IS FULL OF SPUNK!
THIS JUST WILL NOT DO. 'SPECIALLY ON MY BIRTHDAY!
I'VE BEEN CENSORED BREW
OH NO!
THE AUTHORS APOLOGIZE UNRESERVEDLY FOR ALL PHRASES USING THE WORD 'SPUNK' AS A COMICAL INNUENDO. AT THE TIME OF WRITING WE WERE UNAWARE OF THE WORD'S DOUBLE MEANING.

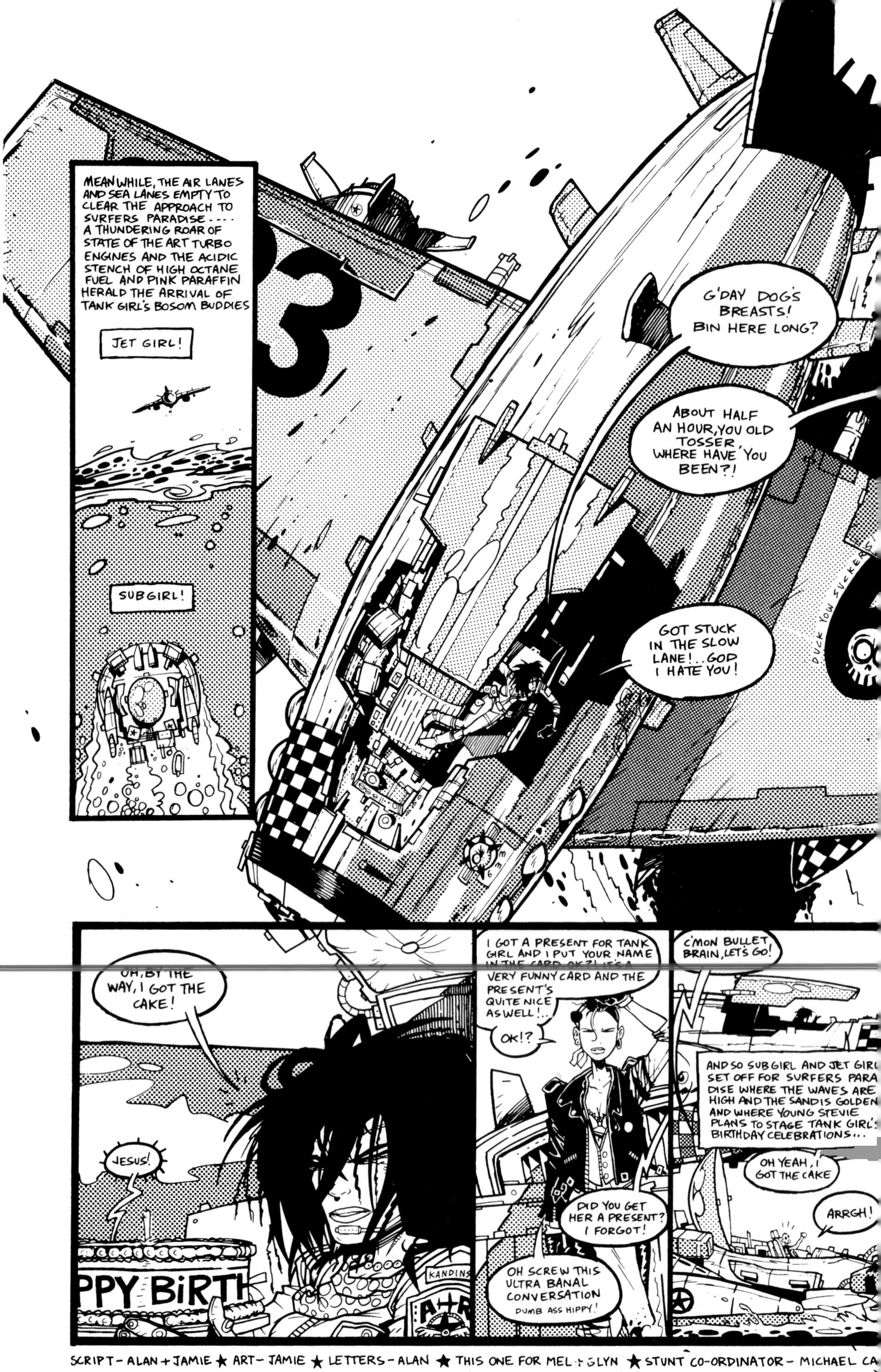
MEANWHILE, THE AIR LANES AND SEA LANES EMPTY TO CLEAR THE APPROACH TO SURFERS PARADISE.... A THUNDERING ROAR OF STATE OF THE ART TURBO ENGINES AND THE ACIDIC STENCH OF HIGH OCTANE FUEL AND PINK PARAFFIN HERALD THE ARRIVAL OF TANK GIRL'S BOSOM BUDDIES
JET GIRL!
SUBGIRL!
G'DAY DOG'S BREASTS! BIN HERE LONG?
ABOUT HALF AN HOUR, YOU OLD TOSSER, WHERE HAVE YOU BEEN?!
GOT STUCK IN THE SLOW LANE!.. GOD I HATE YOU!
DUCK YOU SUCKERS
OH, BY THE WAY, I GOT THE CAKE!
JESUS!
PPY BiRTH
KANDINS
I GOT A PRESENT FOR TANK GIRL AND I PUT YOUR NAME
VERY FUNNY CARD AND THE PRESENT'S QUITE NICE AS WELL!..
OK!?
DID YOU GET HER A PRESENT? I FORGOT!
OH SCREW THIS ULTRA BANAL CONVERSATION DUMB ASS HIPPY!
C'MON BULLET BRAIN, LET'S GO!
AND SO SUBGIRL AND JET GIRL SET OFF FOR SURFERS PARADISE WHERE THE WAVES ARE HIGH AND THE SAND IS GOLDEN AND WHERE YOUNG STEVIE PLANS TO STAGE TANK GIRL'S BIRTHDAY CELEBRATIONS...
OH YEAH, I GOT THE CAKE
ARRGH!

SCRIPT – ALAN + JAMIE ★ ART – JAMIE ★ LETTERS – ALAN ★ THIS ONE FOR MEL + GLYN ★ STUNT CO-ORDINATOR – MICHAEL CA

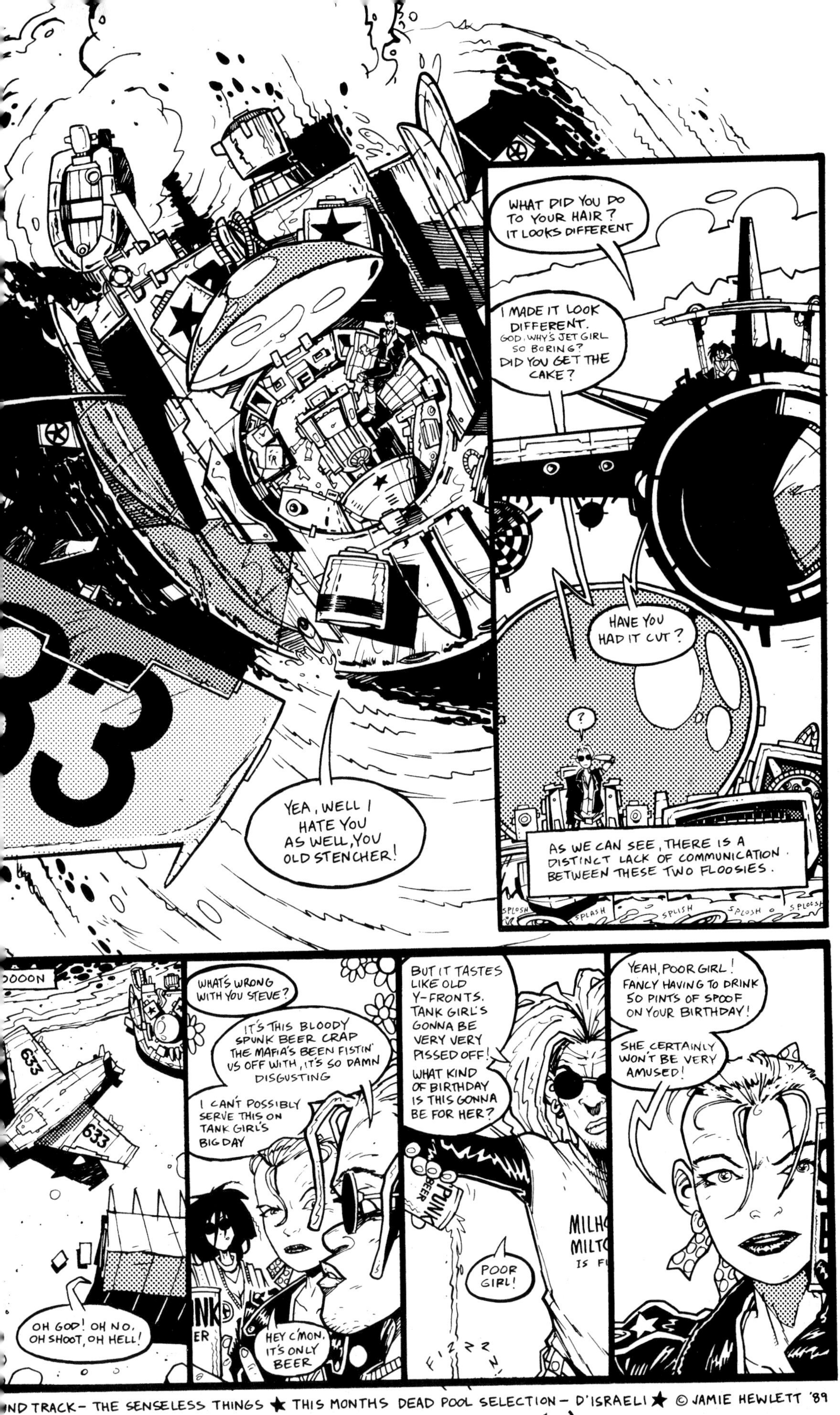

WHAT DID YOU DO TO YOUR HAIR? IT LOOKS DIFFERENT
I MADE IT LOOK DIFFERENT. GOD, WHY'S JET GIRL SO BORING? DID YOU GET THE CAKE?
HAVE YOU HAD IT CUT?
?
YEA, WELL I HATE YOU AS WELL, YOU OLD STENCHER!
AS WE CAN SEE, THERE IS A DISTINCT LACK OF COMMUNICATION BETWEEN THESE TWO FLOOSIES.
SPLOSH
SPLASH
SPLISH
SPLOSH
SPLOOSH
DOOON
633
633
OH GOD! OH NO, OH SHOOT, OH HELL!
WHAT'S WRONG WITH YOU STEVE?
IT'S THIS BLOODY SPUNK BEER CRAP THE MAFIA'S BEEN FISTIN' US OFF WITH, IT'S SO DAMN DISGUSTING
I CAN'T POSSIBLY SERVE THIS ON TANK GIRL'S BIG DAY
HEY C'MON, IT'S ONLY BEER
BUT IT TASTES LIKE OLD Y-FRONTS. TANK GIRL'S GONNA BE VERY VERY PISSED OFF!
WHAT KIND OF BIRTHDAY IS THIS GONNA BE FOR HER?
POOR GIRL!
FIZZZZ
YEAH, POOR GIRL! FANCY HAVING TO DRINK 50 PINTS OF SPOOF ON YOUR BIRTHDAY!
SHE CERTAINLY WON'T BE VERY AMUSED!

ND TRACK – THE SENSELESS THINGS ★ THIS MONTHS DEAD POOL SELECTION – D'ISRAELI ★ © JAMIE HEWLETT '89

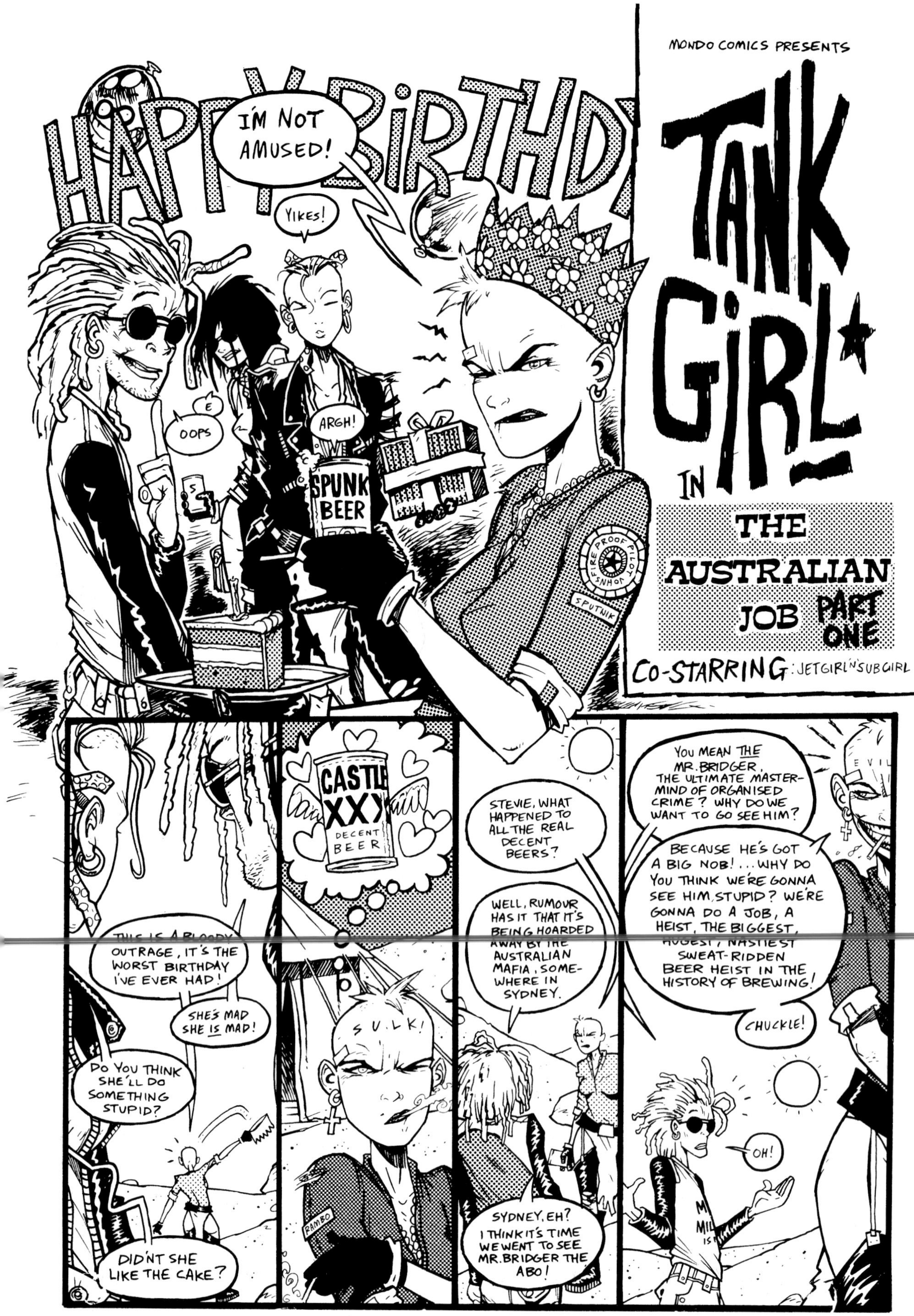
MONDO COMICS PRESENTS
TANK GIRL
IN
THE AUSTRALIAN JOB PART ONE
CO-STARRING: JETGIRL 'N' SUBGIRL
HAPPY BIRTHDAY
I'M NOT AMUSED!
YIKES!
OOPS
ARGH!
SPUNK BEER
FIRE PROOF PILOT SHOVS
SPUTNIK
THIS IS A BLOODY OUTRAGE, IT'S THE WORST BIRTHDAY I'VE EVER HAD!
SHE'S MAD SHE IS MAD!
DO YOU THINK SHE'LL DO SOMETHING STUPID?
DIDN'T SHE LIKE THE CAKE?
CASTLE XXX DECENT BEER
SULK!
RAMBO
STEVIE, WHAT HAPPENED TO ALL THE REAL DECENT BEERS?
WELL, RUMOUR HAS IT THAT IT'S BEING HOARDED AWAY BY THE AUSTRALIAN MAFIA, SOMEWHERE IN SYDNEY.
SYDNEY, EH? I THINK IT'S TIME WE WENT TO SEE MR. BRIDGER THE ABO!
YOU MEAN THE MR. BRIDGER, THE ULTIMATE MASTERMIND OF ORGANISED CRIME? WHY DO WE WANT TO GO SEE HIM?
BECAUSE HE'S GOT A BIG NOB! ... WHY DO YOU THINK WE'RE GONNA SEE HIM, STUPID? WE'RE GONNA DO A JOB, A HEIST, THE BIGGEST, HUGEST, NASTIEST SWEAT-RIDDEN BEER HEIST IN THE HISTORY OF BREWING!
CHUCKLE!
OH!

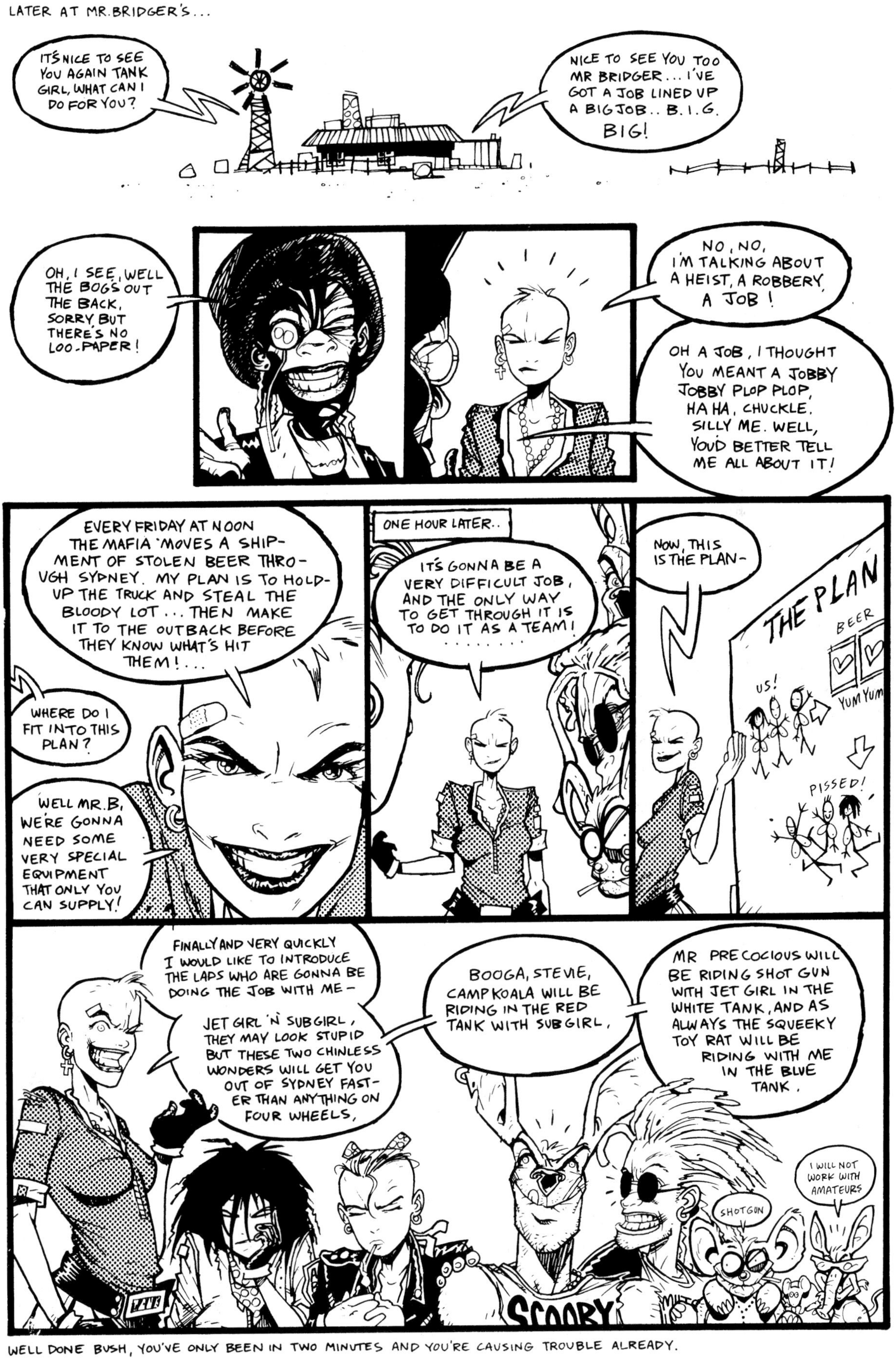
LATER AT MR.BRIDGER'S...
IT'S NICE TO SEE YOU AGAIN TANK GIRL, WHAT CAN I DO FOR YOU?
NICE TO SEE YOU TOO MR BRIDGER... I'VE GOT A JOB LINED UP A BIG JOB.. B. I. G. BIG!
OH, I SEE, WELL THE BOG'S OUT THE BACK, SORRY, BUT THERE'S NO LOO-PAPER!
NO, NO, I'M TALKING ABOUT A HEIST, A ROBBERY, A JOB!
OH A JOB, I THOUGHT YOU MEANT A JOBBY JOBBY PLOP PLOP, HA HA, CHUCKLE. SILLY ME. WELL, YOU'D BETTER TELL ME ALL ABOUT IT!
EVERY FRIDAY AT NOON THE MAFIA MOVES A SHIPMENT OF STOLEN BEER THROUGH SYDNEY. MY PLAN IS TO HOLD-UP THE TRUCK AND STEAL THE BLOODY LOT... THEN MAKE IT TO THE OUTBACK BEFORE THEY KNOW WHAT'S HIT THEM!...
WHERE DO I FIT INTO THIS PLAN?
WELL MR.B, WE'RE GONNA NEED SOME VERY SPECIAL EQUIPMENT THAT ONLY YOU CAN SUPPLY!
ONE HOUR LATER..
IT'S GONNA BE A VERY DIFFICULT JOB, AND THE ONLY WAY TO GET THROUGH IT IS TO DO IT AS A TEAM! ....
NOW, THIS IS THE PLAN-
THE PLAN
BEER
US!
YUM YUM
PISSED!
FINALLY AND VERY QUICKLY I WOULD LIKE TO INTRODUCE THE LADS WHO ARE GONNA BE DOING THE JOB WITH ME-
JET GIRL 'N' SUBGIRL, THEY MAY LOOK STUPID BUT THESE TWO CHINLESS WONDERS WILL GET YOU OUT OF SYDNEY FASTER THAN ANYTHING ON FOUR WHEELS,
BOOGA, STEVIE, CAMP KOALA WILL BE RIDING IN THE RED TANK WITH SUBGIRL,
MR PRECOCIOUS WILL BE RIDING SHOT GUN WITH JET GIRL IN THE WHITE TANK, AND AS ALWAYS THE SQUEEKY TOY RAT WILL BE RIDING WITH ME IN THE BLUE TANK.
SHOTGUN
I WILL NOT WORK WITH AMATEURS
SCOOBY
WELL DONE BUSH, YOU'VE ONLY BEEN IN TWO MINUTES AND YOU'RE CAUSING TROUBLE ALREADY.

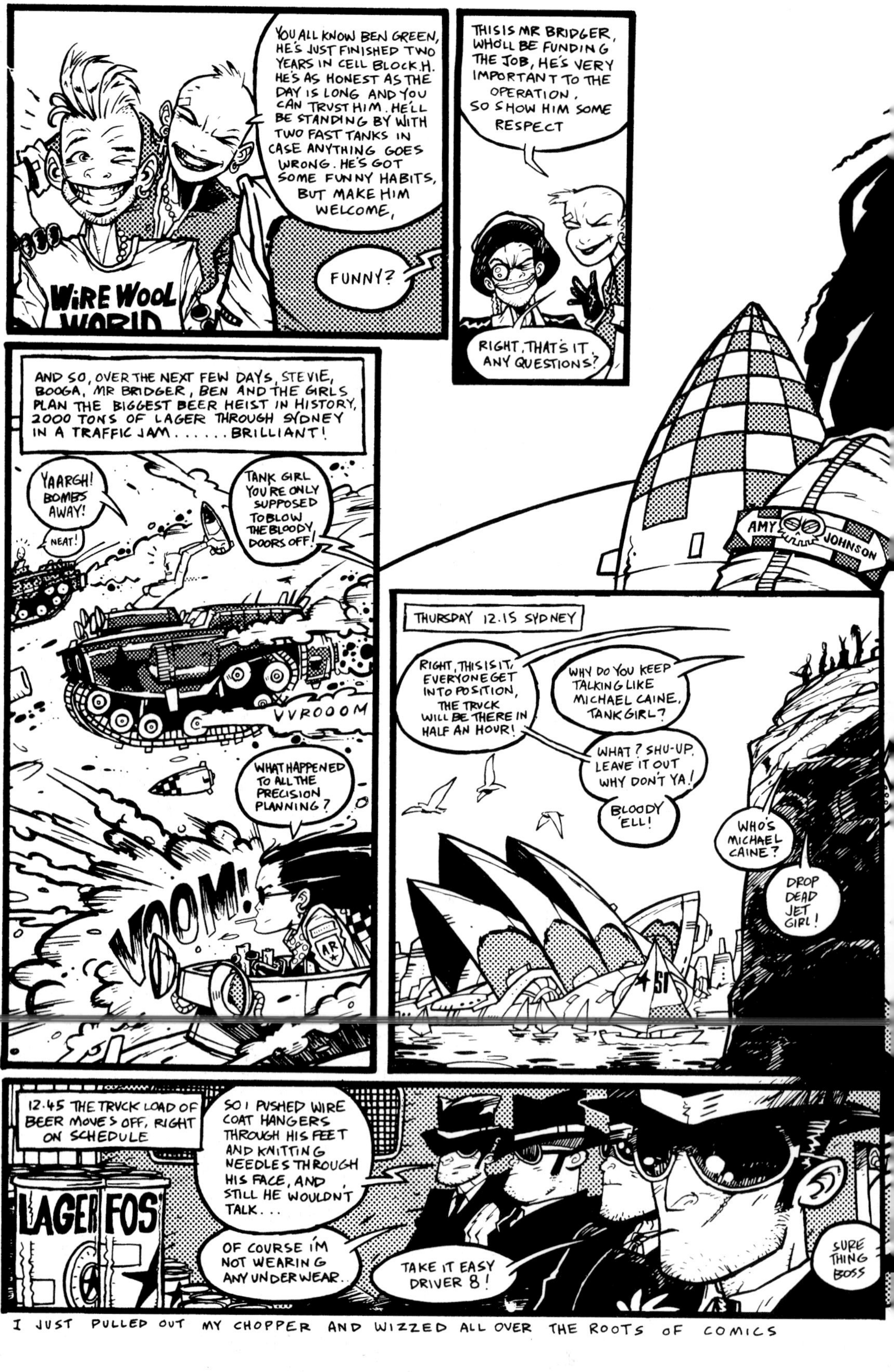
YOU ALL KNOW BEN GREEN, HE'S JUST FINISHED TWO YEARS IN CELL BLOCK H. HE'S AS HONEST AS THE DAY IS LONG AND YOU CAN TRUST HIM. HE'LL BE STANDING BY WITH TWO FAST TANKS IN CASE ANYTHING GOES WRONG. HE'S GOT SOME FUNNY HABITS, BUT MAKE HIM WELCOME,
FUNNY?
WIRE WOOL WORLD
THIS IS MR BRIDGER, WHO'LL BE FUNDING THE JOB, HE'S VERY IMPORTANT TO THE OPERATION, SO SHOW HIM SOME RESPECT
RIGHT, THAT'S IT, ANY QUESTIONS?
AND SO, OVER THE NEXT FEW DAYS, STEVIE, BOOGA, MR BRIDGER, BEN AND THE GIRLS PLAN THE BIGGEST BEER HEIST IN HISTORY, 2000 TONS OF LAGER THROUGH SYDNEY IN A TRAFFIC JAM......BRILLIANT!
YAARGH! BOMBS AWAY!
NEAT!
TANK GIRL YOU'RE ONLY SUPPOSED TO BLOW THE BLOODY DOORS OFF!
VVROOOM
WHAT HAPPENED TO ALL THE PRECISION PLANNING?
VOOM!
AMY JOHNSON
THURSDAY 12.15 SYDNEY
RIGHT, THIS IS IT, EVERYONE GET INTO POSITION, THE TRUCK WILL BE THERE IN HALF AN HOUR!
WHY DO YOU KEEP TALKING LIKE MICHAEL CAINE, TANK GIRL?
WHAT? SHU-UP, LEAVE IT OUT WHY DON'T YA!
BLOODY 'ELL!
WHO'S MICHAEL CAINE?
DROP DEAD JET GIRL!
12.45 THE TRUCK LOAD OF BEER MOVES OFF, RIGHT ON SCHEDULE
SO I PUSHED WIRE COAT HANGERS THROUGH HIS FEET AND KNITTING NEEDLES THROUGH HIS FACE, AND STILL HE WOULDN'T TALK...
OF COURSE I'M NOT WEARING ANY UNDERWEAR...
TAKE IT EASY DRIVER 8!
SURE THING BOSS
LAGER
FOS
I JUST PULLED OUT MY CHOPPER AND WIZZED ALL OVER THE ROOTS OF COMICS

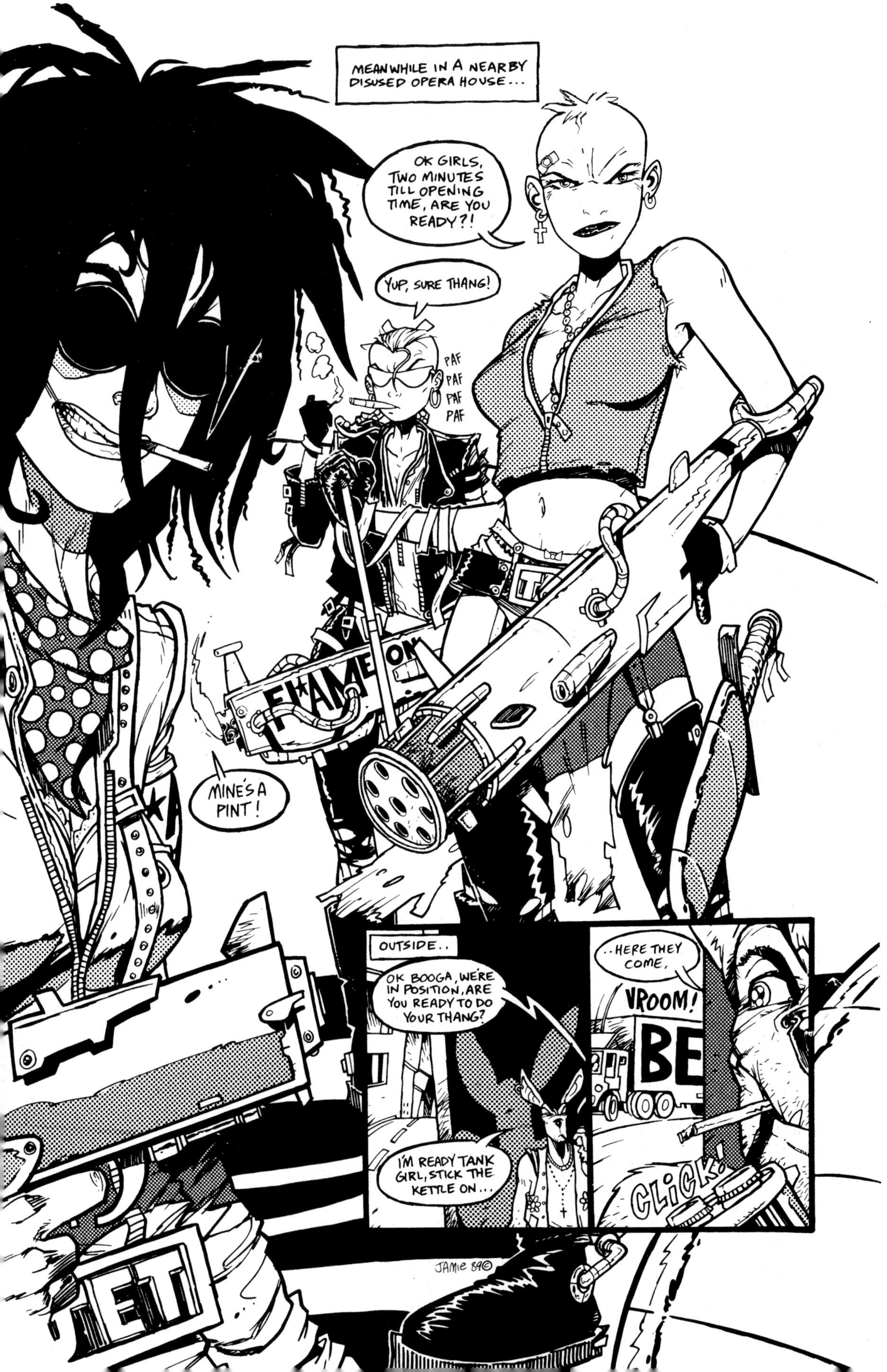
MEANWHILE IN A NEARBY DISUSED OPERA HOUSE...
OK GIRLS, TWO MINUTES TILL OPENING TIME, ARE YOU READY?!
YUP, SURE THANG!
PAF PAF PAF PAF
FLAME ON
MINE'S A PINT!
OUTSIDE..
OK BOOGA, WE'RE IN POSITION, ARE YOU READY TO DO YOUR THANG?
I'M READY TANK GIRL, STICK THE KETTLE ON...
..HERE THEY COME.
VROOM!
BE
CLICK!
JAMIE 89©

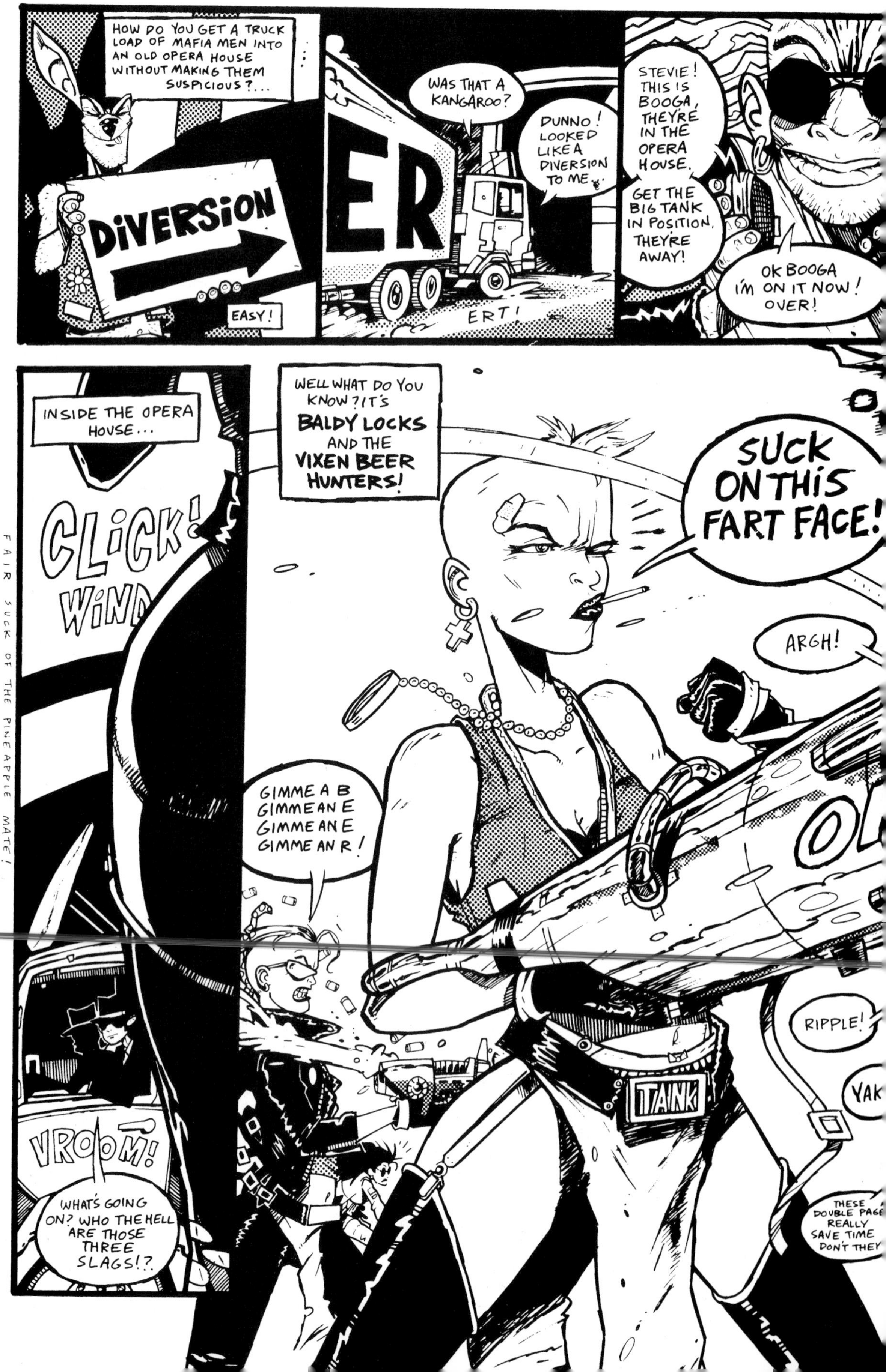

HOW DO YOU GET A TRUCK LOAD OF MAFIA MEN INTO AN OLD OPERA HOUSE WITHOUT MAKING THEM SUSPICIOUS?...
DIVERSION
EASY!
WAS THAT A KANGAROO?
DUNNO! LOOKED LIKE A DIVERSION TO ME.
ER
ERT!
STEVIE! THIS IS BOOGA, THEY'RE IN THE OPERA HOUSE.
GET THE BIG TANK IN POSITION, THEY'RE AWAY!
OK BOOGA I'M ON IT NOW! OVER!
INSIDE THE OPERA HOUSE...
CLICK!
WIND
WELL WHAT DO YOU KNOW?! IT'S BALDY LOCKS AND THE VIXEN BEER HUNTERS!
SUCK ON THIS FART FACE!
ARGH!
GIMME A B GIMME AN E GIMME AN E GIMME AN R!
RIPPLE!
YAK
TANK
VROOM!
WHAT'S GOING ON? WHO THE HELL ARE THOSE THREE SLAGS!?
THESE DOUBLE PAGE REALLY SAVE TIME DON'T THEY
FAIR SUCK OF THE PINEAPPLE MATE!

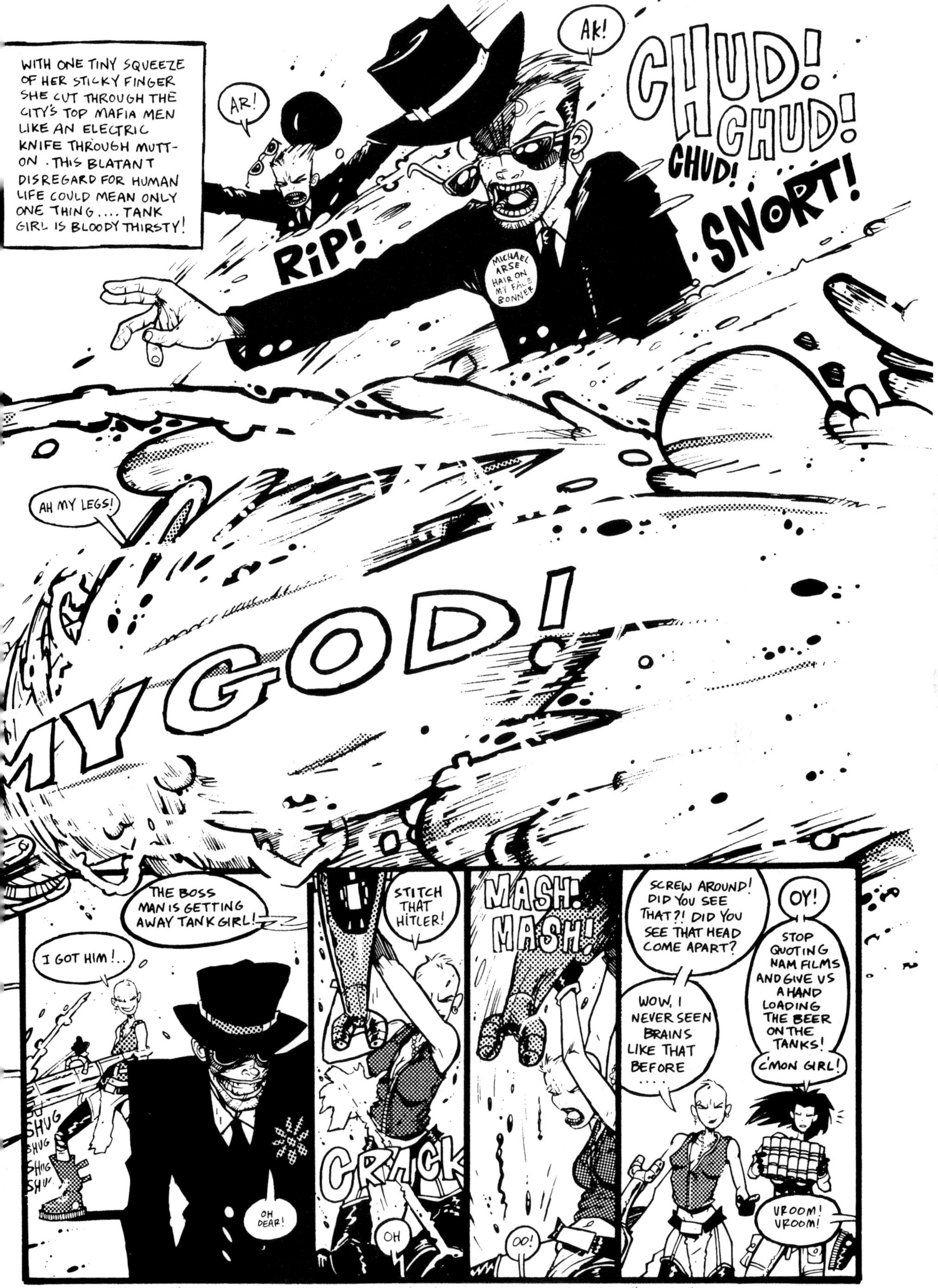
WITH ONE TINY SQUEEZE OF HER STICKY FINGER SHE CUT THROUGH THE CITY'S TOP MAFIA MEN LIKE AN ELECTRIC KNIFE THROUGH MUTT-ON. THIS BLATANT DISREGARD FOR HUMAN LIFE COULD MEAN ONLY ONE THING.... TANK GIRL IS BLOODY THIRSTY!
AR!
AK!
CHUD! CHUD! CHUD!
SNORT!
RIP!
MICHAEL ARSE HAIR ON MY FACE BONNER
AH MY LEGS!
MY GOD!
THE BOSS MAN IS GETTING AWAY TANK GIRL!
I GOT HIM!..
SHUG SHUG SHUG SHUG
OH DEAR!
STITCH THAT HITLER!
CRACK
OH
MASH! MASH!
OO!
SCREW AROUND! DID YOU SEE THAT?! DID YOU SEE THAT HEAD COME APART?
WOW, I NEVER SEEN BRAINS LIKE THAT BEFORE ....
OY!
STOP QUOTING NAM FILMS AND GIVE US A HAND LOADING THE BEER ON THE TANKS!
C'MON GIRL!
VROOM! VROOM!

SLICING UP EYEBALLS I WANT YOU TO KNOW GIRLIE SO GROOVIE I WANT YOU TO KNOW

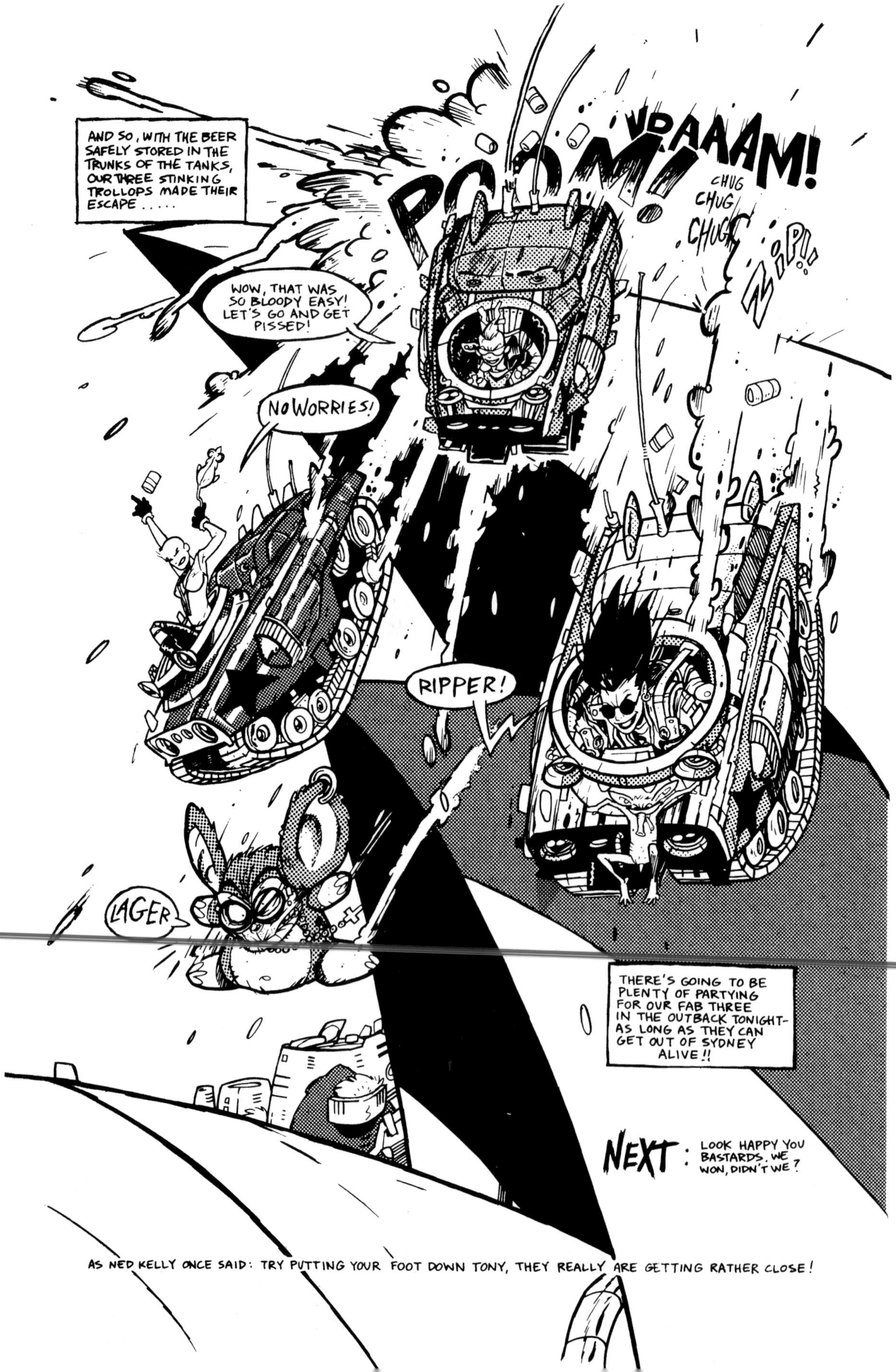

AND SO, WITH THE BEER SAFELY STORED IN THE TRUNKS OF THE TANKS, OUR THREE STINKING TROLLOPS MADE THEIR ESCAPE .....
VRAAAM!
POOM!
CHUG CHUG CHUG
ZIP!!
WOW, THAT WAS SO BLOODY EASY! LET'S GO AND GET PISSED!
NO WORRIES!
RIPPER!
LAGER
THERE'S GOING TO BE PLENTY OF PARTYING FOR OUR FAB THREE IN THE OUTBACK TONIGHT- AS LONG AS THEY CAN GET OUT OF SYDNEY ALIVE!!
NEXT: LOOK HAPPY YOU BASTARDS. WE WON, DIDN'T WE?
AS NED KELLY ONCE SAID: TRY PUTTING YOUR FOOT DOWN TONY, THEY REALLY ARE GETTING RATHER CLOSE!

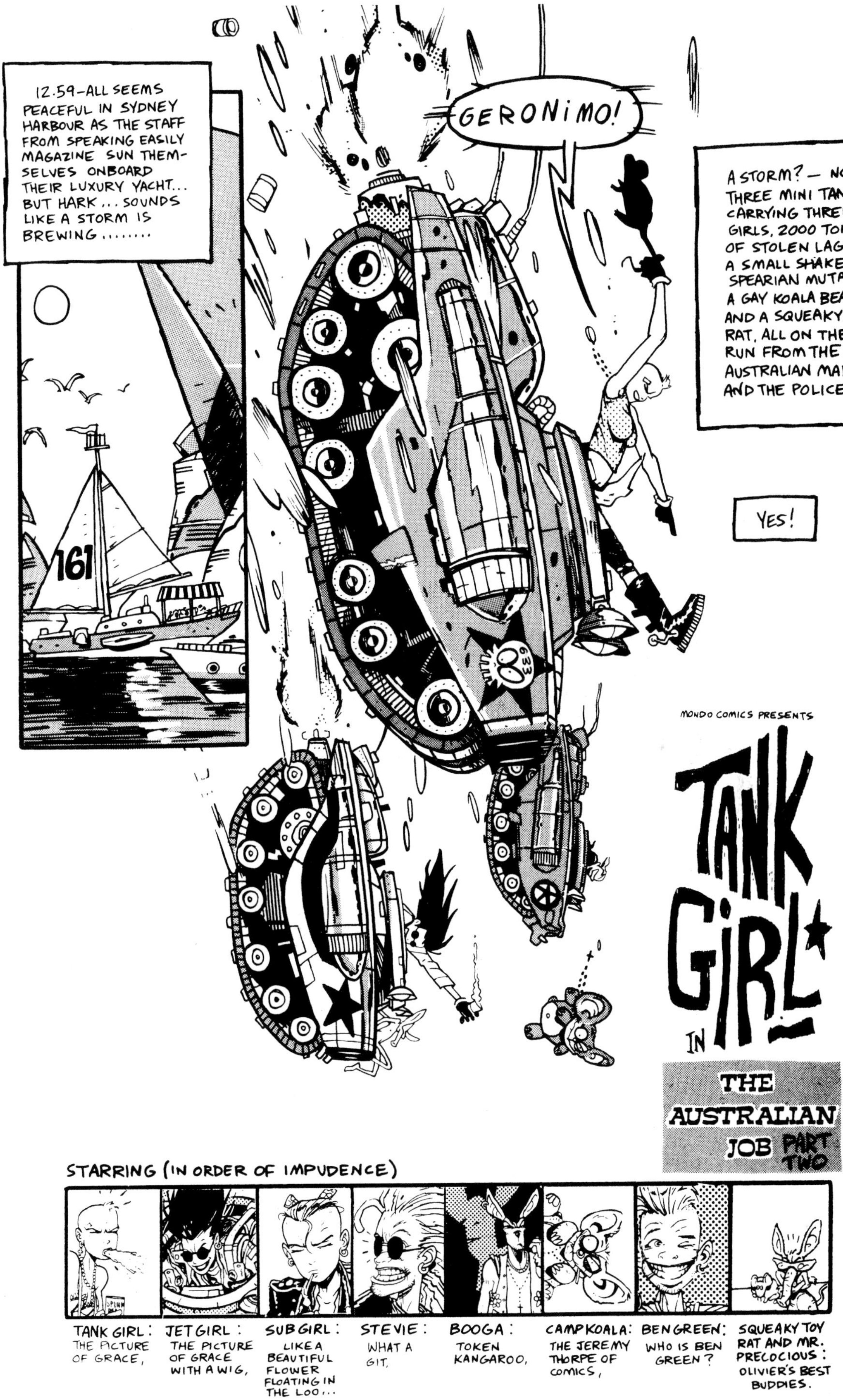
12:59–ALL SEEMS PEACEFUL IN SYDNEY HARBOUR AS THE STAFF FROM SPEAKING EASILY MAGAZINE SUN THEMSELVES ONBOARD THEIR LUXURY YACHT... BUT HARK... SOUNDS LIKE A STORM IS BREWING........
161
GERONiMO!
A STORM?— NO! THREE MINI TANKS CARRYING THREE GIRLS, 2000 TONS OF STOLEN LAGER, A SMALL SHAKESPEARIAN MUTANT, A GAY KOALA BEAR AND A SQUEAKY TOY RAT, ALL ON THE RUN FROM THE AUSTRALIAN MAFIA AND THE POLICE?—
YES!
MONDO COMICS PRESENTS
TANK GIRL
IN
THE AUSTRALIAN JOB PART TWO
STARRING (IN ORDER OF IMPUDENCE)
TANK GIRL: THE PICTURE OF GRACE,
JET GIRL: THE PICTURE OF GRACE WITH A WIG,
SUB GIRL: LIKE A BEAUTIFUL FLOWER FLOATING IN THE LOO...
STEVIE: WHAT A GIT,
BOOGA: TOKEN KANGAROO,
CAMP KOALA: THE JEREMY THORPE OF COMICS,
BEN GREEN: WHO IS BEN GREEN?
SQUEAKY TOY RAT AND MR. PRECOCIOUS: OLIVIER'S BEST BUDDIES.

SCRIPT - ALAN + JAMIE ★ ART - JAMIE ★ LETTERS - ALAN ★ STUNTS - MIKE SMITH ★ © JAMIE HEWLETT

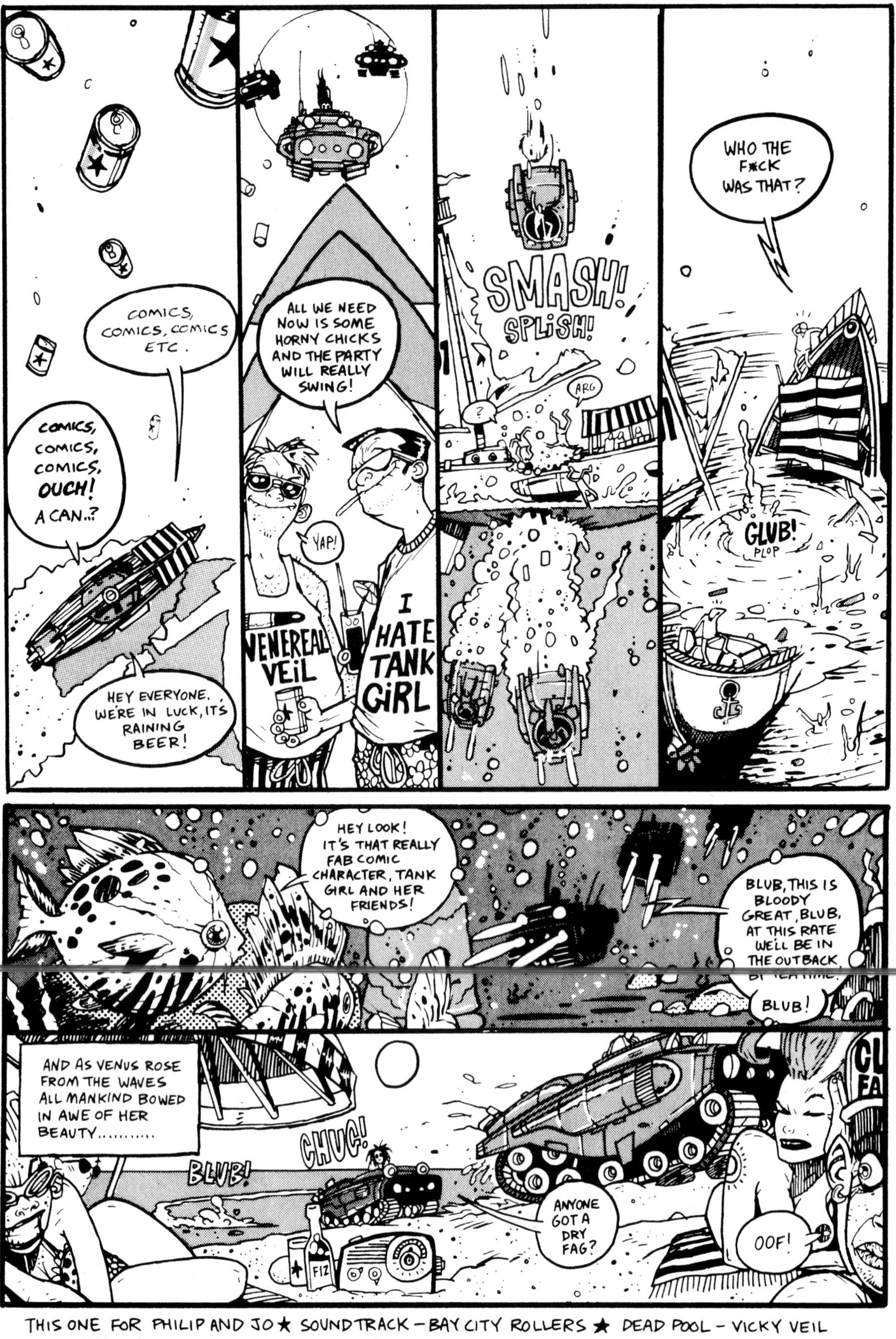

COMICS, COMICS, COMICS ETC.
COMICS, COMICS, COMICS, OUCH! A CAN..?
HEY EVERYONE, WE'RE IN LUCK, IT'S RAINING BEER!
ALL WE NEED NOW IS SOME HORNY CHICKS AND THE PARTY WILL REALLY SWING!
YAP!
VENEREAL VEIL
I HATE TANK GIRL
SMASH!
SPLISH!
ARG
WHO THE F*CK WAS THAT?
GLUB!
PLOP
HEY LOOK! IT'S THAT REALLY FAB COMIC CHARACTER, TANK GIRL AND HER FRIENDS!
BLUB, THIS IS BLOODY GREAT, BLUB, AT THIS RATE WE'LL BE IN THE OUTBACK
BLUB!
AND AS VENUS ROSE FROM THE WAVES ALL MANKIND BOWED IN AWE OF HER BEAUTY..........
CHUG!
BLUB!
ANYONE GOT A DRY FAG?
OOF!

THIS ONE FOR PHILIP AND JO ★ SOUNDTRACK - BAY CITY ROLLERS ★ DEAD POOL - VICKY VEIL

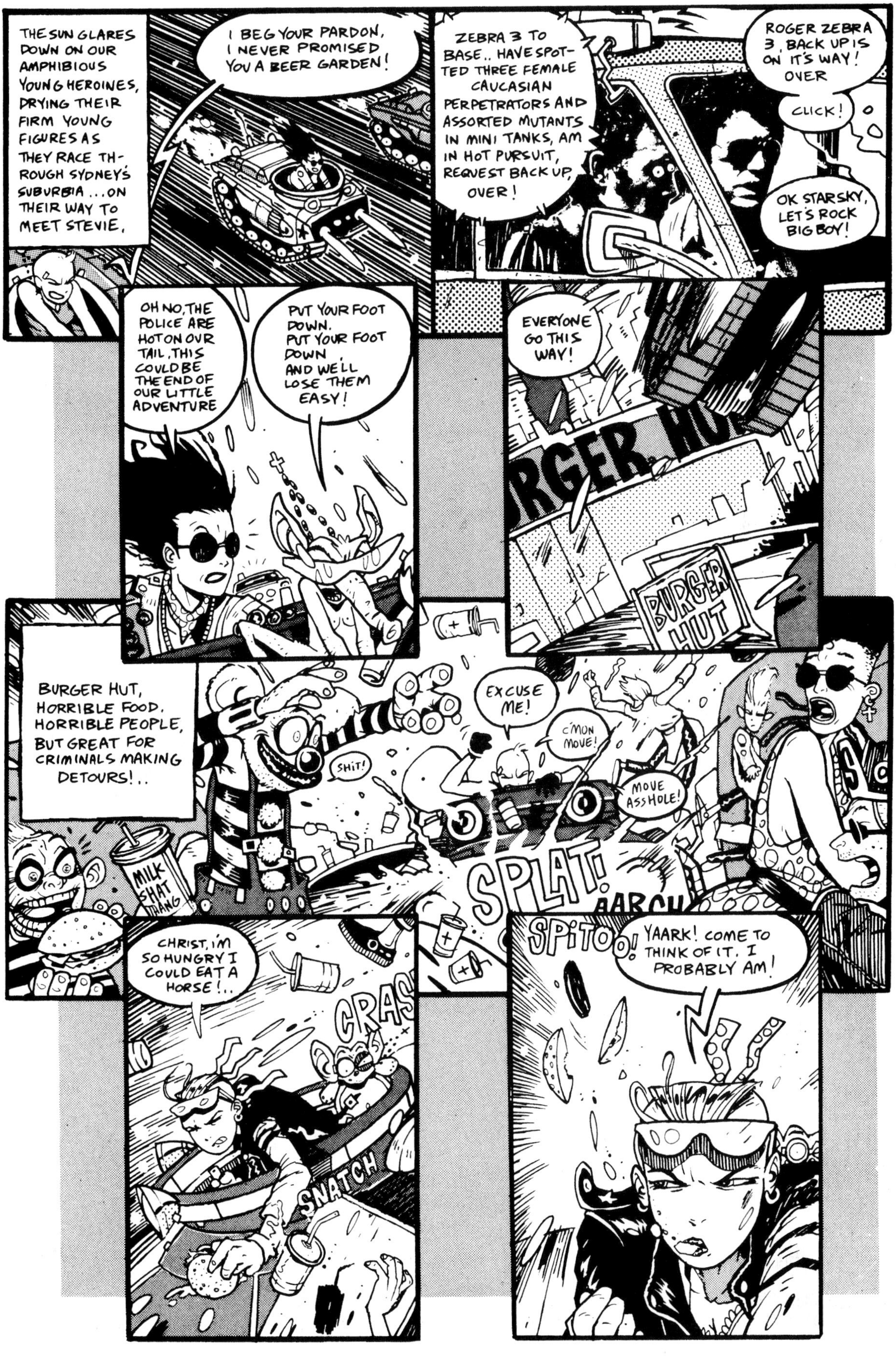
THE SUN GLARES DOWN ON OUR AMPHIBIOUS YOUNG HEROINES, DRYING THEIR FIRM YOUNG FIGURES AS THEY RACE THROUGH SYDNEY'S SUBURBIA ...ON THEIR WAY TO MEET STEVIE,
I BEG YOUR PARDON, I NEVER PROMISED YOU A BEER GARDEN!
ZEBRA 3 TO BASE.. HAVE SPOTTED THREE FEMALE CAUCASIAN PERPETRATORS AND ASSORTED MUTANTS IN MINI TANKS, AM IN HOT PURSUIT, REQUEST BACK UP, OVER!
ROGER ZEBRA 3, BACK UP IS ON IT'S WAY! OVER
CLICK!
OK STARSKY, LET'S ROCK BIG BOY!
OH NO, THE POLICE ARE HOT ON OUR TAIL, THIS COULD BE THE END OF OUR LITTLE ADVENTURE
PUT YOUR FOOT DOWN. PUT YOUR FOOT DOWN AND WE'LL LOSE THEM EASY!
EVERYONE GO THIS WAY!
BURGER HUT
BURGER HUT
BURGER HUT, HORRIBLE FOOD, HORRIBLE PEOPLE, BUT GREAT FOR CRIMINALS MAKING DETOURS!..
EXCUSE ME!
C'MON MOVE!
SHIT!
MOVE ASSHOLE!
MILK SHAT THANG
SPLAT!
AARCH
CHRIST, I'M SO HUNGRY I COULD EAT A HORSE!..
CRAS
SNATCH
SPITOO!
YAARK! COME TO THINK OF IT. I PROBABLY AM!

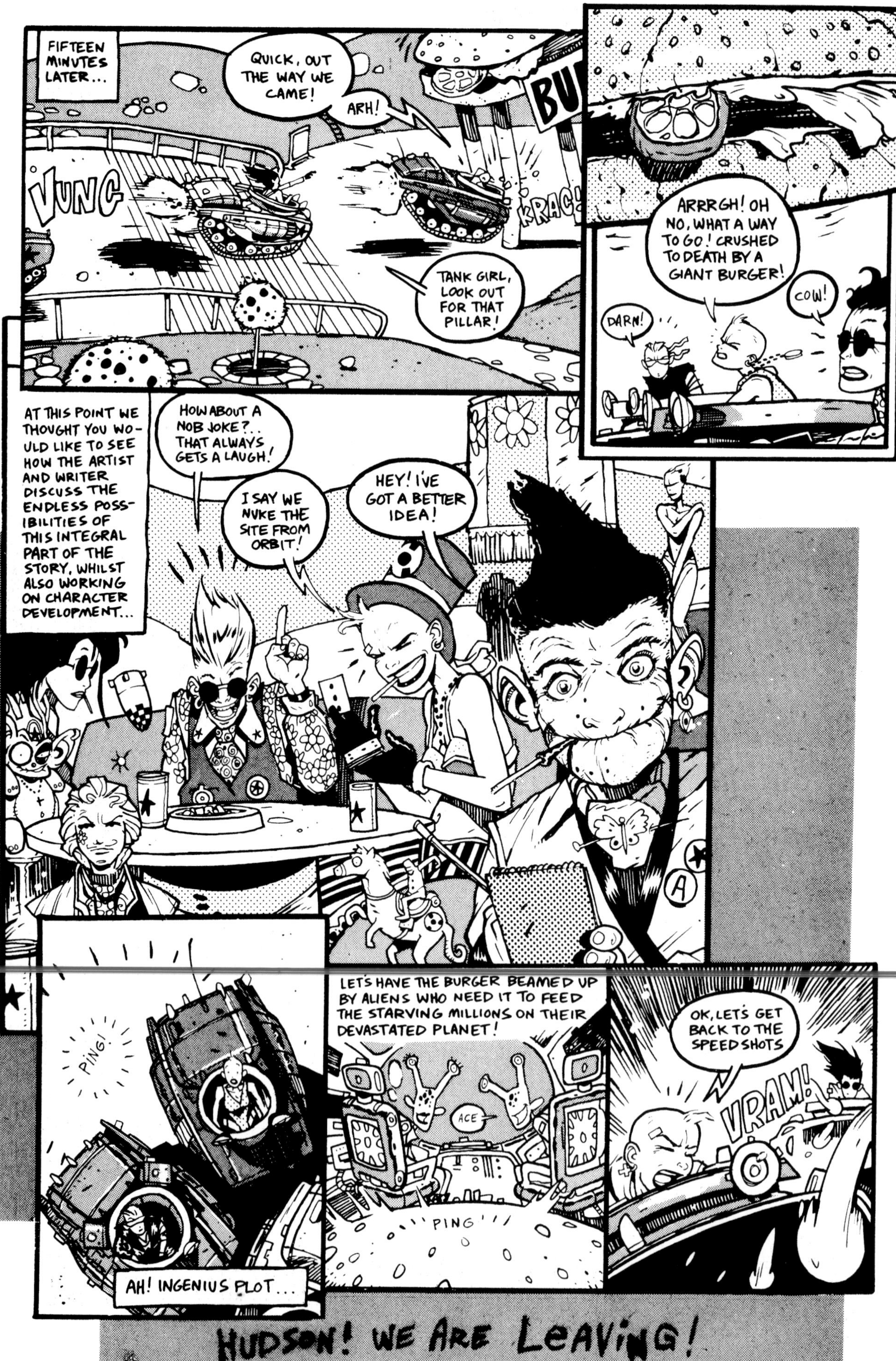
FIFTEEN MINUTES LATER...
QUICK, OUT THE WAY WE CAME!
ARH!
VUNG
KRAC
TANK GIRL, LOOK OUT FOR THAT PILLAR!
ARRRGH! OH NO, WHAT A WAY TO GO! CRUSHED TO DEATH BY A GIANT BURGER!
DARN!
COW!
AT THIS POINT WE THOUGHT YOU WOULD LIKE TO SEE HOW THE ARTIST AND WRITER DISCUSS THE ENDLESS POSSIBILITIES OF THIS INTEGRAL PART OF THE STORY, WHILST ALSO WORKING ON CHARACTER DEVELOPMENT...
HOW ABOUT A NOB JOKE?.. THAT ALWAYS GETS A LAUGH!
I SAY WE NUKE THE SITE FROM ORBIT!
HEY! I'VE GOT A BETTER IDEA!
PING!
AH! INGENIUS PLOT...
LET'S HAVE THE BURGER BEAMED UP BY ALIENS WHO NEED IT TO FEED THE STARVING MILLIONS ON THEIR DEVASTATED PLANET!
ACE
PING
OK, LET'S GET BACK TO THE SPEED SHOTS
VRAM!
HUDSON! WE ARE LEAVING!

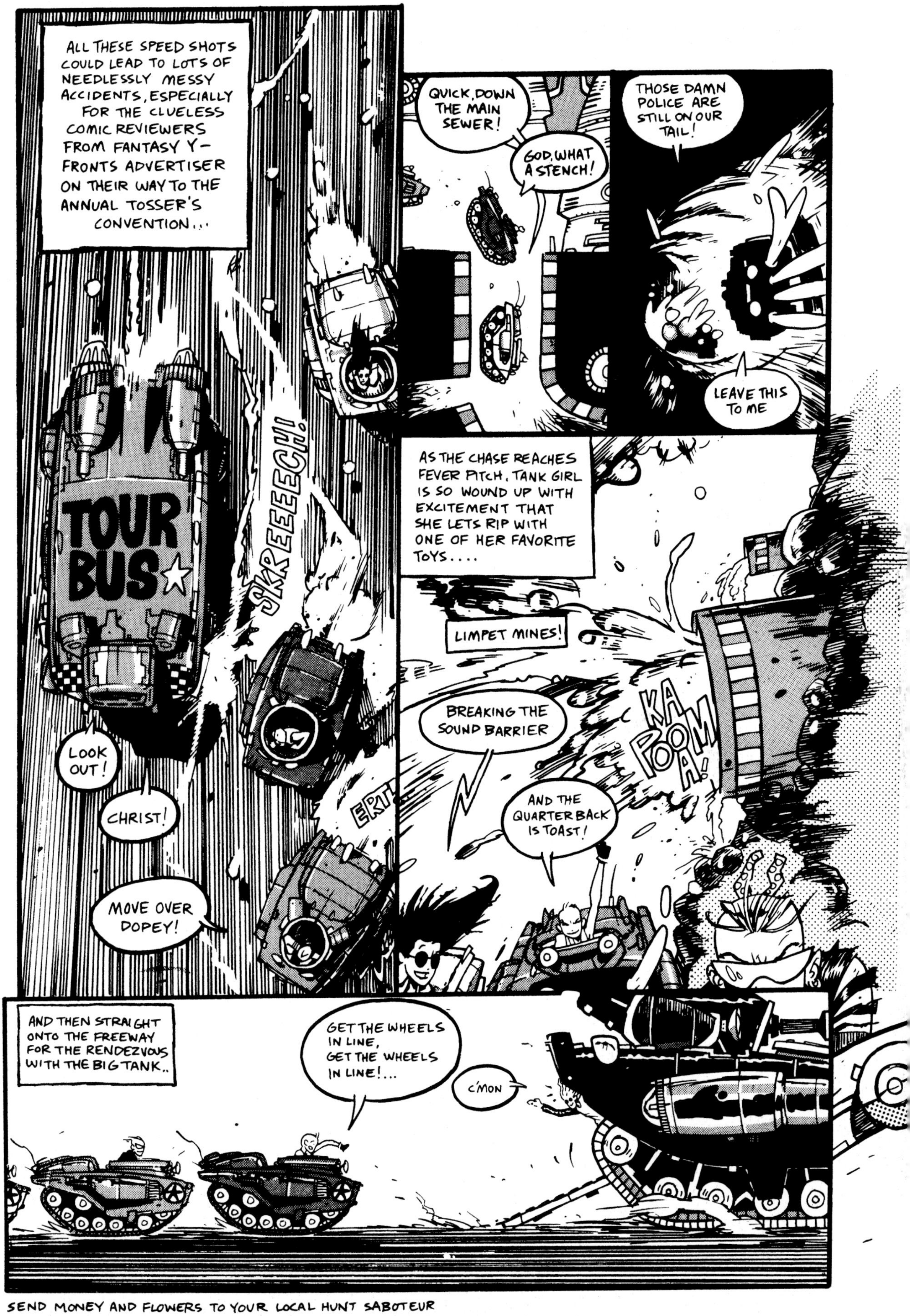

ALL THESE SPEED SHOTS COULD LEAD TO LOTS OF NEEDLESSLY MESSY ACCIDENTS, ESPECIALLY FOR THE CLUELESS COMIC REVIEWERS FROM FANTASY Y-FRONTS ADVERTISER ON THEIR WAY TO THE ANNUAL TOSSER'S CONVENTION...
TOUR BUS
SKREEEECH!
LOOK OUT!
CHRIST!
MOVE OVER DOPEY!
QUICK, DOWN THE MAIN SEWER!
GOD, WHAT A STENCH!
THOSE DAMN POLICE ARE STILL ON OUR TAIL!
LEAVE THIS TO ME
AS THE CHASE REACHES FEVER PITCH, TANK GIRL IS SO WOUND UP WITH EXCITEMENT THAT SHE LETS RIP WITH ONE OF HER FAVORITE TOYS....
LIMPET MINES!
BREAKING THE SOUND BARRIER
KA POOM A!
AND THE QUARTER BACK IS TOAST!
AND THEN STRAIGHT ONTO THE FREEWAY FOR THE RENDEZVOUS WITH THE BIG TANK..
GET THE WHEELS IN LINE, GET THE WHEELS IN LINE!...
C'MON

SEND MONEY AND FLOWERS TO YOUR LOCAL HUNT SABOTEUR

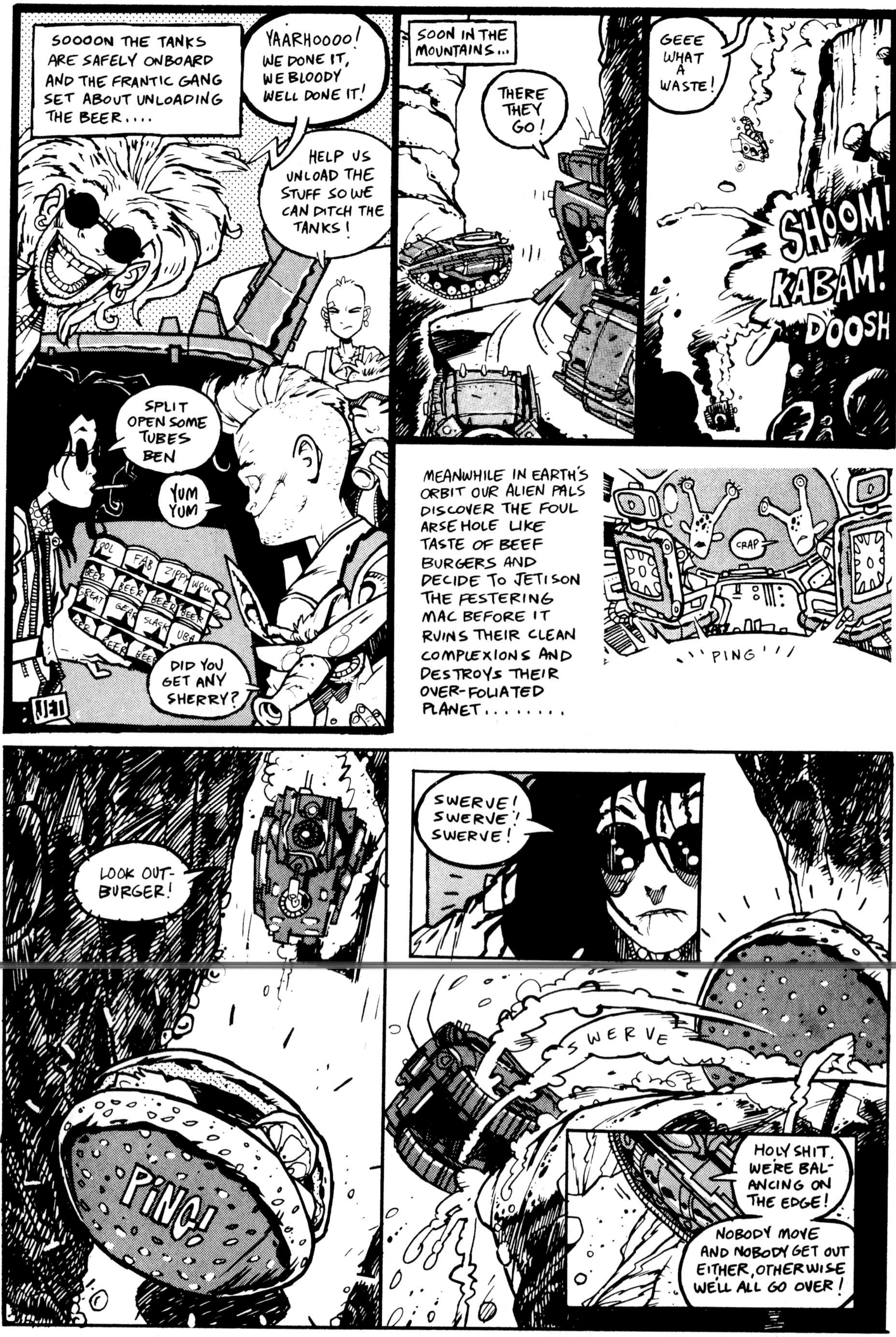

SOOOON THE TANKS ARE SAFELY ONBOARD AND THE FRANTIC GANG SET ABOUT UNLOADING THE BEER....
YAARHOOOO! WE DONE IT, WE BLOODY WELL DONE IT!
HELP US UNLOAD THE STUFF SO WE CAN DITCH THE TANKS!
SPLIT OPEN SOME TUBES BEN
YUM YUM
COOL
FAB
ZIPPY
WOW
BEER
BEER
GREAT
GEAR
BEER
BEER
SLASK
UBA
BEER
BEER
DID YOU GET ANY SHERRY?
SOON IN THE MOUNTAINS...
THERE THEY GO!
GEEE WHAT A WASTE!
SHOOM!
KABAM!
DOOSH
MEANWHILE IN EARTH'S ORBIT OUR ALIEN PALS DISCOVER THE FOUL ARSE HOLE LIKE TASTE OF BEEF BURGERS AND DECIDE TO JETISON THE FESTERING MAC BEFORE IT RUINS THEIR CLEAN COMPLEXIONS AND DESTROYS THEIR OVER-FOLIATED PLANET........
CRAP
PING
LOOK OUT- BURGER!
PING!
SWERVE! SWERVE! SWERVE!
SWERVE
HOLY SHIT, WE'RE BALANCING ON THE EDGE!
NOBODY MOVE AND NOBODY GET OUT EITHER, OTHERWISE WE'LL ALL GO OVER!

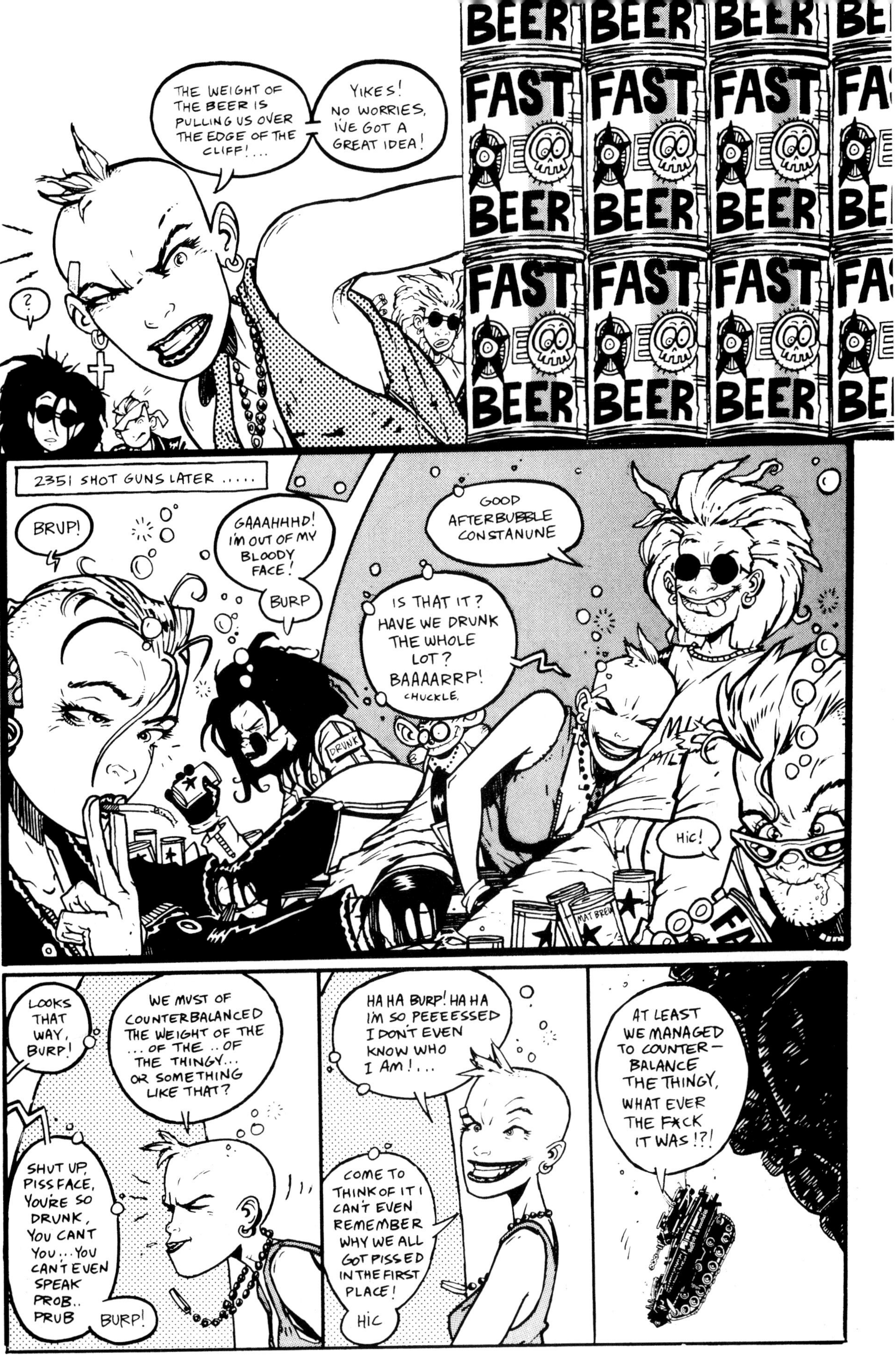
BEER
FAST
BEER
THE WEIGHT OF THE BEER IS PULLING US OVER THE EDGE OF THE CLIFF!...
YIKES! NO WORRIES, I'VE GOT A GREAT IDEA!
?
2351 SHOT GUNS LATER .....
BRUP!
GAAAHHHD! I'M OUT OF MY BLOODY FACE!
BURP
GOOD AFTERBUBBLE CONSTANUNE
IS THAT IT? HAVE WE DRUNK THE WHOLE LOT? BAAAARRP! CHUCKLE.
DRUNK
Hic!
LOOKS THAT WAY, BURP!
WE MUST OF COUNTERBALANCED THE WEIGHT OF THE ... OF THE .. OF THE THINGY... OR SOMETHING LIKE THAT?
SHUT UP, PISSFACE, YOU'RE SO DRUNK, YOU CAN'T YOU... YOU CAN'T EVEN SPEAK PROB.. PRUB
BURP!
HA HA BURP! HA HA I'M SO PEEEESSED I DON'T EVEN KNOW WHO I AM!...
COME TO THINK OF IT I CAN'T EVEN REMEMBER WHY WE ALL GOT PISSED IN THE FIRST PLACE!
HIC
AT LEAST WE MANAGED TO COUNTER-BALANCE THE THINGY, WHAT EVER THE F*CK IT WAS!?!

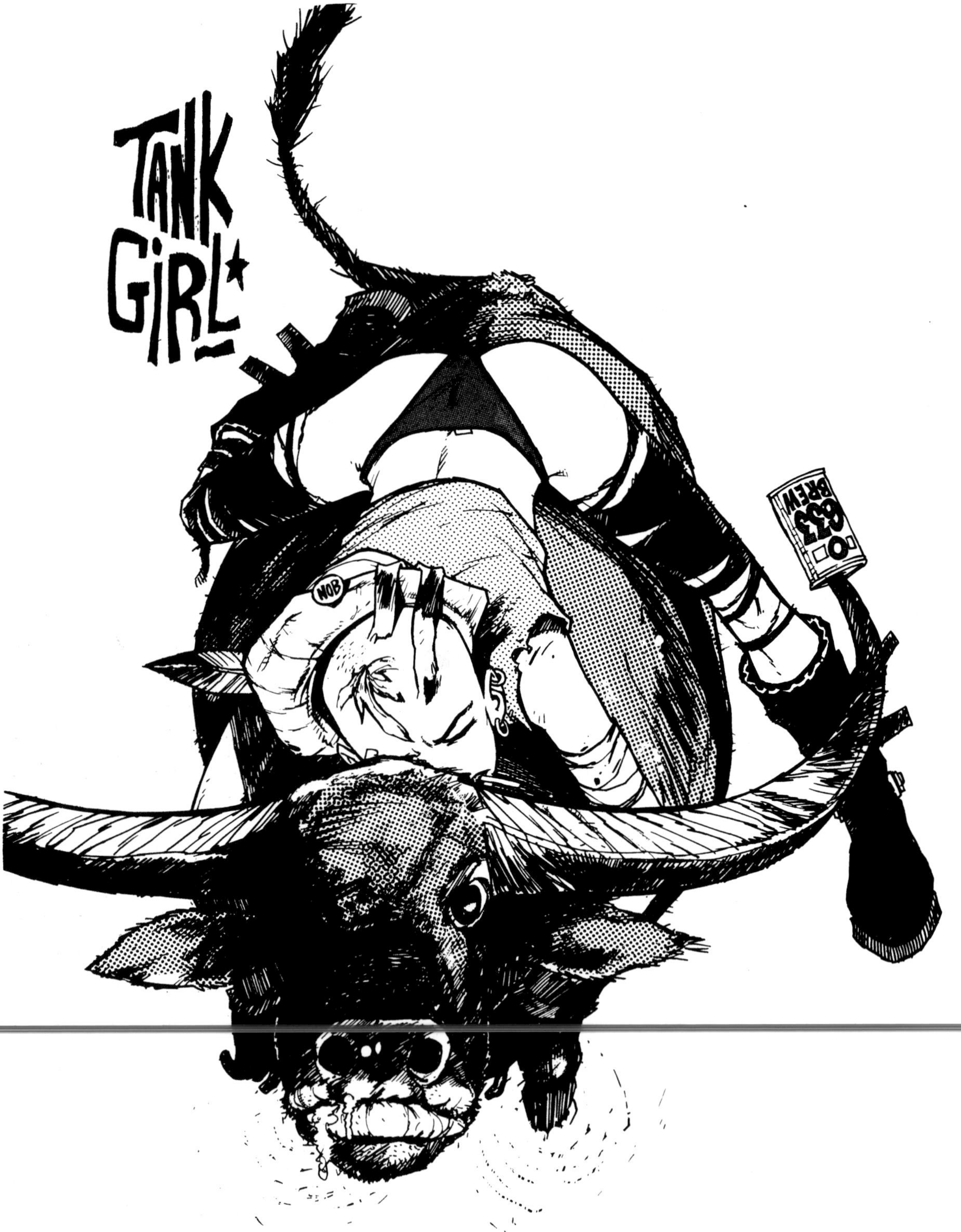
TANK GIRL
MOB

SOME TIMES WHEN I'M ASLEEP I DREAM THAT I CAN FLY. IT'S NOT REALLY FLYING, SOMETIMES I DREAM THAT I'M RUNNING AWAY FROM THE ARMY DOWN PAST THE PUB NEAR STEVIES HOUSE.... AND I START LEAPING, OVER ROCKS AND BUSHES ..... AND THEN I FEEL MY HEART KIND OF TUGGING UPWARDS AND I PUT MY ARMS OUT LIKE WINGS.... AND RAISE MY LEGS UP TO MY CHEST LIKE UNDERCARRIAGE .... THEN I JUST GLIDE ALONG... LEAVING THE ARMY BEHIND ME... GOD I'M F*CKED......

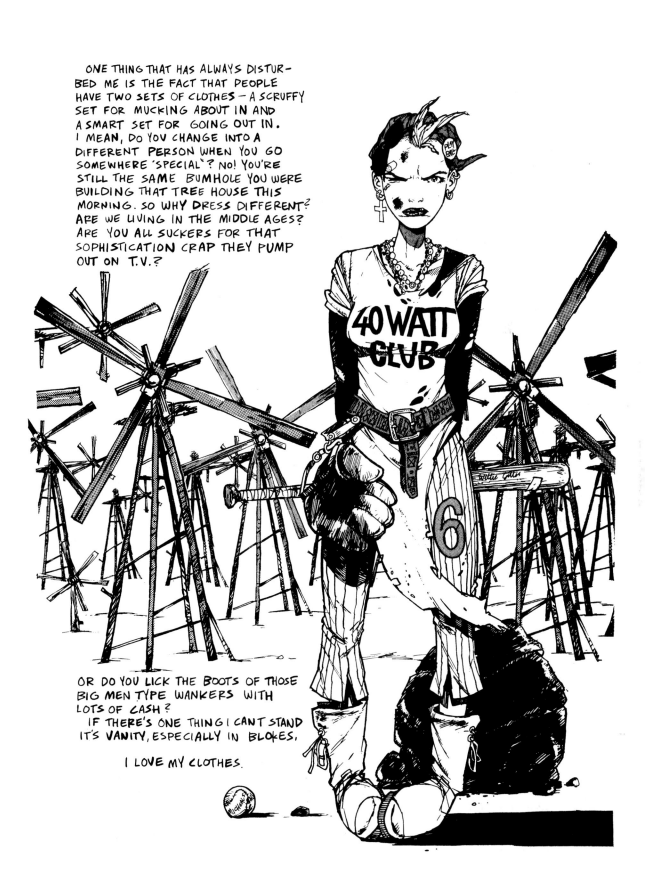

ONE THING THAT HAS ALWAYS DISTUR-
BED ME IS THE FACT THAT PEOPLE
HAVE TWO SETS OF CLOTHES — A SCRUFFY
SET FOR MUCKING ABOUT IN AND
A SMART SET FOR GOING OUT IN.
I MEAN, DO YOU CHANGE INTO A
DIFFERENT PERSON WHEN YOU GO
SOMEWHERE 'SPECIAL'? NO! YOU'RE
STILL THE SAME BUMHOLE YOU WERE
BUILDING THAT TREE HOUSE THIS
MORNING. SO WHY DRESS DIFFERENT?
ARE WE LIVING IN THE MIDDLE AGES?
ARE YOU ALL SUCKERS FOR THAT
SOPHISTICATION CRAP THEY PUMP
OUT ON T.V.?

OR DO YOU LICK THE BOOTS OF THOSE
BIG MEN TYPE WANKERS WITH
LOTS OF CASH?
    IF THERE'S ONE THING I CAN'T STAND
IT'S VANITY, ESPECIALLY IN BLOKES.

        I LOVE MY CLOTHES.

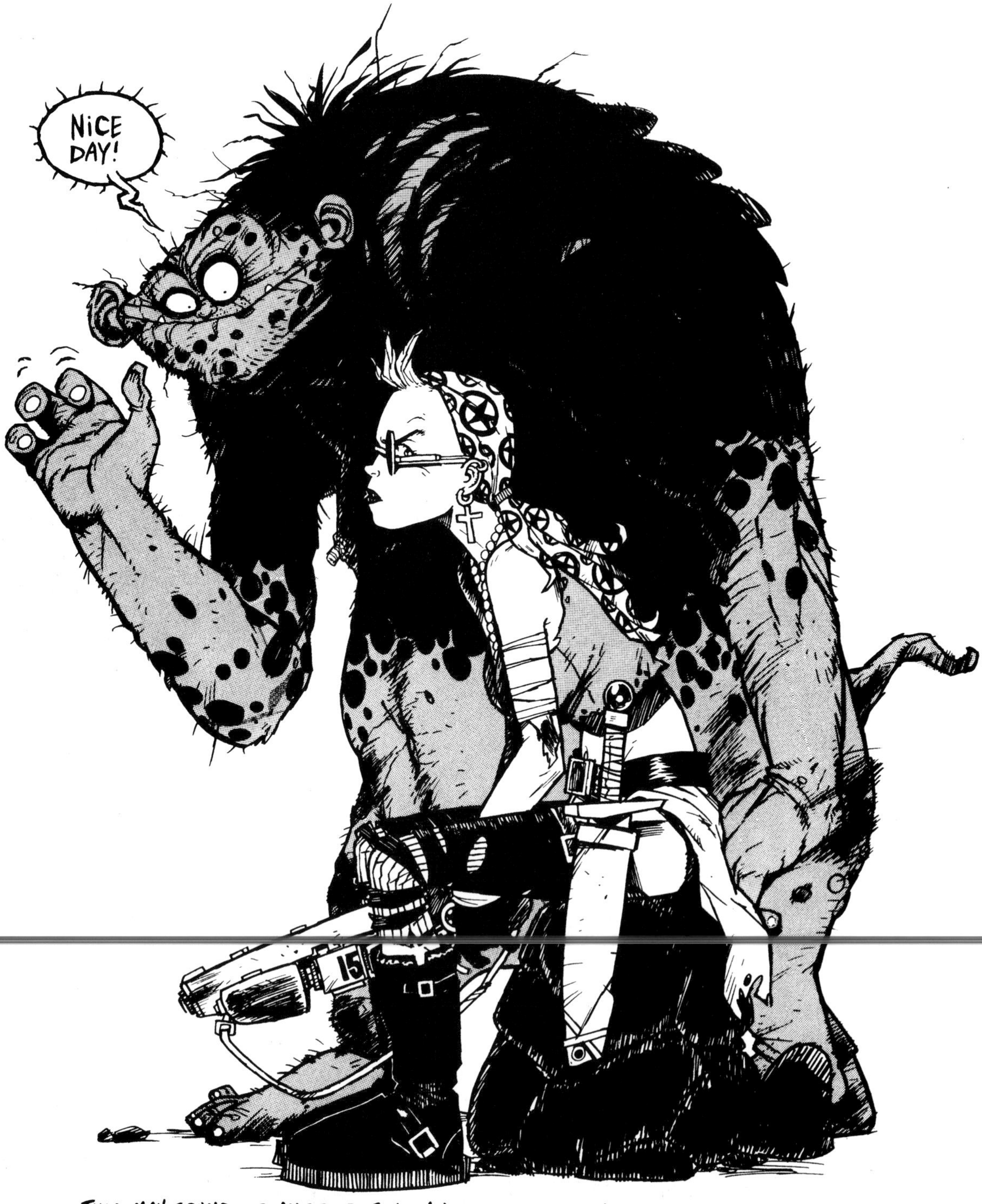
NICE DAY!

THIS MAY SOUND STRANGE, BUT I CAN TELL WHEN IT'S GOING TO RAIN.... REALLY! I'M FEELING VERY ODD OF LATE. I'VE BEEN ACTING VERY ODD TOO, TALKING TO MYSELF, GRINNING AND LAUGHING FOR NO REASON. SOME THING'S GOING ON. MY LIFE SEEMS TO BE COMING TOGETHER, TAKING SOME REAL DIRECTION. THIS JUST WON'T DO ... THE TIMES THEY ARE A CHANGIN.

I HAD A VISION.
I LAY HALF ASLEEP IN THE DIRT, THE SUNSET
BEHIND THE HILLS AND BURNT MY SKIN,
AND IN MY DREAM I SAW A THRONE — MY THRONE,
BUILT ON THE TOWER OF MY LIFE.
   WHEN I WOKE ALL I COULD THINK OF WAS MY
VISION; ETCHED SO CLEARLY ON MY MIND.
   I WORKED FOR THREE DAYS AND THREE NIGHTS
WITH NO FOOD OR DRINK, UNTIL MY VISION
HAD BECOME A REALITY — PERFECT IN EVERY
DETAIL,
   I PONDERED THE SIGNIFICANCE OF THIS
EDIFICE AND SHOOK OFF MY TRANCE ....
   I FELT TIRED,
   I FELT LONELY,
   I FELT CONFUSED,
   I FELT SO BLOODY CONFUSED,
   I FELT LIKE A RIGHT PRAT!

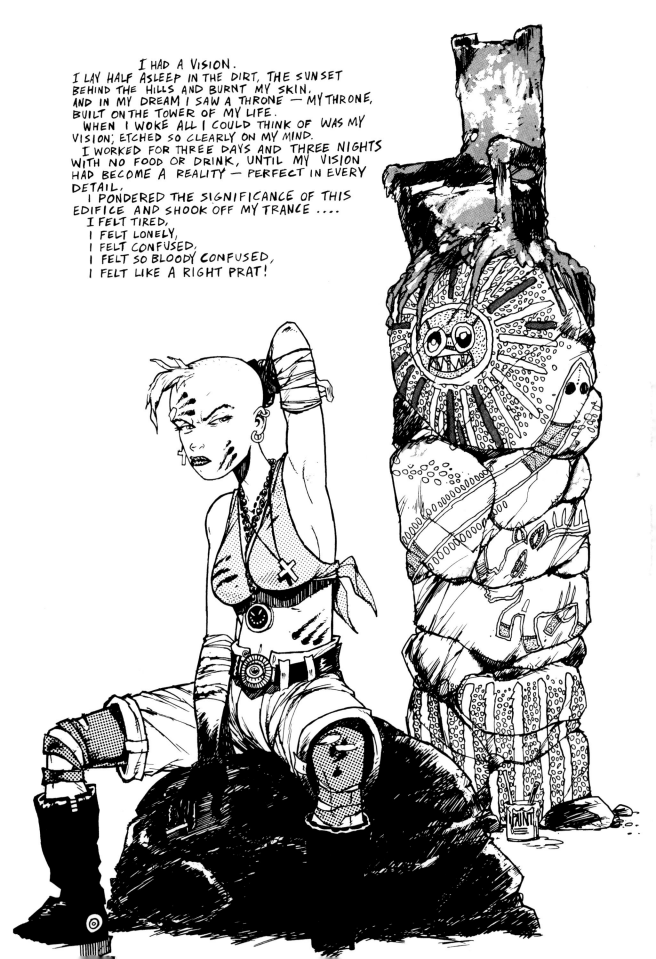

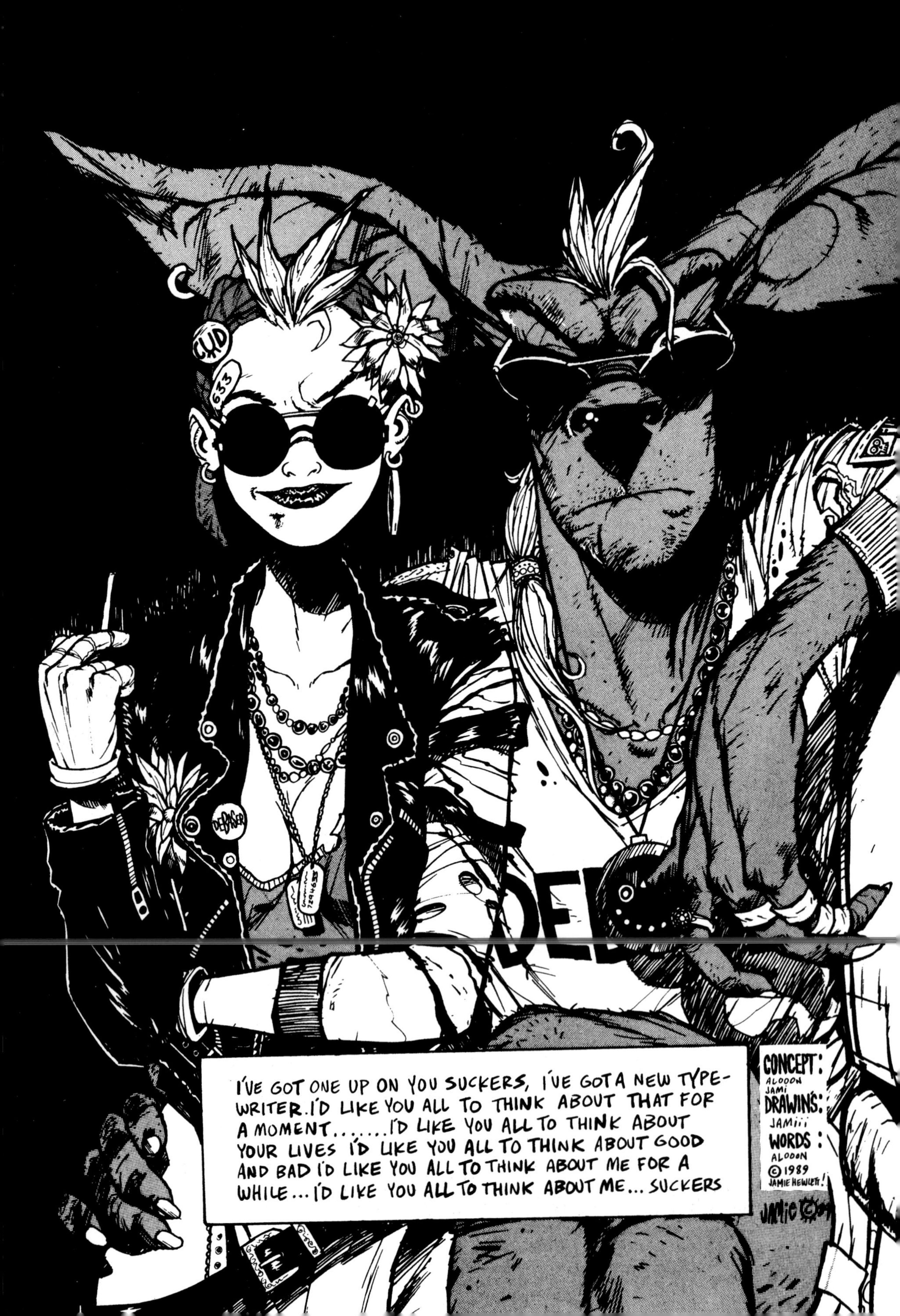

I'VE GOT ONE UP ON YOU SUCKERS, I'VE GOT A NEW TYPE-WRITER. I'D LIKE YOU ALL TO THINK ABOUT THAT FOR A MOMENT....... I'D LIKE YOU ALL TO THINK ABOUT YOUR LIVES I'D LIKE YOU ALL TO THINK ABOUT GOOD AND BAD I'D LIKE YOU ALL TO THINK ABOUT ME FOR A WHILE... I'D LIKE YOU ALL TO THINK ABOUT ME... SUCKERS
CONCEPT: ALOOON JAMI
DRAWINS: JAMiii
WORDS: ALOOON
© 1989 JAMIE HEWLETT!

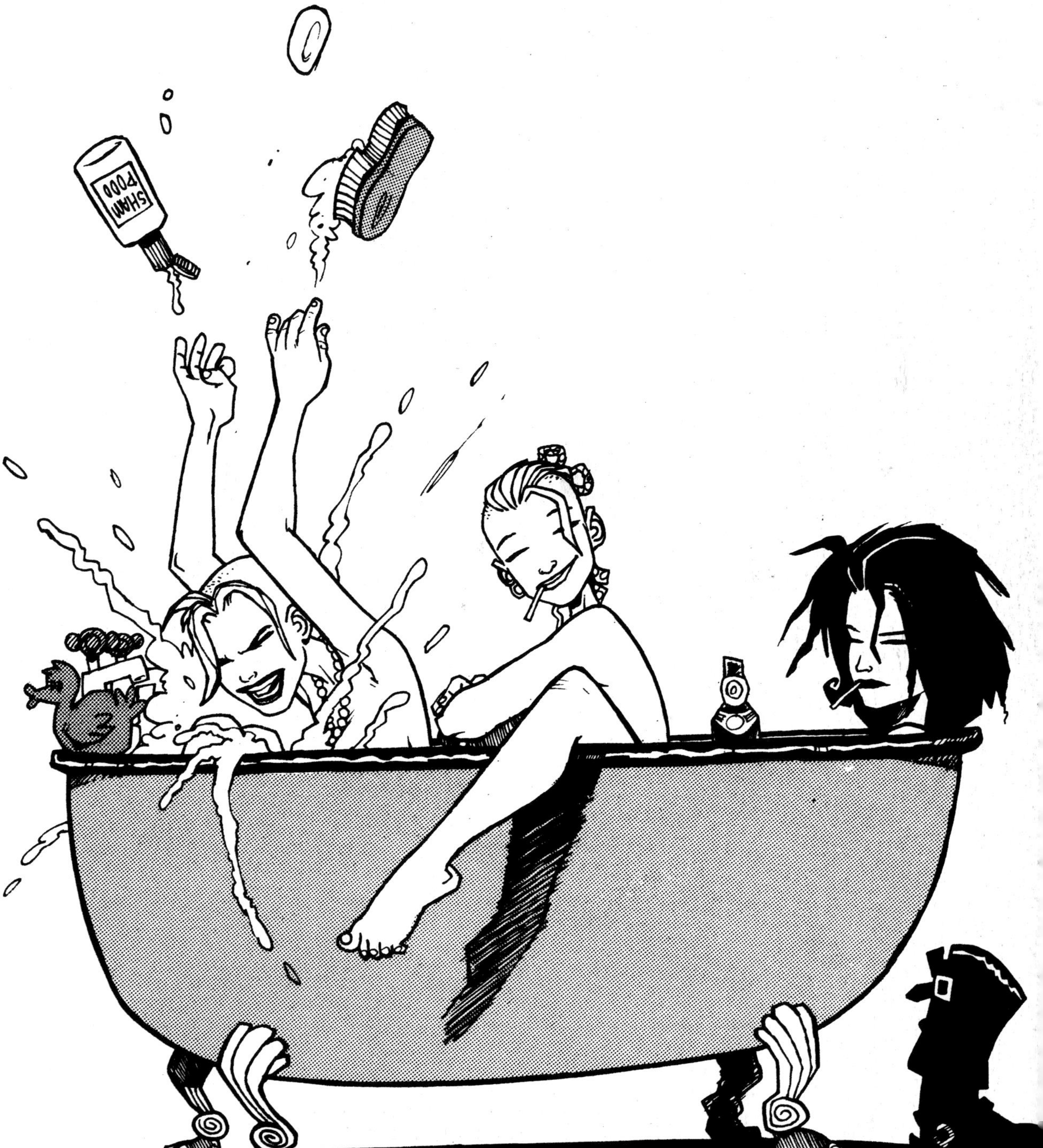
SHAM POO

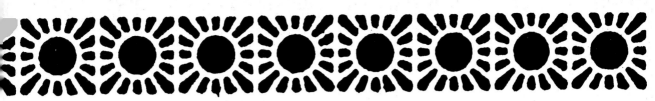

THIS ONE FOR MICK JONES ★

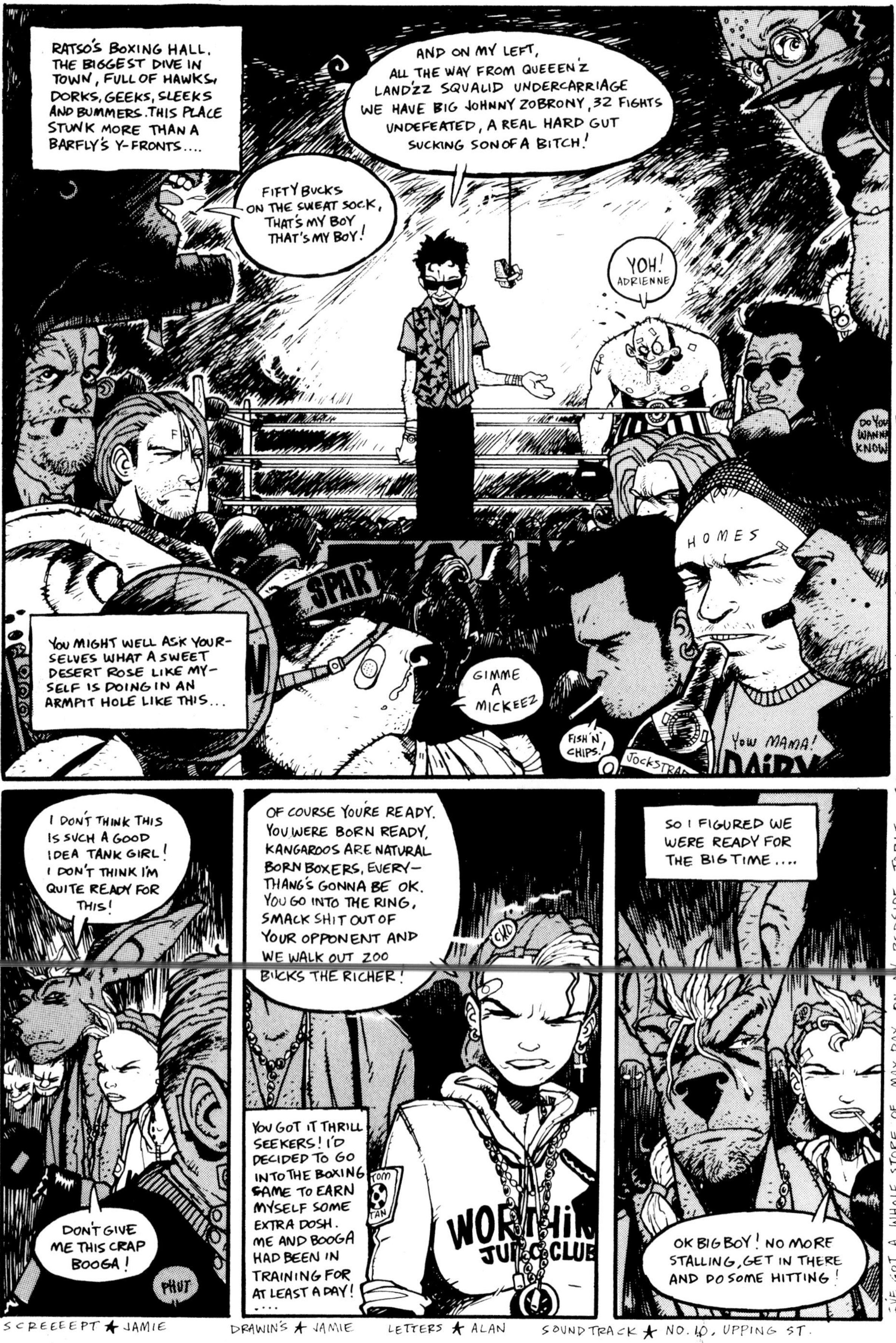
RATSO'S BOXING HALL. THE BIGGEST DIVE IN TOWN, FULL OF HAWKS, DORKS, GEEKS, SLEEKS AND BUMMERS. THIS PLACE STUNK MORE THAN A BARFLY'S Y-FRONTS....
AND ON MY LEFT, ALL THE WAY FROM QUEEEN'Z LAND'ZZ SQUALID UNDERCARRIAGE WE HAVE BIG JOHNNY ZOBRONY, 32 FIGHTS UNDEFEATED, A REAL HARD GUT SUCKING SON OF A BITCH!
FIFTY BUCKS ON THE SWEAT SOCK, THAT'S MY BOY THAT'S MY BOY!
YOH! ADRIENNE
DO YOU WANNA KNOW
HOMES
SPAR
YOU MIGHT WELL ASK YOURSELVES WHAT A SWEET DESERT ROSE LIKE MYSELF IS DOING IN AN ARMPIT HOLE LIKE THIS...
GIMME A MICKEEZ
FISH 'N' CHIPS!
JOCKSTRAP
YOU MAMA!
DAIRY
I DON'T THINK THIS IS SUCH A GOOD IDEA TANK GIRL! I DON'T THINK I'M QUITE READY FOR THIS!
DON'T GIVE ME THIS CRAP BOOGA!
PHUT
OF COURSE YOU'RE READY. YOU WERE BORN READY, KANGAROOS ARE NATURAL BORN BOXERS, EVERYTHANG'S GONNA BE OK. YOU GO INTO THE RING, SMACK SHIT OUT OF YOUR OPPONENT AND WE WALK OUT 200 BUCKS THE RICHER!
YOU GOT IT THRILL SEEKERS! I'D DECIDED TO GO INTO THE BOXING GAME TO EARN MYSELF SOME EXTRA DOSH. ME AND BOOGA HAD BEEN IN TRAINING FOR AT LEAST A DAY! ....
TOM TAN
WORTHING JUDO CLUB
SO I FIGURED WE WERE READY FOR THE BIG TIME....
OK BIG BOY! NO MORE STALLING, GET IN THERE AND DO SOME HITTING!

I'VE GOT A WHOLE STORE OF MAX PAX ON MY BEDSIDE TABLE SO THAT WHEN YOU CAN'T GO ON NO MORE I WILL still be Able!

SCREEEEPT ★ JAMIE DRAWIN'S ★ JAMIE LETTERS ★ ALAN SOUNDTRACK ★ NO. 10, UPPING ST.

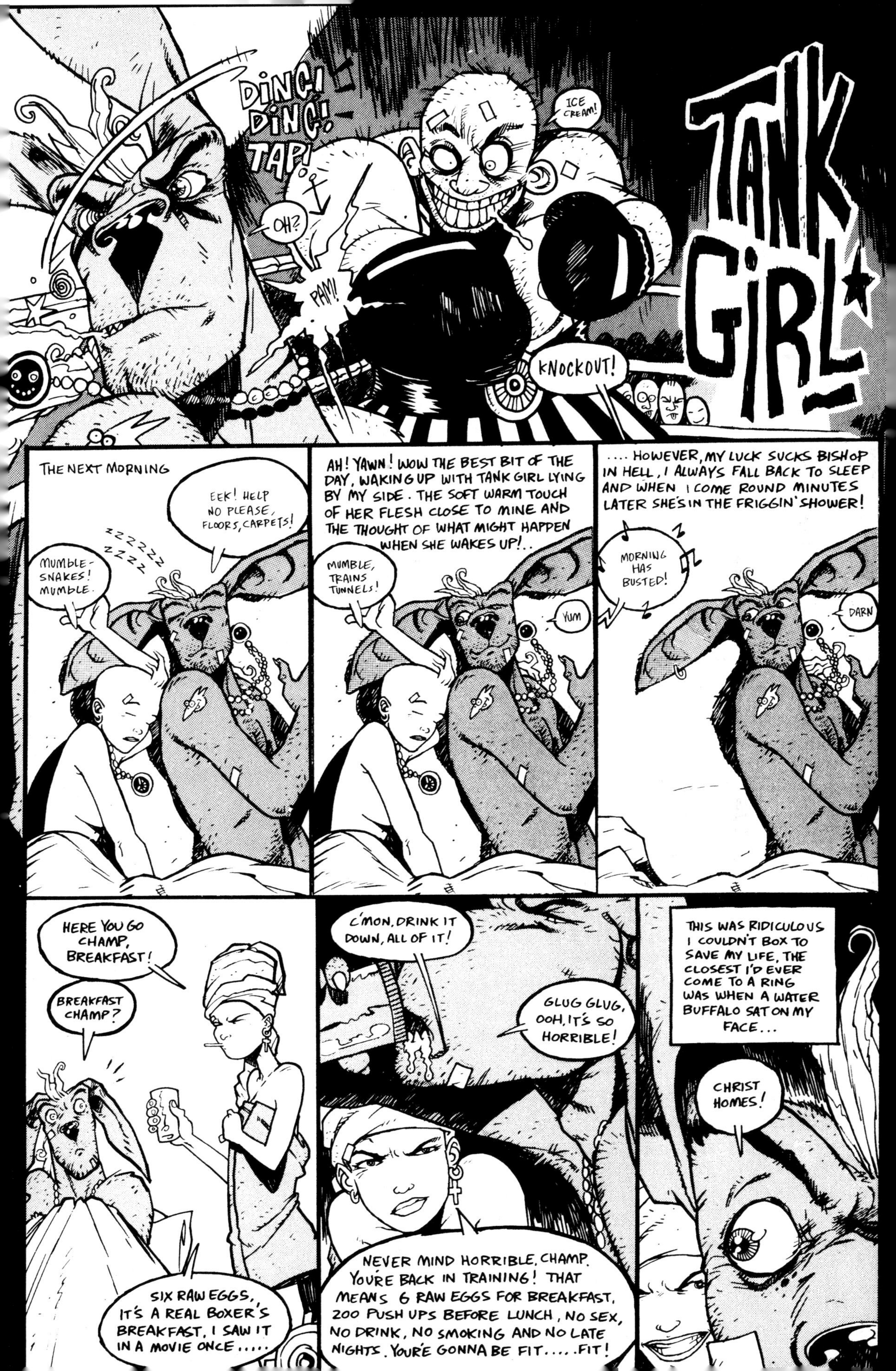
DING! DING! TAP!
OH?
ICE CREAM!
TANK GIRL
PAM!
KNOCKOUT!
THE NEXT MORNING
EEK! HELP NO PLEASE, FLOORS, CARPETS!
ZZZZZZ ZZZZ
MUMBLE-SNAKES! MUMBLE.
AH! YAWN! WOW THE BEST BIT OF THE DAY, WAKING UP WITH TANK GIRL LYING BY MY SIDE. THE SOFT WARM TOUCH OF HER FLESH CLOSE TO MINE AND THE THOUGHT OF WHAT MIGHT HAPPEN WHEN SHE WAKES UP!..
MUMBLE, TRAINS TUNNELS!
YUM
.... HOWEVER, MY LUCK SUCKS BISHOP IN HELL, I ALWAYS FALL BACK TO SLEEP AND WHEN I COME ROUND MINUTES LATER SHE'S IN THE FRIGGIN' SHOWER!
MORNING HAS BUSTED!
DARN
HERE YOU GO CHAMP, BREAKFAST!
BREAKFAST CHAMP?
SIX RAW EGGS, IT'S A REAL BOXER'S BREAKFAST. I SAW IT IN A MOVIE ONCE.....
C'MON, DRINK IT DOWN, ALL OF IT!
GLUG GLUG, OOH, IT'S SO HORRIBLE!
NEVER MIND HORRIBLE, CHAMP. YOU'RE BACK IN TRAINING! THAT MEANS 6 RAW EGGS FOR BREAKFAST, 200 PUSH UPS BEFORE LUNCH, NO SEX, NO DRINK, NO SMOKING AND NO LATE NIGHTS. YOU'RE GONNA BE FIT.....FIT!
THIS WAS RIDICULOUS I COULDN'T BOX TO SAVE MY LIFE, THE CLOSEST I'D EVER COME TO A RING WAS WHEN A WATER BUFFALO SAT ON MY FACE...
CHRIST HOMES!

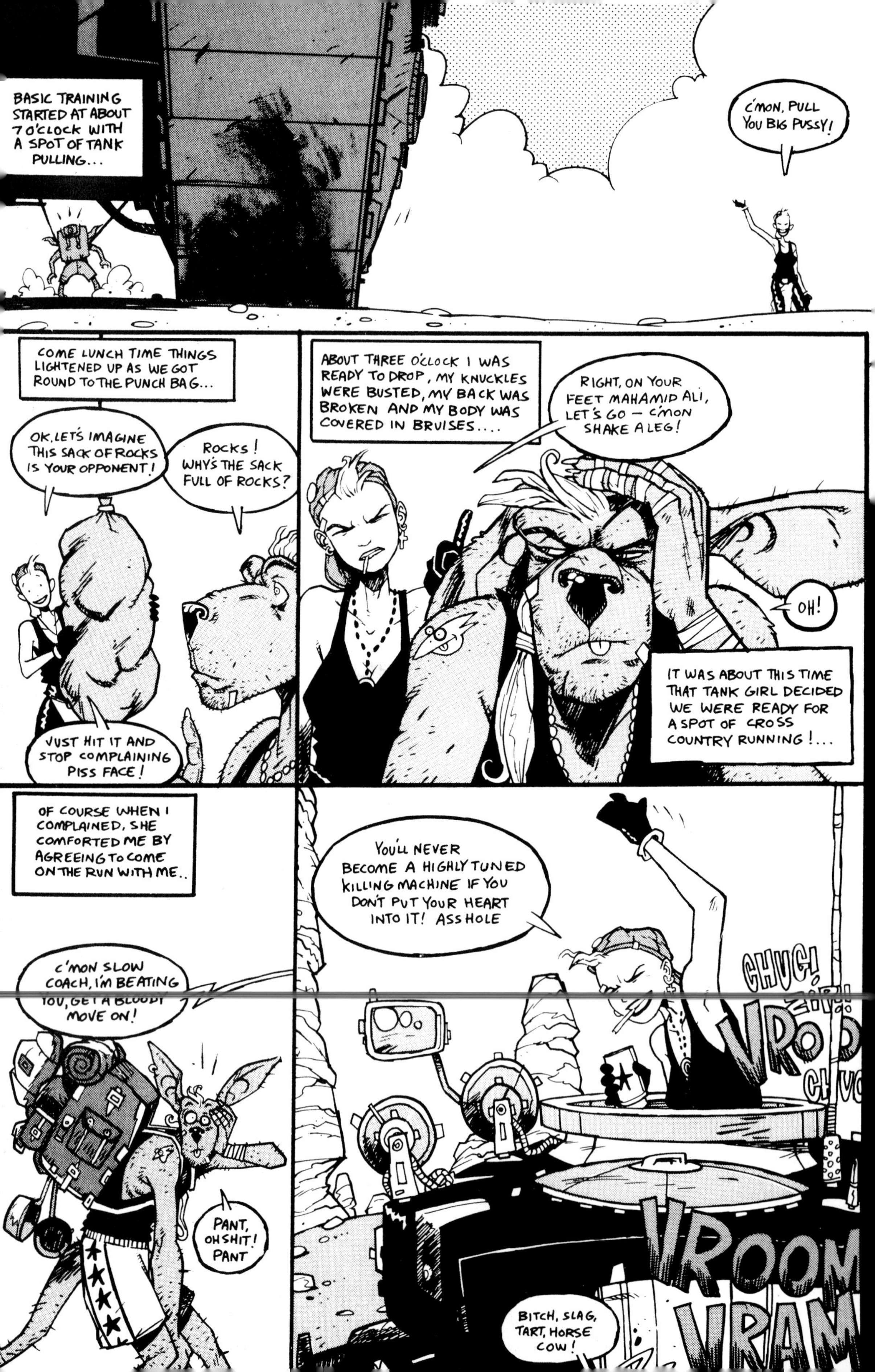
BASIC TRAINING STARTED AT ABOUT 7 O'CLOCK WITH A SPOT OF TANK PULLING...
C'MON, PULL YOU BIG PUSSY!
COME LUNCH TIME THINGS LIGHTENED UP AS WE GOT ROUND TO THE PUNCH BAG...
OK, LET'S IMAGINE THIS SACK OF ROCKS IS YOUR OPPONENT!
ROCKS! WHY'S THE SACK FULL OF ROCKS?
JUST HIT IT AND STOP COMPLAINING PISS FACE!
ABOUT THREE O'CLOCK I WAS READY TO DROP, MY KNUCKLES WERE BUSTED, MY BACK WAS BROKEN AND MY BODY WAS COVERED IN BRUISES....
RIGHT, ON YOUR FEET MAHAMID ALI, LET'S GO — C'MON SHAKE A LEG!
OH!
IT WAS ABOUT THIS TIME THAT TANK GIRL DECIDED WE WERE READY FOR A SPOT OF CROSS COUNTRY RUNNING!...
OF COURSE WHEN I COMPLAINED, SHE COMFORTED ME BY AGREEING TO COME ON THE RUN WITH ME..
C'MON SLOW COACH, I'M BEATING YOU, GET A BLOODY MOVE ON!
PANT, OH SHIT! PANT
YOU'LL NEVER BECOME A HIGHLY TUNED KILLING MACHINE IF YOU DON'T PUT YOUR HEART INTO IT! ASSHOLE
CHUG!
VROO
VROOM
VRAM
BITCH, SLAG, TART, HORSE COW!

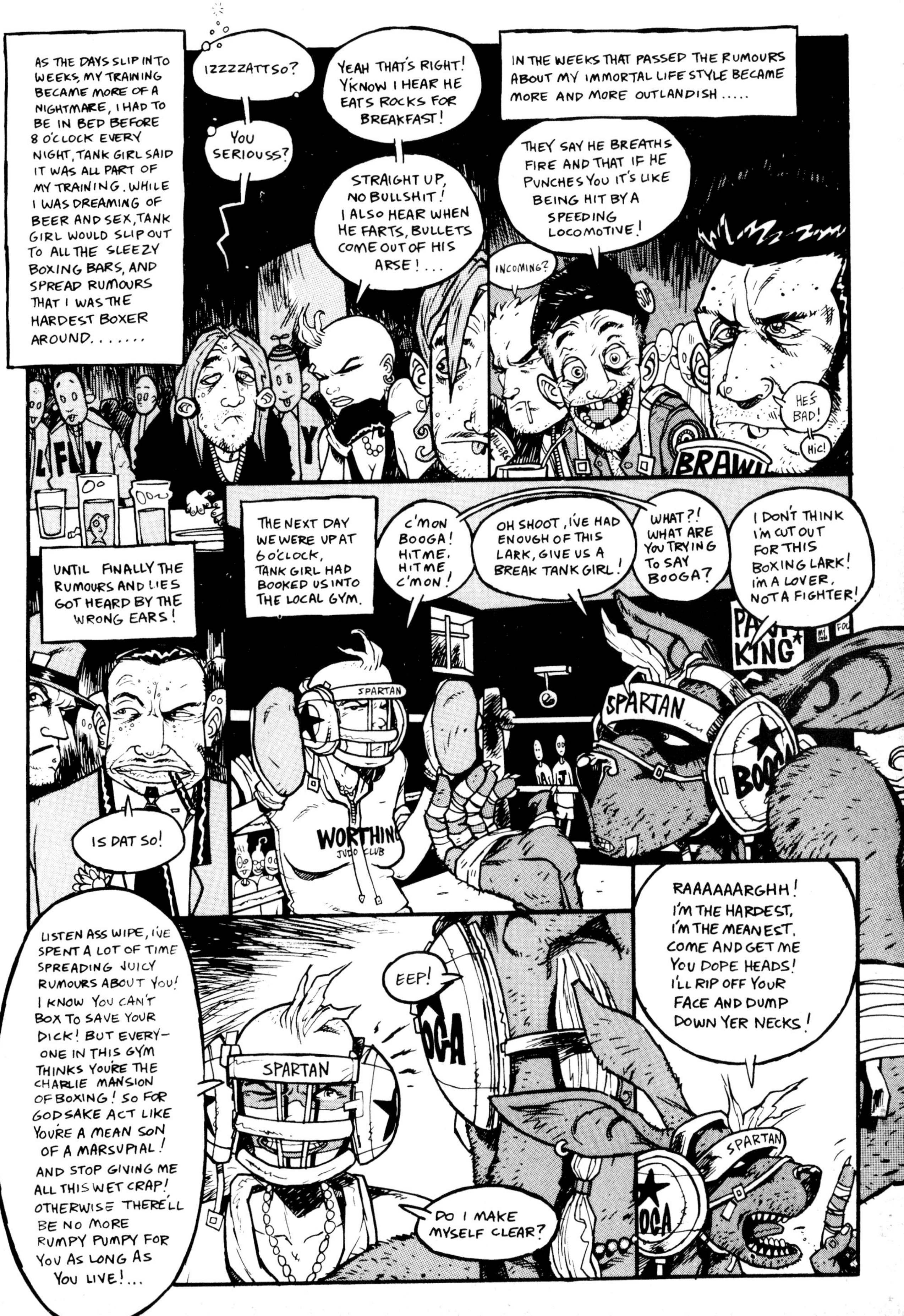

AS THE DAYS SLIP INTO WEEKS, MY TRAINING BECAME MORE OF A NIGHTMARE, I HAD TO BE IN BED BEFORE 8 O'CLOCK EVERY NIGHT, TANK GIRL SAID IT WAS ALL PART OF MY TRAINING. WHILE I WAS DREAMING OF BEER AND SEX, TANK GIRL WOULD SLIP OUT TO ALL THE SLEEZY BOXING BARS, AND SPREAD RUMOURS THAT I WAS THE HARDEST BOXER AROUND.......
IZZZZATTSO?
YEAH THAT'S RIGHT! Y'KNOW I HEAR HE EATS ROCKS FOR BREAKFAST!
YOU SERIOUSS?
STRAIGHT UP, NO BULLSHIT! I ALSO HEAR WHEN HE FARTS, BULLETS COME OUT OF HIS ARSE!...
IN THE WEEKS THAT PASSED THE RUMOURS ABOUT MY IMMORTAL LIFE STYLE BECAME MORE AND MORE OUTLANDISH.....
THEY SAY HE BREATHS FIRE AND THAT IF HE PUNCHES YOU IT'S LIKE BEING HIT BY A SPEEDING LOCOMOTIVE!
INCOMING?
HE'S BAD!
HIC!
BRAWL
UNTIL FINALLY THE RUMOURS AND LIES GOT HEARD BY THE WRONG EARS!
IS DAT SO!
THE NEXT DAY WE WERE UP AT 6 O'CLOCK, TANK GIRL HAD BOOKED US INTO THE LOCAL GYM.
C'MON BOOGA! HIT ME. HIT ME, C'MON!
OH SHOOT, I'VE HAD ENOUGH OF THIS LARK, GIVE US A BREAK TANK GIRL!
WHAT?! WHAT ARE YOU TRYING TO SAY BOOGA?
I DON'T THINK I'M CUT OUT FOR THIS BOXING LARK! I'M A LOVER, NOT A FIGHTER!
KING
SPARTAN
WORTHING JUDO CLUB
SPARTAN
BOOGA
LISTEN ASS WIPE, I'VE SPENT A LOT OF TIME SPREADING JUICY RUMOURS ABOUT YOU! I KNOW YOU CAN'T BOX TO SAVE YOUR DICK! BUT EVERYONE IN THIS GYM THINKS YOU'RE THE CHARLIE MANSION OF BOXING! SO FOR GODSAKE ACT LIKE YOU'RE A MEAN SON OF A MARSUPIAL! AND STOP GIVING ME ALL THIS WET CRAP! OTHERWISE THERE'LL BE NO MORE RUMPY PUMPY FOR YOU AS LONG AS YOU LIVE!...
EEP!
SPARTAN
DO I MAKE MYSELF CLEAR?
RAAAAAARGHH! I'M THE HARDEST, I'M THE MEANEST, COME AND GET ME YOU DOPE HEADS! I'LL RIP OFF YOUR FACE AND DUMP DOWN YER NECKS!
SPARTAN

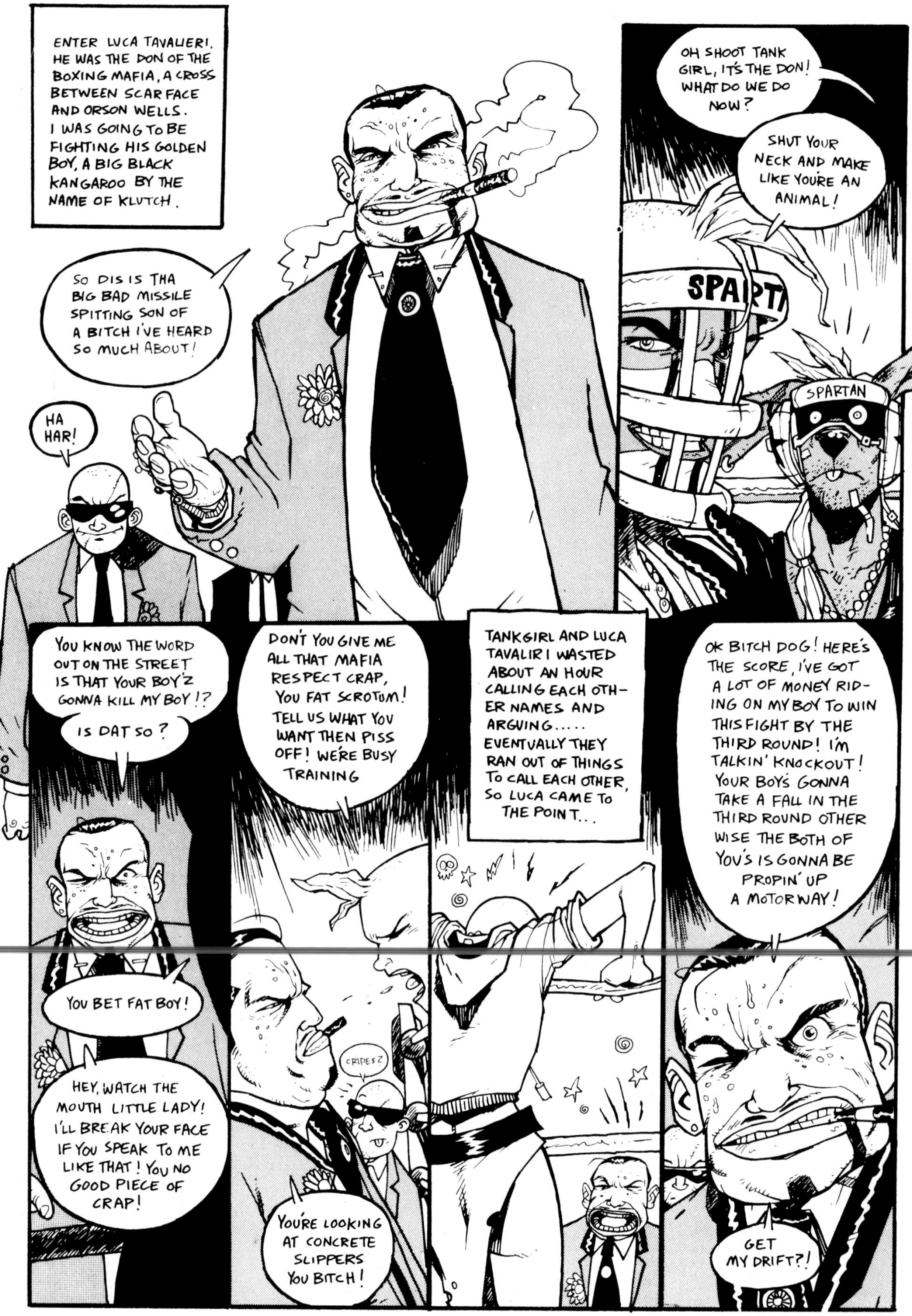
ENTER LUCA TAVALIERI. HE WAS THE DON OF THE BOXING MAFIA, A CROSS BETWEEN SCARFACE AND ORSON WELLS. I WAS GOING TO BE FIGHTING HIS GOLDEN BOY, A BIG BLACK KANGAROO BY THE NAME OF KLUTCH.
SO DIS IS THA BIG BAD MISSILE SPITTING SON OF A BITCH I'VE HEARD SO MUCH ABOUT!
HA HAR!
OH SHOOT TANK GIRL, IT'S THE DON! WHAT DO WE DO NOW?
SHUT YOUR NECK AND MAKE LIKE YOU'RE AN ANIMAL!
SPARTAN
SPARTAN
YOU KNOW THE WORD OUT ON THE STREET IS THAT YOUR BOY'Z GONNA KILL MY BOY!?
IS DAT SO?
YOU BET FAT BOY!
HEY, WATCH THE MOUTH LITTLE LADY! I'LL BREAK YOUR FACE IF YOU SPEAK TO ME LIKE THAT! YOU NO GOOD PIECE OF CRAP!
DON'T YOU GIVE ME ALL THAT MAFIA RESPECT CRAP, YOU FAT SCROTUM! TELL US WHAT YOU WANT THEN PISS OFF! WE'RE BUSY TRAINING
CRIPES!
YOU'RE LOOKING AT CONCRETE SLIPPERS YOU BITCH!
TANKGIRL AND LUCA TAVALIRI WASTED ABOUT AN HOUR CALLING EACH OTHER NAMES AND ARGUING..... EVENTUALLY THEY RAN OUT OF THINGS TO CALL EACH OTHER, SO LUCA CAME TO THE POINT...
OK BITCH DOG! HERE'S THE SCORE, I'VE GOT A LOT OF MONEY RIDING ON MY BOY TO WIN THIS FIGHT BY THE THIRD ROUND! I'M TALKIN' KNOCKOUT! YOUR BOY'S GONNA TAKE A FALL IN THE THIRD ROUND OTHERWISE THE BOTH OF YOU'S IS GONNA BE PROPIN' UP A MOTORWAY!
GET MY DRIFT?!

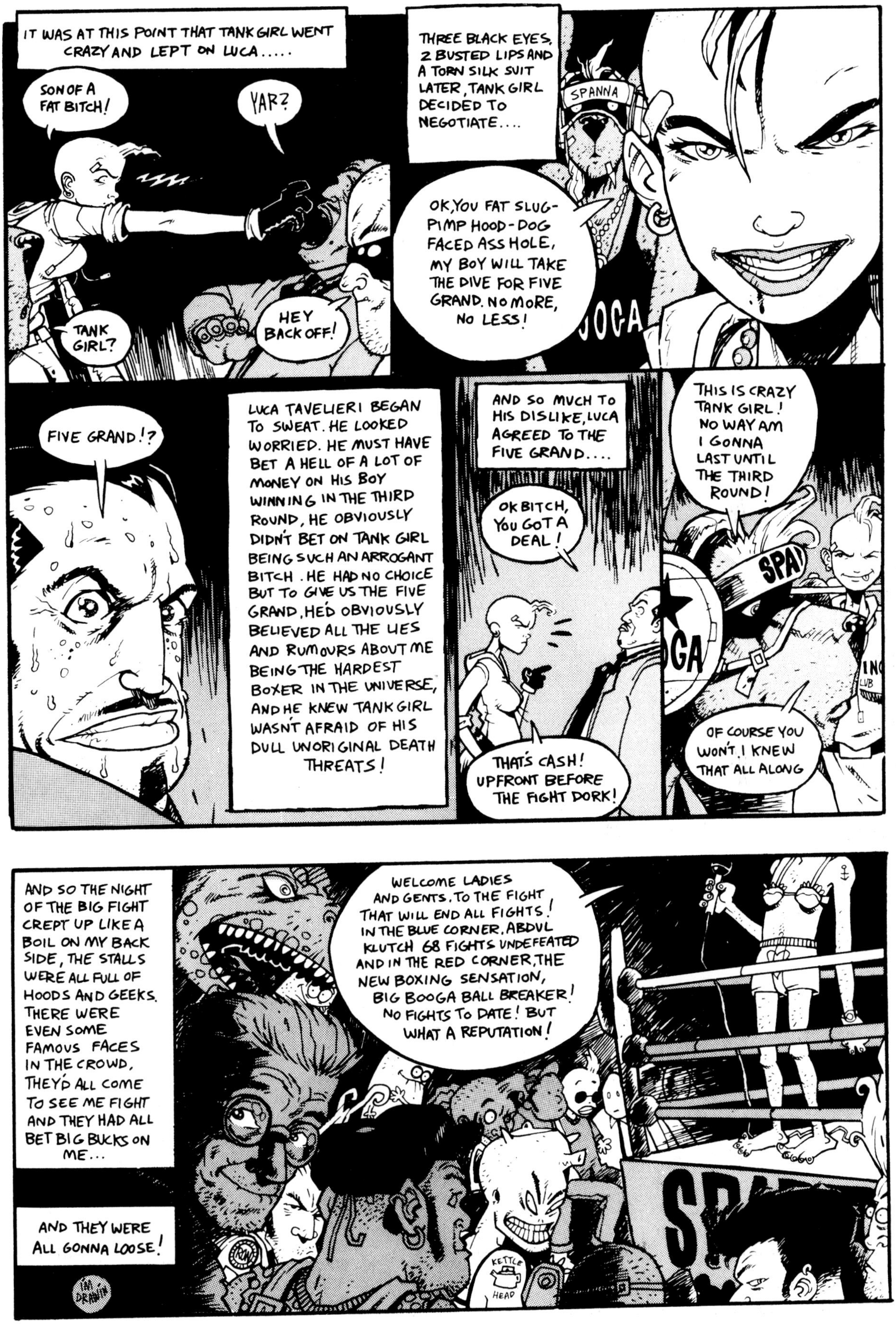
IT WAS AT THIS POINT THAT TANK GIRL WENT CRAZY AND LEPT ON LUCA.....
SON OF A FAT BITCH!
YAR?
TANK GIRL?
HEY BACK OFF!
THREE BLACK EYES, 2 BUSTED LIPS AND A TORN SILK SUIT LATER, TANK GIRL DECIDED TO NEGOTIATE....
SPANNA
OK, YOU FAT SLUG-PIMP HOOD-DOG FACED ASS HOLE, MY BOY WILL TAKE THE DIVE FOR FIVE GRAND. NO MORE, NO LESS!
FIVE GRAND!?
LUCA TAVELIERI BEGAN TO SWEAT. HE LOOKED WORRIED. HE MUST HAVE BET A HELL OF A LOT OF MONEY ON HIS BOY WINNING IN THE THIRD ROUND, HE OBVIOUSLY DIDN'T BET ON TANK GIRL BEING SUCH AN ARROGANT BITCH. HE HAD NO CHOICE BUT TO GIVE US THE FIVE GRAND, HE'D OBVIOUSLY BELIEVED ALL THE LIES AND RUMOURS ABOUT ME BEING THE HARDEST BOXER IN THE UNIVERSE, AND HE KNEW TANK GIRL WASN'T AFRAID OF HIS DULL UNORIGINAL DEATH THREATS!
AND SO MUCH TO HIS DISLIKE, LUCA AGREED TO THE FIVE GRAND....
OK BITCH, YOU GOT A DEAL!
THAT'S CASH! UPFRONT BEFORE THE FIGHT DORK!
THIS IS CRAZY TANK GIRL! NO WAY AM I GONNA LAST UNTIL THE THIRD ROUND!
OF COURSE YOU WON'T, I KNEW THAT ALL ALONG
AND SO THE NIGHT OF THE BIG FIGHT CREPT UP LIKE A BOIL ON MY BACK SIDE, THE STALLS WERE ALL FULL OF HOODS AND GEEKS. THERE WERE EVEN SOME FAMOUS FACES IN THE CROWD, THEY'D ALL COME TO SEE ME FIGHT AND THEY HAD ALL BET BIG BUCKS ON ME...
WELCOME LADIES AND GENTS, TO THE FIGHT THAT WILL END ALL FIGHTS! IN THE BLUE CORNER, ABDUL KLUTCH 68 FIGHTS UNDEFEATED AND IN THE RED CORNER, THE NEW BOXING SENSATION, BIG BOOGA BALL BREAKER! NO FIGHTS TO DATE! BUT WHAT A REPUTATION!
KETTLE HEAD
AND THEY WERE ALL GONNA LOOSE!

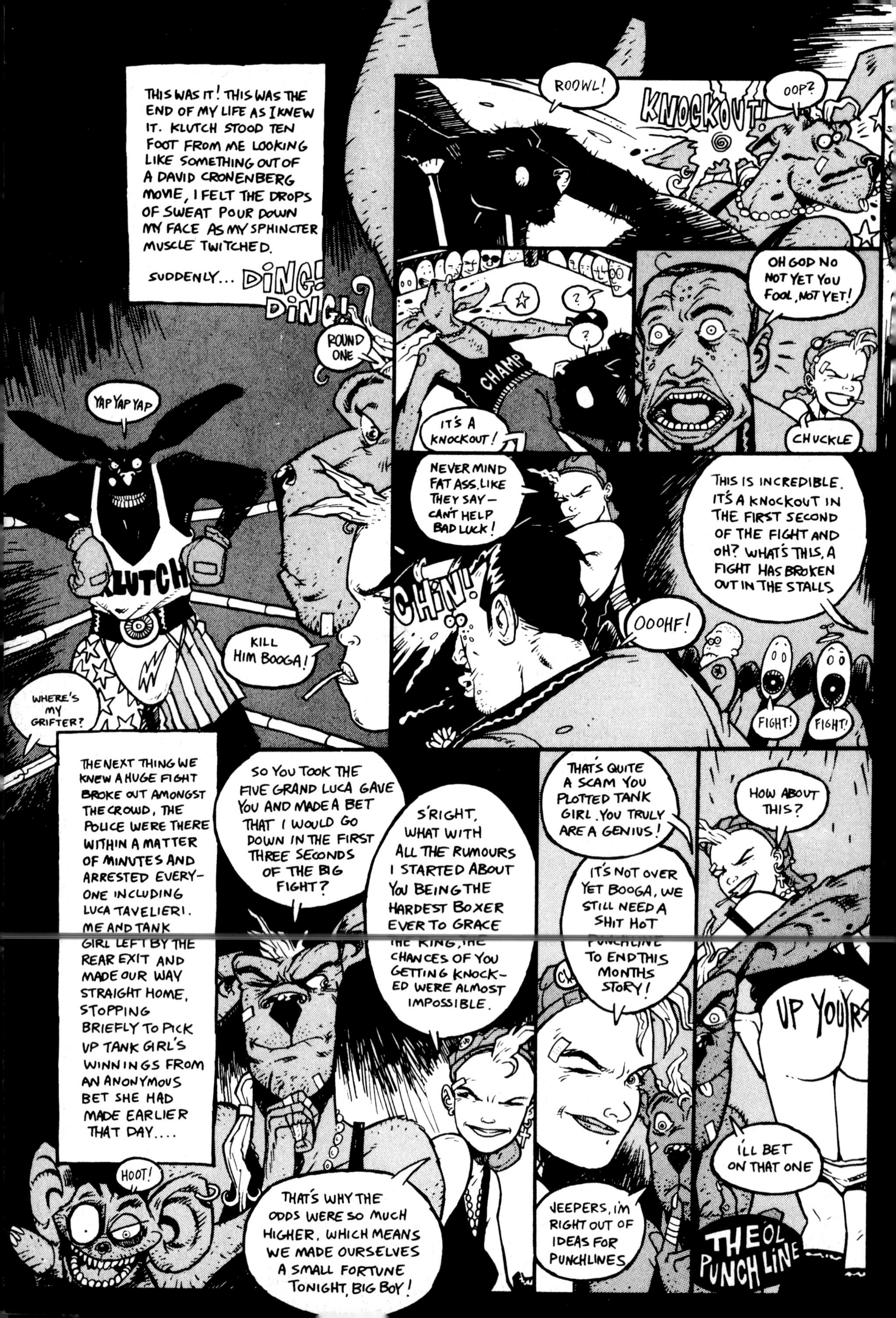
THIS WAS IT! THIS WAS THE END OF MY LIFE AS I KNEW IT. KLUTCH STOOD TEN FOOT FROM ME LOOKING LIKE SOMETHING OUT OF A DAVID CRONENBERG MOVIE, I FELT THE DROPS OF SWEAT POUR DOWN MY FACE AS MY SPHINCTER MUSCLE TWITCHED.
SUDDENLY... DING! DING!
ROUND ONE
YAP YAP YAP
KLUTCH
KILL HIM BOOGA!
WHERE'S MY GRIFTER?
ROOWL!
KNOCKOUT!
OOP?
CHAMP
IT'S A KNOCKOUT!
OH GOD NO NOT YET YOU FOOL, NOT YET!
CHUCKLE
NEVER MIND FAT ASS. LIKE THEY SAY— CAN'T HELP BAD LUCK!
CHIN!
OOOHF!
THIS IS INCREDIBLE. IT'S A KNOCKOUT IN THE FIRST SECOND OF THE FIGHT AND OH? WHAT'S THIS, A FIGHT HAS BROKEN OUT IN THE STALLS
FIGHT!
FIGHT!
THE NEXT THING WE KNEW A HUGE FIGHT BROKE OUT AMONGST THE CROWD, THE POLICE WERE THERE WITHIN A MATTER OF MINUTES AND ARRESTED EVERY-ONE INCLUDING LUCA TAVELIERI. ME AND TANK GIRL LEFT BY THE REAR EXIT AND MADE OUR WAY STRAIGHT HOME, STOPPING BRIEFLY TO PICK UP TANK GIRL'S WINNINGS FROM AN ANONYMOUS BET SHE HAD MADE EARLIER THAT DAY....
HOOT!
SO YOU TOOK THE FIVE GRAND LUCA GAVE YOU AND MADE A BET THAT I WOULD GO DOWN IN THE FIRST THREE SECONDS OF THE BIG FIGHT?
S'RIGHT, WHAT WITH ALL THE RUMOURS I STARTED ABOUT YOU BEING THE HARDEST BOXER EVER TO GRACE THE RING, THE CHANCES OF YOU GETTING KNOCK-ED WERE ALMOST IMPOSSIBLE.
THAT'S WHY THE ODDS WERE SO MUCH HIGHER, WHICH MEANS WE MADE OURSELVES A SMALL FORTUNE TONIGHT, BIG BOY!
THAT'S QUITE A SCAM YOU PLOTTED TANK GIRL. YOU TRULY ARE A GENIUS!
IT'S NOT OVER YET BOOGA, WE STILL NEED A SHIT HOT PUNCHLINE TO END THIS MONTHS STORY!
JEEPERS, I'M RIGHT OUT OF IDEAS FOR PUNCHLINES
HOW ABOUT THIS?
UP YOURS
I'LL BET ON THAT ONE
THE OL PUNCH LINE

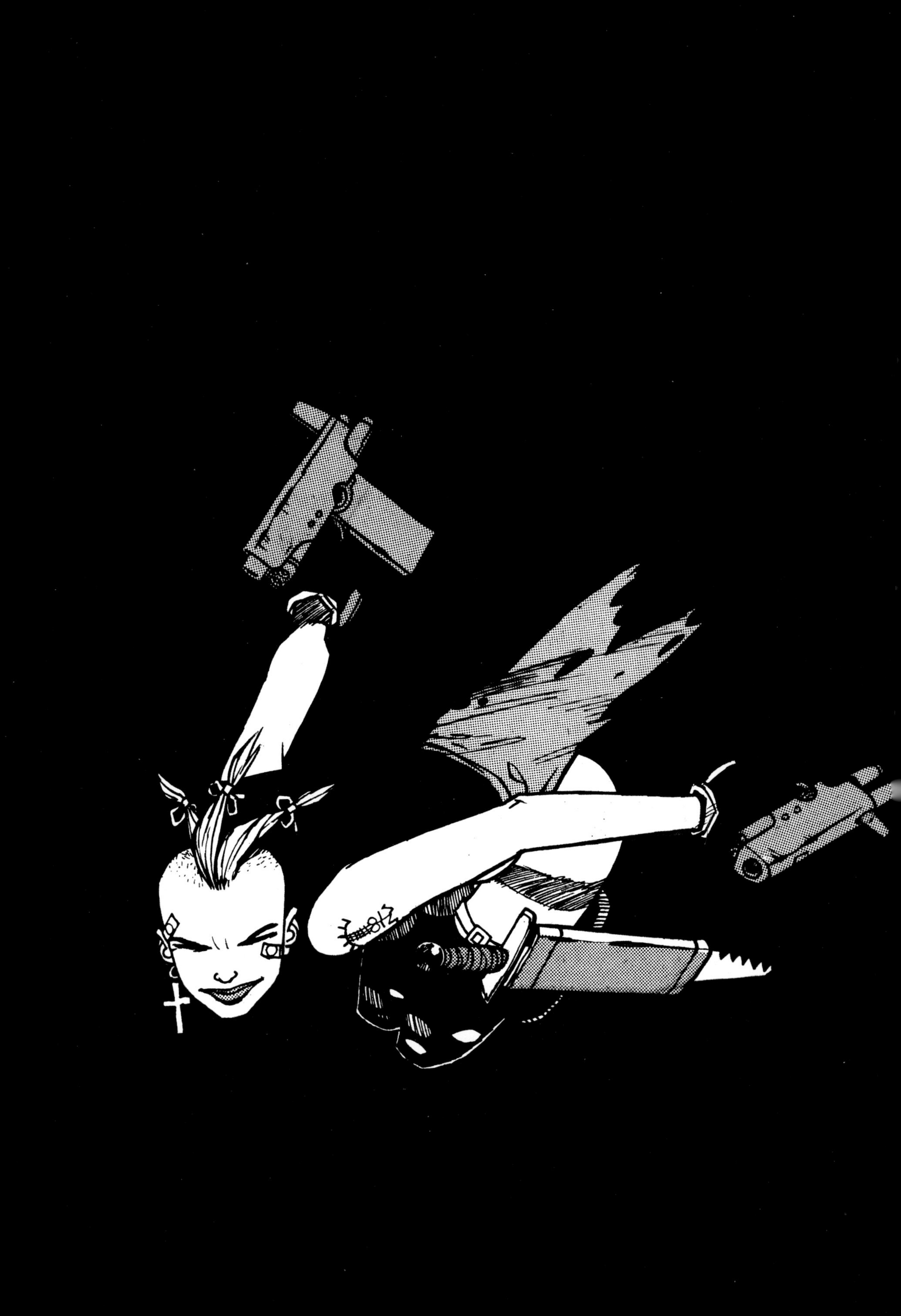

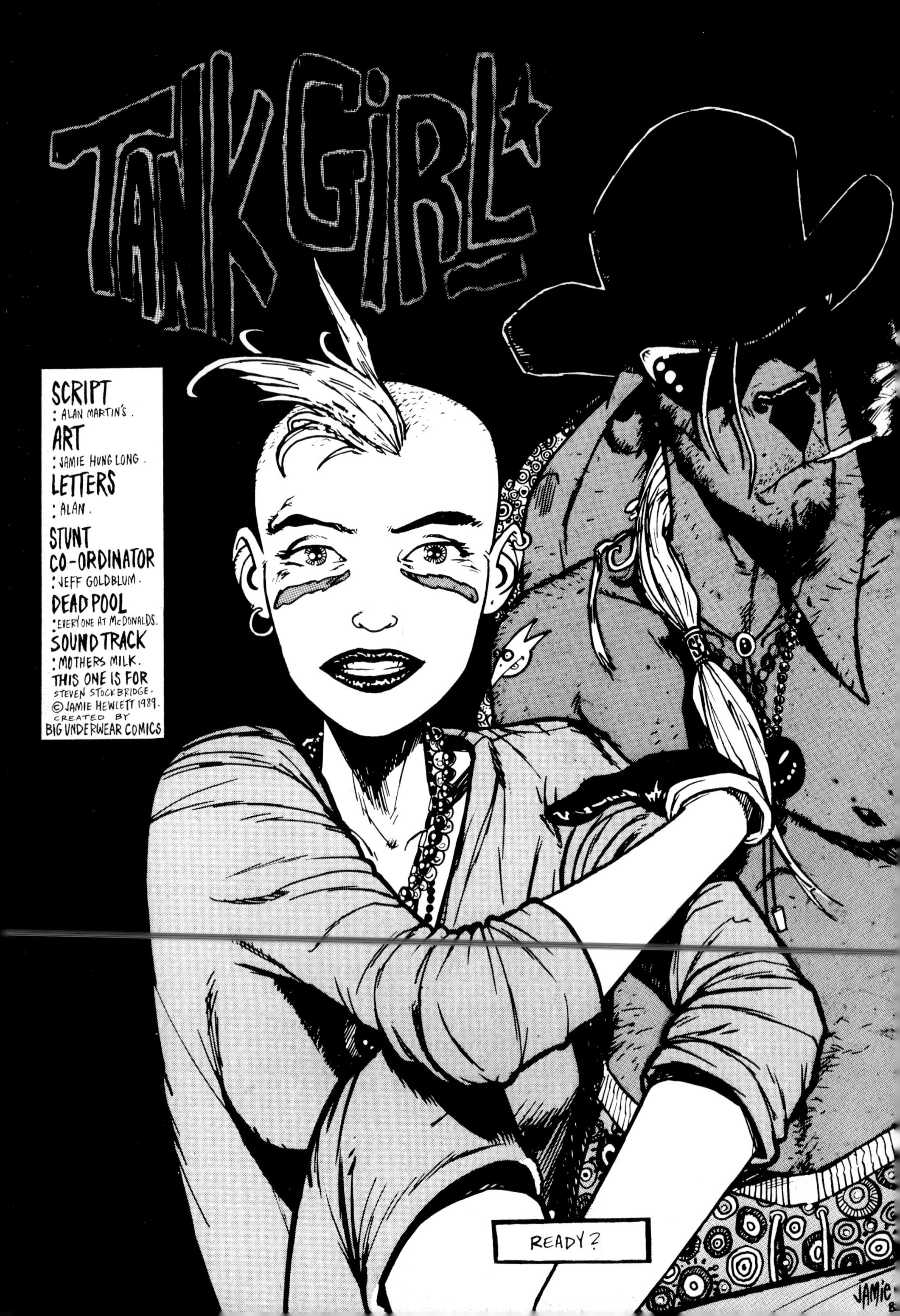
TANK GIRL
SCRIPT
: ALAN MARTIN'S.
ART
: JAMIE HUNG LONG.
LETTERS
: ALAN.
STUNT CO-ORDINATOR
: JEFF GOLDBLUM.
DEAD POOL
: EVERYONE AT McDONALDS.
SOUND TRACK
: MOTHERS MILK.
THIS ONE IS FOR
STEVEN STOCKBRIDGE.
© JAMIE HEWLETT 1989.
CREATED BY
BIG UNDERWEAR COMICS
READY?
JAMIE

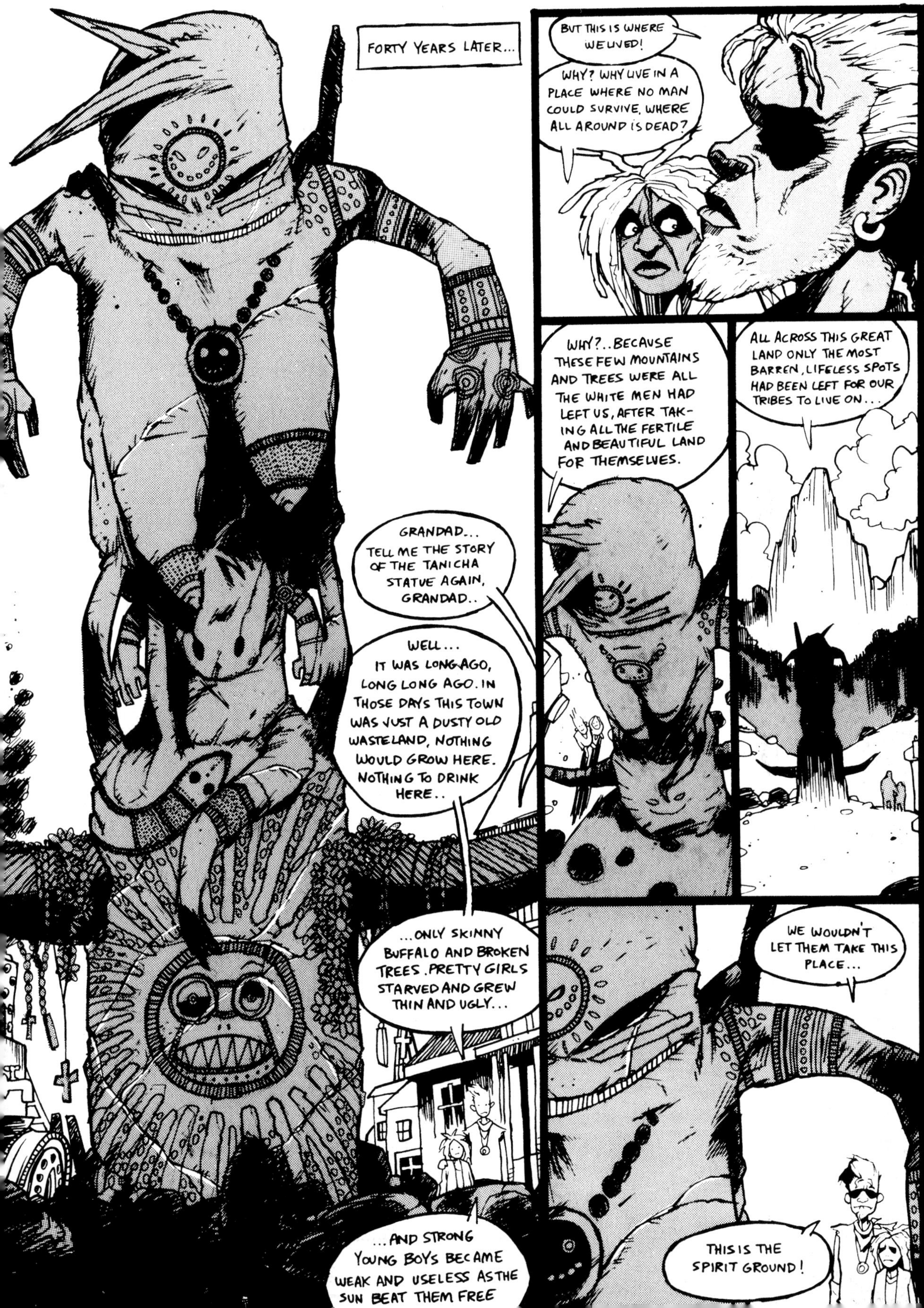
FORTY YEARS LATER...
BUT THIS IS WHERE WE LIVED!
WHY? WHY LIVE IN A PLACE WHERE NO MAN COULD SURVIVE, WHERE ALL AROUND IS DEAD?
WHY?.. BECAUSE THESE FEW MOUNTAINS AND TREES WERE ALL THE WHITE MEN HAD LEFT US, AFTER TAKING ALL THE FERTILE AND BEAUTIFUL LAND FOR THEMSELVES.
ALL ACROSS THIS GREAT LAND ONLY THE MOST BARREN, LIFELESS SPOTS HAD BEEN LEFT FOR OUR TRIBES TO LIVE ON...
GRANDAD... TELL ME THE STORY OF THE TANICHA STATUE AGAIN, GRANDAD..
WELL... IT WAS LONG AGO, LONG LONG AGO. IN THOSE DAYS THIS TOWN WAS JUST A DUSTY OLD WASTELAND, NOTHING WOULD GROW HERE. NOTHING TO DRINK HERE..
...ONLY SKINNY BUFFALO AND BROKEN TREES. PRETTY GIRLS STARVED AND GREW THIN AND UGLY...
...AND STRONG YOUNG BOYS BECAME WEAK AND USELESS AS THE SUN BEAT THEM FREE
WE WOULDN'T LET THEM TAKE THIS PLACE...
THIS IS THE SPIRIT GROUND!

MISSION SEEMED IMPOSSIBLE, WE HAD TO SAVE THE SHOW!

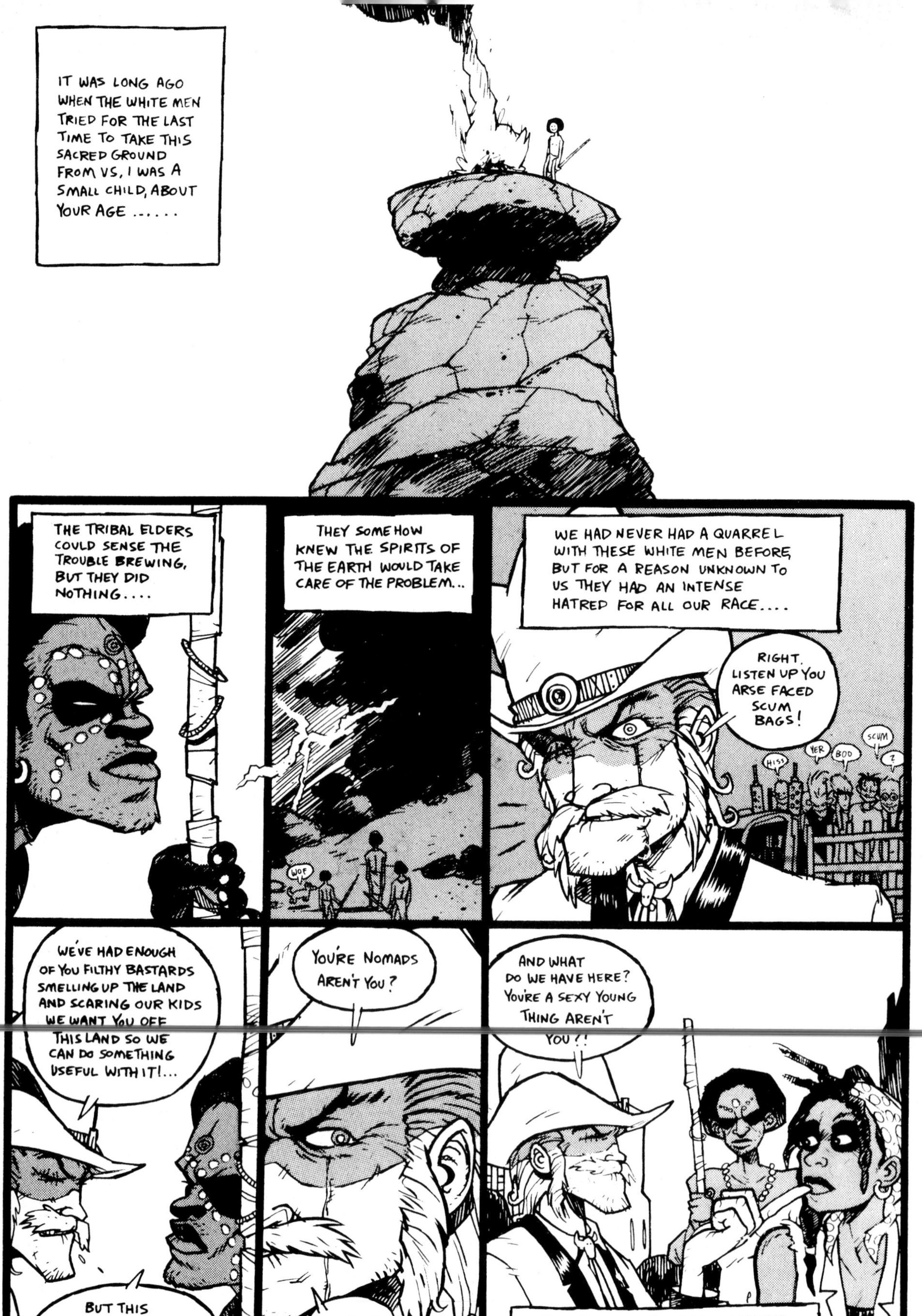
IT WAS LONG AGO WHEN THE WHITE MEN TRIED FOR THE LAST TIME TO TAKE THIS SACRED GROUND FROM US, I WAS A SMALL CHILD, ABOUT YOUR AGE ......
THE TRIBAL ELDERS COULD SENSE THE TROUBLE BREWING, BUT THEY DID NOTHING....
THEY SOMEHOW KNEW THE SPIRITS OF THE EARTH WOULD TAKE CARE OF THE PROBLEM...
WOF
WE HAD NEVER HAD A QUARREL WITH THESE WHITE MEN BEFORE, BUT FOR A REASON UNKNOWN TO US THEY HAD AN INTENSE HATRED FOR ALL OUR RACE....
RIGHT. LISTEN UP YOU ARSE FACED SCUM BAGS!
HISS
YER
BOO
SCUM
?
WE'VE HAD ENOUGH OF YOU FILTHY BASTARDS SMELLING UP THE LAND AND SCARING OUR KIDS WE WANT YOU OFF THIS LAND SO WE CAN DO SOMETHING USEFUL WITH IT!...
BUT THIS IS THE ONLY LAND WE HAVE LEFT, WHERE WILL WE GO?
YOU'RE NOMADS AREN'T YOU?
SO JUST PISS OFF!
AND WHAT DO WE HAVE HERE? YOU'RE A SEXY YOUNG THING AREN'T YOU?!
THE FATHER OF THESE MEN SEEMED TO TAKE A SHINE TO MY ELDER SISTER...

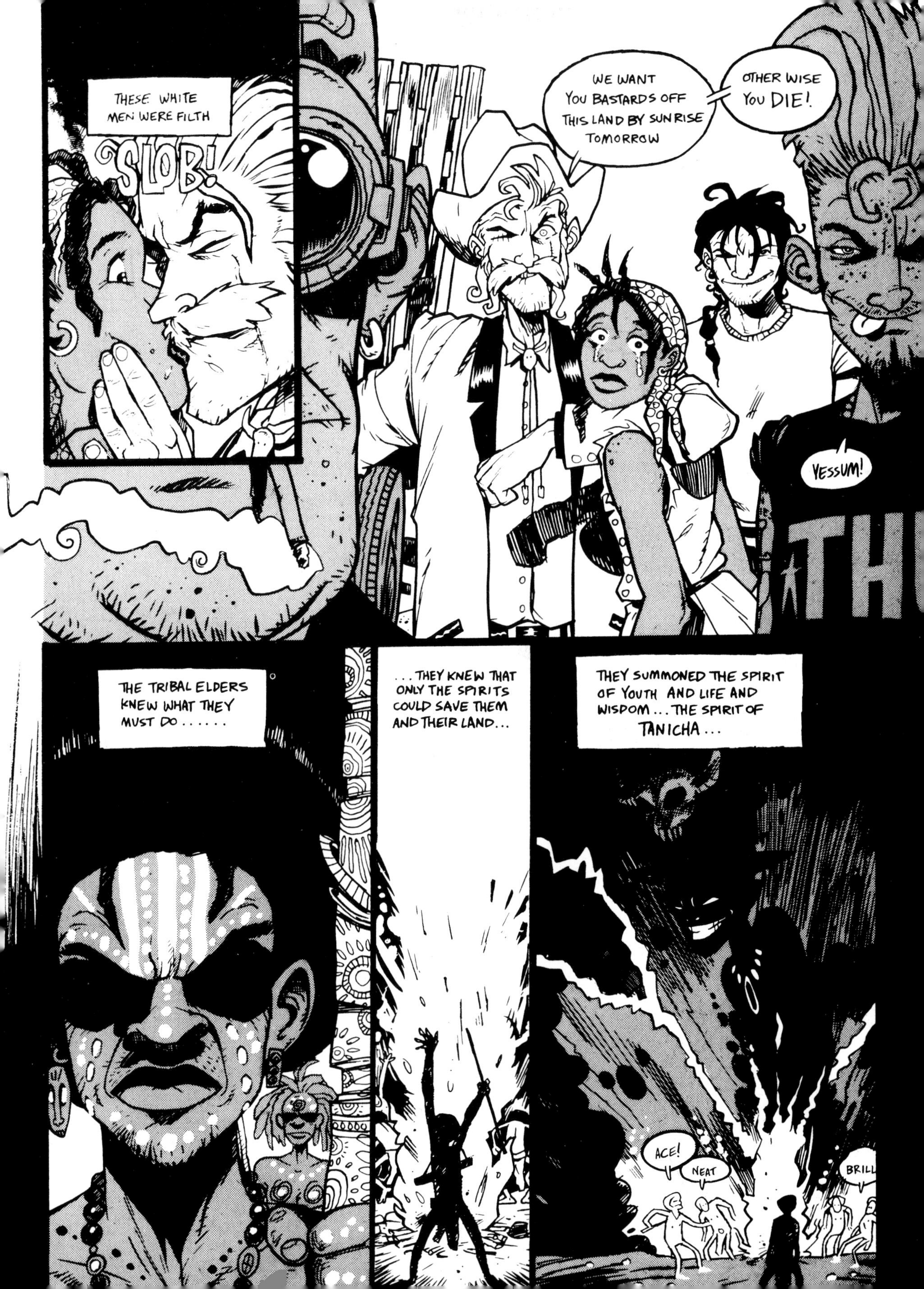

THESE WHITE MEN WERE FILTH
SLOB!
WE WANT YOU BASTARDS OFF THIS LAND BY SUNRISE TOMORROW
OTHER WISE YOU DIE!
YESSUM!
THU
THE TRIBAL ELDERS KNEW WHAT THEY MUST DO......
...THEY KNEW THAT ONLY THE SPIRITS COULD SAVE THEM AND THEIR LAND...
THEY SUMMONED THE SPIRIT OF YOUTH AND LIFE AND WISDOM... THE SPIRIT OF TANICHA...
ACE!
NEAT
BRILL

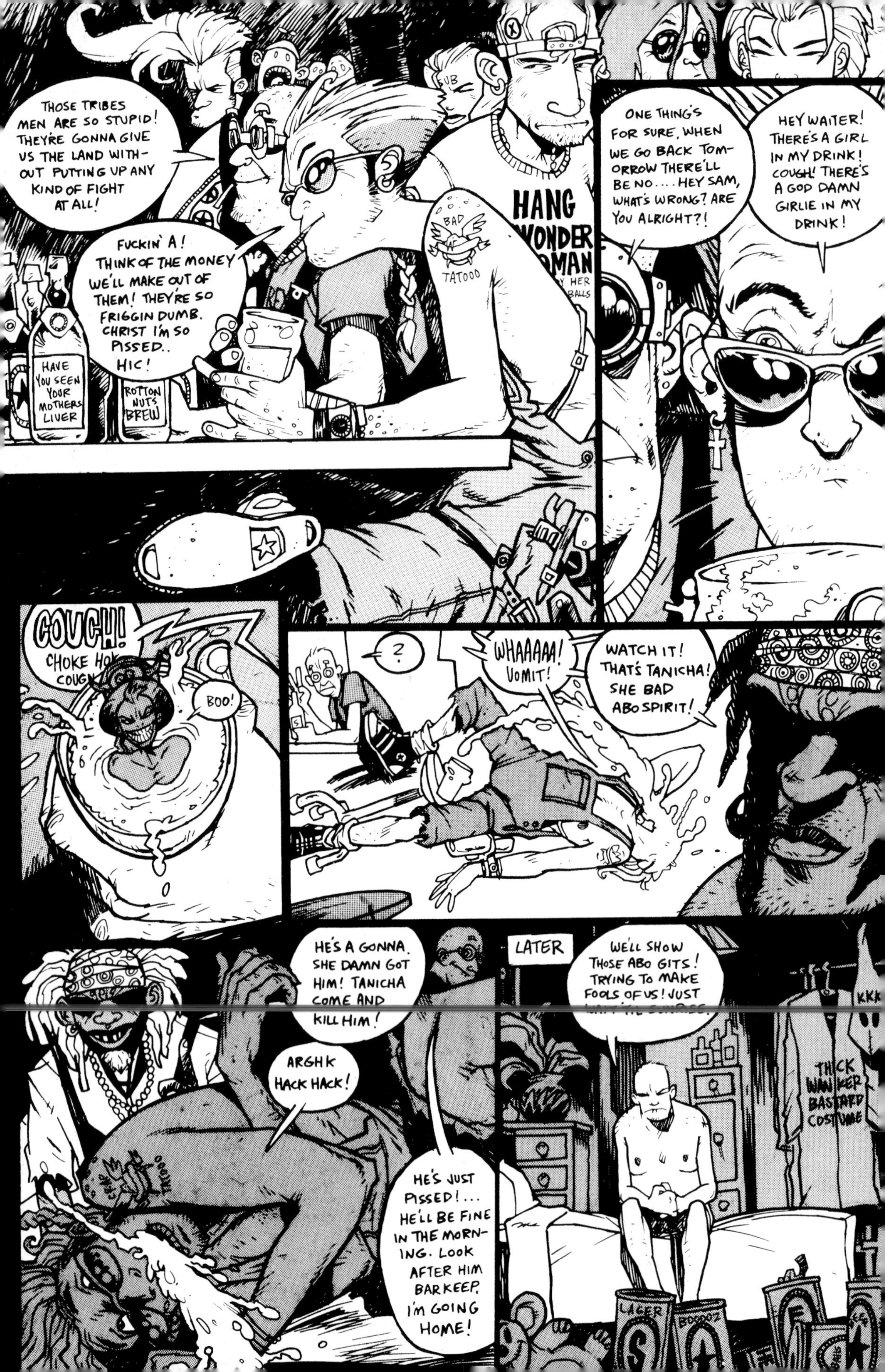
THOSE TRIBES MEN ARE SO STUPID! THEY'RE GONNA GIVE US THE LAND WITH-OUT PUTTING UP ANY KIND OF FIGHT AT ALL!
FUCKIN' A! THINK OF THE MONEY WE'LL MAKE OUT OF THEM! THEY'RE SO FRIGGIN DUMB. CHRIST I'M SO PISSED.. HIC!
HAVE YOU SEEN YOUR MOTHERS LIVER
ROTTON NUTS BREW
SUB
BAD TATOOO
HANG
ONE THING'S FOR SURE, WHEN WE GO BACK TOM-ORROW THERE'LL BE NO.... HEY SAM, WHAT'S WRONG? ARE YOU ALRIGHT?!
HEY WAITER! THERE'S A GIRL IN MY DRINK! COUGH! THERE'S A GOD DAMN GIRLIE IN MY DRINK!
COUGH!
CHOKE
BOO!
?
WHAAAAA! VOMIT!
WATCH IT! THAT'S TANICHA! SHE BAD ABO SPIRIT!
HE'S A GONNA. SHE DAMN GOT HIM! TANICHA COME AND KILL HIM!
ARGHK HACK HACK!
HE'S JUST PISSED!... HE'LL BE FINE IN THE MORN-ING. LOOK AFTER HIM BARKEEP, I'M GOING HOME!
LATER
WE'LL SHOW THOSE ABO GITS! TRYING TO MAKE FOOLS OF US! JUST
KKK
THICK WANKER BASTARD COSTUME

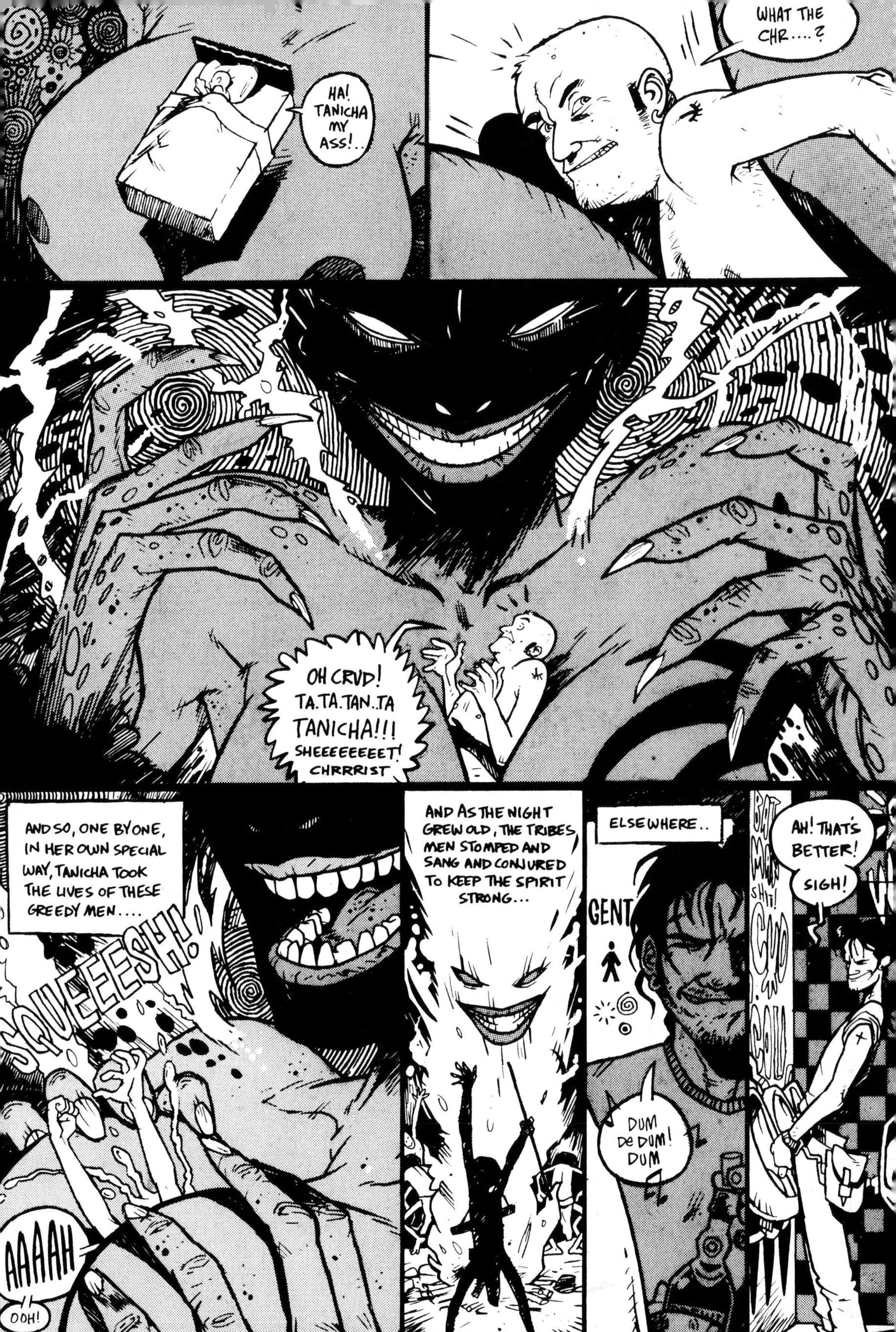

HA! TANICHA MY ASS!..
WHAT THE CHR....?
OH CRUD! TA.TA.TAN..TA TANICHA!!! SHEEEEEEEET! CHRRRIST
AND SO, ONE BY ONE, IN HER OWN SPECIAL WAY, TANICHA TOOK THE LIVES OF THESE GREEDY MEN....
SQUEEESH!
AAAAH
OOH!
AND AS THE NIGHT GREW OLD, THE TRIBES MEN STOMPED AND SANG AND CONJURED TO KEEP THE SPIRIT STRONG...
ELSEWHERE..
GENT
DUM DE DUM! DUM
AH! THAT'S BETTER!
SIGH!

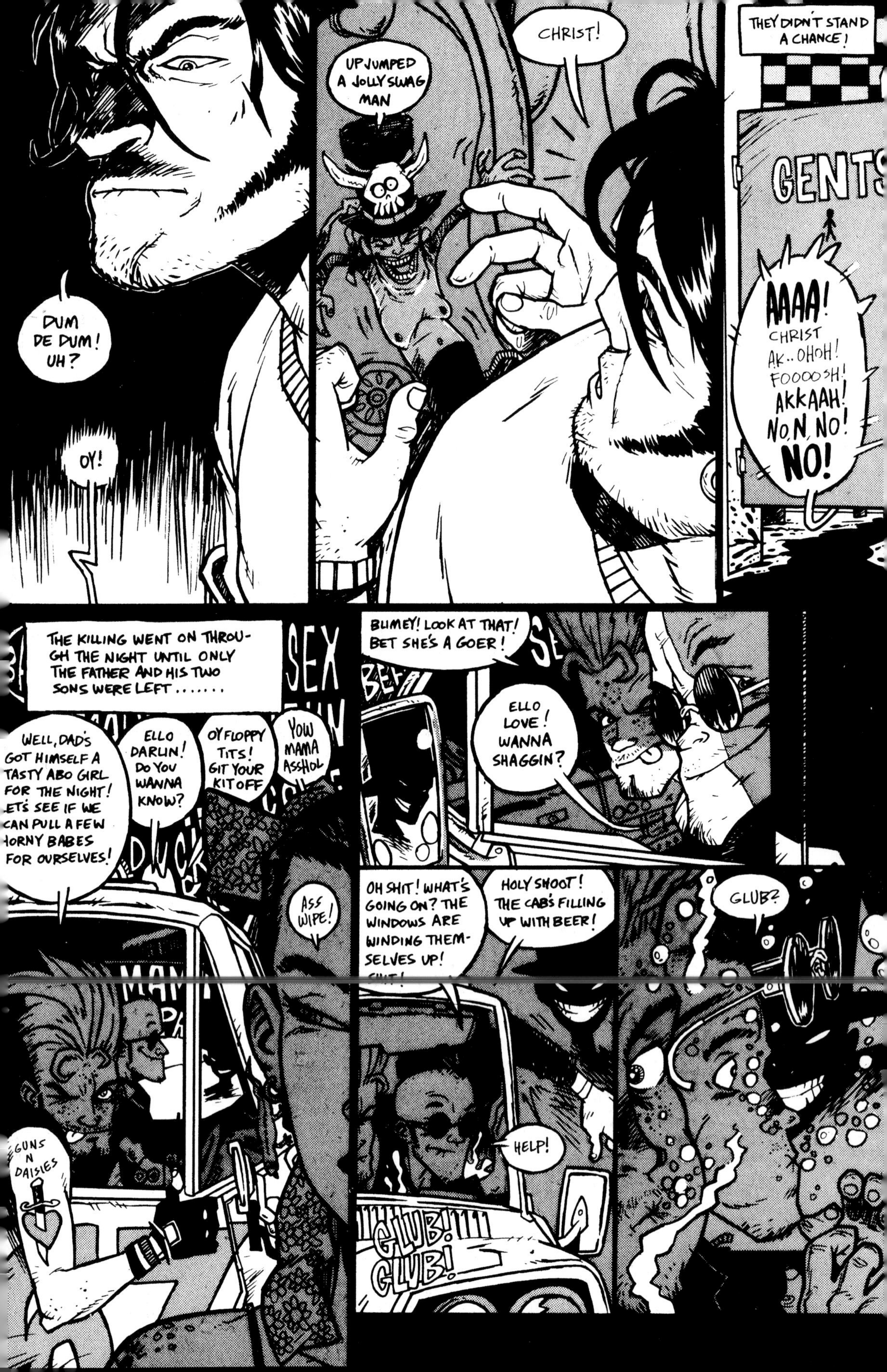
DUM DE DUM! UH?
OY!
UP JUMPED A JOLLY SWAG MAN
CHRIST!
THEY DIDN'T STAND A CHANCE!
GENTS
AAAA! CHRIST AK..OHOH! FOOOOSH! AKKAAH! NO,N, NO! NO!
THE KILLING WENT ON THROUGH THE NIGHT UNTIL ONLY THE FATHER AND HIS TWO SONS WERE LEFT.......
SEX
WELL, DAD'S GOT HIMSELF A TASTY ABO GIRL FOR THE NIGHT! ETS SEE IF WE CAN PULL A FEW ORNY BABES FOR OURSELVES!
ELLO DARLIN! DO YOU WANNA KNOW?
OY FLOPPY TITS! GIT YOUR KIT OFF
YOW MAMA ASSHOL
ASS WIPE!
BLIMEY! LOOK AT THAT! BET SHE'S A GOER!
ELLO LOVE! WANNA SHAGGIN?
OH SHIT! WHAT'S GOING ON? THE WINDOWS ARE WINDING THEMSELVES UP!
HOLY SHOOT! THE CAB'S FILLING UP WITH BEER!
GLUB?
GUNS N DAISIES
HELP!
GLUB! GLUB!

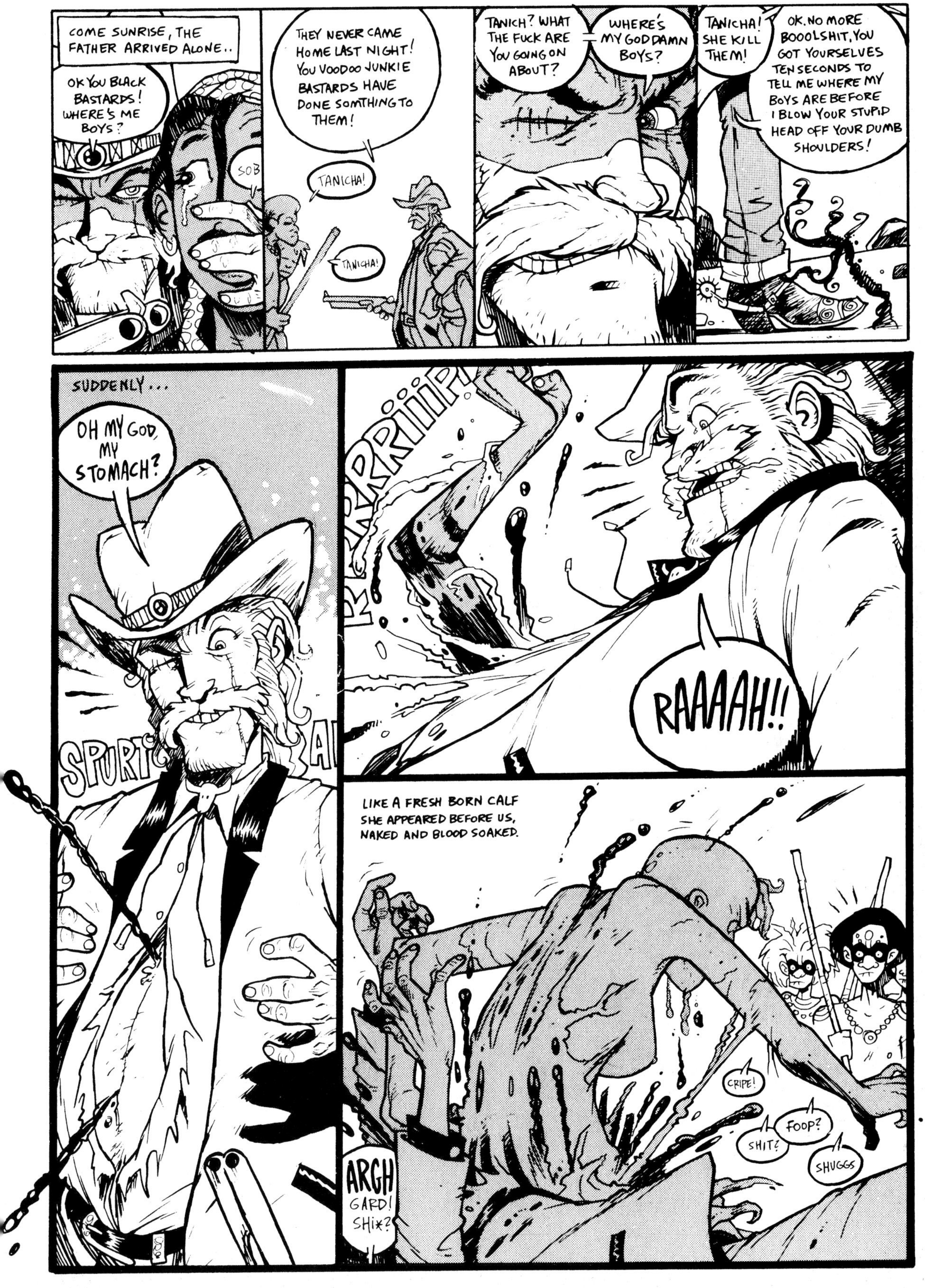
COME SUNRISE, THE FATHER ARRIVED ALONE..
OK YOU BLACK BASTARDS! WHERE'S ME BOYS?
SOB
THEY NEVER CAME HOME LAST NIGHT! YOU VOODOO JUNKIE BASTARDS HAVE DONE SOMTHING TO THEM!
TANICHA!
TANICHA!
TANICH? WHAT THE FUCK ARE YOU GOING ON ABOUT?
WHERE'S MY GODDAMN BOYS?
TANICHA! SHE KILL THEM!
OK. NO MORE BOOOLSHIT, YOU GOT YOURSELVES TEN SECONDS TO TELL ME WHERE MY BOYS ARE BEFORE I BLOW YOUR STUPID HEAD OFF YOUR DUMB SHOULDERS!
SUDDENLY...
OH MY GOD, MY STOMACH?
SPURT
RRRRRIIIIP
RAAAAH!!
LIKE A FRESH BORN CALF SHE APPEARED BEFORE US, NAKED AND BLOOD SOAKED.
ARGH
GARD! SHI*?
CRIPE!
FOOP?
SHIT?
SHUGGS

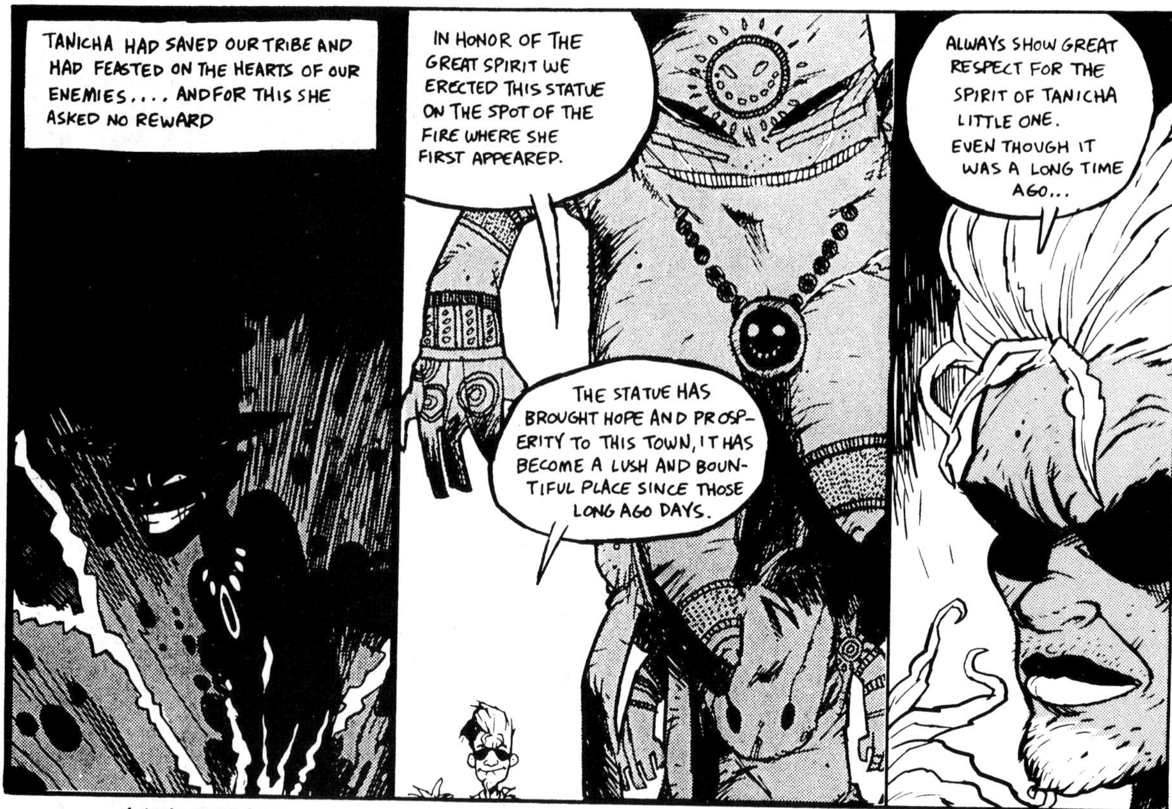
TANICHA HAD SAVED OUR TRIBE AND HAD FEASTED ON THE HEARTS OF OUR ENEMIES.... AND FOR THIS SHE ASKED NO REWARD
IN HONOR OF THE GREAT SPIRIT WE ERECTED THIS STATUE ON THE SPOT OF THE FIRE WHERE SHE FIRST APPEARED.
THE STATUE HAS BROUGHT HOPE AND PROSPERITY TO THIS TOWN, IT HAS BECOME A LUSH AND BOUNTIFUL PLACE SINCE THOSE LONG AGO DAYS.
ALWAYS SHOW GREAT RESPECT FOR THE SPIRIT OF TANICHA LITTLE ONE.
EVEN THOUGH IT WAS A LONG TIME AGO...

.... A LONG TIME AGO

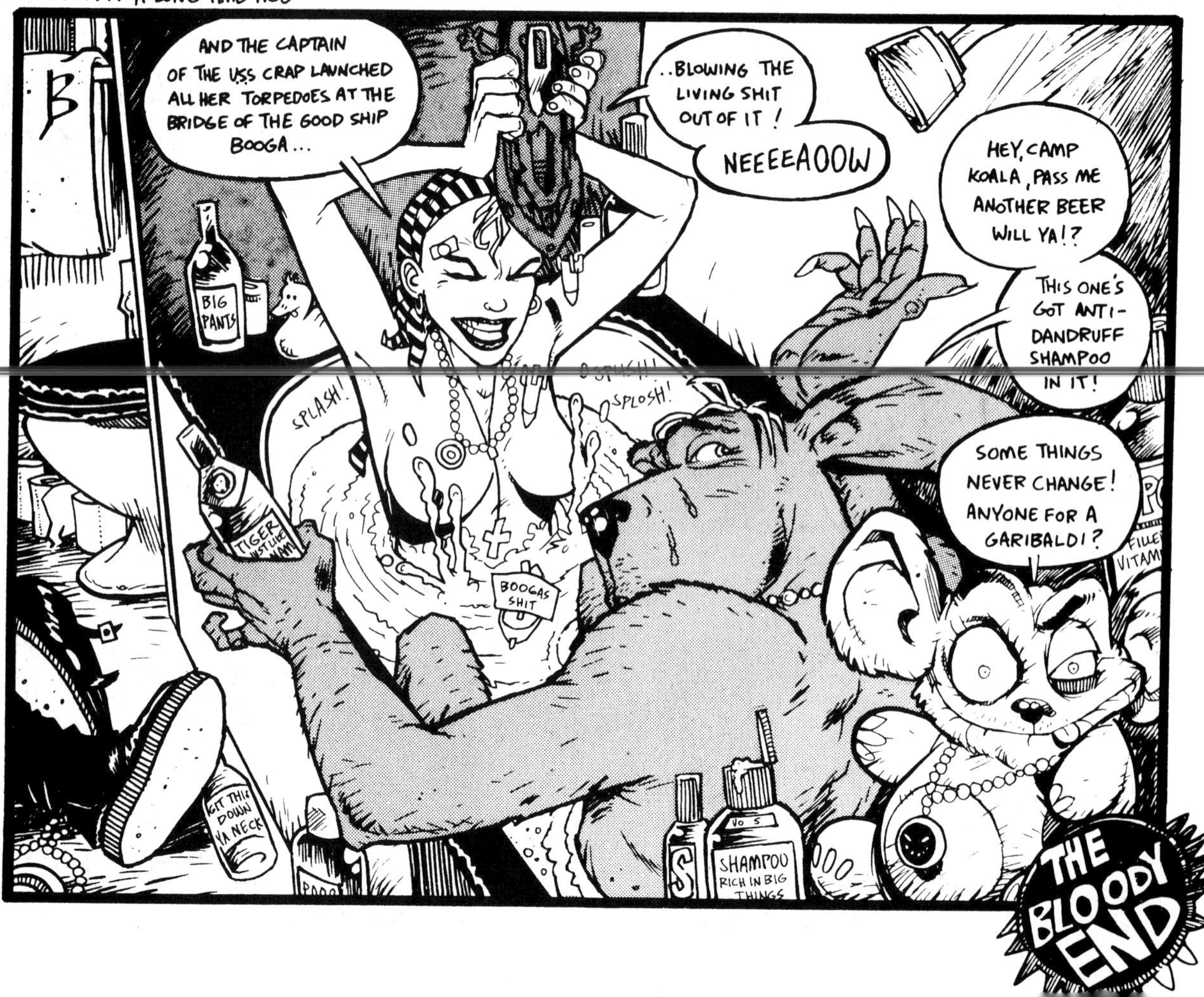
AND THE CAPTAIN OF THE U.S.S CRAP LAUNCHED ALL HER TORPEDOES AT THE BRIDGE OF THE GOOD SHIP BOOGA...
..BLOWING THE LIVING SHIT OUT OF IT!
NEEEEAOOW
HEY, CAMP KOALA, PASS ME ANOTHER BEER WILL YA!?
THIS ONE'S GOT ANTI-DANDRUFF SHAMPOO IN IT!
SOME THINGS NEVER CHANGE! ANYONE FOR A GARIBALDI?
BIG PANTS
SPLASH!
SPLOSH!
BOOGAS SHIT
GIT THIS DOWN YA NECK
SHAMPOO RICH IN BIG THINGS
THE BLOODY END

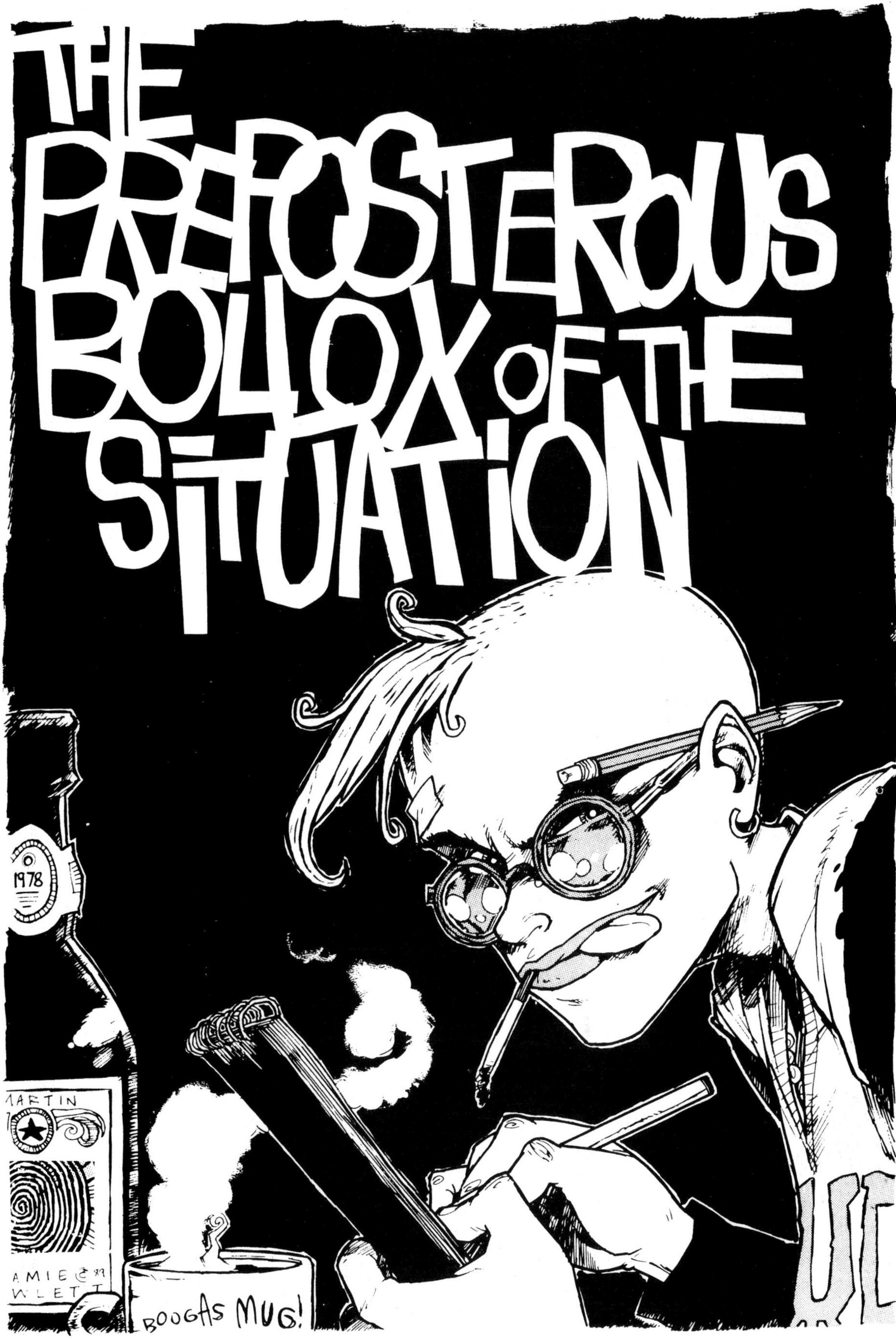
THE PREPOSTEROUS BOLLOX OF THE SITUATION
1978
MARTIN
BOOGAS MUG!

CRIPT
CRIPTIC
CRITIC

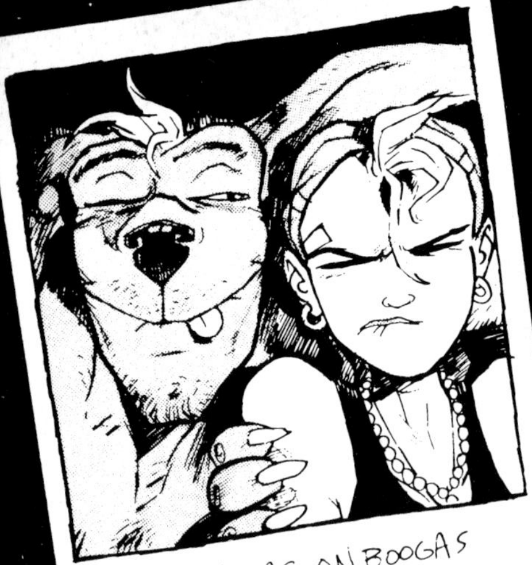

BOOGA AND ME ON BOOGAS BIRTHDAY X

DEAR MOM,

I KNOW IT'S BEEN A LONG TIME SINCE I LAST WROTE TO YOU, BUT THINGS HAVE BEEN GETTING RATHER HECTIC.

I'M ALRIGHT THOUGH. I'M TAKING REAL GOOD CARE OF MYSELF.

I'VE GOT A FEW THINGS TO TELL YOU ABOUT, SO I'LL START WITH THE GOSSIP FIRST...

I HAVEN'T SEEN MUCH OF STEVIE LATELY (YOU REMEMBER STEVIE, HE WAS THE ONE WHO DRANK ALL OF YOUR CHRISTMAS SHERRY AND CLOGGED UP THE SINK WITH PUKE), HE COMES TO VISIT EVERY NOW AND THEN. I THINK HE'S A BIT JEALOUS OF MY NEW BOYFRIEND. HE'S A KANGAROO CALLED BOOGA. HE'S REALLY CUTE BUT HE DRESSES FOR SHIT.

I THINK HE WANTS TO MARRY ME.

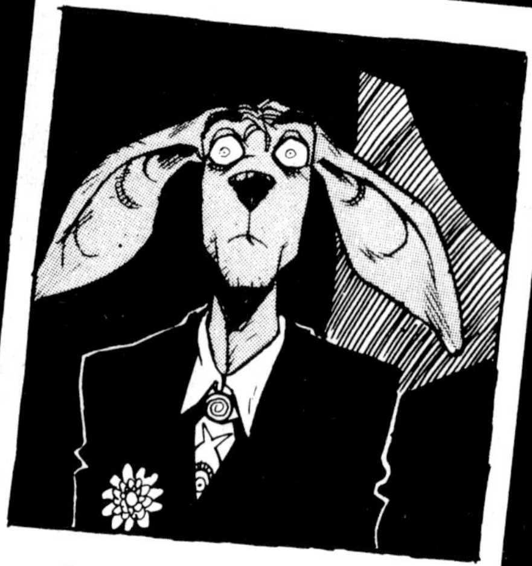

BOOGA GOES TO CHURCH!

PERVIS
peter DUNCAN

THIS IS YOU

WELL, YOU KNOW ME, I NEVER WANTED TO GET MARRIED, I ESPECIALLY DON'T WANT TO NOW, I MEAN I CAN'T. I MEAN, OH I'LL TELL YOU ABOUT THAT LATER.

Hello mum! Love BOOGA! XXX

ANYWAY, DO YOU REMEMBER THOSE TWO GIRLS WHO USED TO COME ROUND OUR HOUSE AFTER SUNDAY SCHOOL AND TRY ON YOUR UNDERWEAR? WELL THEY COME TO SEE ME QUITE A BIT. THE BORING ONE WITH BLACK HAIR FLIES A JET PLANE AND THE OTHER ONE (THE ONE YOU LIKED) DRIVES A SUBMARINE. WE'RE ALL TRYING TO GET A BASEBALL TEAM TOGETHER FOR NEXT SUMMER.

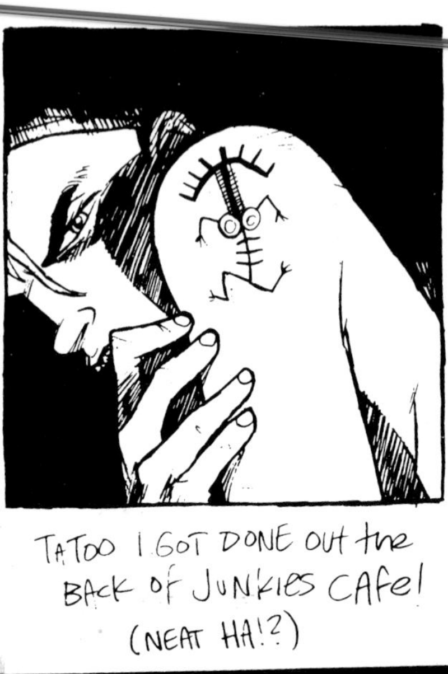

TATOO I GOT DONE out the BACK of JUNKIES CAFE! (NEAT HA!?)

DOCTOR NO

WELL, THAT'S ALL THE BORING STUFF. NOW, I'VE GOT SOME THINGS TO TELL YOU AND I DON'T WANT YOU GETTING ALL UPSET. AND I DON'T WANT

TEETH TEETH TEETH TEETH

UNDERNEATH

YOU THINKING THAT YOUR DAUGHTER HAS GONE ALL WIERD AND SHIT.

BUT— DO YOU REMEMBER WHEN I WAS A KID AND YOU TOOK ME TO THAT FORTUNE-TELLER WOMAN AND SHE SAID THAT MY NAME MEANT 'THE RULE BREAKER' AND THAT I WOULD SOMEDAY BREAK ALL THE ESTABLISHED LAWS OF LIFE?

WELL MOM, IT WAS TRUE, IT'S HAPPENING! BUT I'M NOT JUST BREAKING RULES FOR THE SAKE OF IT, THERE SEEMS TO BE A REASON FOR EVERYTHING I DO. IT'S LIKE SOME KIND OF FORCE TAKING OVER MY LIFE.

I'M NOT SCARED OF THAT.

THERE ARE SO MANY STUPID PEOPLE, SO MANY STUPID LAWS. SHIT.

WHEN I GET TO SEE YOU NEXT I'LL EXPLAIN EXACTLY WHAT I'M ON ABOUT. BUT IT'S BIG!

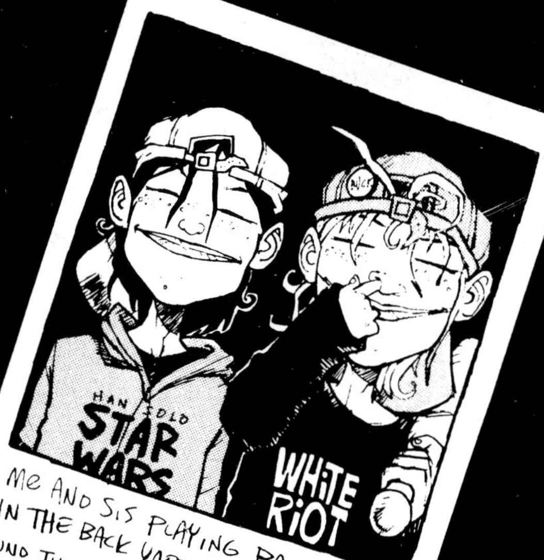

HAN SOLO
STAR WARS
WHITE RIOT

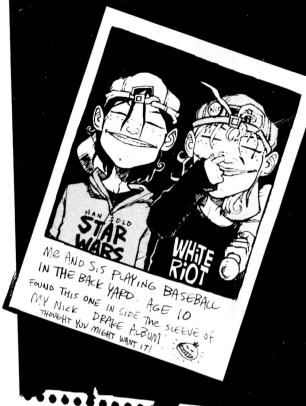

ME AND SIS PLAYING BASEBALL IN THE BACK YARD. AGE 10

FOUND THIS ONE INSIDE THE SLEEVE OF MY NICK DRAKE ALBUM! THOUGHT YOU MIGHT WANT IT!

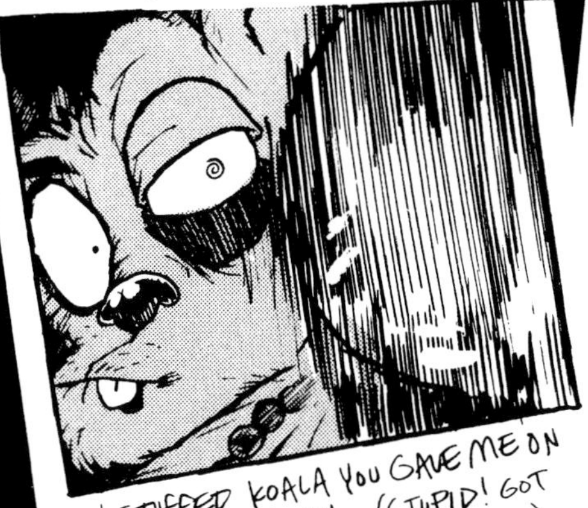

MY STUFFED KOALA YOU GAVE ME ON MY 15TH BIRTHDAY — (STUPID! GOT MY FINGER IN FRONT OF LENSE)

PERVIS PETER'S TEETH PETER DUNCAN

PEOPLE WORLD WIDE ARE LIVING A LIE. AND RUN THEIR LIVES AROUND A SYSTEM THAT IS COMPLETE BOLLOCKS.

ENCLOSED IS A SHORT NOTE THAT MUST BE GIVEN TO ONE OF MY FRIENDS IF ANYTHING SHOULD HAPPEN TO ME. THEY'LL KNOW WHAT IT MEANS.

I'D BETTER GO NOW, BEFORE BOOGA USES ALL THE SHOWER WATER. IT'S A HARD LIFE LIVING IN A TANK.

WELL, SO LONG MOM, HOPE TO SEE YOU SOON, LOVE,

YOUR DAUGHTER,

TANK GIRL XXX

P.S. THANKS FOR ALL THE WALNUTS AND TANGERINES

P.P.S. HOPE YOU LIKE ALL THE PHOTOS.

FART

KEEP THIS SAFE

A POWERFUL LAVATORY CLEANER,
THIS WILL WORK,
THE SIMPLEST EQUATION IN THE WORLD,
THIS IS HOW IT WILL BE DONE.
I HERBY STATE—
THE SIMPLEST EQUATION.
EVERY ONE ALLOWED
THIS WILL WORK. T.G.

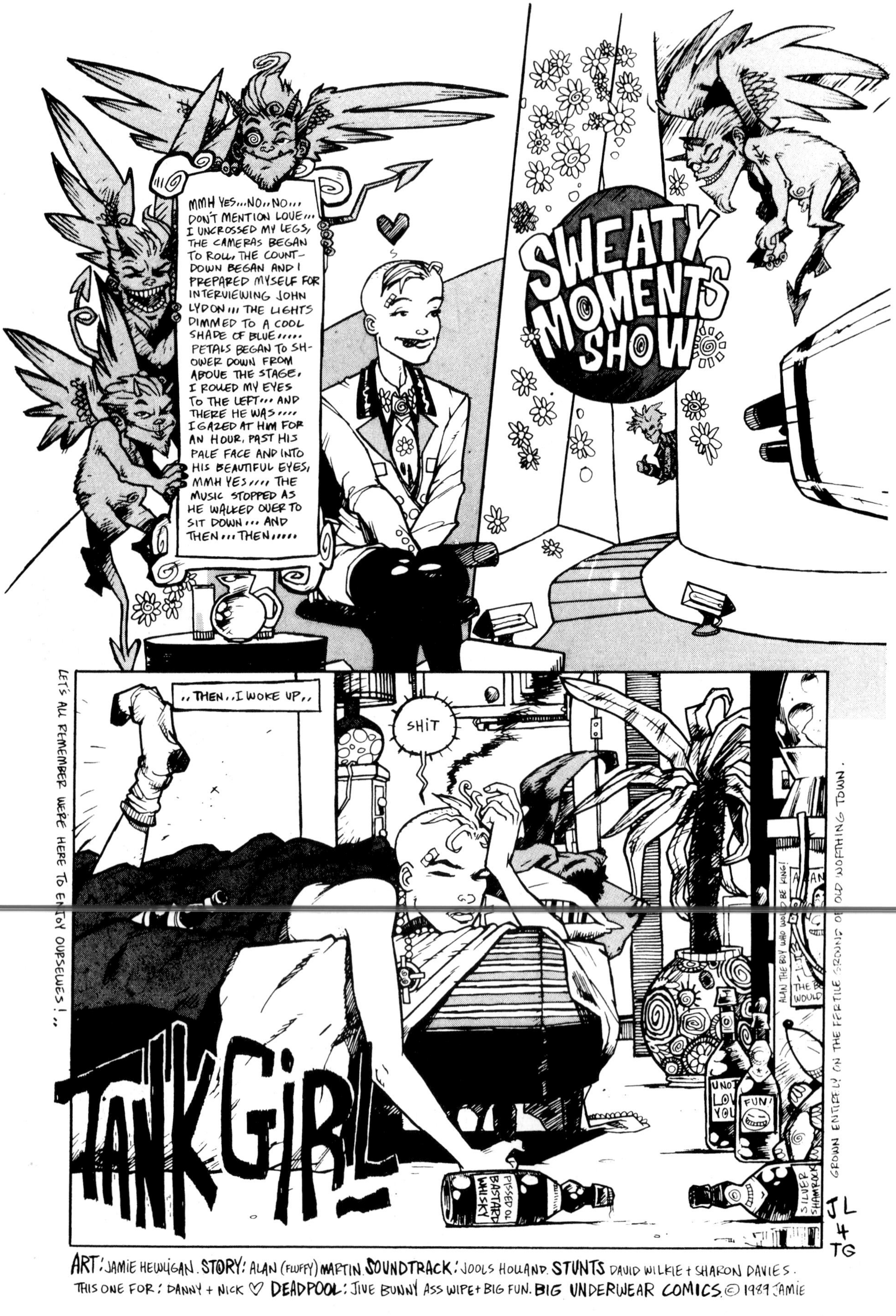
MMH YES... NO... NO... DON'T MENTION LOVE... I UNCROSSED MY LEGS, THE CAMERAS BEGAN TO ROLL, THE COUNT-DOWN BEGAN AND I PREPARED MYSELF FOR INTERVIEWING JOHN LYDON... THE LIGHTS DIMMED TO A COOL SHADE OF BLUE..... PETALS BEGAN TO SHOWER DOWN FROM ABOVE THE STAGE, I ROLLED MY EYES TO THE LEFT... AND THERE HE WAS.... I GAZED AT HIM FOR AN HOUR, PAST HIS PALE FACE AND INTO HIS BEAUTIFUL EYES, MMH YES.... THE MUSIC STOPPED AS HE WALKED OVER TO SIT DOWN... AND THEN... THEN.....
SWEATY MOMENTS SHOW
LET'S ALL REMEMBER WE'RE HERE TO ENJOY OURSELVES!..
..THEN..I WOKE UP..
SHIT
ALAN THE BOY WHO WOULD BE KING!
GROWN ENTIRELY ON THE FERTILE GROUND OF OLD WORTHING TOWN.
TANK GIRL
PISSED OL BASTARD WHISKY
FUN!
SILVER SHAMROCK
JL 4 TG

ART: JAMIE HEWLIGAN. STORY: ALAN (FLUFFY) MARTIN. SOUNDTRACK: JOOLS HOLLAND. STUNTS DAVID WILKIE + SHARON DAVIES.
THIS ONE FOR: DANNY + NICK ♡ DEADPOOL: JIVE BUNNY ASS WIPE + BIG FUN. BIG UNDERWEAR COMICS. © 1989 JAMIE

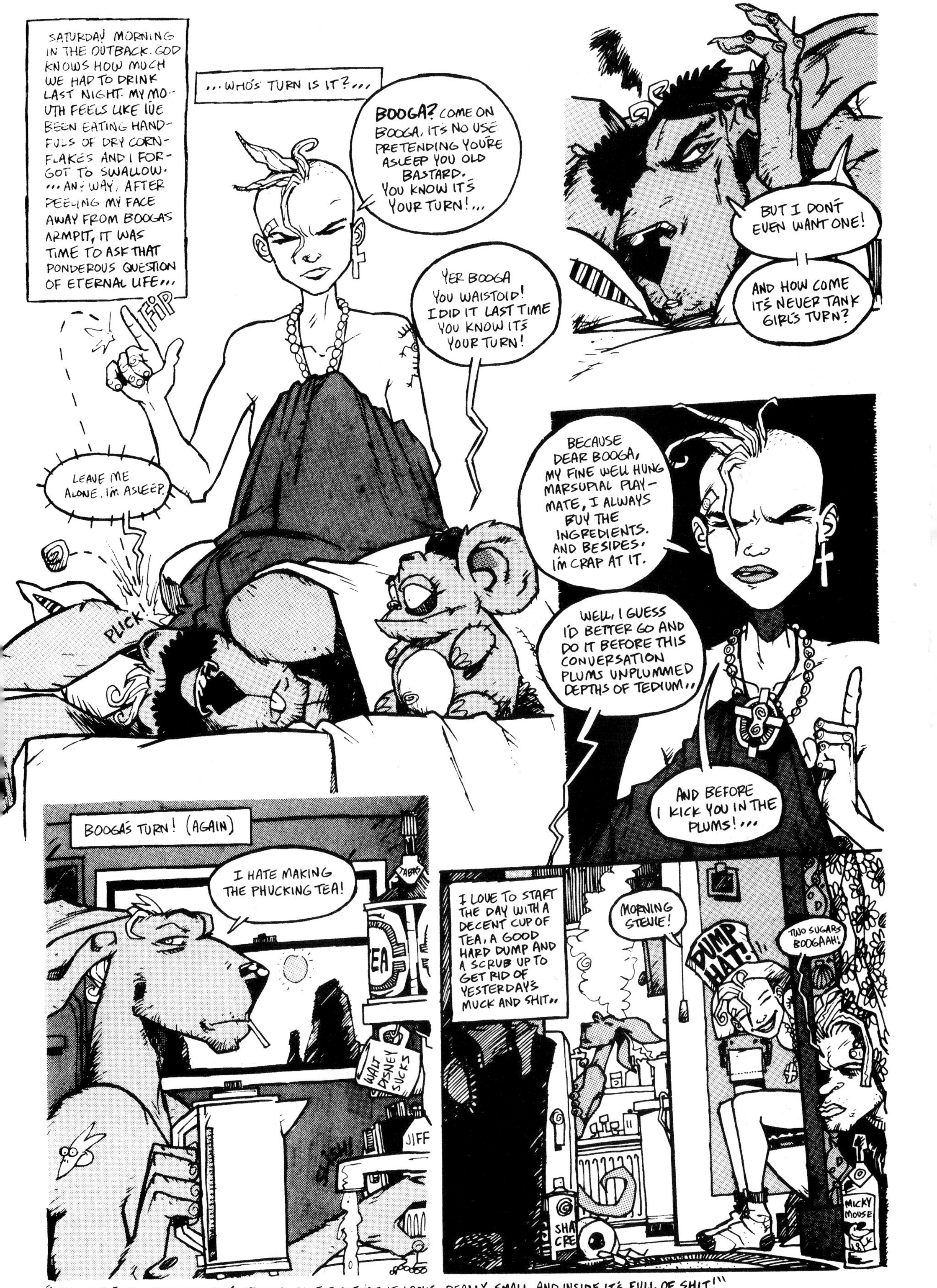
SATURDAY MORNING IN THE OUTBACK. GOD KNOWS HOW MUCH WE HAD TO DRINK LAST NIGHT. MY MOUTH FEELS LIKE I'VE BEEN EATING HANDFULS OF DRY CORNFLAKES AND I FORGOT TO SWALLOW. ... ANY WAY, AFTER PEELING MY FACE AWAY FROM BOOGAS ARMPIT, IT WAS TIME TO ASK THAT PONDEROUS QUESTION OF ETERNAL LIFE...
...WHO'S TURN IS IT?...
BOOGA? COME ON BOOGA, IT'S NO USE PRETENDING YOU'RE ASLEEP YOU OLD BASTARD. YOU KNOW IT'S YOUR TURN!...
FLIP
LEAVE ME ALONE. I'M ASLEEP.
PLICK
YER BOOGA YOU WAISTOID! I DID IT LAST TIME YOU KNOW IT'S YOUR TURN!
BUT I DON'T EVEN WANT ONE!
AND HOW COME IT'S NEVER TANK GIRL'S TURN?
BECAUSE DEAR BOOGA, MY FINE WELL HUNG MARSUPIAL PLAYMATE, I ALWAYS BUY THE INGREDIENTS. AND BESIDES, I'M CRAP AT IT.
WELL, I GUESS I'D BETTER GO AND DO IT BEFORE THIS CONVERSATION PLUMS UNPLUMMED DEPTHS OF TEDIUM..
AND BEFORE I KICK YOU IN THE PLUMS!...
BOOGA'S TURN! (AGAIN)
I HATE MAKING THE PHUCKING TEA!
TEA
WALT DISNEY SUCKS
JIFF
I LOVE TO START THE DAY WITH A DECENT CUP OF TEA, A GOOD HARD DUMP AND A SCRUB UP TO GET RID OF YESTERDAY'S MUCK AND SHIT..
MORNING STEVIE!
DUMP HAT!
TWO SUGARS BOOGAAH!
MICKY MOUSE

"MY TANK IS JUST LIKE DOCTOR WHO'S TARDIS, ON THE OUTSIDE IT LOOKS REALLY SMALL AND INSIDE IT'S FULL OF SHIT!"

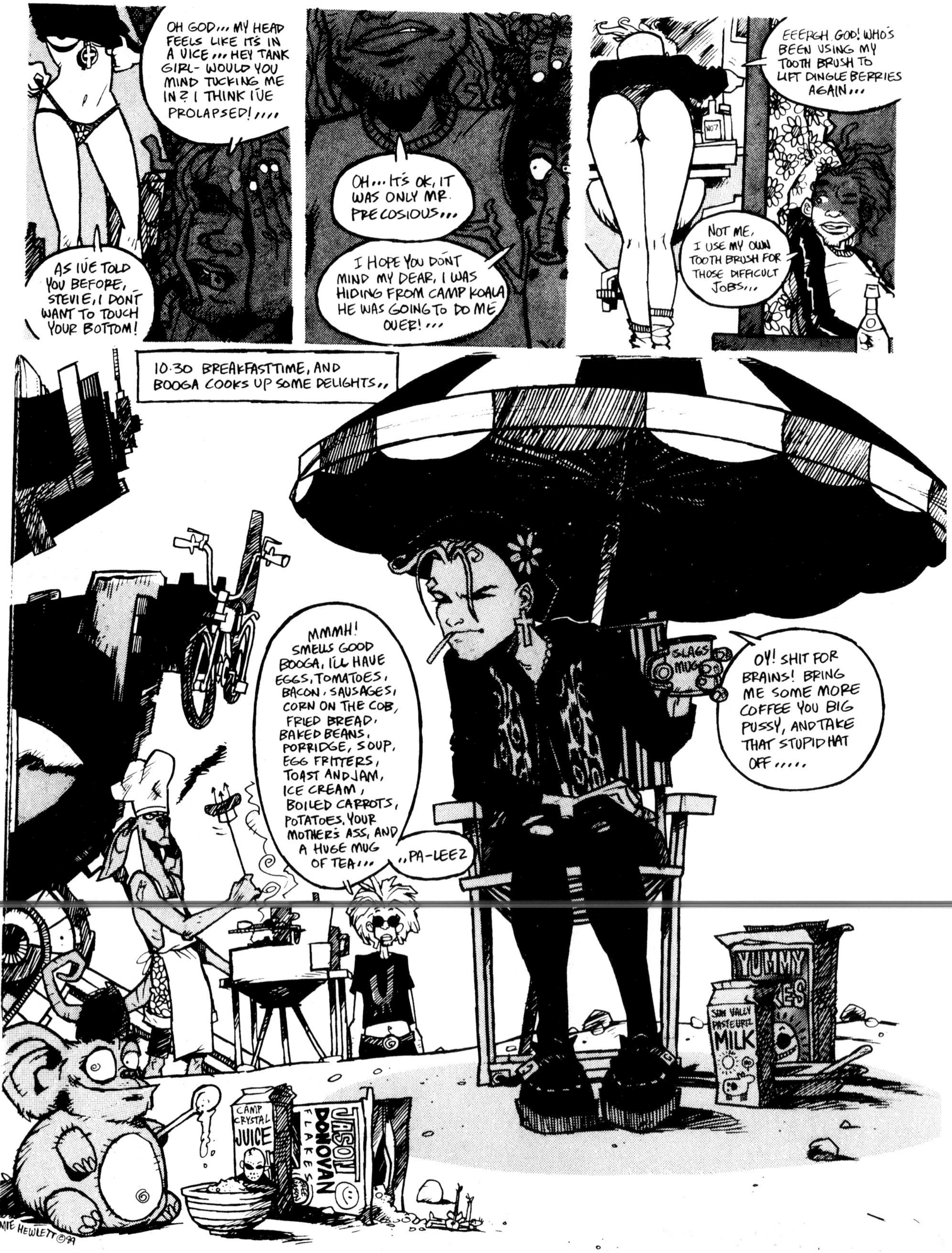
OH GOD... MY HEAD FEELS LIKE IT'S IN A VICE... HEY TANK GIRL- WOULD YOU MIND TUCKING ME IN? I THINK I'VE PROLAPSED!....
AS I'VE TOLD YOU BEFORE, STEVIE, I DON'T WANT TO TOUCH YOUR BOTTOM!
OH... IT'S OK, IT WAS ONLY MR. PRECOSIOUS...
I HOPE YOU DON'T MIND MY DEAR, I WAS HIDING FROM CAMP KOALA HE WAS GOING TO DO ME OVER!...
EEERGH GOD! WHO'S BEEN USING MY TOOTH BRUSH TO LIFT DINGLE BERRIES AGAIN...
NO7
NOT ME, I USE MY OWN TOOTH BRUSH FOR THOSE DIFFICULT JOBS...
10.30 BREAKFASTTIME, AND BOOGA COOKS UP SOME DELIGHTS..
MMMH! SMELLS GOOD BOOGA, I'LL HAVE EGGS, TOMATOES, BACON, SAUSAGES, CORN ON THE COB, FRIED BREAD, BAKED BEANS, PORRIDGE, SOUP, EGG FRITTERS, TOAST AND JAM, ICE CREAM, BOILED CARROTS, POTATOES, YOUR MOTHER'S ASS, AND A HUGE MUG OF TEA...
..PA-LEEZ
SLAGS MUG
OY! SHIT FOR BRAINS! BRING ME SOME MORE COFFEE YOU BIG PUSSY, AND TAKE THAT STUPID HAT OFF.....
YUMMY
MILK
CAMP CRYSTAL JUICE
JASON DONOVAN FLAKES
MIE HEWLETT ©99

feelings flying round, round up in the AIR!

SFP.

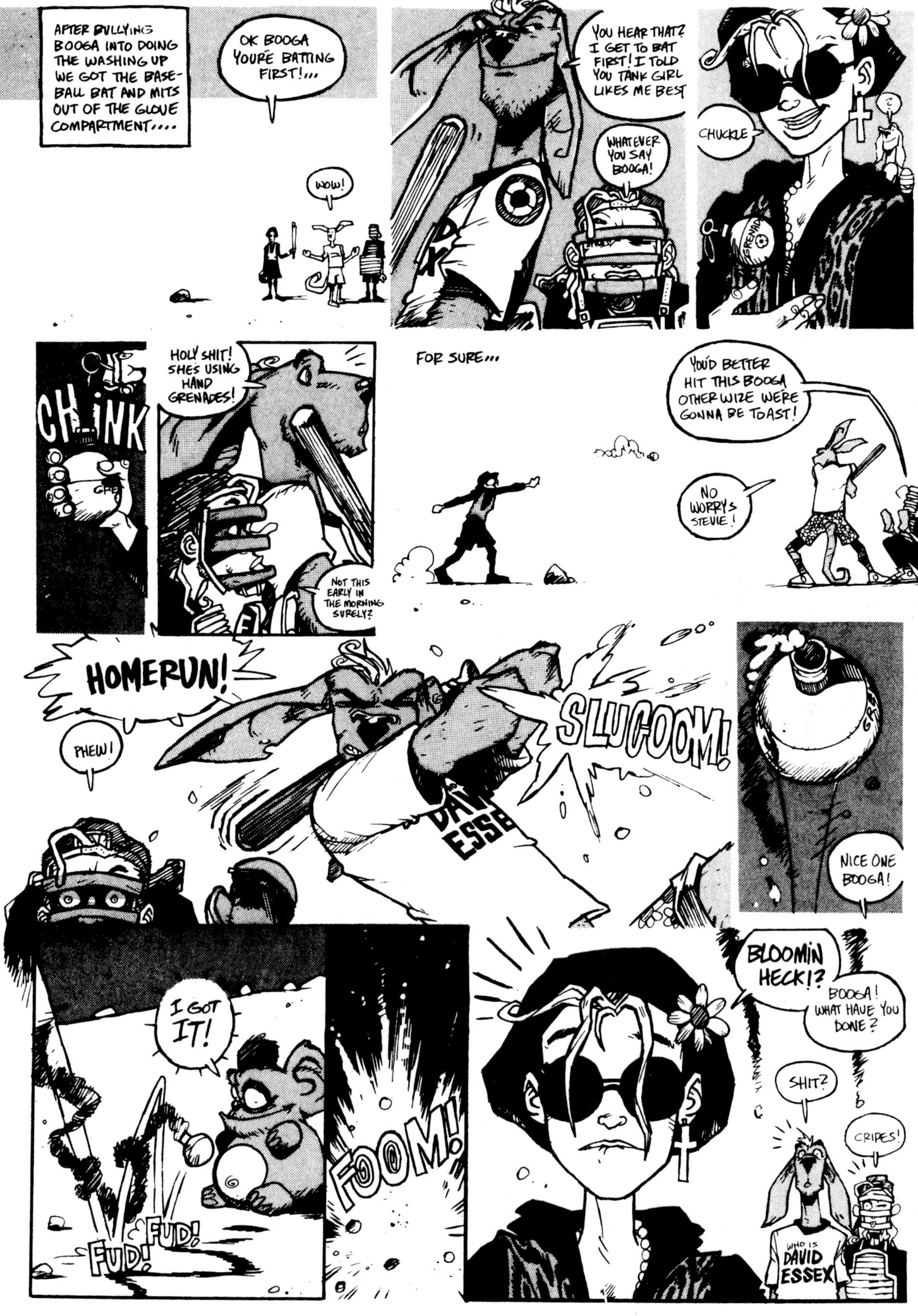
AFTER BULLYING BOOGA INTO DOING THE WASHING UP WE GOT THE BASE-BALL BAT AND MITS OUT OF THE GLOVE COMPARTMENT....
OK BOOGA YOU'RE BATTING FIRST!...
WOW!
YOU HEAR THAT? I GET TO BAT FIRST! I TOLD YOU TANK GIRL LIKES ME BEST
WHATEVER YOU SAY BOOGA!
CHUCKLE
CHINK
HOLY SHIT! SHE'S USING HAND GRENADES!
NOT THIS EARLY IN THE MORNING SURELY?
FOR SURE...
YOU'D BETTER HIT THIS BOOGA OTHERWIZE WE'RE GONNA BE TOAST!
NO WORRY'S STEVIE!
HOMERUN!
PHEW!
SLUCOOM!
DAVID ESSEX
NICE ONE BOOGA!
I GOT IT!
FUD!
FUD!
FOOM!
BLOOMIN HECK!?
BOOGA! WHAT HAVE YOU DONE?
SHIT?
CRIPES!
WHO IS DAVID ESSEX

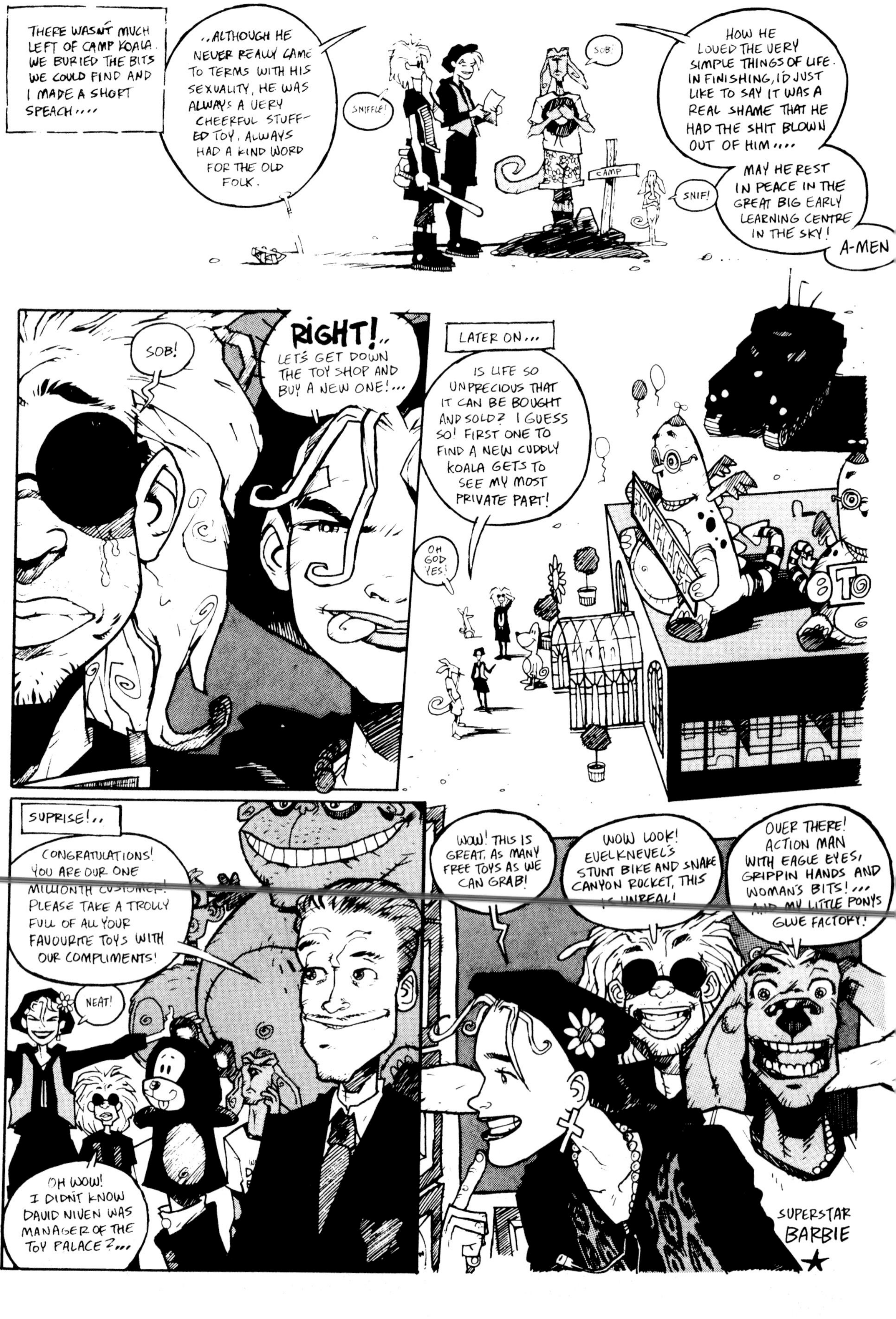
THERE WASN'T MUCH LEFT OF CAMP KOALA. WE BURIED THE BITS WE COULD FIND AND I MADE A SHORT SPEACH....
..ALTHOUGH HE NEVER REALLY CAME TO TERMS WITH HIS SEXUALITY, HE WAS ALWAYS A VERY CHEERFUL STUFFED TOY, ALWAYS HAD A KIND WORD FOR THE OLD FOLK.
SNIFFLE!
SOB!
HOW HE LOVED THE VERY SIMPLE THINGS OF LIFE. IN FINISHING, I'D JUST LIKE TO SAY IT WAS A REAL SHAME THAT HE HAD THE SHIT BLOWN OUT OF HIM....
CAMP
SNIF!
MAY HE REST IN PEACE IN THE GREAT BIG EARLY LEARNING CENTRE IN THE SKY!
A-MEN
SOB!
RIGHT!.. LET'S GET DOWN THE TOY SHOP AND BUY A NEW ONE!...
LATER ON...
IS LIFE SO UNPRECIOUS THAT IT CAN BE BOUGHT AND SOLD? I GUESS SO! FIRST ONE TO FIND A NEW CUDDLY KOALA GETS TO SEE MY MOST PRIVATE PART!
OH GOD YES!
TOY PALACE
SUPRISE!..
CONGRATULATIONS! YOU ARE OUR ONE MILLIONTH CUSTOMER! PLEASE TAKE A TROLLY FULL OF ALL YOUR FAVOURITE TOYS WITH OUR COMPLIMENTS!
NEAT!
OH WOW! I DIDN'T KNOW DAVID NIVEN WAS MANAGER OF THE TOY PALACE?...
WOW! THIS IS GREAT, AS MANY FREE TOYS AS WE CAN GRAB!
WOW LOOK! EVELKNEVEL'S STUNT BIKE AND SNAKE CANYON ROCKET, THIS IS UNREAL!
OVER THERE! ACTION MAN WITH EAGLE EYES, GRIPPIN HANDS AND WOMAN'S BITS!... AND MY LITTLE PONYS GLUE FACTORY!
SUPERSTAR BARBIE

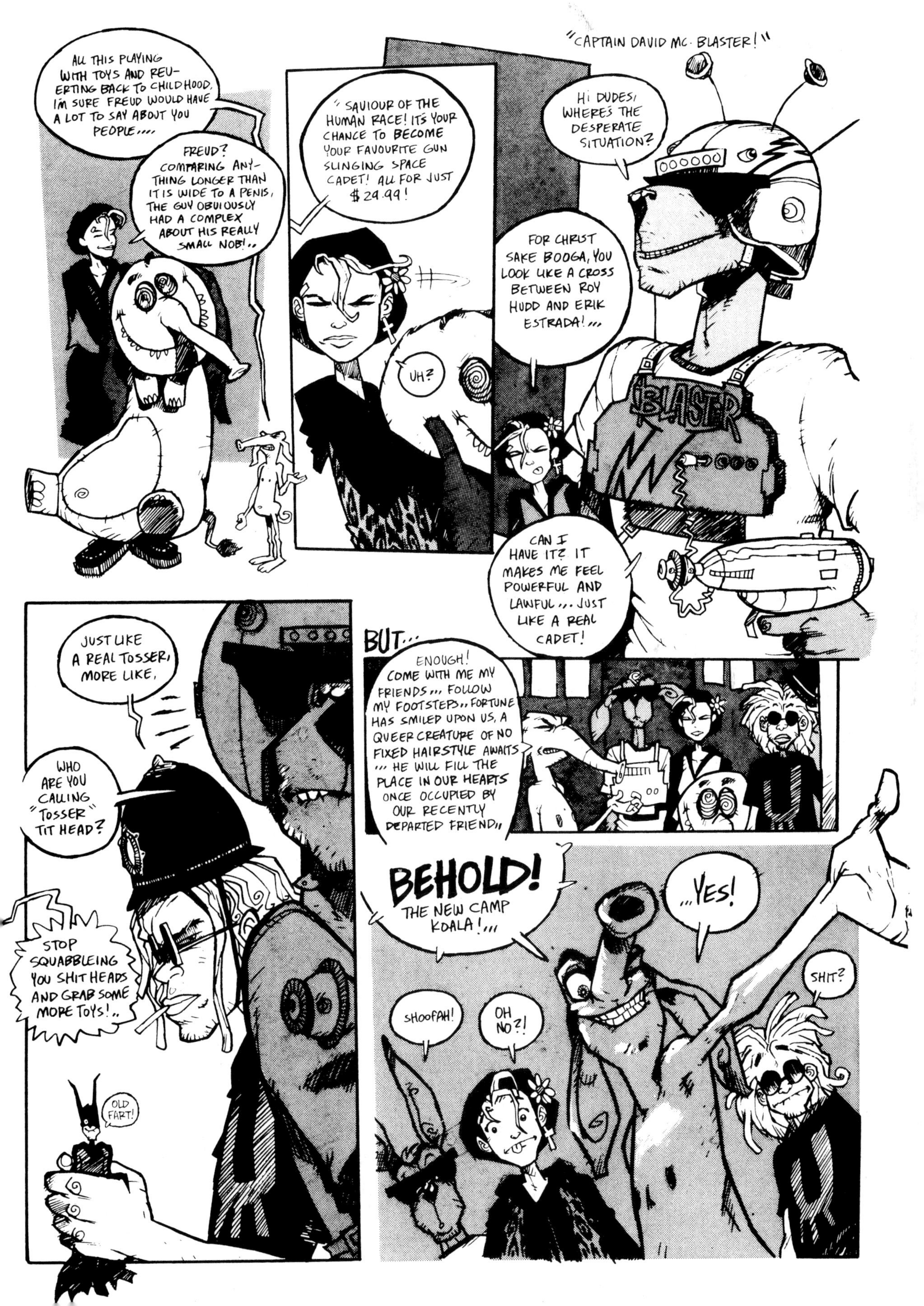

ALL THIS PLAYING WITH TOYS AND REVERTING BACK TO CHILDHOOD, I'M SURE FREUD WOULD HAVE A LOT TO SAY ABOUT YOU PEOPLE....
FREUD? COMPARING ANYTHING LONGER THAN IT IS WIDE TO A PENIS, THE GUY OBVIOUSLY HAD A COMPLEX ABOUT HIS REALLY SMALL NOB!..
"SAVIOUR OF THE HUMAN RACE! IT'S YOUR CHANCE TO BECOME YOUR FAVOURITE GUN SLINGING SPACE CADET! ALL FOR JUST $29.99!
UH?
"CAPTAIN DAVID MC. BLASTER!"
Hi DUDES, WHERE'S THE DESPERATE SITUATION?
FOR CHRIST SAKE BOOGA, YOU LOOK LIKE A CROSS BETWEEN ROY HUDD AND ERIK ESTRADA!...
BLASTER
CAN I HAVE IT? IT MAKES ME FEEL POWERFUL AND LAWFUL... JUST LIKE A REAL CADET!
JUST LIKE A REAL TOSSER, MORE LIKE,
WHO ARE YOU CALLING "TOSSER" TIT HEAD?
STOP SQUABBLEING YOU SHIT HEADS AND GRAB SOME MORE TOYS!..
OLD FART!
BUT...
ENOUGH! COME WITH ME MY FRIENDS... FOLLOW MY FOOTSTEPS.. FORTUNE HAS SMILED UPON US, A QUEER CREATURE OF NO FIXED HAIRSTYLE AWAITS... HE WILL FILL THE PLACE IN OUR HEARTS ONCE OCCUPIED BY OUR RECENTLY DEPARTED FRIEND..
BEHOLD! THE NEW CAMP KOALA!...
...YES!
SHOOFAH!
OH NO?!
SHIT?

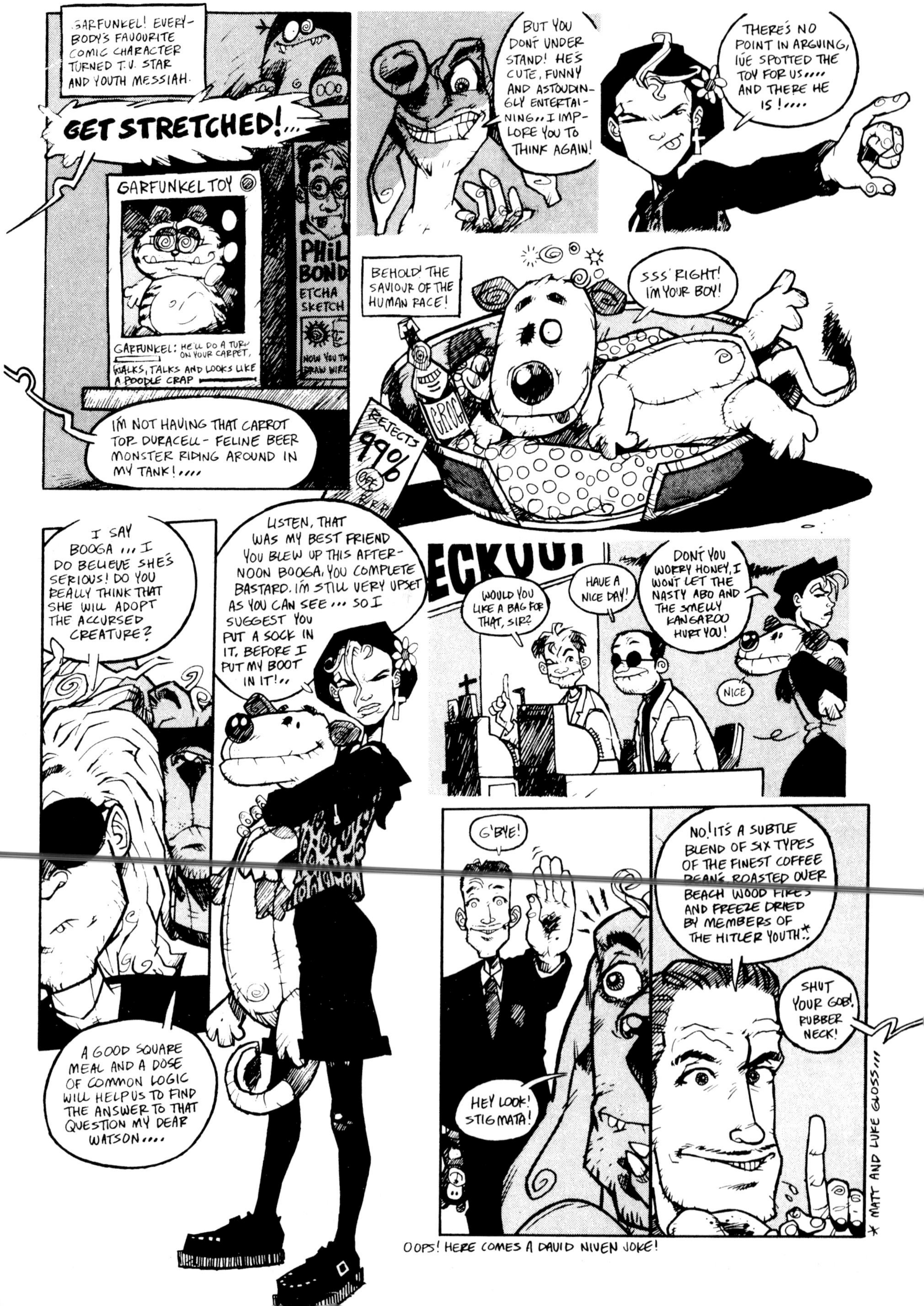
GARFUNKEL! EVERY-BODY'S FAVOURITE COMIC CHARACTER TURNED T.V. STAR AND YOUTH MESSIAH.
GET STRETCHED!....
GARFUNKEL TOY
GARFUNKEL: HE'LL DO A TURD ON YOUR CARPET, WALKS, TALKS AND LOOKS LIKE A POODLE CRAP
PHIL BOND ETCHA SKETCH
I'M NOT HAVING THAT CARROT TOP- DURACELL- FELINE BEER MONSTER RIDING AROUND IN MY TANK!....
BUT YOU DON'T UNDER STAND! HE'S CUTE, FUNNY AND ASTOUDINGLY ENTERTAINING,, I IMPLORE YOU TO THINK AGAIN!
THERE'S NO POINT IN ARGUING, I'VE SPOTTED THE TOY FOR US..... AND THERE HE IS!....
BEHOLD! THE SAVIOUR OF THE HUMAN RACE!
SSS' RIGHT! I'M YOUR BOY!
REJECTS 99% OFF
GROG
I SAY BOOGA ,,, I DO BELIEVE SHE'S SERIOUS! DO YOU REALLY THINK THAT SHE WILL ADOPT THE ACCURSED CREATURE?
LISTEN, THAT WAS MY BEST FRIEND YOU BLEW UP THIS AFTERNOON BOOGA, YOU COMPLETE BASTARD. I'M STILL VERY UPSET AS YOU CAN SEE... SO I SUGGEST YOU PUT A SOCK IN IT, BEFORE I PUT MY BOOT IN IT!,,
A GOOD SQUARE MEAL AND A DOSE OF COMMON LOGIC WILL HELP US TO FIND THE ANSWER TO THAT QUESTION MY DEAR WATSON....
ECKOUT
WOULD YOU LIKE A BAG FOR THAT, SIR?
HAVE A NICE DAY!
DON'T YOU WORRY HONEY, I WON'T LET THE NASTY ABO AND THE SMELLY KANGAROO HURT YOU!
NICE
G'BYE!
NO! IT'S A SUBTLE BLEND OF SIX TYPES OF THE FINEST COFFEE BEANS ROASTED OVER BEACH WOOD FIRES AND FREEZE DRIED BY MEMBERS OF THE HITLER YOUTH*.
SHUT YOUR GOB! RUBBER NECK!
HEY LOOK! STIGMATA!
* MATT AND LUKE GLOSS,,,
OOPS! HERE COMES A DAVID NIVEN JOKE!

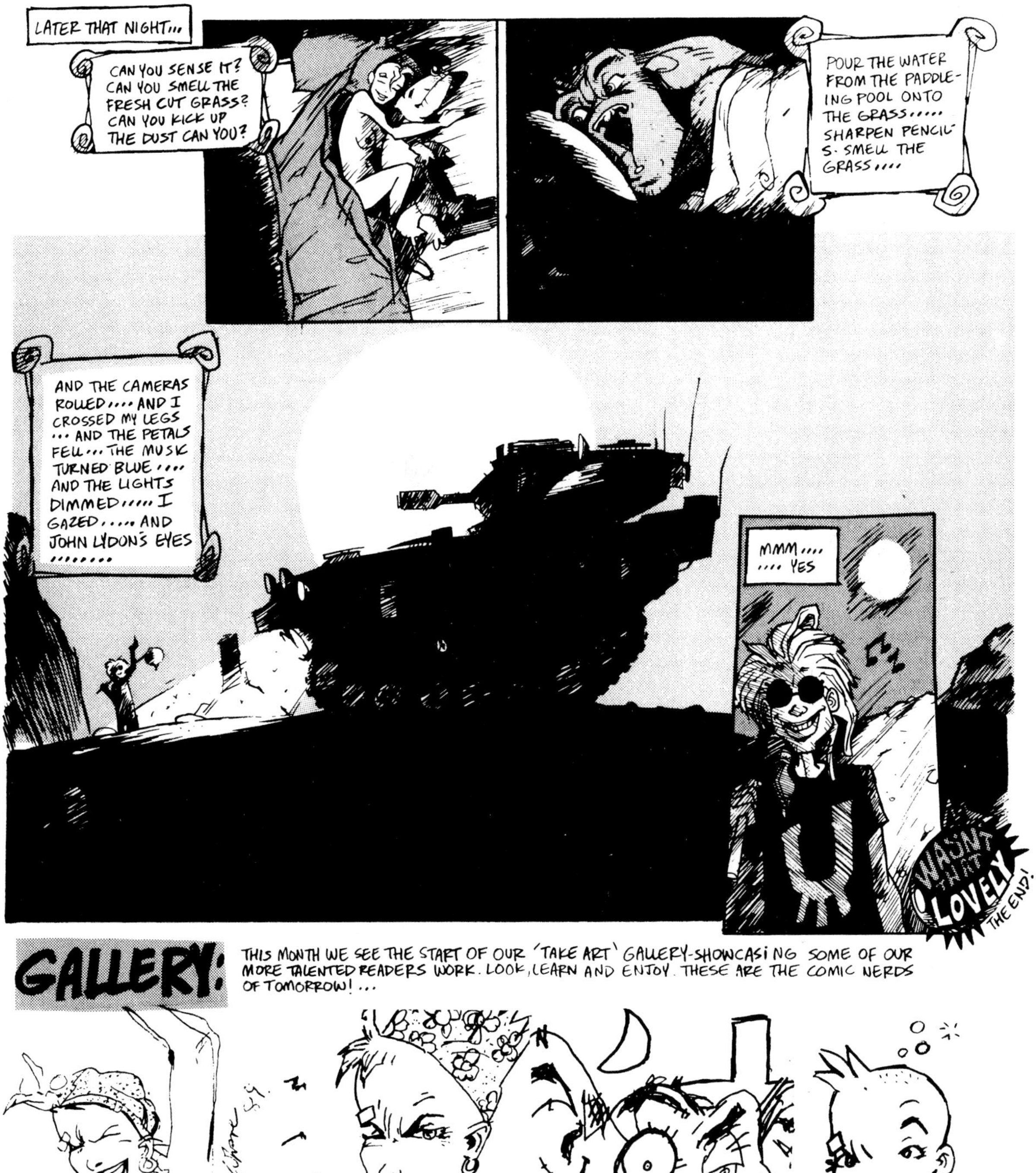
LATER THAT NIGHT...
CAN YOU SENSE IT? CAN YOU SMELL THE FRESH CUT GRASS? CAN YOU KICK UP THE DUST CAN YOU?
POUR THE WATER FROM THE PADDLE-ING POOL ONTO THE GRASS..... SHARPEN PENCIL-S. SMELL THE GRASS.....
AND THE CAMERAS ROLLED.... AND I CROSSED MY LEGS ... AND THE PETALS FELL... THE MUSK TURNED BLUE.... AND THE LIGHTS DIMMED...... I GAZED..... AND JOHN LYDON'S EYES ....
MMM.... ....YES
WASN'T THAT LOVELY
THE END!

GALLERY:

THIS MONTH WE SEE THE START OF OUR 'TAKE ART' GALLERY-SHOWCASING SOME OF OUR MORE TALENTED READERS WORK. LOOK, LEARN AND ENJOY. THESE ARE THE COMIC NERDS OF TOMORROW! ...

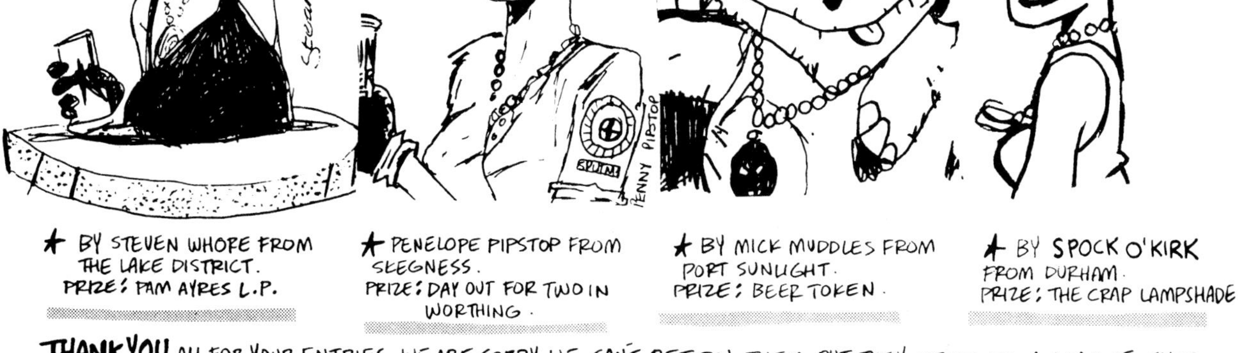

★ BY STEVEN WHORE FROM THE LAKE DISTRICT.
PRIZE: PAM AYRES L.P.

★ PENELOPE PIPSTOP FROM SKEGNESS.
PRIZE: DAY OUT FOR TWO IN WORTHING.

★ BY MICK MUDDLES FROM PORT SUNLIGHT.
PRIZE: BEER TOKEN.

★ BY SPOCK O'KIRK FROM DURHAM.
PRIZE: THE CRAP LAMPSHADE.

THANK YOU ALL FOR YOUR ENTRIES. WE ARE SORRY WE CAN'T RETURN THEM BUT THEY WERE ALL A LOAD OF SHIT.

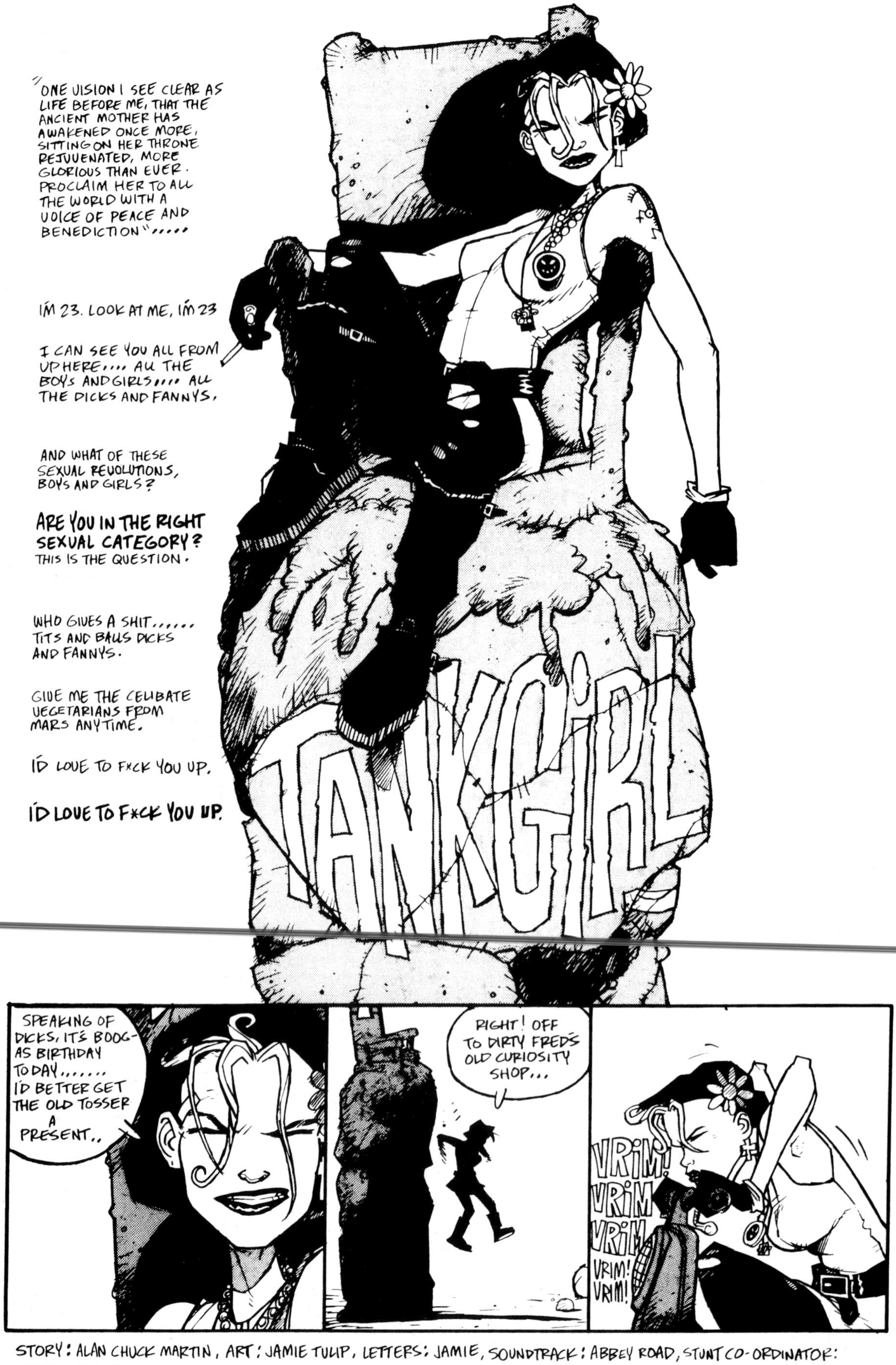
"ONE VISION I SEE CLEAR AS LIFE BEFORE ME, THAT THE ANCIENT MOTHER HAS AWAKENED ONCE MORE, SITTING ON HER THRONE REJUVENATED, MORE GLORIOUS THAN EVER. PROCLAIM HER TO ALL THE WORLD WITH A VOICE OF PEACE AND BENEDICTION"......
I'M 23. LOOK AT ME, I'M 23
I CAN SEE YOU ALL FROM UP HERE.... ALL THE BOYS AND GIRLS.... ALL THE DICKS AND FANNYS.
AND WHAT OF THESE SEXUAL REVOLUTIONS, BOYS AND GIRLS?
ARE YOU IN THE RIGHT SEXUAL CATEGORY? THIS IS THE QUESTION.
WHO GIVES A SHIT...... TITS AND BALLS DICKS AND FANNYS.
GIVE ME THE CELIBATE VEGETARIANS FROM MARS ANYTIME.
I'D LOVE TO F*CK YOU UP.
I'D LOVE TO F*CK YOU UP.
TANK GIRL
SPEAKING OF DICKS, IT'S BOOGAS BIRTHDAY TODAY...... I'D BETTER GET THE OLD TOSSER A PRESENT..
RIGHT! OFF TO DIRTY FRED'S OLD CURIOSITY SHOP...
VRIM! VRIM! VRIM! VRIM! VRIM!

STORY: ALAN CHUCK MARTIN, ART: JAMIE TULIP, LETTERS: JAMIE, SOUNDTRACK: ABBEY ROAD, STUNT CO-ORDINATOR: STRETCH ARMSTRONG, DEADPOOL: THE BLOKE FROM THE RADION AUTOMATC ADVERT, THIS ONE FOR NICK, JAMIE ©1990.

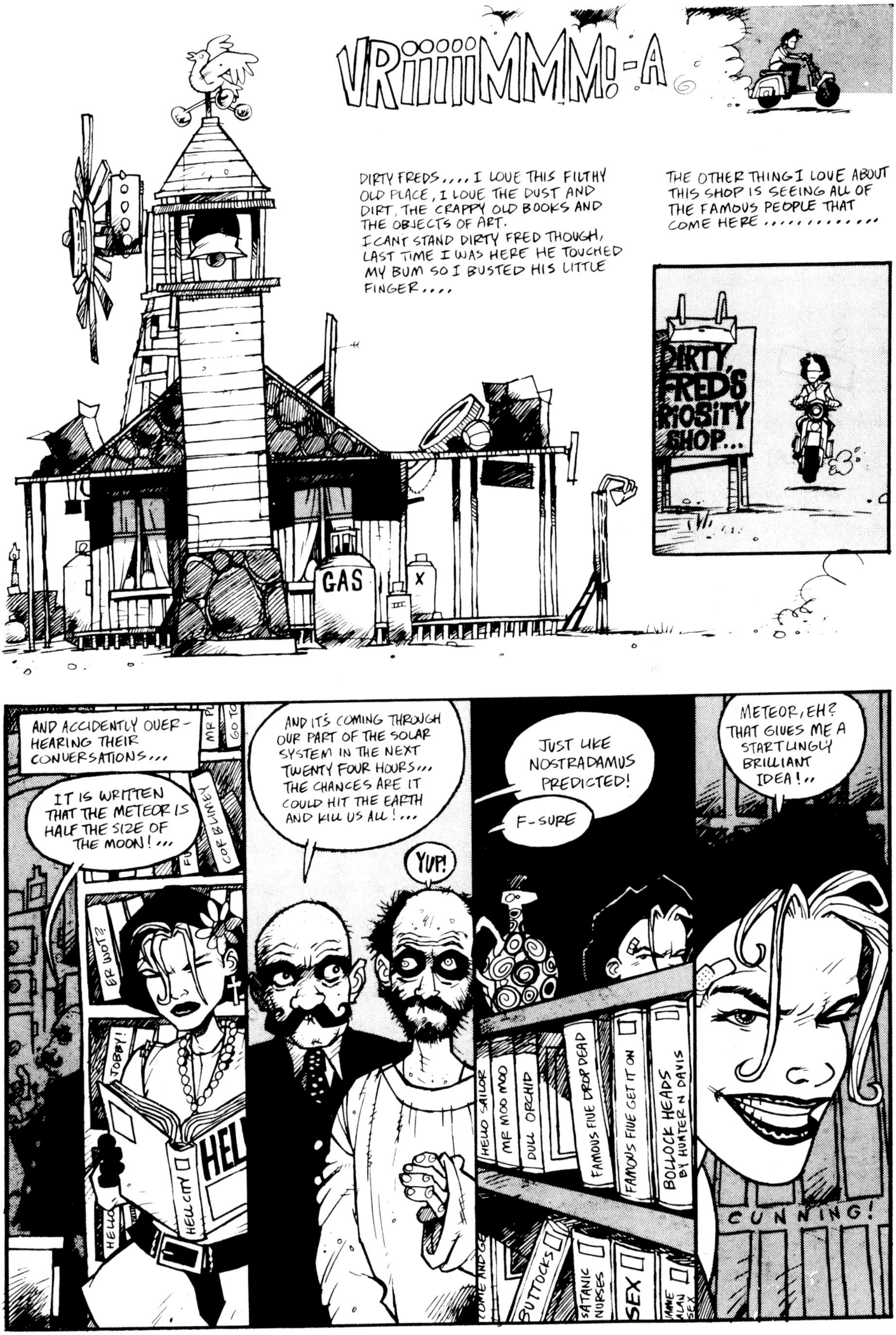
VRooooooiiiiiMMMM!-A
DIRTY FREDS,,,, I LOVE THIS FILTHY OLD PLACE, I LOVE THE DUST AND DIRT, THE CRAPPY OLD BOOKS AND THE OBJECTS OF ART.
I CAN'T STAND DIRTY FRED THOUGH, LAST TIME I WAS HERE HE TOUCHED MY BUM SO I BUSTED HIS LITTLE FINGER,,,,
THE OTHER THING I LOVE ABOUT THIS SHOP IS SEEING ALL OF THE FAMOUS PEOPLE THAT COME HERE,,,,,,,,,,,,
GAS
DIRTY FRED'S RIOSITY SHOP...
AND ACCIDENTLY OVER-HEARING THEIR CONVERSATIONS,,,
IT IS WRITTEN THAT THE METEOR IS HALF THE SIZE OF THE MOON!,,,
AND IT'S COMING THROUGH OUR PART OF THE SOLAR SYSTEM IN THE NEXT TWENTY FOUR HOURS,,, THE CHANCES ARE IT COULD HIT THE EARTH AND KILL US ALL!,,,
YUP!
JUST LIKE NOSTRADAMUS PREDICTED!
F-SURE
METEOR, EH? THAT GIVES ME A STARTLINGLY BRILLIANT IDEA!,,
CUNNING!
COR BLIMEY
ER WOT?
JOBBY!
HELL CITY
HELLO SAILOR
MR MOO MOO
DULL ORCHID
FAMOUS FIVE DROP DEAD
FAMOUS FIVE GET IT ON
BOLLOCK HEADS BY HUNTER N DAVIS
SUTTOCKS
SATANIC NURSES
SEX
JAMIE ALAN SEX

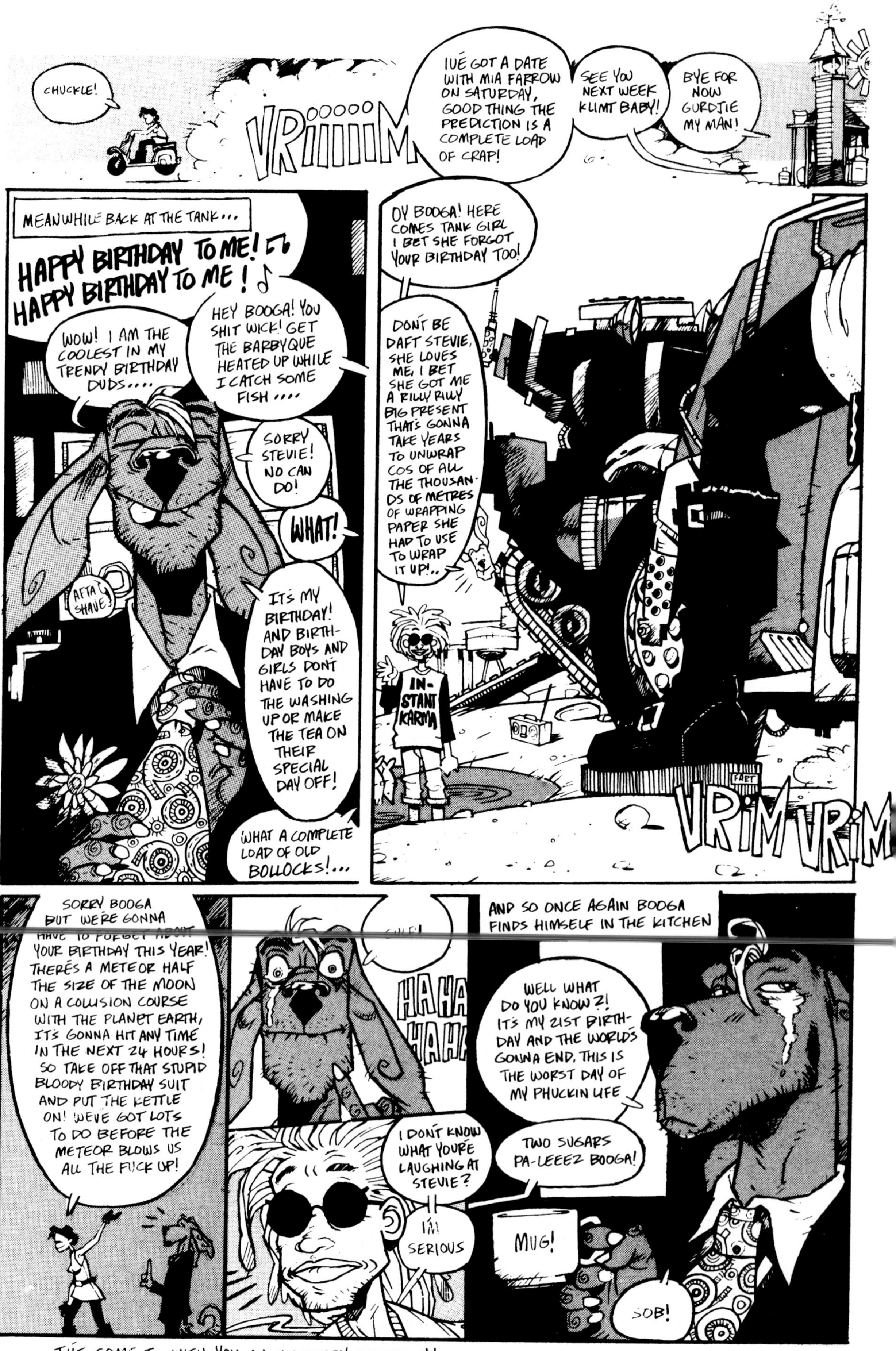
CHUCKLE!
VRiiiiiiMoooooo
IVE GOT A DATE WITH MIA FARROW ON SATURDAY, GOOD THING THE PREDICTION IS A COMPLETE LOAD OF CRAP!
SEE YOU NEXT WEEK KLIMT BABY!
BYE FOR NOW GURDJIE MY MAN!
MEANWHILE BACK AT THE TANK...
HAPPY BIRTHDAY TO ME! HAPPY BIRTHDAY TO ME!
WOW! I AM THE COOLEST IN MY TRENDY BIRTHDAY DUDS....
HEY BOOGA! YOU SHIT WICK! GET THE BARBYQUE HEATED UP WHILE I CATCH SOME FISH....
SORRY STEVIE! NO CAN DO!
WHAT!
AFTA SHAVE
ITS MY BIRTHDAY! AND BIRTHDAY BOYS AND GIRLS DONT HAVE TO DO THE WASHING UP OR MAKE THE TEA ON THEIR SPECIAL DAY OFF!
WHAT A COMPLETE LOAD OF OLD BOLLOCKS!...
OY BOOGA! HERE COMES TANK GIRL I BET SHE FORGOT YOUR BIRTHDAY TOO!
DONT BE DAFT STEVIE, SHE LOVES ME, I BET SHE GOT ME A RILLY RILLY BIG PRESENT THATS GONNA TAKE YEARS TO UNWRAP COS OF ALL THE THOUSANDS OF METRES OF WRAPPING PAPER SHE HAD TO USE TO WRAP IT UP!..
INSTANT KARMA
FART
VRiM VRiM
SORRY BOOGA BUT WE'RE GONNA HAVE TO FORGET ABOUT YOUR BIRTHDAY THIS YEAR! THERES A METEOR HALF THE SIZE OF THE MOON ON A COLLISION COURSE WITH THE PLANET EARTH, ITS GONNA HIT ANY TIME IN THE NEXT 24 HOURS! SO TAKE OFF THAT STUPID BLOODY BIRTHDAY SUIT AND PUT THE KETTLE ON! WE'VE GOT LOTS TO DO BEFORE THE METEOR BLOWS US ALL THE FUCK UP!
HAHA HAHA
I DONT KNOW WHAT YOURE LAUGHING AT STEVIE?
IM SERIOUS
AND SO ONCE AGAIN BOOGA FINDS HIMSELF IN THE KITCHEN
WELL WHAT DO YOU KNOW? ITS MY 21ST BIRTHDAY AND THE WORLDS GONNA END. THIS IS THE WORST DAY OF MY PHUCKIN LIFE
TWO SUGARS PA-LEEEZ BOOGA!
MUG!
SOB!
IVE COME TO WISH YOU AN UNHAPPY BIRTHDAY!...

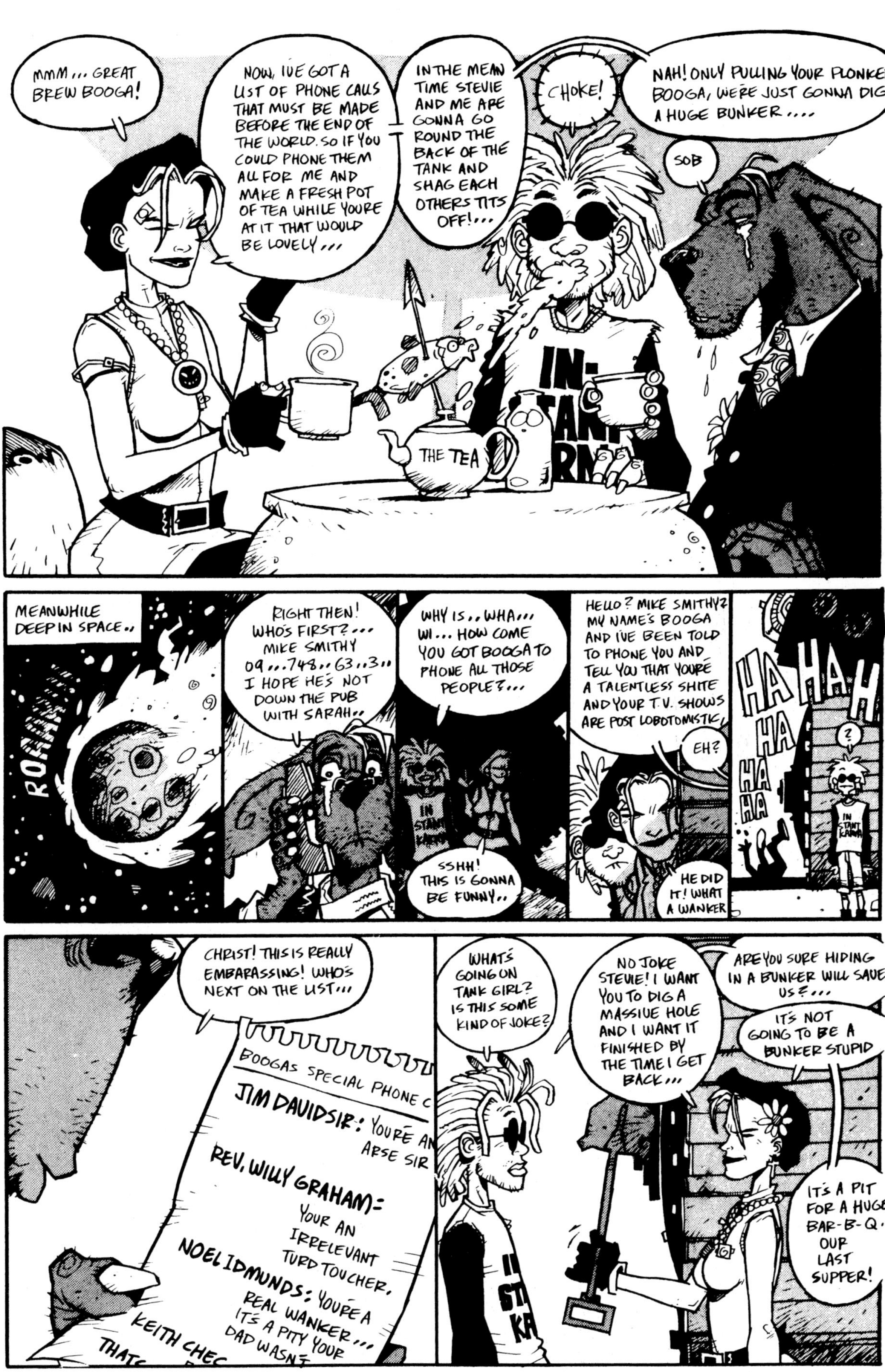
MMM... GREAT BREW BOOGA!
NOW, IVE GOT A LIST OF PHONE CALLS THAT MUST BE MADE BEFORE THE END OF THE WORLD. SO IF YOU COULD PHONE THEM ALL FOR ME AND MAKE A FRESH POT OF TEA WHILE YOURE AT IT THAT WOULD BE LOVELY...
IN THE MEAN TIME STEVIE AND ME ARE GONNA GO ROUND THE BACK OF THE TANK AND SHAG EACH OTHERS TITS OFF!...
CHOKE!
NAH! ONLY PULLING YOUR PLONKER BOOGA, WE'RE JUST GONNA DIG A HUGE BUNKER....
SOB
THE TEA
MEANWHILE DEEP IN SPACE..
ROARRR
RIGHT THEN! WHO'S FIRST?... MIKE SMITHY 09...748...63...3... I HOPE HE'S NOT DOWN THE PUB WITH SARAH..
WHY IS.. WHA... WI... HOW COME YOU GOT BOOGA TO PHONE ALL THOSE PEOPLE?...
SSHH! THIS IS GONNA BE FUNNY..
HELLO? MIKE SMITHY? MY NAME'S BOOGA AND I'VE BEEN TOLD TO PHONE YOU AND TELL YOU THAT YOU'RE A TALENTLESS SHITE AND YOUR T.V. SHOWS ARE POST LOBOTOMISTIC,
EH?
HE DID IT! WHAT A WANKER
HA HA HA HA HA HA
?
CHRIST! THIS IS REALLY EMBARASSING! WHO'S NEXT ON THE LIST...
BOOGAS SPECIAL PHONE C
JIM DAVIDSIR: YOU'RE AN ARSE SIR
REV. WILLY GRAHAM: YOUR AN IRRELEVANT TURD TOUCHER.
NOEL IDMUNDS: YOU'RE A REAL WANKER... IT'S A PITY YOUR DAD WASN'T
KEITH CHEC
THAT'S
WHAT'S GOING ON TANK GIRL? IS THIS SOME KIND OF JOKE?
NO JOKE STEVIE! I WANT YOU TO DIG A MASSIVE HOLE AND I WANT IT FINISHED BY THE TIME I GET BACK...
ARE YOU SURE HIDING IN A BUNKER WILL SAVE US?...
IT'S NOT GOING TO BE A BUNKER STUPID
IT'S A PIT FOR A HUGE BAR-B-Q. OUR LAST SUPPER!

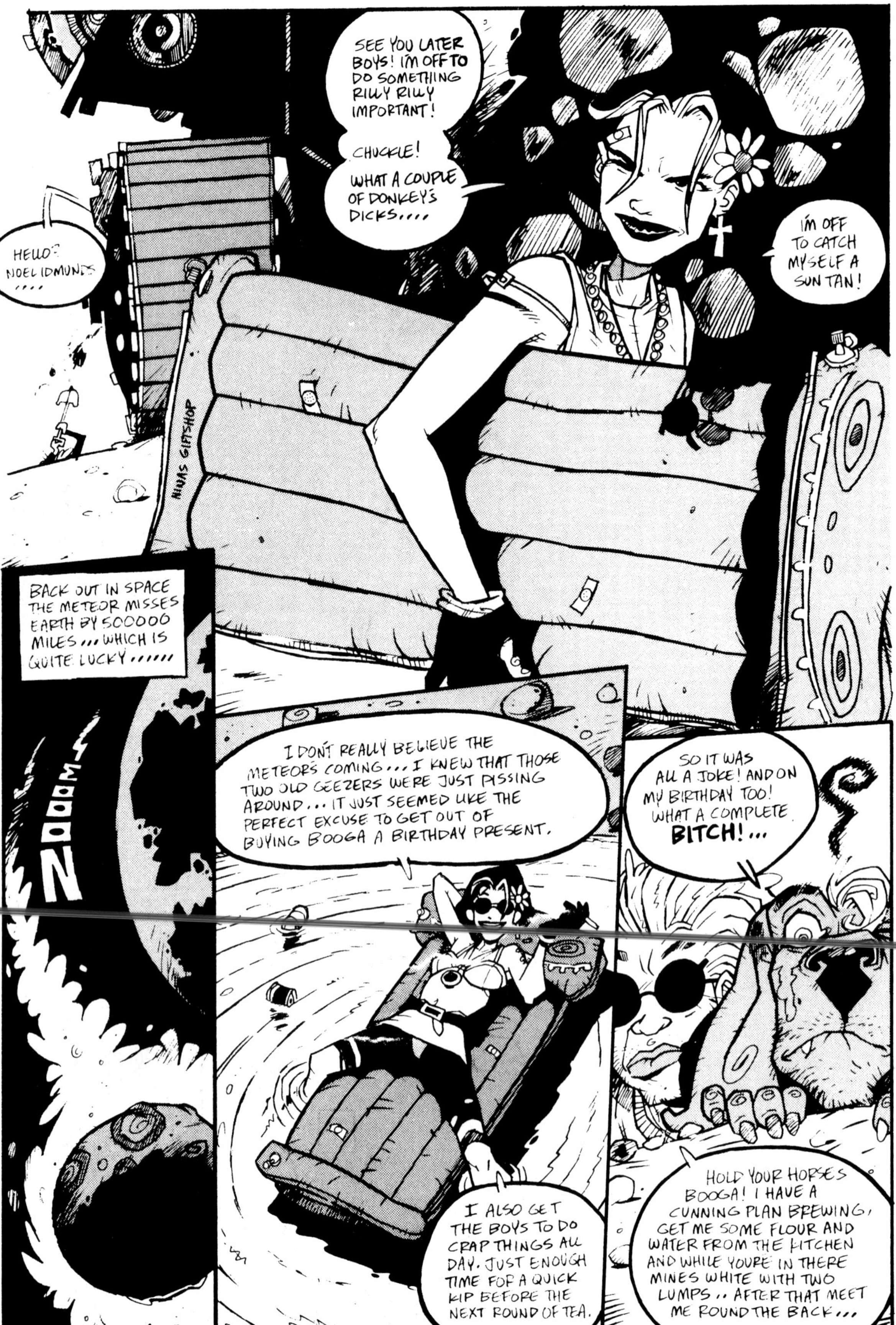
SEE YOU LATER BOYS! I'M OFF TO DO SOMETHING RILLY RILLY IMPORTANT!
CHUCKLE!
WHAT A COUPLE OF DONKEY'S DICKS,,,,
HELLO? NOEL IDMUNDS ,,,,
I'M OFF TO CATCH MYSELF A SUN TAN!
NINAS GIFTSHOP
BACK OUT IN SPACE THE METEOR MISSES EARTH BY 500000 MILES,,,, WHICH IS QUITE LUCKY,,,,,,
ZOOOM
I DON'T REALLY BELIEVE THE METEOR'S COMING,,, I KNEW THAT THOSE TWO OLD GEEZERS WERE JUST PISSING AROUND,,, IT JUST SEEMED LIKE THE PERFECT EXCUSE TO GET OUT OF BUYING BOOGA A BIRTHDAY PRESENT.
I ALSO GET THE BOYS TO DO CRAP THINGS ALL DAY. JUST ENOUGH TIME FOR A QUICK KIP BEFORE THE NEXT ROUND OF TEA.
SO IT WAS ALL A JOKE! AND ON MY BIRTHDAY TOO! WHAT A COMPLETE BITCH!...
HOLD YOUR HORSES BOOGA! I HAVE A CUNNING PLAN BREWING, GET ME SOME FLOUR AND WATER FROM THE KITCHEN AND WHILE YOU'RE IN THERE MINES WHITE WITH TWO LUMPS,, AFTER THAT MEET ME ROUND THE BACK,,,

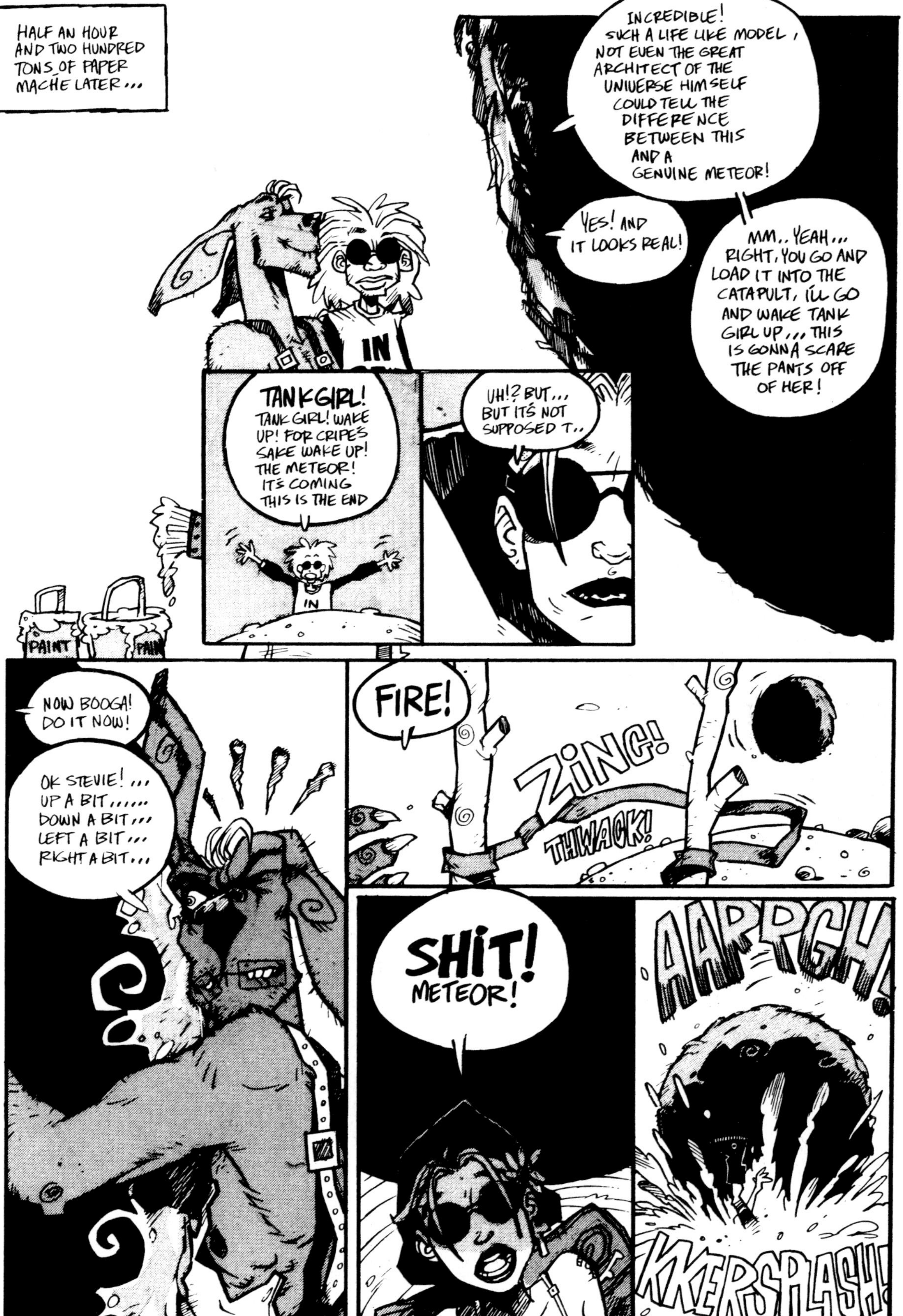
HALF AN HOUR AND TWO HUNDRED TONS OF PAPER MACHE LATER...
INCREDIBLE! SUCH A LIFE LIKE MODEL, NOT EVEN THE GREAT ARCHITECT OF THE UNIVERSE HIMSELF COULD TELL THE DIFFERENCE BETWEEN THIS AND A GENUINE METEOR!
YES! AND IT LOOKS REAL!
MM.. YEAH... RIGHT, YOU GO AND LOAD IT INTO THE CATAPULT, I'LL GO AND WAKE TANK GIRL UP... THIS IS GONNA SCARE THE PANTS OFF OF HER!
TANK GIRL! TANK GIRL! WAKE UP! FOR CRIPE'S SAKE WAKE UP! THE METEOR! IT'S COMING THIS IS THE END
UH!? BUT... BUT IT'S NOT SUPPOSED T..
PAINT
NOW BOOGA! DO IT NOW!
OK STEVIE!... UP A BIT...... DOWN A BIT... LEFT A BIT... RIGHT A BIT...
FIRE!
ZING!
THWACK!
SHIT! METEOR!
AARRGH!
KKERSPLASH!

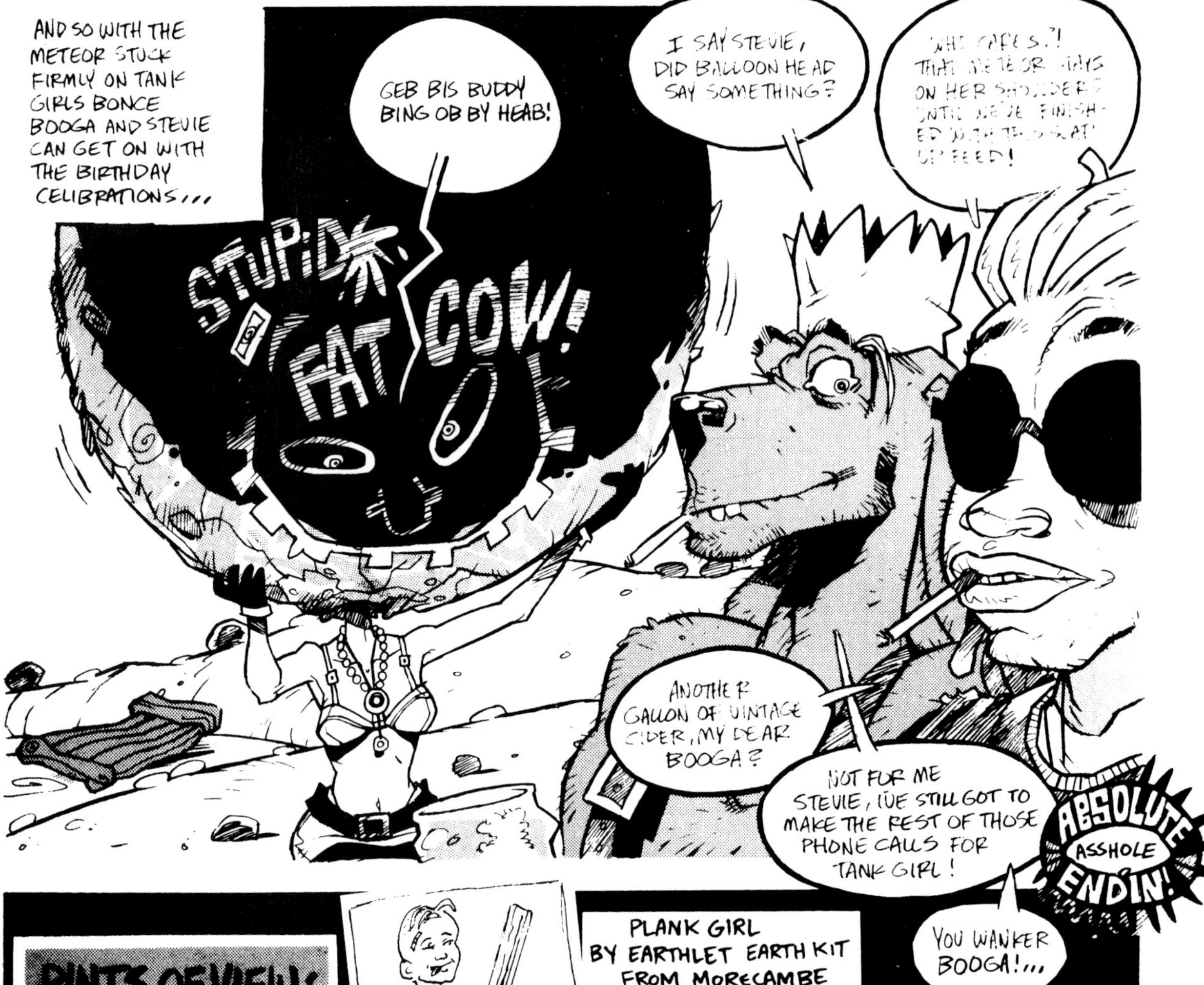
AND SO WITH THE METEOR STUCK FIRMLY ON TANK GIRLS BONCE BOOGA AND STEVIE CAN GET ON WITH THE BIRTHDAY CELIBRATIONS...
GEB BIS BUDDY BING OB BY HEAB!
I SAY STEVIE, DID BALLOON HEAD SAY SOMETHING?
WHO CARES?! THAT METEOR STAYS ON HER SHOULDERS UNTIL WE'VE FINISHED WITH THIS SCAT UP FEED!
STUPID FAT COW!
ANOTHER GALLON OF VINTAGE CIDER, MY DEAR BOOGA?
NOT FOR ME STEVIE, I'VE STILL GOT TO MAKE THE REST OF THOSE PHONE CALLS FOR TANK GIRL!
ABSOLUTE ASSHOLE ENDIN!
YOU WANKER BOOGA!...

PINTS OF VIEW:

CORRESPONDENCE WITH OUR FANS.....

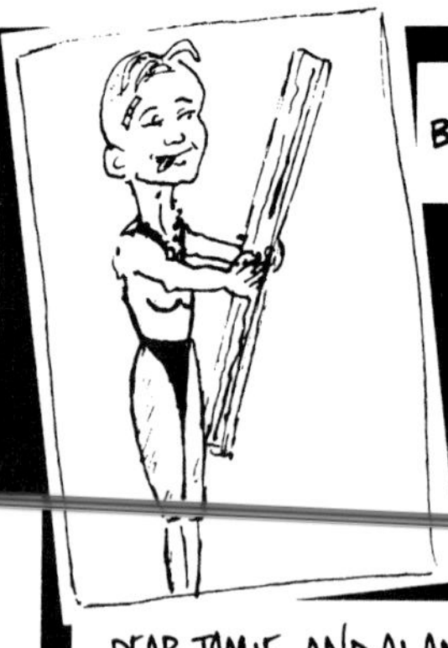

PLANK GIRL
BY EARTHLET EARTH KIT
FROM MORECAMBE

Dear Jamie and Alan,
Could we see again the scene from part two of the 'Australian Job' when Sub Girl grabs the burger. This is our most favorite ever,
Yours Hopefully,
The Chocolate Biscuit Club,
Chelmsford xxx

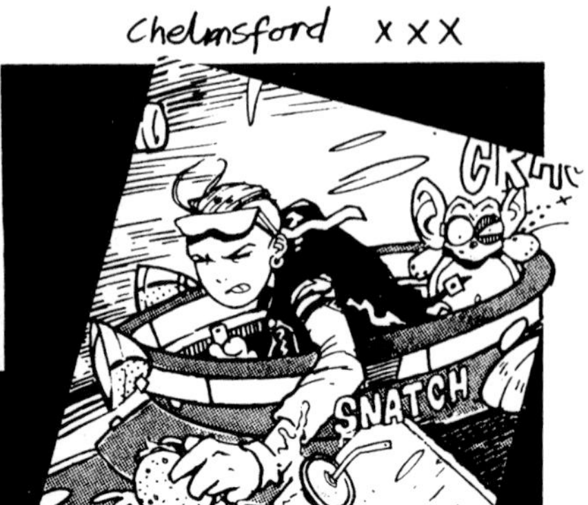
SNATCH

YOUR WISH IS OUR COMMAND!

DEAR JAMIE + ALAN
ON THE 4th OF DECEMBER 1989 I WAS LYING IN BED WITH REALLY SWOLLEN TESTICLES. SHORTLY, MY COPY OF DEADLINE No 14 WAS DELIVERED. AFTER READING THE ISH I SHOT MY LOAD ALL OVER THE LIVING ROOM CARPET.
YOURS, SPOCK O'KIRK
BOURNVILLE GRDN CITY

DEAR SPOCK,
CHEERS!
LOVE J+A

DEAR JAMIE AND ALAN,
I NOTICED THAT IN TANK GIRL #8 ON PAGE FIVE, FRAME 4, TANK GIRL IS WEARING A RING IN HER EAR, BUT IN THE NEXT FRAME SHE IS SPORTING A CROSS. HOW DO YOU EXPLAIN THIS DRASTIC MISTAKE?
BARRY HEADWOUND,
LITTLE-HAMPTON.

DEAR BARRY,
IF YOU EVER EVEN COME WITHIN TEN MILES OF OUR HOUSE WE WILL BREAK YOUR SHIT FILLED RETARDED SKULL, LOVE J+A

EPITAPH.

NOT NEXT YEAR, NOT THE NEXT ONE, NOT THE YEAR AFTER THAT. BUT AGES FROM HERE,

CLAD IN LOVE STAINED SLEEPING BAGS, DYING WITH FEET WRAPPED IN ENDLESS SHIRTS AND PILLOW CASES,

CRUMBLING. WITH 99 FLAKES CLUTCHED BETWEEN THUMB AND PALM, DRIPPING YELLOW CREAM FROM TWIG FINGERS, BASKING OUR WHITE HAIRED CHESTS ON GREEN GRASSED PARKS UNDER PURPLE SKIES. LAUGHING OVER COFFEE AFTER BATH TUBS OF COFFEE HAVE PASSED THROUGH OUR GUTS. HUDDLED, LONELY, UNDER HEAPED CLOTHES. HERE LAY US...

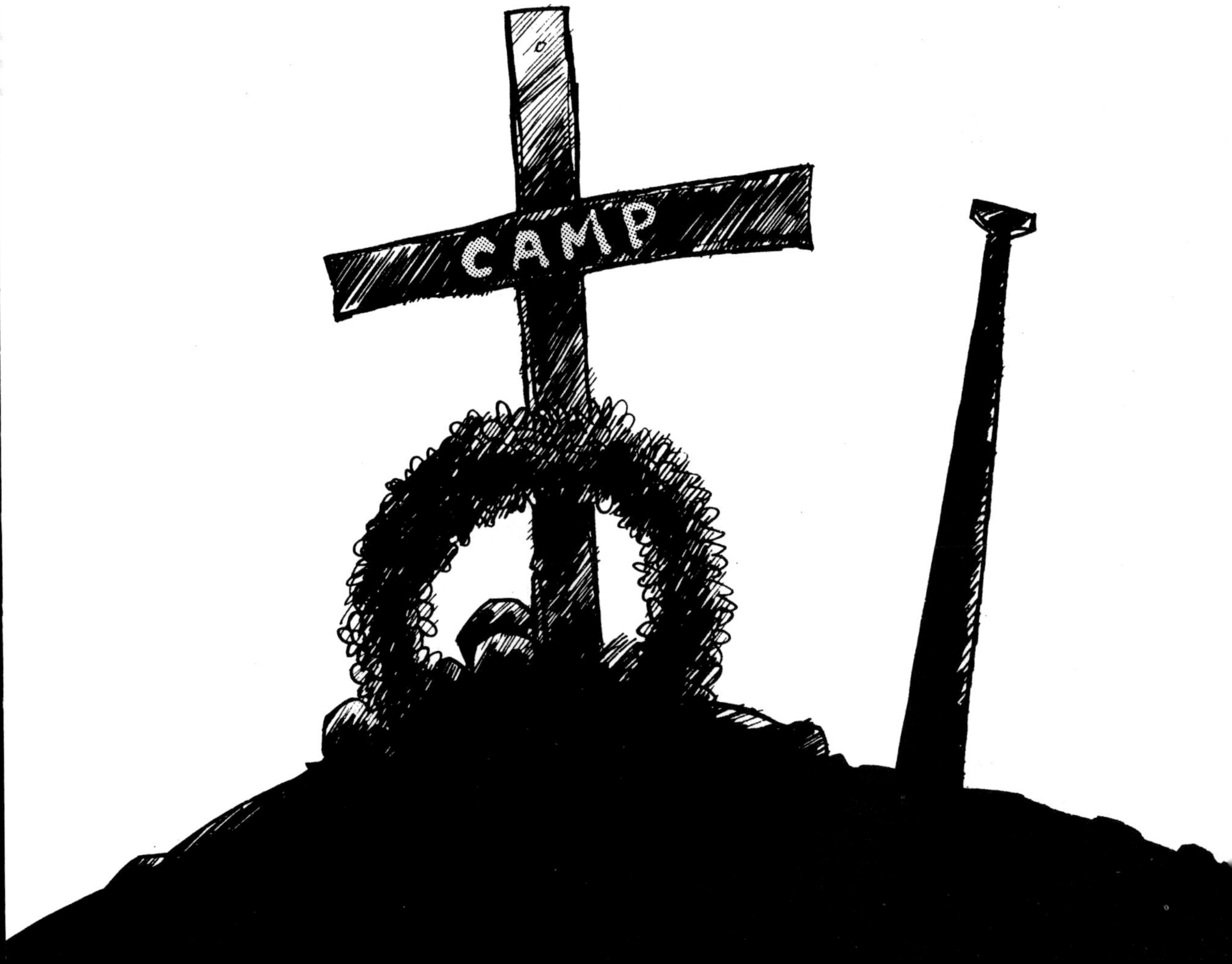
CAMP

CUT AND DRESS TANK GIRL

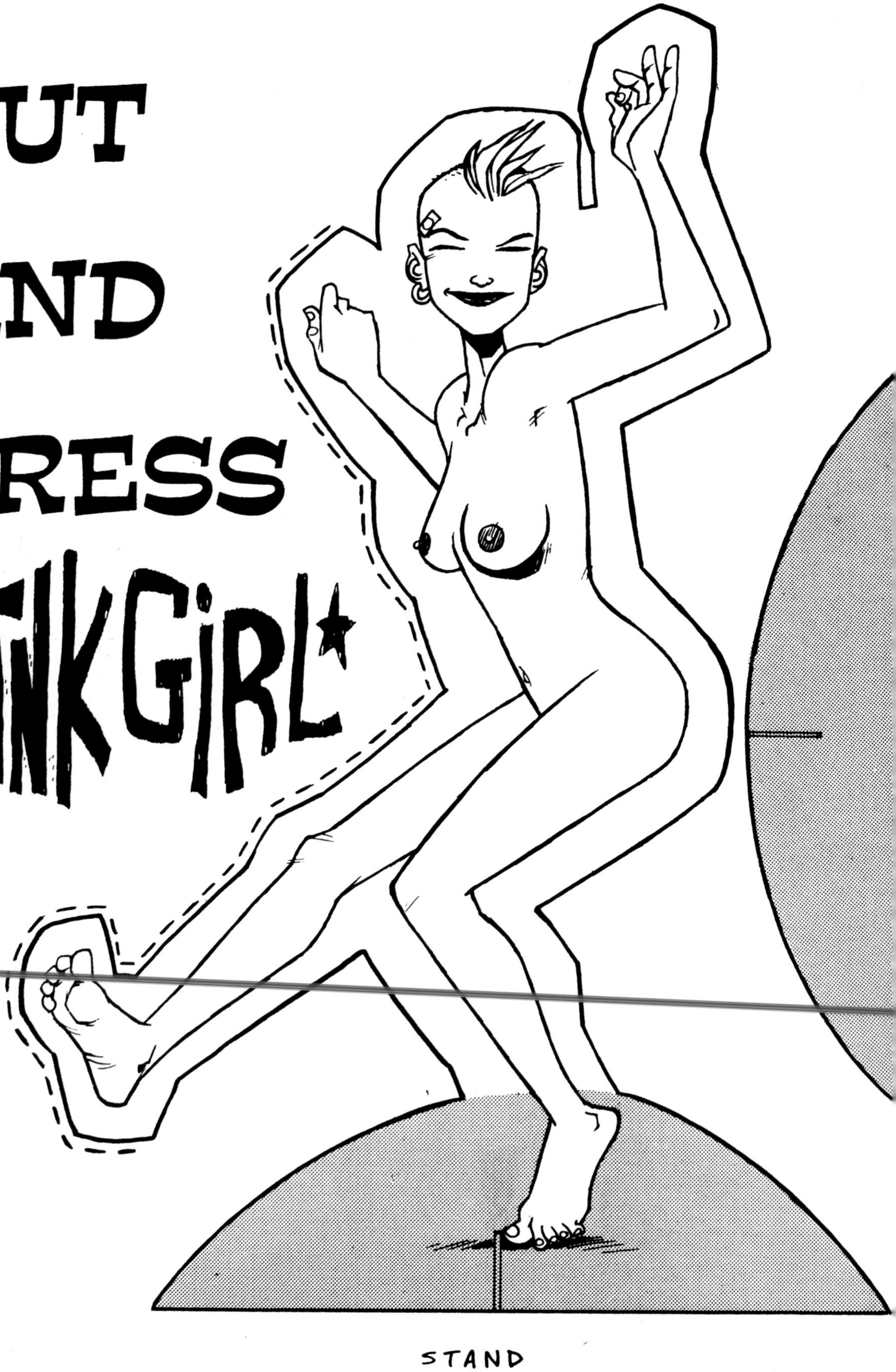
STAND

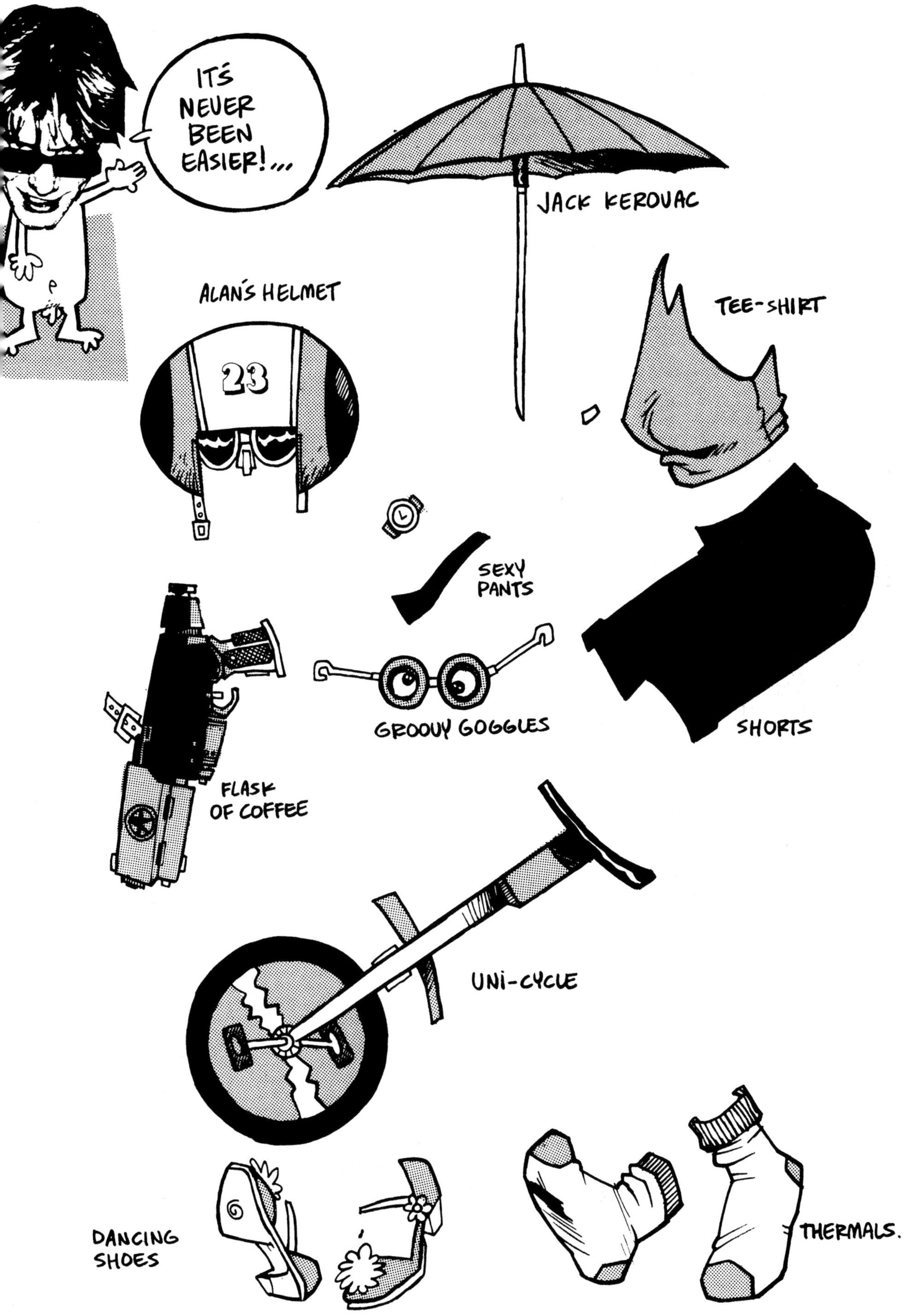
IT'S NEVER BEEN EASIER!...
JACK KEROUAC
ALAN'S HELMET
23
TEE-SHIRT
SEXY PANTS
GROOVY GOGGLES
SHORTS
FLASK OF COFFEE
UNI-CYCLE
DANCING SHOES
THERMALS.

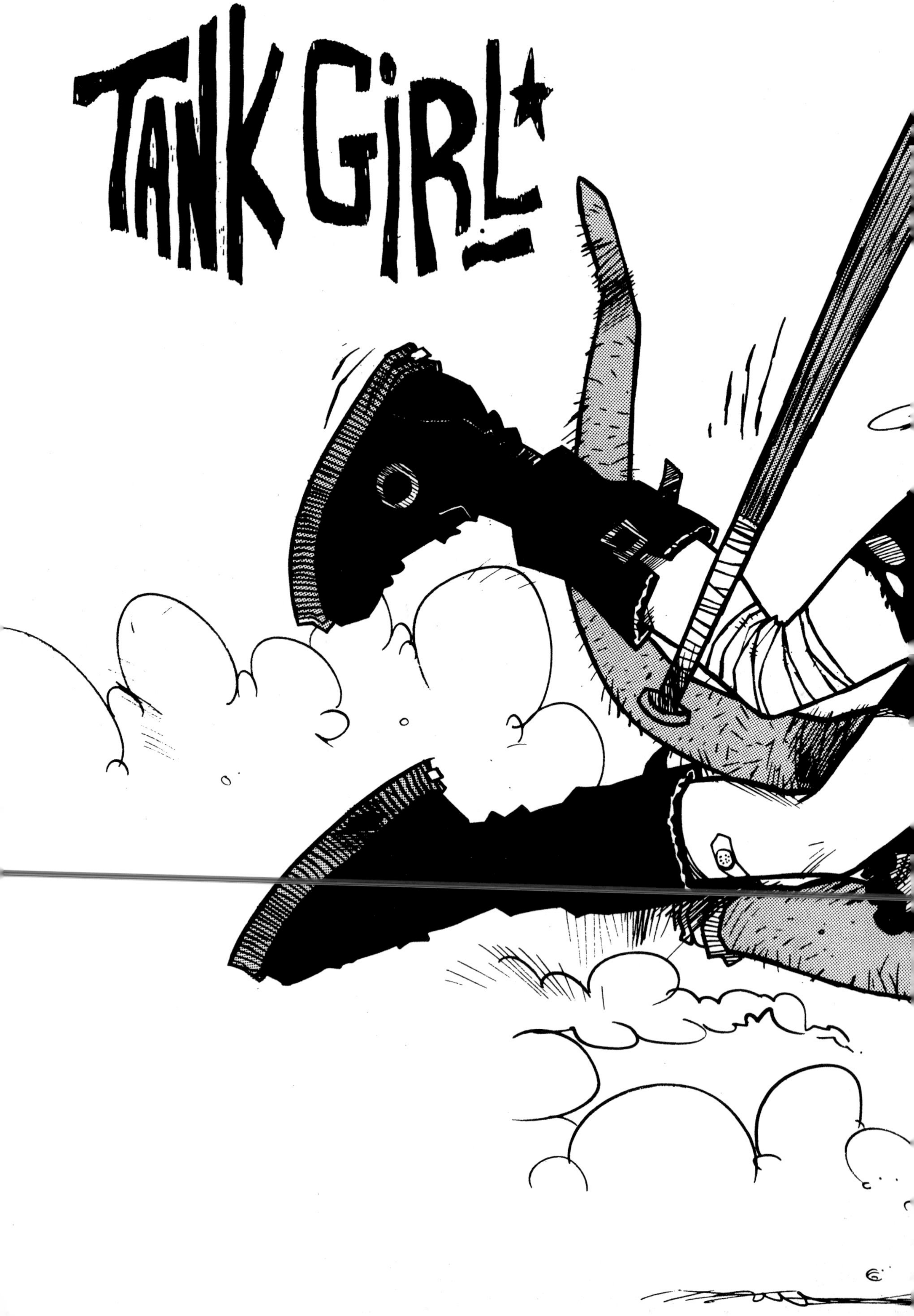
TANK GIRL

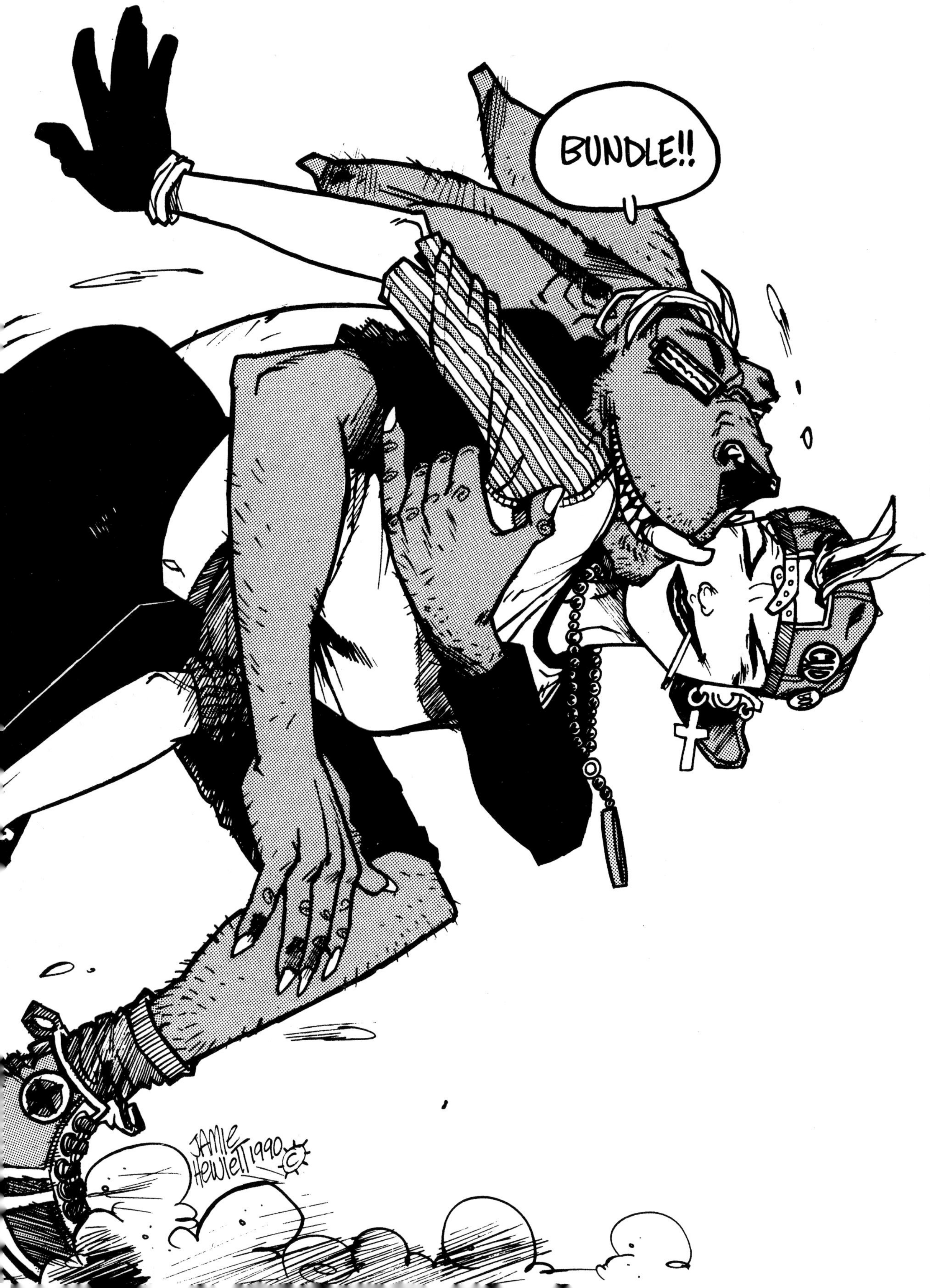
BUNDLE!!
JAMIE HEWLETT 1990 ©

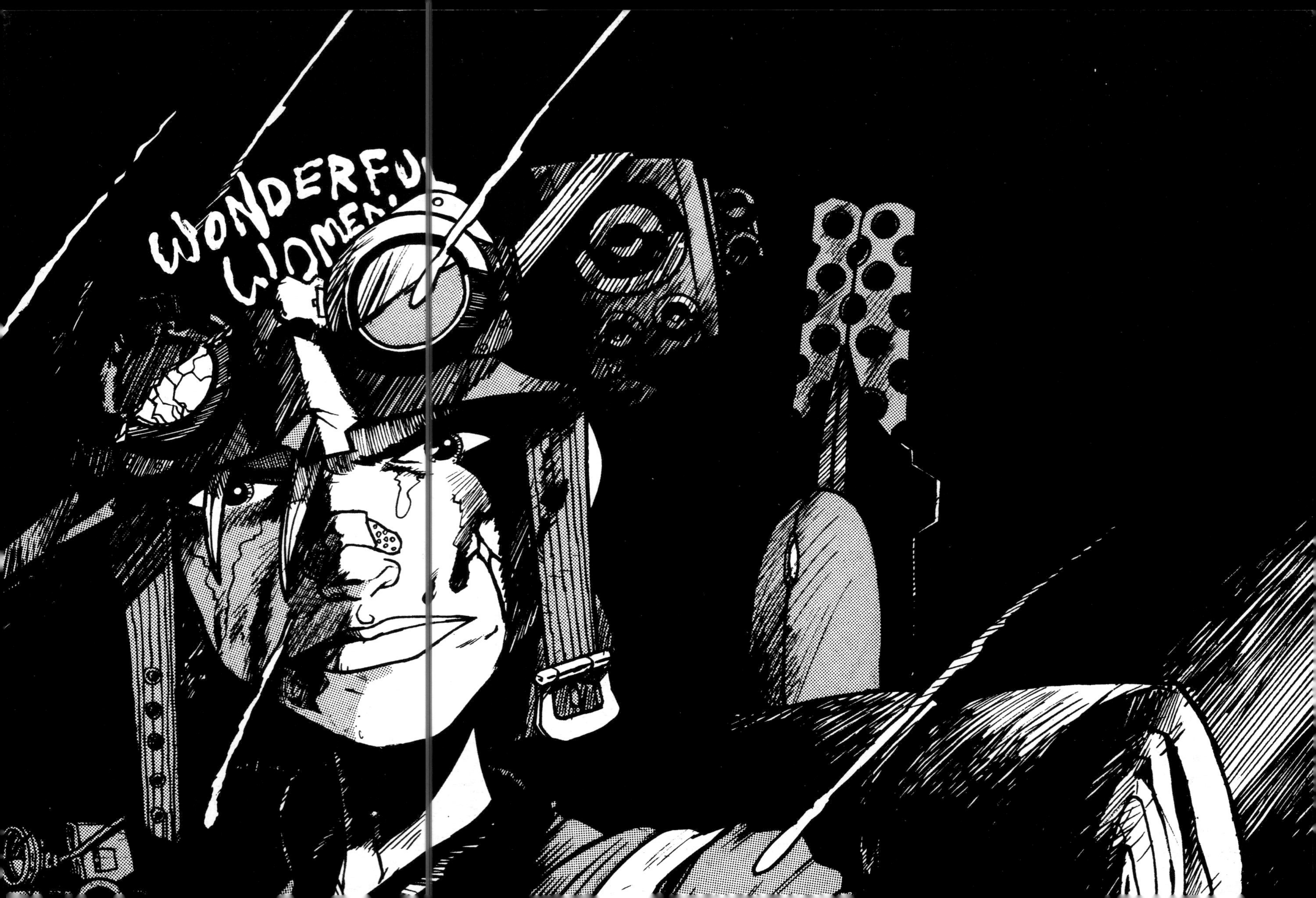
WONDERFUL WOMEN!

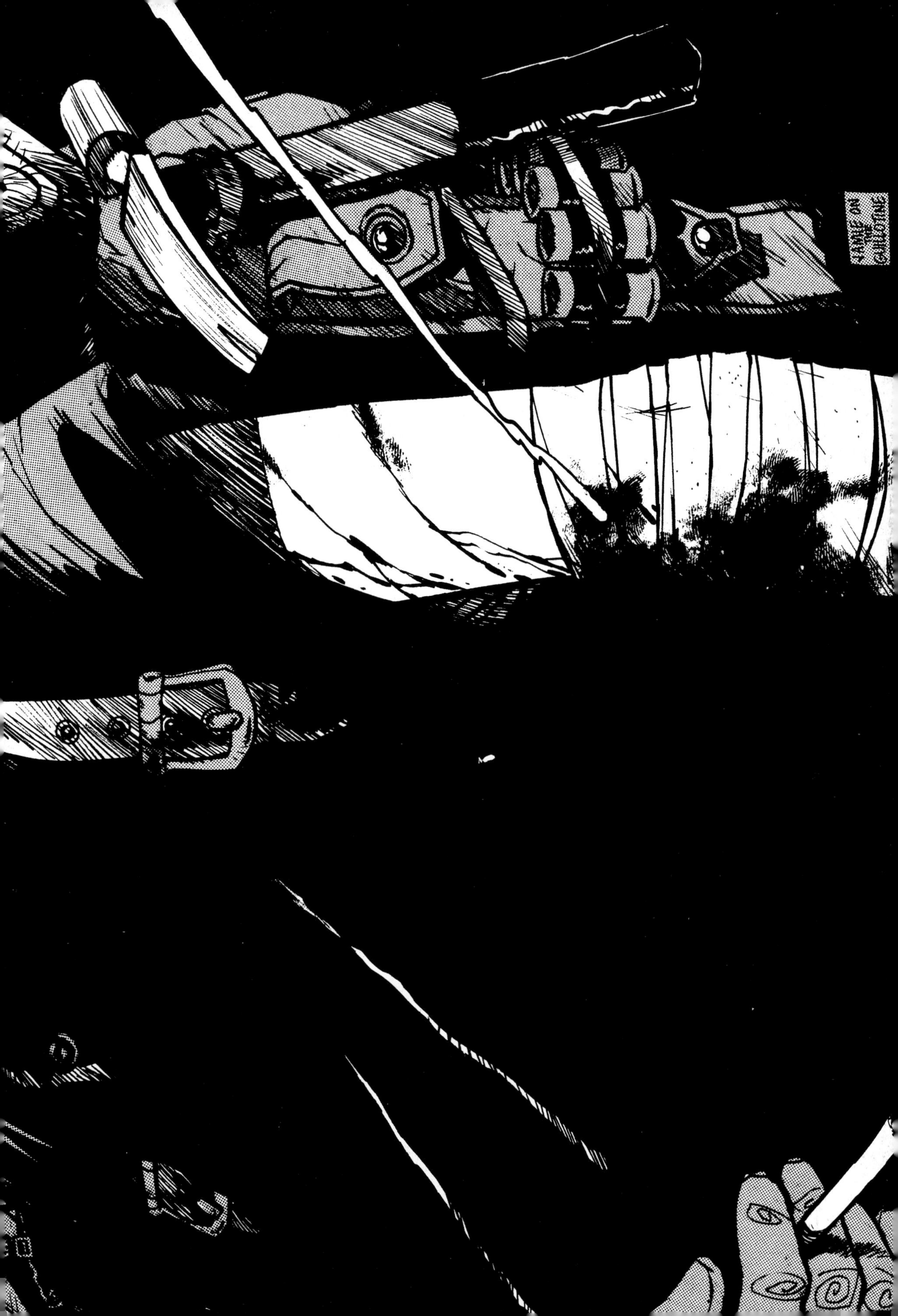
JAMIE ON THE GUILLOTINE

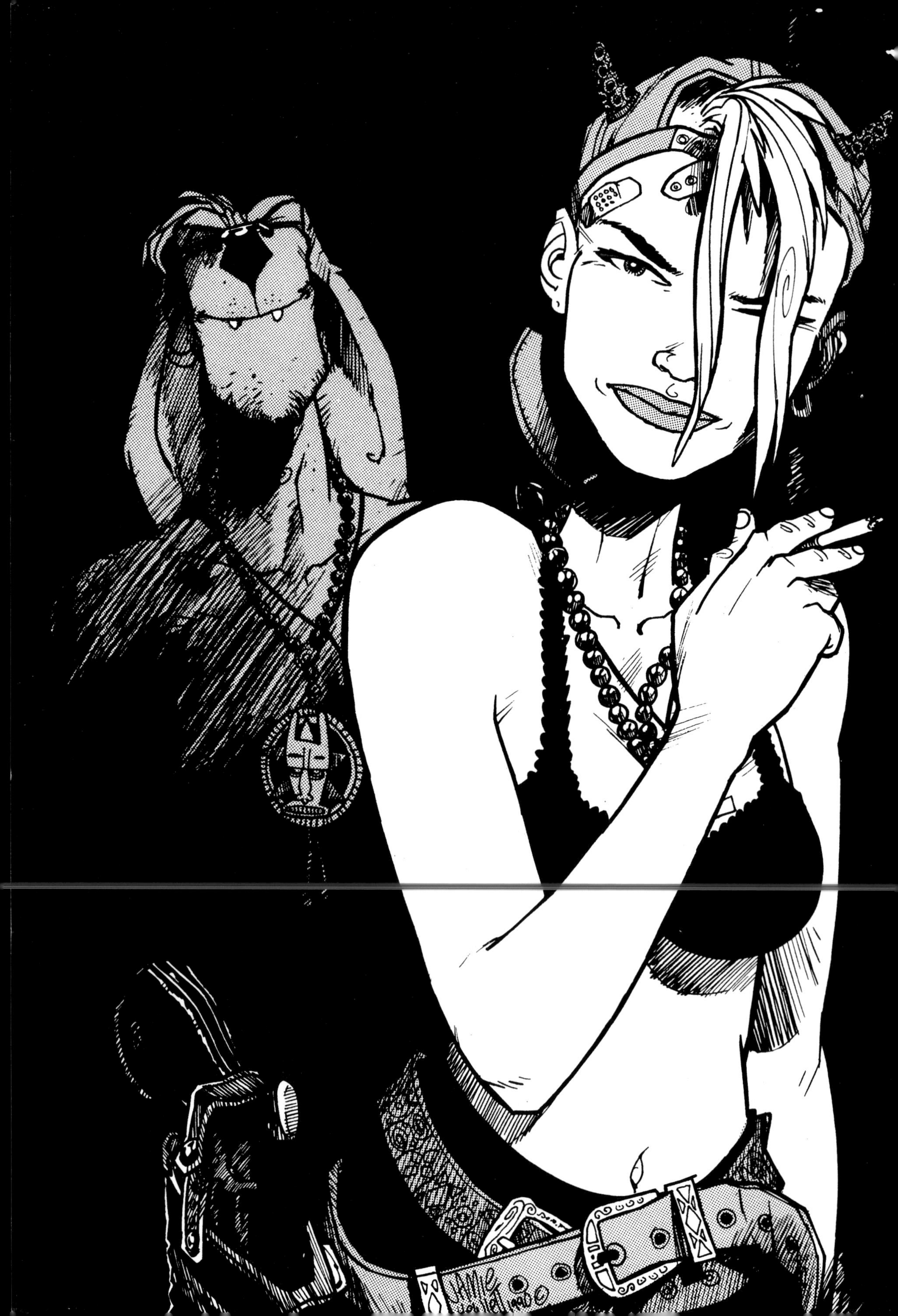

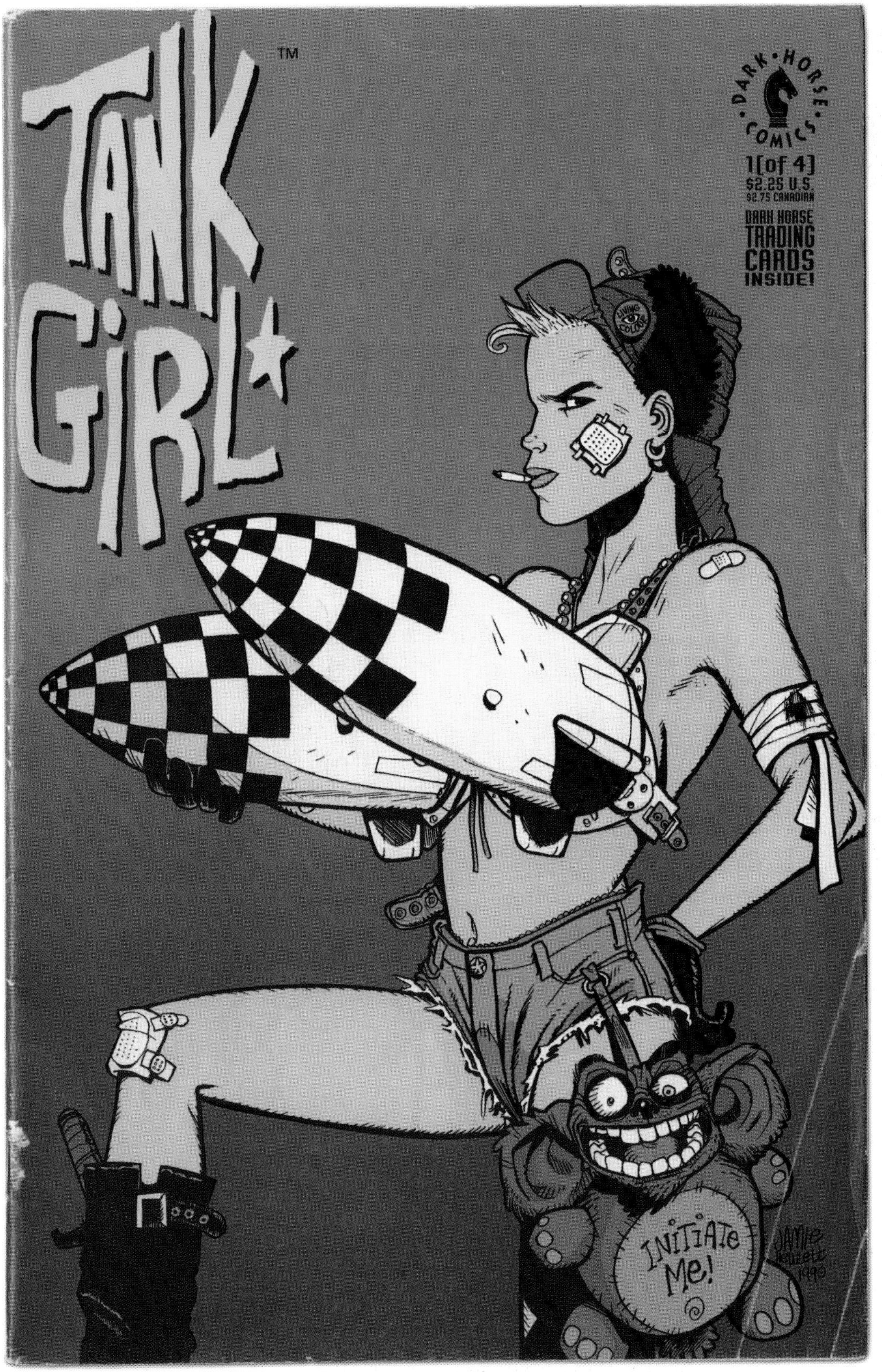
TANK GIRL™
DARK HORSE COMICS
1 [of 4]
$2.25 U.S.
$2.75 CANADIAN
DARK HORSE TRADING CARDS INSIDE!
INITIATE ME!
JAMIE HEWLETT 1990

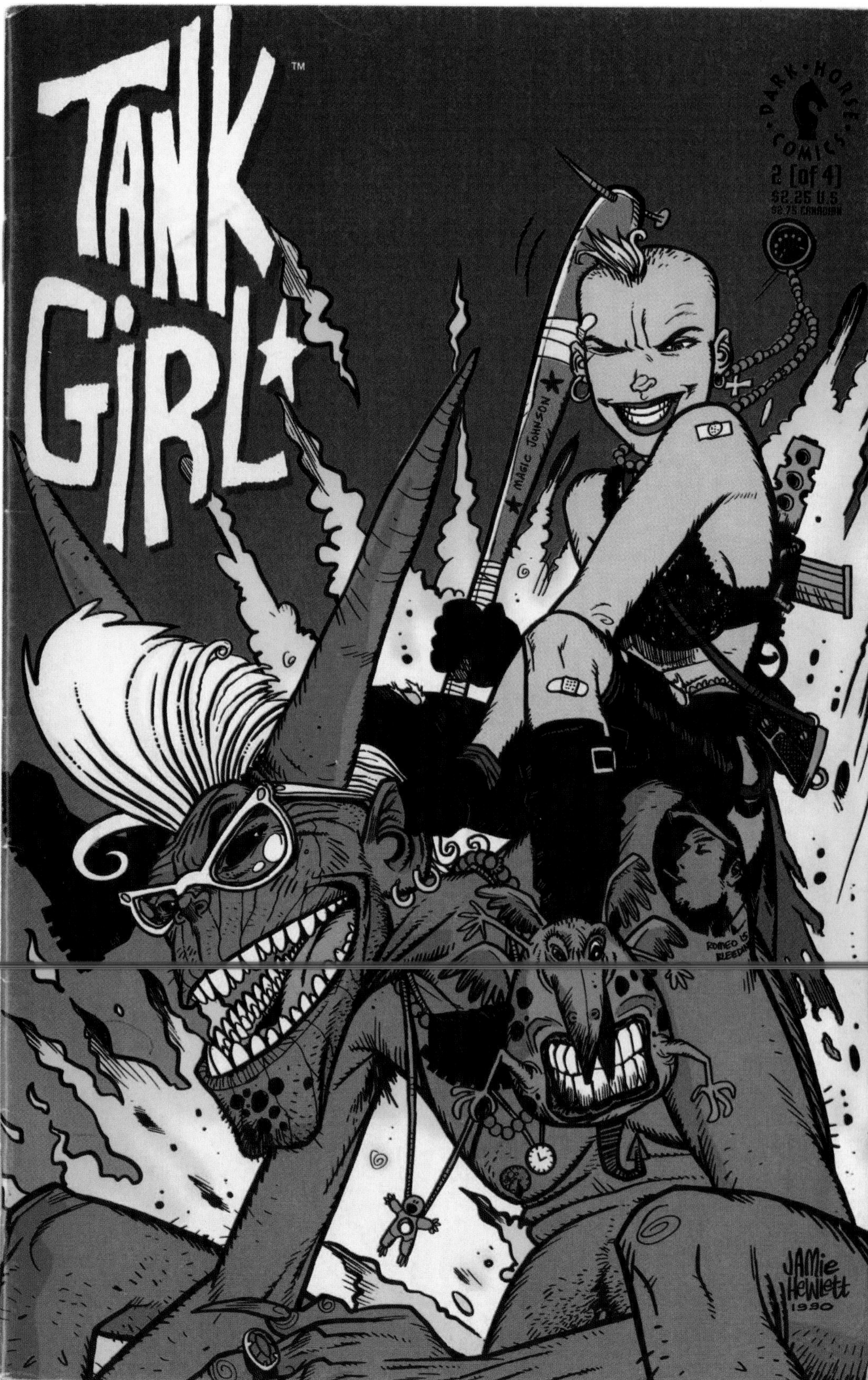
TANK GIRL™
DARK HORSE COMICS
2 [of 4]
$2.25 U.S.
$2.75 CANADIAN
MAGIC JOHNSON
ROMEO IS
JAMIE HEWLETT 1990

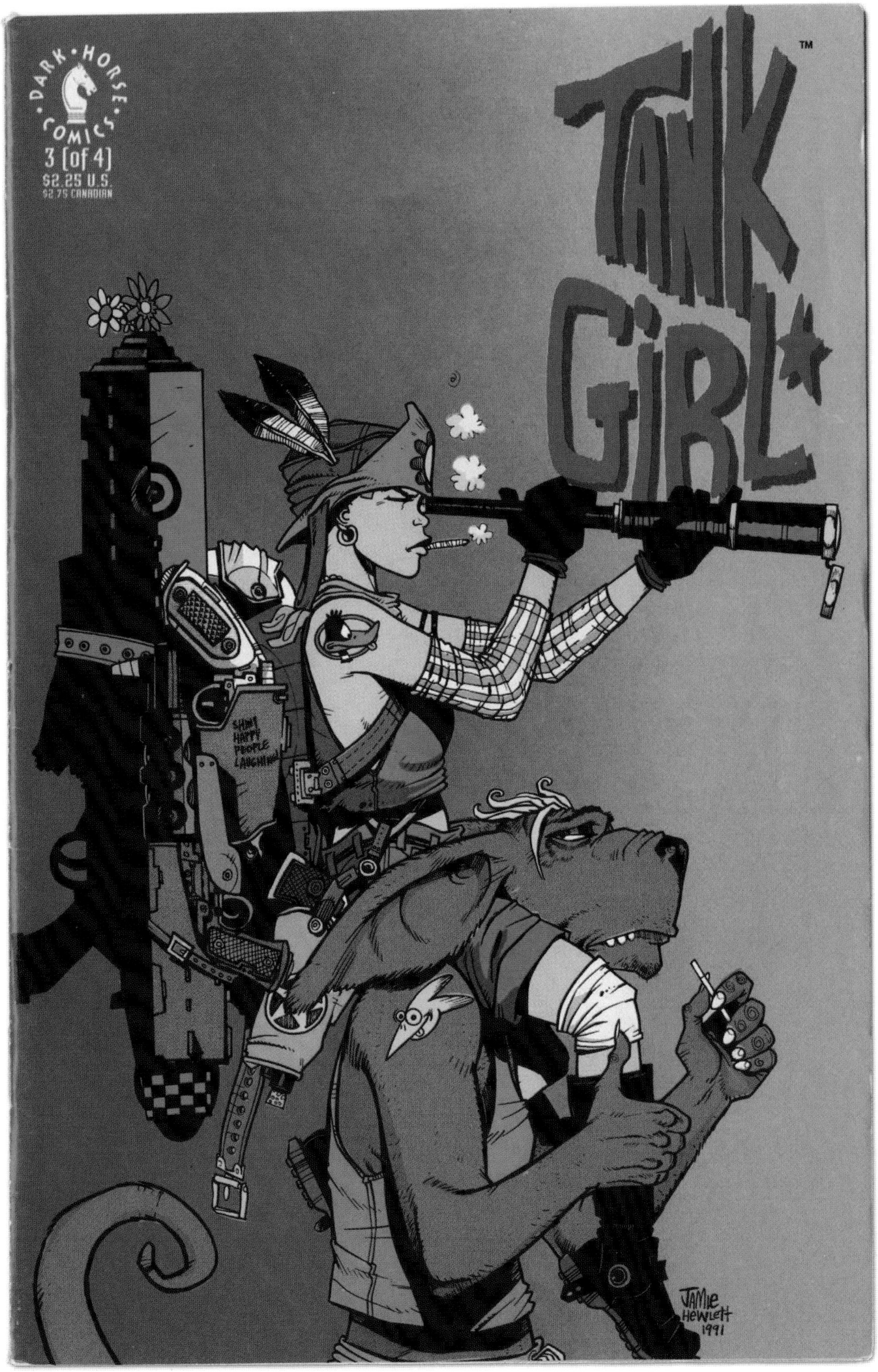
DARK HORSE COMICS
3 (of 4)
$2.25 U.S.
$2.75 CANADIAN
TANK GIRL™
SHINY HAPPY PEOPLE LAUGHING!
JAMIE HEWLETT 1991

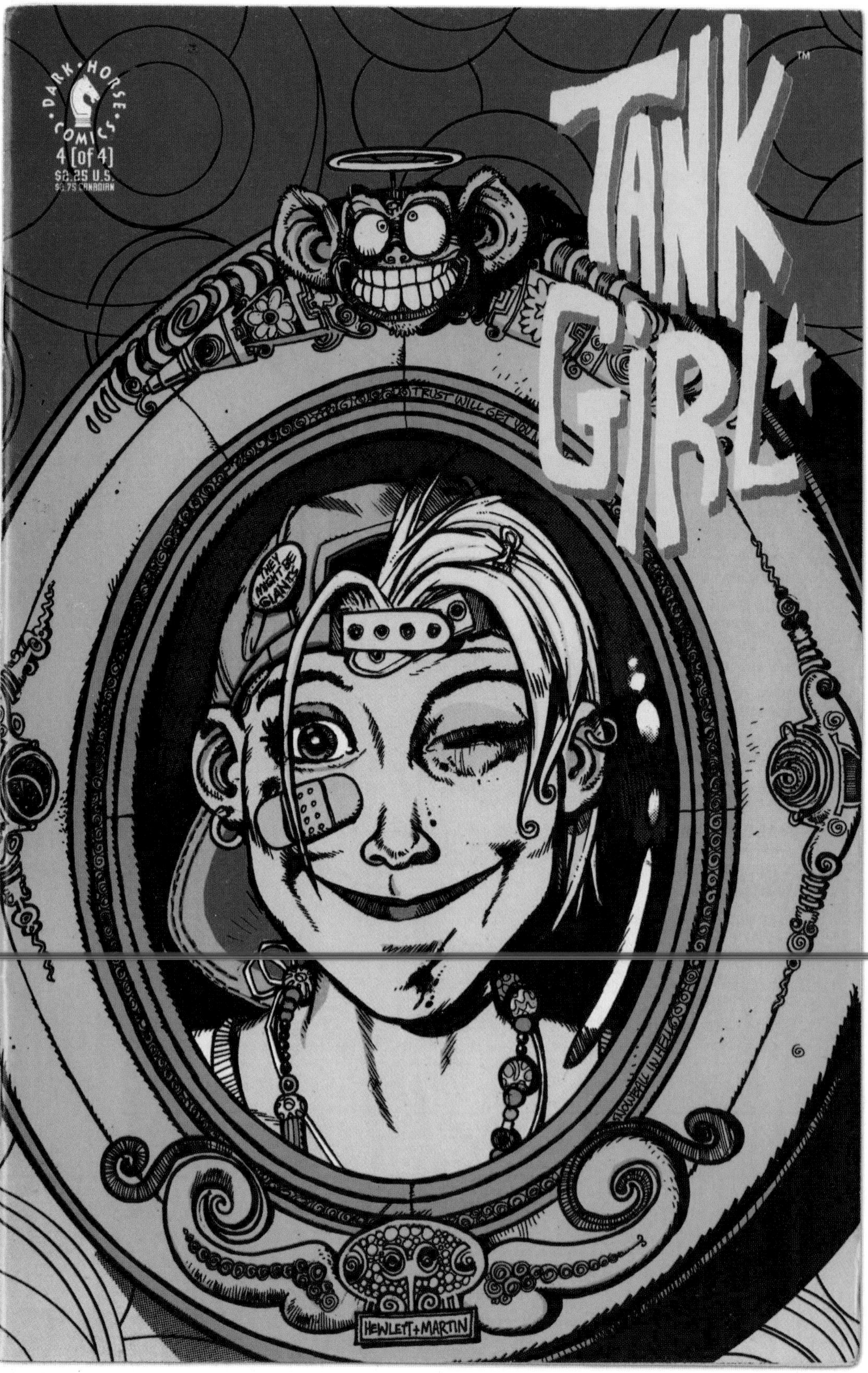
DARK HORSE COMICS
4 [of 4]
$2.25 U.S.
CANADIAN
TANK GIRL
THEY MIGHT BE GIANTS
HEWLETT + MARTIN